AMERICAN PROBLEMS

What should be done?

Debates from "The Advocates"

AMERICAN PROBLEMS

What should be done?

Debates from "The Advocates"

Compiled, with Introductions, Commentaries, and Exercises by

JOHN D. MAY, Ph. D.

NATIONAL PRESS BOOKS

The transcripts adapted for use in this book were derived from television programs produced by, and copyrighted in the names of, WGBH-TV and KCET-TV and financed by grants from the Corporation for Public Broadcasting and the Ford Foundation.

Library of Congress Catalog Card Number: 72-97840
International Standard Book Numbers;
0-87484-232-8 (paper)
0-87484-233-6 (cloth)

Manufactured in the United States of America

National Press Books,
850 Hansen Way,
Palo Alto, California 94304

This book was set in Palatino by Applied Typographic Systems and was printed and bound by Levison McNally Company. The designer was Nancy Sears, who also designed the cover, from a photograph supplied by the staff of "The Advocates" at WGBH-TV, Boston. The editor was Richard W. Bare and production was supervised by Michelle Hogan.

Contents

ix   Introduction

ELECTIONS AND LEGISLATION

1   DEBATE ONE   Should the congressional seniority system be abolished?

> *Participants:* U.S. Senator **Bob Packwood** (R-Ore.); **Jack Anderson**, newspaper columnist; **James Jackson Kilpatrick**, newspaper columnist; Professor **Charles O. Jones**, department of political science, University of Pittsburgh; U.S. Representative **Philip Crane** (R-Ill.); U.S. Representative **Donald Fraser** (D-Minn.)

43   DEBATE TWO   Should the government subsidize all campaigns for office?

> *Participants:* Journalist **Britt Hume**, associate newspaper columnist; **Philip Stern**, author of The Great Treasury Raid; U.S. Representative **John Ashbrook** (R-Ohio); **Charlene Mitchell**, 1968 Communist Party candidate for President (on film); **Kipp Dawson**, Leader of the Socialist Workers Party (on film); **Raymond Miller**, leader of the Abolish Port Authority Party (on film); **Lar Daly**, "America First" candidate for office; **Dr. Herbert Alexander**, director of the Citizen's Research Foundation; **Jerome Medalie**, Boston attorney and campaigner for election reform; **T. Coleman Andrews**, chairman of the American Independent Party (on film)

76   DEBATE THREE   Should the federal government register voters for presidential elections?

> *Participants:* U.S. Representative **Morris Udall** (D-Ariz.); U.S. Senator **Peter Dominick** (R-Colo.); **Robert Nisbet**, professor of sociology,

*Other than moderator and advocate

University of California at Riverside; **Andrew Hacker**, professor of government, Cornell University; **Ramsey Clark**, former Attorney General of the U.S.

INTER-GOVERNMENTAL RELATIONS

106   DEBATE FOUR   Should congress adopt president nixon's general revenue-sharing plan?

Participants: Mayor **Richard Lugar** of Indianapolis; Governor **John Love** of Colorado, immediate past chairman of the National Governors' Conference; **Melville Ulmer**, professor of economics, University of Maryland; U.S. Senator **Adlai Stevenson III** (D-Ill.); **Dr. John O. Wilson**, assistant director, U.S. Office of Economic Opportunity and former professor of economics at Yale University; Governor **Ronald Reagan** of California (on film; Mayor **Carl Stokes** of Cleveland (on film); Mayor **James Tate** of Philadelphia (on film); Governor **Nelson Rockefeller** of New York (on film); Mayor **Kenneth Gibson** of Newark (on film)

135   DEBATE FIVE   Should the federal government compel suburbs to accept low-income housing?

Participants: **Paul Davidoff**, director of the Suburban Action Institute; **Sumner Wolsky**, member of the Lexington, Mass., Town Meeting; **Cecil Rouson**, former lieutenant of Malcolm X and president of the Woodmere Park Improvement Association of Greensboro, N.C.; **Randy Hamilton**, executive director, Institute for Local Self-Government; **Edgar Olsen**, professor of economics, University of Virginia; **Herbert Franklin**, director of the National Urban Coalition's Urban Growth Program

JUDICIAL PROCEDURES AND INDIVIDUAL RIGHTS

167   DEBATE SIX   Should your state adopt a pre-trial preventive detention law?

Participants: **Tim Murphy**, Superior Court judge, District of Columbia; **Donald Santarelli**, associate deputy attorney general of the U.S.; Sergeant **Hugh Williams**, Newark police officer and Fellow at the Center for Criminal Justice of Harvard University; **Alan Dershowitz**, professor of law, Harvard University; **Sir Arthur James**, judge of the Queen's Bench Division, Supreme Court Judicature of the United Kingdom

193   DEBATE SEVEN   Should television be allowed to broadcast criminal trials with the consent of the defendant?

Participants: **Marshall McLuhan**, author (on film); **Evelle Younger**, attorney general of California and former district attorney of Los Angeles County (on film); **Thomas Brennan**, chief justice of the Supreme Court of Michigan; **Joseph A. Ball**, former president of the American College of Trial Lawyers and current member of the American Bar Association's advisory committee for television and motion pictures; **Grant Cooper**, member of the A.B.A's Fair Trial and Free Press Commission, former president of the American College of Trial Lawyers, former defense attorney for Sirhan Sirhan; **Dr. Charles Wahl**, professor of psychiatry, U.C.L.A.; **Richard Jencks**, president of the Broadcast Group of C.B.S.; **Walter Cronkite**, newscaster (on film)

219   DEBATE EIGHT   Should colleges adopt a fixed rule expelling any student who uses obstruction, sit-ins, or other illegal physical force as a means of persuasion?

Participants: **Dr. James Hester**, president of New York University; Governor **Louis B. Nunn** of Kentucky, chairman of the State University's board of trustees; **Tom Gerety**, Harvard Law School student and former leader of disruptive demonstrations at Yale University; **Dr. James P. Dixon**, president of Antioch College; **Alan Dershowitz**, professor of law, Harvard University; **William Sloan Coffin**, chaplain at Yale University (on film)

SOCIAL POLICY

241   DEBATE NINE   Should the u.s. government make contraceptives available to every american, including teenagers, and conduct an educational campaign to limit population?

Participants: **Kenneth E. F. Watt**, professor of zoology, University of California at Davis; U.S. Representative **Edward Koch** (D-N.Y.); **Dr. Ansley Coale**, head of population research at Princeton University (on film); **Dr. Karl Taeuber**, professor of sociology, Wisconsin University, and urban population expert with the Rand Corporation; the Reverend **Billy Graham** (on film); **Mrs. Carl Cohan**, mother of eight; **Dr. Victor Rosenblum**, president of Reed College; **Stephanie Mills**, recent valedictorian of Mills College

261 DEBATE TEN Should criminal penalties for the use of marijuana be abolished?

Participants: **Dr. Joel Fort**, public health specialist and author of *The Pleasure Seekers;* **Margaret Mead**, professor of anthropology, Columbia University; **Dr. Reese Jones**, professor of psychiatry at University of California, California Medical School and adviser on marijuana for the National Institute of Mental Health; **Dr. Thomas J. Ungerleider**, professor of psychiatry at U.C.L.A. and adviser to the Governor's Committee on Drug Abuse; **Philip Quellet**, former marijuana user; U.S. Senator **George Murphy** (R-Cal.)

ECOLOGY AND RESOURCE-DEVELOPMENT

282 DEBATE ELEVEN Should the trans-alaska pipeline be constructed?

Participants: **Eban Hobson**, executive director of the Alaska Federation of Natives (on film); U.S. Senator **Ted Stevens** (R-Alaska); **Ed Patton**, president of Alyeska Pipeline Co.; **Willie Willoya** and **Lloyd Elasanga**, Alaska natives (on film); **David Brower**, president of Friends of the Earth; **Ross Mullins**, member of the Cordova Fish Union (on film); U.S. Representative **Les Aspin** (D-Wis.); **Ed Fortier**, executive editor of Alaska magazine

307 DEBATE TWELVE Should there be a moratorium on the construction of nuclear power plants?

Participants: **Dr. John D. Gofman**, professor of medical physics, biomedical laboratory of Lawrence Radiation Laboratory, Berkeley, Calif.; U.S. Senator **Mike Gravel** (D-Alaska); **Joseph Swidler**, chairman, New York State Public Service Commission; **Dr. Leonard Sagan**, associate director of environmental medicine, Palo Alto (California) Medical Clinic; **Merril Eisenbud**, professor of environmental medicine, New York University Medical Center

Moderators: **Victor Palmieri**, president of Great Southwest Corporation of Los Angeles, attorney, former member of California commissions on metropolitan problems and urban problems; **Roger Fisher**, professor of interntional law at Harvard University and founder of "The Advocates."

Advocates: **Howard Miller**, associate professor of law, University of Southern California; **William Rusher**, publisher of *The National Review*, board member of the American Conservative Union, former associate counsel to the Internal Security Subcommittee of the U.S. Senate; **J. Daniel Mahoney**, attorney and chairman of the Conservative Party of New York; **Kevin O'Connell**, California attorney; **Max Greenberg**, California attorney; **Lisle Baker**, Boston attorney; **Evan Semerjian**, Boston attorney; **John Havelock**, former attorney general of Alaska; **Judith Hope**, California attorney

Introduction

This book has been designed to serve two needs. It has been designed, first, to serve the need for understanding issues that have lately commanded the attention of Americans. Among these issues are violence on the streets and on college campuses, use and abuse of drugs, operations of the United States Congress, relations between Federal and State and local organs of government, due process of law, over-population, and pollution.

The second need which this book has been designed to serve is the need for critical sophistication. By "critical sophistication" I mean ability to distinguish between sound and spurious arguments, between solid and spurious evidence, between reason and rubbish in controversies about what should be done. This kind of ability, cultivated among the many rather than just the few, is peculiarly vital to the survival of popular government.

In a book called *The Secret of Democracy* (Vanguard Press, 1955) a Frenchwoman named Suzanne Labin asks this question: "What sort of education should the people be given in order to exert genuine control over public affairs?" She answers in these words:

> They should certainly know more than they know now, but above all, they should know more fundamental things. They should learn to dis-

tinguish the sound of truth from that of lies [and] the popular demagogue from the honest reformer, to grasp the frontiers between reality and Utopia, to estimate the hierarchy of dangers, to be open to the objections and aspirations of others, to . . . distinguish hypotheses from certainties and causes from effects, to stick to the subject, to understand that every law has only the finite field of validity imposed by necessary and fruitful approximations, to detect flaws in reasoning, vicious circles, abusive interpolations and extrapolations, [and] to recognize the coarser threads of voluntary or involuntary sophism. . . .

In order to undergo this vital kind of learning experience—in order to be "immunized against demagogy, Utopia, or casuistry"—Labin suggests that people need "systematic exercises in tracking down error, misinterpretation, nonsense, double meaning, evasion, exaggeration, tricks, lies. . . ." Armed with such knowledge, citizens would not necessarily be able to devise solutions to vexing current problems; but they *would* be able to make wise *choices* among alternative courses of action that are brought to their attention. They would be equipped, one might say, with a genuine civic education, as contrasted with the rote learning of sacred texts, with the ingestion of miscellaneous facts, or with conditioned reverence for Old Glory.

This book, I hope, not only will acquaint you with some of the facts and the arguments that have been marshalled in connection with current controversies, but also will enable you to do mental exercises of the kind prescribed by Suzanne Labin. Accordingly, this book differs from most anthologies of documents dealing with current issues. It is distinctive on the following counts.

First, our focus of attention is not just on identifying problems; it is on canvassing and appraising proposed *solutions*. The documents comprising this volume deal not just with versions of what has been happening, but with versions of what needs to happen.

Second, we examine antagonistic versions of what should be done. Each treatment of a problem takes the form of a debate—a modified form of a court trial—in which one man espouses a specified policy, another opposes that policy, and each calls upon and cross-examines an array of more or less expert witnesses. These debates have been adapted from the educational television series called "The Advocates."*

---

*My adaptations are based on transcripts supplied by the executive producer on behalf of the Corporation for Public Broadcasting and WGBH Educational Foundation Inc. I have tried to retain the flavor and the substance of what originally was recorded in these tran-

Third, we inspect evidence, testimony, and reasoning provided by serious, responsible sources. This approach marks a contrast with the practice of subjecting students to the effusions of figures whose sole claim to attention consists of having grabbed a headline which bestows upon them the mystical accolade "relevant."

Fourth, several of the debates, especially those appearing early in the collection, are followed by Commentaries. These cite particular examples of recurrent argumentational devices, with emphasis given to fallacious arguments.

Finally, readers are supplied with direct, and I hope irresistible, invitations to do the work of responsible citizens. These invitations take the form of "suggested exercises" following most of the debates. The exercises do not test one's vocabulary. They do not concentrate on recalling just what spokesman made what assertion. They test for grasp of principal lines of argument, for detection of logical fallacies, for alertness to arbitrary assumptions and extraneous evidence, and for apprehension of conspicuous omissions: in short for sensitivity—as Suzanne Labin would say—to voluntary or involuntary sophism.

---

scripts, while working for brevity and coherence. This editorial operation has proved to be a delicate one: verbal statements which seem clear enough when heard often prove to be baffling when merely read. From the original transcripts I have deleted standard prefatory announcements, closing announcements about future programs, background statements by the moderator (some of which have been worked into my "overviews"), some allusions to guest decision-makers, most statements of welcome and thanks addressed by the moderator to successive witnesses, plainly repetitious remarks, and verbiage that is tantamount to stuttering. I have approached punctuation from the standpoint of achieving clarity of ideas rather than utmost fidelity to the participants' original rhythms of speech. On occasion I have inserted words in brackets to clarify an apparent intention or to encapsulate deleted remarks. I also have done a bit of transposing. This has been done exclusively so as to bring together separate but overlapping opening statements by rival advocates.

Responsibility for these editorial adaptations, including any distortion of what participants in the debates originally said, rests exclusively with me.

Should the congressional seniority system be abolished?

OVERVIEW

"The seniority system" is a phrase crudely describing a prominent and controversial aspect of the method by which authority is apportioned among members of the United States Congress. The phrase is crude and even misleading because it suggests that authority is apportioned *directly* according to the age of Representatives and Senators. Actually, while the seniority system does operate so that older Congressmen frequently surpass younger ones in authority, the connection between age and authority is indirect.

In the Congress, as contrasted with most other legislatures outside the United States, individual shares of authority are closely related to membership on, and rank in, standing committees. Each bill introduced to a house of the Congress is first referred to a specific committee on the basis of its subject matter. Most of the lawmaking work gets done in committee. Bills finding favor with committee majorities stand an excellent chance of receiving majority support on the floor of the House of Representatives and the Senate. Other bills rarely survive. Consequently, an individual Congressman's influence depends on his committee assignments and on his rank within committee. Every member is entitled to the

1

same number of assignments, but some assignments are more widely coveted than others. The most powerful Representatives and Senators, other than general officers such as the Speaker of the House and the Majority Leader of the Senate, are generally the top-ranking members of those committees exercising the widest jurisdiction. Among these are the committees on appropriations, finance (or ways and means, in which tax bills are written), and foreign relations.

For all practical purposes, individual committee assignments and committee rankings are determined by members of the party holding a majority of seats in the House and the Senate. On the issue of organizing Congress, co-partisans act in unison on the basis of customary principles used in deciding who gets what office. "Seniority" since the early 1900's has been one of those principles; but the concept means different things, and carries varying weight, in shaping committee *assignments* and determining committee *rank*.

With respect to assignments, seniority is measured not in terms of age or total legislative experience, but in terms of continuous membership in the House or Senate. When two candidates of the same party seek to fill one vacancy on a given committee, the "senior" candidate, in the sense specified, gets the nod, if all other considerations are equal.* However, these other considerations are numerous, and they do not always balance out. They include the home States or districts of rival candidates (there is a strong attempt to maintain sectional diversity), personal education and experience (legal training, for example, is an asset for a prospective Judiciary Committee member), and political considerations (endorsements from party wheelhorses and interest groups are important, as is one's reputation as a liberal, moderate, or conservative).

With respect to rank, seniority is measured in terms of continuous membership on a given committee. There are two seniority ladders for each committee: one for Democrats and one for Republicans. The majority party's senior man, in the sense specified here, becomes the committee chairman. The minority party's senior man becomes the committee's

---

*In the Senate, Democrats and Republicans differ somewhat in their use of seniority. In consequence of a guideline sponsored by Lyndon Johnson when he was Majority Leader, a Democratic senior man gets his *first* choice of a committee ahead of a junior man, but a junior man's first choice takes precedence over a senior man's *second* choice (each Senator serving on two committees). The Republicans give more weight to the senior man.

ranking minority member, with privileges and prerogatives exceeding those of his junior co-partisans.*

Use of seniority as a determinant of Congressional position, and hence of power, has frequently encountered objections. One of the latest attacks from outside the Congress emanates from a citizens' group known as Common Cause. Assailants generally argue that the seniority system too often vests authority in men who are senile, technically inept, unrepresentative of their colleagues (because they come from politically safe districts), and enabled to act in an arbitrary manner (because their security of tenure depends so little on popularity with their colleagues). Apologists generally dispute some of the critics' assumptions, while claiming additionally that the seniority system rewards valuable experience and forestalls Congressional disruption. These and other contentions are canvassed in the following debate.

1. OPENING STATEMENTS

1.1 MODERATOR VICTOR PALMIERI: Tonight we're concerned with the rules by which Congress operates. Specifically, our question is this: "Should the Congressional seniority system be abolished?" Advocate Howard Miller says "Yes"; Advocate William Rusher says "No."

1.2 ADVOCATE HOWARD MILLER: No group in the United States promotes people solely on the basis of seniority—except the Congress of the United States. In fact the Congress itself, in governing the groups and agencies that it has power over, does not impose its *own* rule of seniority; and in most cases—civil service, the military, independent agencies—[Congress] imposes . . . retirement at age 65 or 70, the age of most of its own committee chairmen. We simply propose that Congress apply to itself, and to its committee chairmen, the same rules that it applies to others. We [make this proposition] not in anger at age, but in fact with respect. Those who

---

*Committee rank is no trivial or ceremonial matter. Senior members exert more control over the selection of committee staff, get first crack at subcommittee chairmanships, and exert more control in selecting witnesses for hearings and in conducting interrogations. They speak first in moving amendments to proposed bills, play a larger part in managing bills taken to the floor for final action, and get priority in assignment to temporary conference committees which are formed to resolve differences between Senate and House versions of kindred bills.

have served the country well and honorably can now serve it best by agreeing to a change in the system, and by themselves stepping from power.

1.3   ADVOCATE WILLIAM RUSHER: I wouldn't blame you if you were wondering, right now, what on earth can possibly be said in favor of the seniority system. And yet, if you will just keep an open mind until our case can be made, I think you may wind up agreeing with me that few things which look so unappealing to start with have more to be said in their favor when you sit down and think about them. For instance, did you know that the seniority system was instituted in the House of Representatives in 1911 as a reform, to break the tyrannical power of Speaker Joe Cannon*? And are you aware that in fact there actually is no binding seniority rule—that this very night any committee of either house of Congress could, by a simple majority, vote to trim its chairman's powers to any desired extent? And that the whole party caucus can replace any committee chairman overnight, and has, in fact, removed half a dozen of them in the past 25 years?

1.4   What is being presented to us this evening, dressed up as a much-needed reform, is actually just a power grab by a busy little clique that can't be bothered to travel the road of patient service to seats of power in the Congress.

2.   FIRST AFFIRMATIVE WITNESS: DIRECT EXAMINATION

2.1   MILLER: The congress is not doing well. In the final months and weeks of 1970, especially in the Senate of the United States, the nation was presented with the spectacle of a legislative body that had seemingly lost the capacity to decide and the will to act. That is not my statement; it's President Nixon's. At the same time, the Minority Leader of the Senate called the situation one of "chaos" and other senators referred to it as a "disgrace" and an "agony." Six months after the fiscal year had begun, and a year after major appropriations bills had been sent in, Congress

---

*Prior to the end of what was stigmatized as "Cannon Rule," the Speaker possessed immense discretion over assignments of Representatives to standing committees, over what bills went to what committees, and over the terms under which bills reported out of committee could be debated on the floor of the House.

was still wrestling, in frantic last-minute sessions, to pass the basic appropriations bills that run the country. Now of course there are many reasons for that. But . . . the most basic, and simplest to correct, is the seniority system. Under the seniority system, the senior member of a committee is automatically chairman, regardless of any other qualifications or any other factor. And that committee chairman has in fact the most enormous power in the Congress. The result of that seniority system: three-quarters of the committee chairmen in the Senate are 65 or older; two-thirds in the House of Representatives are 65 or over. In an age when most of our domestic problems relate to urban affairs, almost all committee chairmen come from small towns or rural areas in relatively low-population States.

2.2   We propose that that system be changed, that there be other factors besides seniority in choosing committee chairmen, that something else be taken into account. And when that something else *is* taken into account, we will begin to get more responsive, more relevant, and better committee chairmen. With me tonight to propose the abolition of this seniority system is Senator Bob Packwood of Oregon. Senator, is the seniority system important in the operation of the Senate and [House]?

2.3   SEN. BOB PACKWOOD: It's absolutely critical. Not more than 5 percent of the legislation is ever changed on the Senate floor in any significant way. It is handled in committee . . . and as it comes out of committee, in all likelihood, it will pass. And therefore, how the committee operates—and who the chairman is—is very important. Nobody wants to cross the chairman. The chairman has the right to determine what bills will be heard and whether or not certain witnesses will be called. He has the right to demand proxies, or ask for them, and he gets them. In essence the chairman runs the committee, and the committees run Congress.

2.4   MILLER: Do you oppose the seniority system?

2.5   PACKWOOD: Very much. I do oppose it. I've served six years in the State legislature. I've examined every other parliament and congressional body in this world. No other governmental body in the world, let alone in the United States, operates on the seniority system. I think there are a variety of ways that we could replace the seniority system and ask, somehow, that a person be picked on merit, or ability, or anything other than solely age.

2.6   MILLER: Does the seniority system do positive harm in governing our country?

2.7   PACKWOOD: I think it does positive harm, in the sense that power corrupts, and absolute power can corrupt absolutely. To the extent that a chairman is free to do as he wants, to the extent that he's from a one-party State or a one-party district and is elected over and over and over, [he can develop] a tendency to be arbitrary and simply treat the rest of the committee [members] or the Congress with the back of [his] hand.

2.8   MILLER: Would a change in the system really make a difference? Would it make things better?

2.9   PACKWOOD: I think it would make a substantial difference. If a chairman knew that he was going to be elected by his fellow members, if he knew that he was going to be elected by the caucus, . . . and knew he would be elected every two years, it would cause him to think twice, and to pause, before being arbitrary in discretion.

3.   CROSS-EXAMINATION

3.1   RUSHER: Senator, we often hear the criticism that the seniority system greatly enhances and over-represents the South. Is that true, in your opinion?

3.2   PACKWOOD: Not necessarily the South. What it does over-represent are those areas that do not have competitive two-party systems.

3.3   RUSHER: You come from the West. Does it have a competitive two-party system?

3.4   PACKWOOD: It has a very competitive two-party system. It has [for a very long time], in the State of Washington, [elected] two Democrats, both of whom are chairmen.

3.5   RUSHER: Isn't it a fact that in the 20 years between 1947 and 1966, according to a new study by Professor Barbara Hinckley of Cornell, the Western Democrats had only 23 percent of the Democratic Senate seats and yet 35 percent of the Senate chairmanships?

3.6   PACKWOOD: That could very well be true.

3.7   RUSHER: In that case, then, it is not Southern, but Western, seats that are over-represented under the seniority system. Is that right?

3.8   PACKWOOD: I didn't say it was Southern.

3.9   RUSHER: But you did say that it was States that do not have a competitive two-party system.

3.10   PACKWOOD: Basically, you look at the larger States of this Union, you look at the New Yorks, the Ohios, the Pennsylvanias, the Californias—where it's very hard to build up two, three, or four-term incumbencies in the

Senate—and you'll find that year after year, they never have chairmen of significant committees.

3.11 RUSHER: Would you care to guess which State in that same 20-year period, between 1947 and 1966, produced the largest number of committee chairmen in the House of Representatives, of the Democratic party?

3.12 PACKWOOD: Haven't got the foggiest idea.

3.13 RUSHER: Well, it certainly wouldn't be a big State like New York, would it, according to you? And yet it *was* New York.

3.14 PACKWOOD: Could be. They have 45 Congressmen.

3.15 RUSHER: They certainly do. And they happen to be well represented in the House committee chairmanships. Now, wherein are they not represented?

3.16 PACKWOOD: What I said is: [the present system] tends to over-represent those districts where you have non-competitive two-party—

3.17 RUSHER: States, you said.

3.18 PACKWOOD: Well, States or districts. We have many districts in the North that are basically liberal Democrat. They have elected liberals, not conservatives, year after year after year. Mayor [Richard] Daley's wards and precincts in Chicago are good examples [of districts] where Democrats who are not Southerners can be elected time after time.

3.19 RUSHER: Mayor Daley isn't in New York. Which machines do we have in New York to compare with Mayor Daley's?

3.20 PACKWOOD: Fortunately, we have none; and what we do have are crumbling.

3.21 RUSHER: So that that [the power of party machines to keep men in office] is apparently not the explanation for the power of New York in the Democratic chairmanships in the House of Representatives.

3.22 PACKWOOD: Well, it doesn't really make any difference if you're talking about a machine or not. If you've got a district that has been gerrymandered* in such a way that it's 80 percent Republican or 80 percent Democrat, in all likelihood you're going to return the same man year after year.

3.23 RUSHER: You're referring, yes, to so-called "safe districts." In point of fact, are not approximately 85 percent of all the districts in the House of Representatives, according to political scientists, reasonably safe from the standpoint of the incumbent?

3.24 PACKWOOD: I don't think so.

---

*A "gerrymandered" district is one whose boundary lines have been drawn on the basis of narrowly political considerations so as to strengthen one party at the expense of another.

4.   SECOND AFFIRMATIVE WITNESS: DIRECT EXAMINATION

4.1   MILLER: In fact the seniority system, over time, has hurt; and it does provide examples where the leadership is not what it ought to be. To speak to us about some of the problems of the seniority system, we've asked to join us tonight Columnist Jack Anderson. Mr. Anderson, are there examples where the seniority system is not providing leadership that we might say is immediately relevant to the problems that we face?

4.2   COLUMNIST JACK ANDERSON: Yes. The examples are numerous. We can start with the Space Age. We're standing in the 1970's, on the edge of outer space, facing the greatest exploration challenge in human history. Well, to take us to the planets, the seniority system has given us Senate Space Chairman Clint Anderson, age 75, of Albuquerque, New Mexico, and House Space Chairman George Miller, age 79, of Alameda, California. Now, they're both kindly, feeble, ailing old men who were brought up when the modern marvel was the Model T.

4.3   [And] domestically, the nation is plagued by, and polarized by, racial tension. To achieve racial harmony in the United States, the seniority system has given us Senate Judiciary Chairman James Eastland, age 65, of Doddsville, Mississippi. The nation is of course troubled by our restive youth, who feel that their voice isn't being heard. Well, the legislation to reduce the voting age was delayed for months by House Judiciary Chairman Manny Celler, age 82, a great-grandfather. We're polluting our water; we're poisoning our air. And to purify our atmosphere, the seniority system has given us House Interior Chairman Wayne Aspinall, age 74, of Palisades, Colorado, whose career has been devoted to protecting oil and mining interests and some of the other polluters. Our big city ghettoes are tinderboxes, about to explode. To solve the big-city problems, the seniority system has given us a Senate Labor Chairman—he's in line for it—Jennings Randolph, age 68, of Elkins, West Virginia.

4.4   PALMIERI: Mr. Rusher, do you want to interrupt this litany; or do you want to ask what goes with the diet of a committee chairman that keeps him going this long?

5.   CROSS-EXAMINATION

5.1   RUSHER: No desire to interrupt it. I was just waiting for it to be over, that's all. I'd rather ask you some other questions, . . . Mr. Anderson. Would you include in your litany—just to get away from Congress for a moment

—that senile old Alabama reactionary, Justice Hugo Black, at 85? I presume you think he's past—

5.2   ANDERSON: I thought he was on the Supreme Court.

5.3   RUSHER: He is. Does that make him unimportant?

5.4   ANDERSON: Well, I think he ought to be retired. [He and Justice William O. Douglas, age 73,] should be retired because of their age.

5.5   RUSHER: You said, in your column on this subject, that a liberal group, whom you called "the plotters," are trying to line up enough support to strip the worst committee tyrants of their chairmanships. And you list four men at the top of the purge list. Is that correct?

5.6   ANDERSON: Yes.

5.7   RUSHER: One of whom has since died—Mendel Rivers—at the age of 65.

5.8   ANDERSON: But he's been replaced by Edward Hébert, age 70.

5.9   RUSHER: Right. . . . Your former boss, and your predecessor, Drew Pearson used to make predictions. Would you care to make a flat prediction that any proposal that comes before the House Democratic Caucus* this year, and is adopted by it, would in fact result in the removal of a single committee chairman? Conceivably, perhaps, Congressman McMillan is a borderline case.

5.10   ANDERSON: Well, what the Congress does, and what it ought to do, are quite often different things.

5.11   RUSHER: But you're proposing that it abolish the seniority rule, on the grounds that it's going to bring about these great changes. We've heard all the wonderful things that are going to happen, and I want you to make a flat prediction of a particular chairman who will lose his chairmanship as a result of this famous reform.

5.12   ANDERSON: Well, you see, Congressional reform is going to be left up to two men, basically. The two people who are supposed to bring Congress up to date would be Senate Rules Chairman Everett Jordan, age 74, of Saxapahaw, North Carolina, and House Rules Chairman William Colmer, age 80, of Pascagoula, Mississippi.

5.13   PALMIERI: You know, we have a lot of friends out there, in those small towns. It's beginning to get me a little worried.

---

*The Democratic Caucus in the House of Representatives, like its counterpart in the Senate, consists of all the members who are Democrats. On certain matters, the Caucus members bind themselves to cast a unanimous vote on the floor of the House in favor of a measure adopted by a majority of the Caucus. Most common cases of this sort are measures involving personnel: the choice of Speaker of the House and assignments of members to committees.

5.14   RUSHER: I've noticed that Mr. Anderson finds it intensely funny, [here] and in his column too, to list the small towns from which they come. John L. McMillan, from Mullins, South Carolina; William Colmer, from Pascagoula, Mississippi; Mendel Rivers, from a tired industrial suburb of North Charleston; William R. Poage, of Throckmorton County, Texas. What do you think you're proving by those long Miltonic lists of the names of the places they come from?

5.15   ANDERSON: I think I'm proving that the committees of Congress are commanded by tired, inept old men, whose . . . sole claim to power is their ability to outlive their colleagues.

5.16   RUSHER: How many times does a Senator have to be elected, on the average, in order to become a chairman of a committee?

5.17   ANDERSON: I haven't looked into this specifically.

5.18   RUSHER: Would you believe *twice*?

5.19   ANDERSON: Well, that's twelve years.

5.20   RUSHER: Is that too long, to be[come] a chairman of a committee of the United States Senate?

5.21   ANDERSON: I think it's quite possible that a Senator who has only been in the Senate for two years, a man like Packwood here, would have the ability to command a committee of Congress.

5.22   RUSHER: Yes; but is twelve years too long—two terms—to be elected to chair a committee of the United States Senate?

5.23   ANDERSON: Oh, I think that it should be determined entirely upon ability.

5.24   PALMIERI: Let's close with that, gentlemen. It would have made a great spelling bee.

5.25   MILLER: There's an attempt to somehow turn this into a partisan issue. This is not a partisan issue. Mr. Anderson mentioned liberals as well as conservatives, Democrats as well as Republicans. [It is] not an issue of partisanship. Nor is it a power grab, unless it's a power grab for the majority and for an efficiently running Congress. The Congress is the only institution in this country that determines advancement solely on the basis of seniority. Those who would maintain that system have a heavy burden indeed: to [show] why it . . . should be so different.

6.   FIRST NEGATIVE WITNESS: DIRECT EXAMINATION

6.1   RUSHER: In recent years, America's liberals have begun to regret the major role they played in the expansion of Presidential power in the 1930's and 1940's. Under Franklin Roosevelt it all seemed so logical. And the conservatives who opposed it, and warned against it, were so obviously "just biased against Roosevelt." It wasn't until Lyndon Johnson and Richard Nixon came along that these liberals realized, to their sorrow, that powers rashly conferred upon a President you favor are inherited by other Presidents you may not favor; that concentrations of power must be opposed consistently, and not just because our favorites happen to be out of office. Precisely the same considerations apply to this business of the seniority rules in Congress. As I said earlier, [abolition of the seniority system] is presented as a so-called reform; but it is actually just a power grab. A clique of liberals in both Houses, in both parties, have done a little counting, and think they could win one or two more chairmanships if the seniority rule were abolished and the selection of committee chairmen was determined by a vote of the committee members or [of] the whole party caucus. To accomplish this, they are quite ready, and indeed eager, to turn control of this whole vital process of picking the committee chairmen over to whatever faction of the majority party happens to have 51 percent or more of the votes in that party when Congress assembles. Perhaps they *have* counted right, and would gain some further power temporarily. But what if the next Congress, or the one after that, happens to be controlled by a 51 percent majority that the liberals don't like? Does that majority get to replace Senator Fulbright in the Foreign Relations Committee of the Senate, and Congressman Celler, that great liberal, in the Judiciary Committee of the House? What's sauce for the goose, they say, is sauce for the gander.

6.2   To tell us something about the fascinating history of the seniority custom, and to describe some of its great advantages, I call first upon the noted columnist and former editor of the *Richmond News-Leader*, James Jackson Kilpatrick. Mr. Kilpatrick, why was the seniority custom ever introduced in the first place, in the House and the Senate?

6.3   JAMES JACKSON KILPATRICK: It was introduced in the Senate, as I read the history of that period, in an effort to get away from the bitter intra-party fighting of the Twenty-Ninth Congress. There were only 58 Senators then, but they were sick and tired of the delay and confusion attendant upon these popularity contests. In the House, in 1910–1911, there was an effort to get away from the despotic power of Speaker Cannon.

6.4   RUSHER: And by making seniority the rule, [it came about that] the Speaker was no longer able to control the personal choice of the chairmen of the committees. What are the advantages—the absolute and affirmative advantages—of the seniority system in selecting committee chairmen?

6.5   KILPATRICK: The first of them, I think, is to avoid these bitter intra-party quarrels that we have seen in and out of both the Senate and the House in recent years. I vividly remember, because I happened to cover it, the fight in 1967, when Mr. Gilbert of New York and Mr. Burleson of Texas were struggling for a seat—not the chairmanship, but a seat on [the House Ways and Means Committee]. In the end Burleson lost, but he lost by two votes [in the Democratic Caucus], and we're still feeling the bruises of that fight three years ago. We're going through it now in the House, in a fight over the leadership of the [Democratic] party, between Mr. Udall and Mr. Bolling. That fight will leave bruises and wounds. A party can recover from these at the leadership level. But if we had to go through this every two years, for 21 chairmanships with these struggles for power I think the House would be in chaos. And incidentally, my friends have mentioned merit and ability and so forth. It has nothing to do with merit and ability; that's horsefeathers. We're talking about power. And this is what we would have: 21 struggles for power every two years.

6.6   Secondly—and the main thing—is that the seniority system contributes an element of stability in what Mr. Packwood has described as "this dizzying world." It's a brake upon the power of the Presidency. It's a brake upon the impulse of the people. It's a restraint against the automatic power of the 51 percent.

6.7   RUSHER: Does [the seniority system] tend to favor senile old men of the type [of which] we have heard, together with the long funny names of the places that they were born in, from Mr. Jack Anderson?

6.8   KILPATRICK: In the course of time, it does favor older men, of course. But I'm at a point where I see nothing wrong in being more than 65 years old. I see nothing wrong in coming from a small town in the United States of America. I see often great advantages in coming from a small town.

7.   CROSS-EXAMINATION

7.1   MILLER: [About] the leadership battle now in the House: when the time came to choose a successor to Speaker McCormack, do you think the senior Democrat in the House of Representatives should automatically have become Speaker?

7.2   KILPATRICK: Of course not—not Speaker.

7.3   MILLER: Well, now there is a potential bitter battle. We now have the House Majority Leader. If you don't apply seniority to leadership, why apply it to—

7.4   KILPATRICK: You misunderstand the system completely, Mr. Miller. Truly you do.

7.5   MILLER: There are lots of people who misunderstand it with me.

7.6   KILPATRICK: Well, I'll try to educate you if I may. A man who rises to become chairman of a committee will have served on that committee for many years because of his interest in that committee. But the fact that a man wishes to be a floor leader has nothing to do with his seniority. Being a floor leader in either chamber is a tedious, demanding job, and the qualifications or the interests of a man are not necessarily those of a committee chairman.

7.7   MILLER: . . . let me ask you then about the military, where the same problems apply, and where Congress itself has imposed a retirement age of 65 or 70. Should we automatically have the senior military commander become Chief of Naval Operations? Admiral Zumwalt would not have.

7.8   KILPATRICK: You're comparing horses and rabbits here. I've covered the Congress for a long time. I've covered the Pentagon a long time. And it's a rather different matter, the sedentary life of [the Congressman] and that [of] military command.

7.9   MILLER: Well, let me ask you what the difference is. You said it was in terms of power. The Chairman of the Joint Chiefs of Staff cannot be over 65. The Chairman of the House Armed Services Committee, or the Senate Armed Services Committee, may be 75 or 80. The Chairman of the Armed Services Committee has every bit as much power over what happens in this country militarily as the Joint Chiefs of Staff. Why a different standard?

7.10   KILPATRICK: I think of this necessarily in terms of personalities. I know John Stennis—one of the great chairmen of all time on [the Senate Armed Services Committee]. I wouldn't care how old John Stennis was. There's a man—he's not in command of troops; he's in command of a committee.

7.11   MILLER: Tell me about the principle. You see nothing wrong with a man of any age being chairman of an Armed Services Committee, and controlling the military destiny of the country, because his life is sedentary; but you do not approve of that in terms of the Joint Chiefs of Staff.

7.12   KILPATRICK: I think it's a very different matter, if we're talking about the legislative branch of government or the—

7.13   MILLER: But the one thing the Joint Chiefs have in common with the committees, as you mentioned when we were talking about the Speaker, is, they've worked on the problem, they know the problem—all the attributes of knowledge, of age, of experience, all apply. Why the difference?

7.14   KILPATRICK: Because we're dealing here with committee chairmen, who live, as I've said, a fairly sedentary life. Their expertise is wrapped up in the years they have spent sitting in this chair—

7.15   MILLER: You've not heard of long staff assignments in the Pentagon, I take it.

7.16   KILPATRICK: Oh yes, they have some of that, too.

7.17   MILLER: What about private institutions? Is there any other institution in this country, private or public, for whom you recommend this . . . system of promotion only on the basis of seniority?

7.18   KILPATRICK: You said in your opening remarks twice [that] you didn't know of one. You could have looked to Virginia, just across the river. The Virginia General Assembly's committees operate entirely on the seniority system.

7.19   MILLER: Is there anyone that you recommend it for, besides the Congress? Would you have all State legislatures in this country go on the seniority system?

7.20   KILPATRICK: Yes. If it worked as well in the State legislatures as I think it's worked in the Congress, I would recommend it for all of them.

7.21   MILLER: Would you recommend it for private corporations as well?

7.22   KILPATRICK: No. I think there may be different considerations operating in the private sector that do not operate in the public sector.

7.23   MILLER: Well, you'll have to tell me, again, in [the case of] the private sector as with the military; . . . now you *do* have to educate me.

7.24   KILPATRICK: We're dealing with leadership coming up within a private corporation, and the object of a private organization is to make money— which hasn't been the object lately of the Federal government.

7.25   MILLER: It certainly has not. And you think the Federal government is doing that much better than the "failing" private corporations?

7.26   KILPATRICK: I don't think they're doing well at all. I think there are very different considerations that affect the operations of a corporation, in the private market, than those that affect a chamber of the Congress.

7.27   PALMIERI: Isn't it simply a question of democracy operating in the committee?

7.28   KILPATRICK: Oh, democracy *does* operate. If you read Professor Hinckley's study, which is a very valuable book about to come out (Indiana University Press), you will find that democracy *has* worked in the selection of these chairmen. If the South has been well represented in the Democratic chairmanships, it's because the South has held more than half of the Democratic seats in the Congress.*

---

*Barbara Hinckley, *The Seniority System of Congress* (Indiana University Press, 1970).

7.29 PALMIERI: If it's worked, though, it's worked without voting [for chairmen].

8. SECOND NEGATIVE WITNESS: DIRECT EXAMINATION

8.1 RUSHER: If Mr. Miller really wants to know of one other institution in the United States which advances people [of] great age in this way I think Mr. Anderson—who was once, as I understand it, a missionary of the Mormon Church—might tell him that [the Mormons] recently replaced their leader, when he died at the age of 96, with a gentleman who's only 93. So there *are* other institutions that do it. To consider, now, the political aspects here, I call upon Professor Charles O. Jones of the Department of Political Science of the University of Pittsburgh. Professor Jones, just toward the end of Mr. Kilpatrick's cross-examination, we were getting right into the territory: are committee chairmen in fact unrepresentative of their parties in the Congress, as you've studied the matter?

8.2 PROF. CHARLES O. JONES: It all depends, obviously, on what one means by "representation"—the measures you use. Often regionalism is used as the measure of representation. If one relies on that as "representativeness" of a party, in the chairmanship or in the ranking Republican slot, the fact is that it follows quite closely. On the Democratic side, with chairmanships—as has been noted—the West is the most over-represented. And the Republicans follow . . . carefully the regional representation in the party.

8.3 RUSHER: But then—moving from the question of regional representation [to] whether or not a committee chairman actually fairly represents the view of the majority of the members of his committee, or whether he's just up there bossing them by virtue of his seniority: Do committee chairmen in general *not* represent, or *do* they represent, the majority views of their committees?

8.4 JONES: Again, one has to set the boundaries and define precisely what you're talking about in "representation." If we mean the kind of majority that you get on committees, typically the chairmen *do* represent the kind of members that get on committees. Members go on committees for all kinds of reasons. Some members actually want to be on the Merchant Marine and Fisheries Committee. Some members actually want to stay on the Post Office and Civil Service Committee. They go on for a variety of different reasons, and they rise in that position eventually to positions of leadership and are quite representative of the interests on that committee.

8.5   RUSHER: . . . we've heard a lot that suggests that it's very difficult for an able young Congressman or Senator without much seniority, like Senator Packwood, to become a chairman of a committee. Is this in fact the case? Is it difficult for an able man, with some persistence, to become a committee chairman in either house?

8.6   JONES: There are two points, I think, to be made here. First of all, in the post-[World War II] period, [it takes] two [six-year] terms for a Senator, typically, to rise to a position of chairman. It takes eight [two-year] terms for a member in the House of Representatives, typically, to rise to this position. It takes considerably less time to rise to important *sub*committee chairmanships. And there is another point[:] . . . a truly able man, . . . a new, young, interested, involved Senator of the modern era, who has had an impact without being a chairman, or without being a ranking Republican—[his] ability can still come through, in the House of Representatives and the Senate.

9.   CROSS-EXAMINATION

9.1   MILLER: You do think that those Congressmen and Senators that want to be on the Merchant Marine Committee ought to be on that committee, since that's their expressed interest and they may come from a district that [itself] has an interest?

9.2   JONES: Yes, sir.

9.3   MILLER: So in fact if they want to, they should be. But under the seniority system, both in assignment and moving up the ladder, wanting to or having interest is not enough, is it? You must be next in line.

9.4   JONES: Committee *assignments* are *not* based on seniority. They are based primarily on a number of factors: geography, the interest of the member, and so forth.

9.5   MILLER: In which seniority plays a substantial role. But what about moving *up* the committee? Now, if someone has been assigned to the committee against his will, and someone else wants to be on the committee [but] happens to be lower down in seniority, that's it. The more senior man gets the chairman[ship]. Can you defend that?

9.6   JONES: I defend it, of course. . . . A reference has been made to the variety of institutions in this country, and how one proceeds to leadership in those institutions. Practically any social institution, in this country or elsewhere, relies on an experience system. There are varieties of experience systems, to be sure.

9.7   MILLER: Valuing experience, and making it the sole criterion, are two different things. Let's look at one of the effects. You say it's representative. The "swing districts" in this country—the districts that go back and forth (a lot of suburban and urban districts)—never have a chance to have one of their members become a senior, powerful member of Congress, do they? If you're so unfortunate in this country as to live in a district that follows national election returns, and change your Congressman every four or six years, your district will never have power in the Congress, will it?

9.8   JONES: Studies of the specific "swing districts" will show that—particularly with the reapportionment decisions by the Supreme Court—these kinds of districts change. Through redistricting, particularly [the decisions of] 1962 and 1963, . . . the "swing districts" changed; and so it is not the case any longer that . . . we can identify a particular set of districts that cannot continue to re-elect a Congressman.

9.9   MILLER: No, we can't identify the same ones; but the fact of the matter is that as long as seniority is the sole criterion, there will be millions of people living in Congressional districts in this country who never have a chance of having their Congressman be a major power in the Congress.

9.10   JONES: I assume that you're not proposing that we select chairmen based upon the swing districts in this country.

9.11   MILLER: . . . the proposal tonight is whether seniority be the sole criterion —whether experience be the sole criterion. In fact, those districts that are under-represented—in those States who may not get the committee chairmen—aren't those the very districts that have the urban and the suburban problems, the mass transit and the education problems?

9.12   JONES: Not entirely, as has been pointed out. The State with the most chairmanships in the post-war period was New York State.

9.13   MILLER: Well, that's just the one example; but by and large—

9.14   JONES: Well, I haven't memorized the rest.

9.15   MILLER: Well, . . . you should try.

10.   THIRD NEGATIVE WITNESS: DIRECT EXAMINATION

10.1   RUSHER: Now let us hear from a member of the House of Representatives: the gentleman from the Thirteenth Congressional District of the great State of Illinois, Congressman Philip Crane. I must say, Congressman: for a "senile reactionary," you are remarkably well-preserved. How old are you . . . ? And how long have you been in the House of Representatives?

10.2   REP. PHILIP CRANE: I was 40 last November [1970]. I was elected to my first full term in November of [1970]. And I might note that I have been in the Congress just slightly over a year; I'm assigned to [the] Banking and Currency [Committee]; I've moved one third of the way up the seniority ladder in less than a year.

10.3   RUSHER: I understand then that you, despite your relative newness to the Congress and your youth, are in favor of the seniority system.

10.4   CRANE: I am; but I wasn't always. As a former academician, I think I took the typical academician's attitude toward the concept of the seniority rule in Congress. It's been an educational process since getting here. I have since come to believe in the wisdom of the seniority system.

10.5   RUSHER: Is there any truth to the statement we've had repeated again and again tonight, that committee chairmen have too much power?

10.6   CRANE: One has to realize that if a committee chairman has too much power, the committee can take it away from him. And this in fact has been done in better than two-thirds of the committees in the House. . . . A simple majority vote will do it. And in addition to that, there are other checks on committee chairmen's powers. On the one hand, he can be removed—as was done by the Democratic Party [to a] committee chairman just three years ago—by a caucus—

10.7   RUSHER: Was that hard to do?

10.8   CRANE: No. A simple majority on the part of that party can remove him. And finally, a discharge petition is a way of removing a particular bill from consideration by a committee and getting it before the whole House.*

10.9   RUSHER: Yes, but if a bill is being bottled up by a committee chairman, isn't it hard to get it out of his committee?

10.10   CRANE: Not at all. In fact, we did this last summer. We signed the "equality of rights for women" discharge petition. Simple majority in the House. That got it before the House, although it'd been locked up theoretically—

10.11   RUSHER: . . . Well then, why this big demand for change . . . and the abolition of the seniority system?

---

*Under the present discharge rule, a committee can be relieved of control over a bill after it has had the bill 30 days, if a majority of all the House members sign a petition to that effect. The discharge motion, or petition, must be on the calendar of House business at least seven days. Moreover, the petition can be taken up for action only on certain days of the month. But when it *is* taken up, it is "privileged" business; it comes ahead of other matters. Rarely indeed has this procedure been utilized. However, the *availability* of the procedure may forestall the need for its actual *use*.

10 . 12   CRANE: I think [there are] two reasons. One, it's a short-sighted, short-run, seeming advantage to many liberals in both the House and the Senate. In addition to this, however, there is the disposition to seek a scapegoat; and the "senile chairmen" make convenient scapegoats when your pet project does not come out of committee or is not passed.

10 . 13   RUSHER: I notice that Mr. Miller in his opening statement complained . . . about the failure of Congress to act on various matters in this last session, and implicitly blamed this, at least in large part, on the committee chairmen. Was it their fault?

10 . 14   CRANE: No. I would take issue with that evaluation. We have the situation of a Republican President and Democrat-controlled Congress. I think therein lay much of the problem.

10 . 15   RUSHER: One last and very important question: what would be the effect of the abolition of seniority rule?

10 . 16   CRANE: I think it would be a disaster. . . . the blood-letting, the electioneering, the log-rolling, the opportunity for big States to gang up on little States, coupled with the opportunity for outside pressure groups—and I personally experienced that when I got down here with my educational background. I sought Education and Labor and, according to newspaper accounts, the A.F.L.-C.I.O. was responsible in denying me, as well as Shirley Chisholm, an opportunity to get on that committee.

10 . 17   RUSHER: And if they deny you a seat on the committee, think what they could do if only they didn't have the seniority system blocking the way to the chairmanship.

10 . 18   CRANE: Yes indeed.

11.   CROSS-EXAMINATION

11 . 1   MILLER: Congressman, committee chairmen *do* have substantial power, despite this litany of ways to get around them. But you—

11 . 2   CRANE: The powers they enjoy are the powers that are given, [first by the majority party's caucus, which makes "minimal rules" for all committee chairmen, and then by "the committee itself"].

11 . 3   MILLER: [These controls scarcely affect] the committee chairman's power to schedule the meetings, to call up bills. [On] the things that make the committee run, he's very rarely countered, [because of his] threat of retribution.

11.4   CRANE: An arbitrary committee chairman can, and has, in the past, had power taken away from him. And he has to work in a cooperative way with members of the committee.

11.5   MILLER: Those one or two examples of [disciplining] the arbitrary committee chairman—

11.6   CRANE: No, there are a number of examples: in the last 20 years, as I say, better than two-thirds have had power taken away from them.

11.7   MILLER: Tell me, if you were elected from a district that happened to change its Congressman every four years or six years or eight years, perhaps ten—if you were elected from such a district, and you continued to live in that district, and had the interests of that district at heart, how would you explain to your constituents that they forever were to be denied substantial power in the Congress of the United States?

11.8   CRANE: Well, I don't think you can make that claim, because there are instances of people making committee chairmanships within that span of time, even in the House.

11.9   MILLER: Again, the incidental, by and large—

11.10   CRANE: To be sure; but I could, as Professor Jones observed, perhaps make a *sub*committee chairmanship in that period of time. In addition to that, only 22 percent of districts in the United States are, in effect, denied the opportunity to get a committee chairmanship.

11.11   MILLER: That happens to be 40 million Americans. Let me ask you. . . . The reason we're discussing the seniority system is that the longer you're in Congress, the more likely you are to get a committee. Most committee chairmen serve for six, eight, twelve years. Two-thirds in the House are over 65. If two-thirds are over 65 in the House, there are not many young men who get the committee chairman[ships]. How would you explain to those 500,000 constituents in one of those 22 percent districts why they will never have power, but their next-door neighbors will?

11.12   CRANE: You're implicitly assuming that that committee chairman does not represent my constituents' interests. And I won't buy that, because this is that "generation-gap" argument. And the truth of the matter is—

11.13   MILLER: Generation gap!

11.14   CRANE: Right: that there's a generation gap between the leadership of the House and, presumably, the policies and positions taken by our respective parties.

11.15   MILLER: That's the oldest gap in the world. That's the "taxation-without-representation" gap.

11.16   CRANE: Well, except for the fact that I'm 40, and I see a generation gap between myself and the average member of Congress, who's in his middle fifties, and [also between myself and] the "now" generation, . . . that says "Don't trust anyone over 30," all of us in the Congress can be classified as out of touch with the oncoming generation.

11 . 17 MILLER: Tell me your explanation for why this institution should be different—why the men over 65 or 70 in this institution continue to wield power.

11 . 18 CRANE: For a very important reason. Unlike business, or unlike the military, the Congress represents civilized warfare. We have warfare that goes on here on a civilized basis, and I think the objective then should be to minimize the friction, to provide a basis for the greatest degree of harmony, because we are seeking to reconcile conflicting interests.

11 . 19 MILLER: And the basis for that degree of harmony is a chairman of the Rules Committee that, against the wishes of his committee and the Congress, can bottle up civil rights legislation for—years?

11 . 20 CRANE: Now, wait a second. It's *not* against the wishes of his committee. Obviously his committee goes along with that, or the committee would take action and overrule the chairman. And secondly, the entire committee can be discharged from its responsibility by a simple majority . . . in the House.

11 . 21 MILLER: And is it representative of the urban people in this country to have the chairman of [the Senate's] District of Columbia Committee come from a small town in South Carolina?

11 . 22 CRANE: That's happenstance, and that could change tomorrow.

11 . 23 MILLER: The "incidental" examples in your favor are "general," but mine are "happenstance." I have no further questions. Thank you.

11 . 24 RUSHER: (in summation): Just remember this: the powers of chairmen, despite what Mr. Miller has told you about these "overweening" powers, are precisely what the Democratic Caucus has prescribed that they should be, and what the committee members themselves allow them to be. There isn't a single committee chairman in Congress, and never *will* be under the seniority system, that is not under the control of both his own committee membership and his party caucus. Mr. Miller worries about districts (which he says are mostly city districts, forgetting Congressman Emanuel Celler—is *that* just a happenstance?—from Brooklyn, chairman of the House Judiciary Committee). He worries about districts, unlike Celler's, which are forever throwing their Congressmen in and out of office again, and therefore of course can hardly expect as much influence as a district which finds a good man and elects and then re-elects

him—keeps sending him to Washington. What we are seeing, I repeat, is a power grab by people who simply cannot wait for that process to mature. And they are doing a disservice to the cause of the tradition of checks and balances and [of] resistance to the wishes of a powerful transient majority.

12.   THIRD AFFIRMATIVE WITNESS: DIRECT EXAMINATION

12.1   MILLER: . . . The "power grab" has occurred, and the power is now held by the men who've grabbed it: the senior committee chairmen of Congress. And the question is: how to get that power back. You have to look at the arguments that are being made: "A majority of Congressmen [, they say,] should not choose their committee chairmen—a bare 51 percent." Well, that's the basis of the whole electoral system. One man, one vote in the country—thwarted in the Congress. "Only 22 percent of the people in the country live in districts that mean that they won't have senior members of Congress." The fact of the matter is that the way men become chairmen of powerful committees in Congress today, ordains . . . that they by and large come from small towns; by and large are over 65; by and large come from low-population States; by and large are not representative of the urban problem. They may know about it; but the basis of the country is that it's those who represent those people [concerned] make the decisions. As Mr. Kilpatrick himself said, it's a question of power, not of knowledge; so it cannot be said that simply because *they* [the chairmen] may have the knowledge, . . . the people in the district should be condemned to forever being unrepresented. A Congress with old men, and a Congress that does not work—that is what we seek to change.

12.2   To talk to that change, I have asked to join us tonight Congressman Donald Fraser of Minnesota. Congressman Fraser is chairman of the Democratic Study Group, the first group to seek in an organized way a major re-evaluation of the seniority system. Congressman, . . . do the committee chairmen have substantial power?

12.3   REP. DONALD FRASER: They have an enormous amount of power, and it's power that often goes unrestrained, unchecked, unless it reaches an excess that is so far out that some remedial action has to be taken. That doesn't happen very often; but within that outside limit, there is, I think, an excess of power which is not always used for the interests of the country or for the majority group that put them in power.

12.4   MILLER: [Does] the combination of that power and one-party districts and the seniority system hurt in the House of Representatives?

12.5   FRASER: Yes, it hurts. One of the most important ways that it hurts is that the majority *would* have the capacity to mobilize the Congress to move on major issues *except* [for the fact] that it encounters these major blocks of powers which are represented by committee chairmen, who are completely independent. They can tell a Speaker or Majority Leader to just jump, because they have an absolute right to their job. What happens is that the leadership has to get on the telephone, or go pay a call, and plead with the committee chairman to do something. You can't run a democratic institution with this kind of fracturing and diffusion of power, which makes it impossible to respond to the problems of the country.

12.6   MILLER: Would a change in the seniority system lead to this kind of "intra-party civilized warfare" that apparently Congressmen are not grown up enough to deal with? Would it destroy the Congress?

12.7   FRASER: Not at all. Competition is healthy. An excess can probably create problems, but [in general] Congressmen will tend to shy away from an excess. They don't like it. That's one of the reasons there's been too much tolerance of the seniority system. So we need to restore some differences of opinion [and] work them out? [we must] have the [majority party's] caucus work its will, but [we must] try to get chairmen who are *responsive* to the majority will, who will move with the leadership—who will try to make things better.

12.8   MILLER: On balance, would a change in the seniority system bring more responsive chairmen in the House of Representatives, and help it to function better?

12.9   FRASER: If we could exert the power of the [majority party's] caucus (and that's the crucial question: will we exert the will or the power that we have?) with respect to one or two committee chairmen, I think the other committee chairmen would become much more responsive to the interests of the caucus generally.

12.10   PALMIERI: Do you think [a change in the seniority system] would result in a change in any committee chairmanship?

12.11   FRASER: Changing a committee chairman is a tough job. I'm personally involved in seeking to replace one committee chairman, on a committee on which I serve: the chairman of the District of Columbia Committee. I think [the change] would serve the District of Columbia and our Democratic Party.

12.12   PALMIERI: But you're not sure it would happen.

12.13   FRASER: Well, that's the key point.

13.   CROSS-EXAMINATION

13.1   RUSHER: I saw you on the television program in Washington here Sunday, Congressman, and as I understood it, at that time . . . you were not taking the position that you favored the abolition of the seniority system for all committees. You indicated that your ambitions to remove chairmen, or to bring them under tighter control, were pretty much confined to the District of Columbia Committee. Was I wrong? Are you in favor of the total abolition of the seniority system?

13.2   FRASER: The point I made then is the same I have now: I'm prepared to let seniority be a major consideration, and I'm not willing to abandon common sense for that consideration.

13.3   RUSHER: What about this column of Mr. Anderson's, in which he says that a bunch of liberal "plotters" have drawn up a purge list. Are you one of the plotters?

13.4   FRASER: I don't regard it in that light at all—

13.5   RUSHER: Have you got a purge list?

13.6   FRASER: Let me make the point that the committee [is] recommending procedural changes that will make the challenge easier. The committee has Southerners on it; it's got committee chairmen on it; it's got moderates on it. And it [produced] a unanimous report.

13.7   RUSHER: Is there a purge list such as Mr. Anderson reported?

13.8   FRASER: Not to my knowledge, within the Democratic [Study] Group itself.

13.9   RUSHER: Are there plotters, liberal plotters, trying to seize control, as he reported?

13.10   FRASER: No. I don't think there's anybody [who] expects to seize control.

13.11   RUSHER: If this system isn't going to change any chairmen, what good is abolishing the seniority system going to do?

13.12   FRASER: That's the heart of the matter. The question is: Will the Democrats in the House, where I have my experience, exercise the power they have to move from a strict adherence to the seniority system, which after all is only about 25 years old, contrary to other statements [about it] that have been made here?

13.13   RUSHER: That's not my understanding, but perhaps yours is more accurate.

13.14   FRASER: There was a change in 1910, but the seniority system [was] not . . . observed rigidly from 1910 up to 1946.

13.15   RUSHER: It hasn't even been observed *rigidly* since 1946. Half a dozen chairmen have been removed.

13.16   FRASER: That's the point, you see. We *have* on occasion stripped people of seniority.

13 . 17   RUSHER: Well, then, why the need for a change?

13 . 18   FRASER: I gather that you would argue that we shouldn't even have done that—

13 . 19   RUSHER: No; I'm arguing that you have all the powers you need, if you would only exercise them instead of complaining.

13 . 20   FRASER: All right, are you in favor of exercising them?

13 . 21   RUSHER: I am certainly in favor of *your trying to.*

13 . 22   FRASER: But then we're in agreement; then you're on our side.

13 . 23   RUSHER: But then go get a majority of your committee behind you . . . and you can do whatever you want to, with Congressman McMillan or any other chairman, instead of going on television programs to stick your tongue out at him when you don't have the votes to defeat him, which is what you're doing.

13 . 24   FRASER: We'll see whether or not we have the votes—

13 . 25   RUSHER: Mr. Maestro Anderson, the predictor, wasn't prepared to predict that you did, you will notice.

13 . 26   FRASER: Well, [McMillan] has hope down in his heart in the House.

13 . 27   RUSHER: One last question. It is said that the selection of chairmen by the whole party caucus or by the committee members, rather than by seniority, would result in younger leadership. Bearing in mind that the Speakers of the House are elected by the whole party caucus, would you care to guess—or do you perchance know?—what their average age, on election as Speaker, has been, during the whole period of the twentieth century to date?

13 . 28   FRASER: No, I wouldn't guess, but I—

13 . 29   RUSHER: It's over 63 years old. Now what kind of a reform do you suppose *that* is? In favor of youth?

13 . 30   FRASER: Age is not necessarily a disability. . . . All I'm saying is: let's not ignore every consideration *except* seniority; let's bring some common sense to bear.

13 . 31   RUSHER: We are, on the contrary, considering a great many things. We are considering the pressures [brought by] the Presidency, the Speaker of the House, a man like Boss Cannon, and all of the labor and other pressure groups that press upon the Congress; and all of these are blocked by the seniority system. That is what we are considering.

13 . 32   FRASER: As I understand it, you agree with me that we ought to try to use the power we have, and that's all I'm asking—

13 . 33   RUSHER: Do you think that 226 members of the House of Representatives, who right now have at least one committee or subcommittee chairmanship, is a lot or a little?

13.34   FRASER: What we're proposing to do under the reform is to spread the action to more members.

13.35   RUSHER: Well, the action has already been spread to 226 out of the 435 members. That's a pretty big spread, isn't it?

13.36   FRASER: Are you saying [that] 226 have subcommittee chairmanships or chairmanships—

13.37   RUSHER: Yes, sir—or equivalent Republican ranks: ranking Republican on either a committee or a subcommittee.

13.38   FRASER: All I can tell you is that if we adopt the reforms that we are urging, we will limit one member to one subcommittee chairmanship, and that will help—

13.39   RUSHER: If you consult these statistics, I think you may find the situation isn't as bad as you fear.

14.   CLOSING STATEMENTS

14.1   MILLER: The subcommittee chairmen are appointed by the committee chairmen. [The committee chairmen] are the ones that have the power, and out of the 21 House committee chairmen, as we've seen, two-thirds are over 65. That Speaker who's under 65 is younger than two-thirds of his chairmen. What are we talking about? It's a real issue. You live in an urban area. If you have the typical problems that an urban resident has, you are likely to be unrepresented in the Congress in the higher reaches of power. In fact if you're in a majority in this country, you are likely to be unrepresented in Congress in the reaches of power in Congress, and will always be, so long as seniority is the sole determinant for major power in the country. "They also serve, who only stand and wait"—but they don't have to lead.

14.2   RUSHER: There's a lot more to this seniority business than meets the eye. As Mr. Anderson said in his column, the proposal to abolish the seniority rule is basically a plot by a liberal clique in Congress to purge and replace a handful of committee chairmen who are guilty of the crime of disagreeing with them. In order to carry out their purge, these self-styled reformers are ready to violate the great American tradition of careful checks on the power of transient majorities, [and] to turn the House of Representatives, particularly, into a permanent battleground for the control of key committees, featuring the very kind of under-the-table deals and horse-trading and pressure groups that resulted less than a century ago in the rise of Boss Cannon. Congress climbed out of that morass by means of the reform called the "seniority rule," which is valuable precisely because no clique and no boss and no President can tamper with the iron laws of arithmetic. I urge you to reject this slick proposal, which will actually turn back the clock and restore out-and-out caucus and boss rule to Congress.

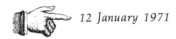 *12 January 1971*

A SUGGESTED EXERCISE

Put yourself in the following situation: You must cast one of two votes that will decide the fate of the "seniority system" as the method of selecting committees of the United States Congress. Your only source of information about that system is the debate (including the descriptive overview) by "The Advocates."

The other vote must be cast by Paul Puzzled. Paul feels as you do about basic values. Like you, moreover, he knows nothing about the seniority system other than what he has read in the debate. He will not cast his vote, however, until you give him the benefit of your advice. He will respond only to careful reasoning based on testimony given in the debate.

Your task, then, is to compose a letter urging Paul to join you in voting either to retain or to abolish the seniority system, and justifying that advice by reference to what was said, and what was conspicuously absent from, the debate by "The Advocates."

COMMENTARY

The foregoing debate serves not only to identify some of the principal lines of argument for and against retaining the seniority system of the United States Congress, but also to illustrate some devices of argument that recur in public controversies. Here is an incomplete inventory of such devices.

Arguing Ad Hominem

Textbooks in logic commonly devote at least one chapter to "informal fallacies," among which they commonly list *argumentum ad hominem*. This

Latin phrase means, most literally, arguing "to the man." More broadly, it means appraising a conclusion by reference to the identity—the character, the motives, the interests—of its proponents or opponents. Since such argumentation deals with content by way of origin, it has aptly been labeled "the genetic fallacy."

This verbiage occurs either in a positive or a negative form. Its positive form consists of lauding a proposal or conclusion on the strength of claims, more or less documented, that men of wisdom and virtue support it. A variant of this technique is to argue that a given conclusion or proposal is sound because large numbers of ordinary people subscribe to it. The Latin name for this variant on *ad hominem* argument is *argumentum ad populum*. An English equivalent is the "plain folks device."

The negative form of this device consists of denouncing a conclusion or proposal on the basis of claims that it is supported by, or is in the interest of, fools and/or knaves.

The debate on the Congressional seniority system (among other debates compiled in *American Problems*) furnished an example of negative *ad hominem* argument. William Rusher used this device when he stigmatized the drive to abolish the seniority system as a "power grab by a busy little clique" of "liberals" (**1.4**, **6.1**, **11.24**, **14**.2; see also Rep. Philip Crane at **10.12**). Thus, Rusher appealed for preservation of the seniority system on the assumption (in part) that its opponents are bad guys. Rusher intimated, moreover, that the villains who oppose the seniority system stand to gain at least a short-run advantage by its abolition.

Such argumentation is basically fallacious.* It serves as a *diversion*. In the domain of logic, it diverts attention from crucial questions about whether a given conclusion follows from a given set of premises, and whether the premises are sound. In the domain of public policy, it diverts attention from central questions about desirable ends and expedient means. To accept *ad hominem* arguments is hazardous indeed, since (a) men endowed with the best of intentions can err in their guesses about means and ends, while (b) 'selfish' men can propound proposals that are sound for others, either because the egotists' interests are congenial to others' interests or because the egotists misconstrue their own interests.

---

*A careful distinction needs to be made, however, between arguing *ad hominem* about what is desirable and/or logical, on the one hand, and arguing *ad hominem* about matters of fact. It is perfectly proper for an attorney to challenge the motives, the interests, and/or the credentials of witnesses who make claims about what they saw or what is true.

Incidentally, one might wonder whether Rusher's choice of *ad hominem* argument was strategically well conceived. Rusher encouraged the impression that behind the controversy over the Congressional 'seniority system' lay a clash between "liberals" and "conservatives." He further implied that the "liberals" stand to gain (while the "conservatives," presumably, stand to lose) from abolition of the 'seniority system.' He thus advanced a line of argument which his opponents, perhaps, would not have dared to voice openly, and which would attract support from "liberals." In so far as Rusher's audience contained a large proportion of "liberals," his *ad hominem* argument would backfire.

The Intentionalist Fallacy

Closely related to *ad hominem* argument is a practice that can be dubbed "the intentionalist fallacy." This consists of confounding the motives or aims that allegedly give rise to a proposal with the result (the function, the actual consequence) that emanates from implementing that proposal.

James Jackson Kilpatrick furnished an example of this practice when he testified (6.3) that the Senate's seniority system was adopted after the Senators tired of their incessant struggles for position, struggles that were not forestalled by the presence of agreed-upon guidelines ("seniority") for distributing offices. This testimony served to suggest that the seniority system put an end—a durable end—to large-scale conflict among Senators. This would imply in turn that the seniority system forestalls, rather than generates, legislative paralysis among Congressmen. Such an inference may be warranted by all the evidence, but it certainly is not warranted by the immediate evidence. It not only confounds *intention* with actual *result*, but also confounds *past* intention (*or* result) with *present* function. Senators in the past may have *hoped* to reduce self-destructive conflict by means of the seniority system. But it remains to be seen whether they hit upon an effective remedy, under present conditions as well as past conditions.

Statistical Nonsense

In a book called *Historians' Fallacies: Toward a Logic of Historical Thought* (Harper and Row, 1970), David Hackett Fischer alludes to "the fallacy of statistical nonsense." This means numerical material that is empty of meaning, usually because some necessary element has been left out. Fischer mentions, as an example, the judgment that since the supply of doctors in Russia increased during the period 1897-1935 from 1,380 to 12,000, then Communism can be credited with considerable "effectiveness."

Such a judgment is questionable on two levels. First, there is the question of whether changes in the supply of doctors suffice to disclose the "effectiveness" of a regime or an ideology. Second, there is the question—assuming that the answer to the first is not negative—of whether reliable information about change in the supply of doctors has been furnished.

The gravity of the second question can be appreciated fully, perhaps, only with the aid of a rudimentary knowledge of Russian history—such as awareness of the date of the Bolshevik, or Communist, revolution. That event took place not in 1897 but in 1918. Accordingly, it is at least *possible* that:

a) the supply of doctors *decreased* after the advent of the Communist regime—from a high of 15,000 in 1918, for example, down to the figure of 12,000 in 1935; or that

b) the *rate of increase* in the supply of doctors was greater during the pre-Communist period than during the Communist period—jumping from 1,380 to 8,000, or by more than 400 percent, in the 21 years between 1897 and 1918, for example, while increasing by 4,000, or only 50 percent, in the years from 1919 to 1935.

Possibilities of this kind are wholly compatible with the statistical information that was given. Consequently, even if we accept the notion that changes in the supply of doctors positively disclose "effectiveness" of regime, and even if we accept the data given at face value, we are in no position to draw any conclusion about regime "effectiveness." The seemingly hard data that has been given is, literally, nonsense. (Similarly, we are in no position to compare the rate of increase during the early Communist years with rates of increase in non-Communist lands).

Two examples of statistical nonsense occurred during the debate on the Congressional seniority system. One was supplied by Howard Miller on behalf of opponents of the seniority system. It consisted of stating (2.1) that three-quarters of the chairmen of standing committees in the Senate, and two-thirds of the chairmen of standing committees in the House of Representatives, are over the age of 65. These figures, together with additional remarks by Miller, surely encouraged the impression that committee chairmen are substantially older, on the average, than non-chairmen. But that impression could easily be false. Since we are given no data concerning the average age of non-chairmen, we are in no position to gauge age-disparities between chairmen and non-chairmen. The figures cited by Miller, to that extent,* are statistically nonsensical.

They also are nonsensical, or at least of doubtful value, in another sense. They shed little light on the subject they were used to elucidate, namely, the value of the Congressional seniority system. Miller suggested, as did one of his witnesses, that many committee chairmen are incapacitated by age both to operate efficiently and to serve as accurate representatives of public opinion. But the link between age, on the one hand, and competence and political representativeness, on the other hand, was merely asserted rather than being established. Moreover, one of Miller's witnesses (Representative Fraser, at **13**.30) denied that such a link exists.

Another example of statistical nonsense was supplied by Rep. Philip Crane on behalf of defenders of the seniority system. Crane used the phrase "two thirds" in alluding (**10**.6, **11**.6) to the number of cases in which House committee chairmen have had "power" taken away from them in the course of the past twenty years. By citing this figure, Crane surely encouraged the impression that committee chairmen chosen by way of the seniority system have *not* been free to act, or have not acted, in an arbitrary, despotic manner. However, Crane was remarkably elusive as to what population he had in mind. The "two thirds" figure *could* mean quite a variety of things, such as:

a) Two out of three men who have chaired committees during the past twenty years have been disciplined after acting in a despotic manner. If this were the case, then it would be hard to sustain the notion that chairmen find it easy to act in a despotic manner without fear of retribution. But equally, it would appear that many men who have become chairmen under the seniority system have committed at least one offense and have had to be punished. To this extent, the system seems to encourage the selection of chairmen who at least are 'despotism-prone.'

---

*To be sure, the figures cited by Miller do lend support to his claim that the Congress is led by men who are older, by and large, than the men who lead many other types of human organizations. But Miller's figures make sense, in the context of the debate, only if they support the contention that the seniority system causes authority to be lodged in the hands of members who are older than other members. The first step toward proving this claim is to establish that the chairmen actually are older than the non-chairmen.

b) Alternatively, two thirds of the "arbitrary" chairmen (at least in the House of Representatives) have been brought to heel during the past twenty years. On this showing, a substantial minority of the "arbitrary" chairmen have *not* been shorn of power. As to whether these "arbitrary" chairmen have comprised a large or a small portion of *all* chairmen, we are left in the dark. Similarly, we are not told whether those "arbitrary" chairmen who have been disciplined (numbering two out of each three who deserve it) were punished immediately after a first "arbitrary" act, or only after a long series of such acts. On this showing, the phrase "two thirds" *could* refer to, or conceal, what actually is a great deal of "arbitrary" behavior on the part of committee chairmen.

c) Again, Representative Crane might be suggesting that in two-thirds of the standing committees of the House during the past twenty years, at least one chairman has been disciplined by his colleagues for wielding too much power. This tells us precious little about the incidence of arbitrary behavior or of discipline against arbitrary chairmen. If there have been ten chairmen per committee over the past twenty years, and if half of these chairmen have been arbitrary in their actions, then the rate of disciplinary action seems to be paltry indeed.

The point, of course, is that we simply do not know what is signified, in the most immediate and direct sense, by Representative Crane's allusion to "two-thirds" of the House committee chairmen. Accordingly, we are confronted here with a piece of statistical nonsense.

Strawmanship

Verbal disputes occasionally give rise to accusations that one's opponent has erected and then attacked a "straw man." This device has not been clearly defined in textbooks, but it seems to comprise the following elements:

a) While ostensibly dealing with a specified issue, institution, or proposal, one deals instead with a more hypothetical issue, institution, or proposal.

b) The hypothetical target is more vulnerable to ridicule than the real thing.

c) The hypothetical target is confounded with the real one.

An example of erecting a straw man was furnished in the debate on the Congressional seniority system. Senator Bob Packwood, having voiced opposition to the seniority system, went on to declare that "there are a variety of ways that we could replace the seniority system and ask, somehow, that a person be picked on merit, or ability, or anything other than solely age" (2.5). This bit of argumentation can be reformulated, without distortion, as follows:

Value assumption: Authority should not be allocated solely on the basis of age.

Practical conclusion: The Congressional seniority system should be discarded.

Such reasoning makes no sense, of course, unless we add an obvious factual-causal assumption: that the seniority system allocates authority solely on the basis of age. This assumption happens to be false. Judging from the overview and the text of the debate, we know that the seniority system imposes at least two criteria for selecting committee chairmen. First, the chairman must be a member of the majority party in the legislative body. Second, among members of the majority party who belong to a given committee, that member with the longest skein of continuous service gets to be the chairman.

This system of allocating authority seems, superficially, more defensible than a system which simply assigns the chair to the oldest member. The seniority system seemingly prevents partisan conflict between a given chairman and the majority in the House or the Senate. The seniority system also seemingly makes it highly probable that the chairman will be richly experienced in matters that normally come before his committee. While these results may be unsatisfactory in the final analysis, they seem more defensible—at least in a culture that does not revere elders—than the hypothetical target attacked by Senator Packwood.

The seniority system surely does make it highly probable that committee chairmen will be older, on average, than non-chairmen. But this result is one of many *concomitants*—among which, perchance, is technical superiority or "merit."

Senator Packwood knows that the Congressional seniority system does *not* allocate authority solely on the basis of age. He does not overtly distort the facts. Instead, he provides a bit of incomplete reasoning, whose terms serve to invite his listeners to erect a straw man.*

---

*A nearly identical example of strawmanship is provided by Howard Miller at paragraph 9.11.

Insidious Omissions

The foregoing discussion made reference to the idea of *missing links* in a chain of argument. A further discussion seems warranted, as a means of delineating what deserve to be called *insidious omissions*. The discussion can start with an excursion into logic, followed by an extension into the domain of political controversy.

In the domain of formal logic, a syllogism is a piece of reasoning in which a stated inference is said to 'follow' from two premises: a major and a minor one. Thus, in the classical syllogism, the major premise is that all men are mortal, the minor premise is that Socrates is a man, and the inference is that Socrates is mortal. Such an argument is 'complete.' If we accept the premises we must accept the conclusion. We need nothing more.

Some arguments, however, are voiced in a manner which leaves them incomplete. These arguments are called *enthymemes*, and they take one of two forms, depending on which kind of premise has been left out. Thus:

	Enthymeme (1)	*Enthymeme (2)*
Major premise:	All men are mortal	—
Minor premise:	—	Socrates is a man
Inference:	Socrates is mortal	Socrates is mortal

Now in some cases, the missing premise is apparent from the context of discussion, and is acceptable to all. To that extent, an enthymeme would deserve to be called *innocuous*. Indeed, under such circumstances the enthymeme is only apparent, because the missing premise is 'present' without being stated.

Rational arguments concerning policy resemble arguments in the domain of logic in some respects. They too require two kinds of statements which can be regarded as counterparts to the major and minor premises in logic. One kind of statement is *normative*. It is an avowed standard for appraising alternative courses of action. In other words, it is a statement of belief about what is good. The other type of indispensable statement is *causal*. It is an assertion about means and ends, an assertion about the probable results flowing from a specified course of action. These pave the way for a *practical conclusion*, stating that some specified course of action should, or should not, be adopted. Thus, a coherent argument about policy could look, for example, like this:

Normative claim:	Prosperity is good.
Causal claim:	Policy p_1 fosters prosperity.
Practical conclusion:	Policy p_1 should be adopted.

Now, in real life, many arguments about policy are formally incomplete because they omit either the normative claim or the causal claim. But among these enthymemes, some surely deserve to be called innocuous. They are innocuous because the missing link is implicit, is readily apparent to all, and is accepted by all. This is most commonly the case with regard to normative claims. Here is an example:

Normative claim:	—
Causal claim:	Policy p_1 fosters prosperity, happiness, and liberty.
Practical conclusion:	Policy p_1 should be adopted.

Although this argument is formally incomplete, it is not really so. The implicit normative claim is that prosperity, happiness, and liberty are good. If I lavish attention on justifying this element of my argument, I waste the time of my listeners, and perhaps forfeit their support. Indeed, if I devote most of my time to extolling prosperity, happiness, and liberty, my listeners might well begin to suspect that I'm trying to conceal my inability to prove my causal claim that my pet project really favors those ends.

But in other cases, the omissions that occur in political argument are of the *insidious* variety. They omit a piece of argument which, if stated explicitly, would encounter a hostile reception. One example of the *insidious omission* has already been identified, in the discussion of strawmanship. It consists of omitting (but implying) a causal claim that is untenable. The omission is reproduced in brackets below:

Normative claim:	Authority should not be allocated solely on the basis of age.
Causal claim:	[The Congressional seniority system allocates authority solely on the basis of age.]
Practical conclusion:	The Congressional seniority system should be discarded.

Another example of the insidious omission occurred in the debate. This one involved the omission of a normative claim. It was furnished by Howard Miller and by Senator Packwood, and it ran approximately as follows:

Since	the Congressional seniority system is a novel, abnormal device among human institutions
Therefore:	The seniority system should be discarded.

What is missing from this bit of reasoning is an explicit normative premise, which can only be the following: *procedural novelty in a human institution is bad.* This belief was not voiced in so many words, but the allusions—to the incidence of "seniority" or "the seniority system" among human institutions—make no sense and do not *work*, unless that norm is accepted. At the same time, if that belief were voiced in so many words, it would probably encounter a cool reception among many listeners. The argument works its subtle way into our minds by not being clearly articulated. It is thus an insidious sort of omission.

Shouldering and Shifting Burdens of Proof

The foregoing discussion gives a somewhat distorted version of an insidious omission emanating from the Affirmative side in the debate. A more accurate version of the argument containing an insidious omission is as follows:

Normative claim:	[Procedural novelty in human institutions normally is bad.]
Causal claim:	The seniority system imposes upon the U.S. Congress a novel procedure.
Practical(?) conclusion:	It is up to the defenders to show why such an eccentricity should be retained.

This bit of reasoning marks an attempt, as the saying goes, to *shift the burden of proof.*

Under Anglo-Saxon law, a person who has been accused of a crime must be presumed innocent until proven guilty. The defense attorney is not obliged to emulate Perry Mason, who invariably clears his client, in the face of seemingly insurmountable evidence, *and* establishes the guilt of sombody else. Jurors are instructed to find a defendant "not guilty" so long as they harbor a "reasonable doubt" about his guilt. Thus, the primary *burden of proof* is upon the prosecutor.*

A similar convention normally governs debates over policy. Here the primary burden of proof rests upon the exponent of innovation (who is usually, but not always, identified with the Affirmative side). The innovator is expected to establish, with some degree of plausibility, that (*a*) a need for change exists, and that (*b*) a specified innovation will meet that need. His opponent customarily engages in denials. He denies that his opponent has established a need or has identified a genuine remedy.

Such a convention often makes life harder for the advocate of change than for his opponent. Accordingly, a skillful debater will attempt, as the clichés suggest, to "turn the tables" or to put his adversary "off balance." This essentially is what Howard Miller attempted to do (especially at 5.25) by way of his claim about the normality of "seniority" or "the seniority system" as a method of allocating authority in human groups. His strategy seems to have been rather effective, since it did not *immediately* elicit appropriate rejoinders, such as these:

a) Procedural novelty is not necessarily a bad thing. Different conditions and goals call for different measures.

b) At any rate, the Congressional seniority system is not markedly different from what other human groups do, directly or indirectly. Top leaders usually are older than subordinates, and usually are senior in terms of length of service as well.

c) Regardless of the truth of this matter, it still is the job of the Affirmative to identify the immediate evils emanating from the seniority system and to show what alternative would provide a remedy.

Some of these rejoinders eventually were voiced by spokesmen for the Negative. Moreover, William Rusher furnished his own example of an attempt to impose the primary burden of proof on his adversaries. This example occurred in the wake of persistent claims on the part of the Affirmative that (*a*) too many committee chairmen are too old to do their

---

*To put this in another way, we can say that the defense attorney is normally privileged to argue *ad ignoratium*, or "to ignorance." He can say, "Since we don't *know* that Smith *did* murder Jones, we must conclude that he did *not*." Similarly, in logic one can argue (fallaciously) that since a given conclusion has not been proved wrong, it must be presumed to be correct. The equivalent in political controversy is to claim that, in the absence of evidence to the contrary, a given policy must be presumed to be expedient.

jobs properly, and—less directly—that (*b*) the seniority system favors rule by elderly chieftains. In some passages (Kilpatrick at **6.8**, and Crane at **11.12–16**), the notion that old age is functionally debilitating was disputed. But at a later point, Rusher challenged the previously guiding assumption that "selection of chairmen by the whole party caucus or by the committee members, rather than by seniority, would result in younger leadership" (**13.27**).

Rusher's method of casting doubt on this assumption (like Miller's references to leader-selecting methods in other groups) involved an appeal to *precedent*. Rusher took note of the fact that certain leaders who have been elected by party caucus, without direct reference to seniority, have been markedly old. Specifically, Speakers of the House of Representatives elected by party caucus during the past 70 years have, on the average, been more than 63 years of age at the time of their election (**13.27-.29**). On the strength of that bit of experience, he challenged Representative Donald Fraser to show grounds for believing that abolition of the seniority system really would rejuvenate the ranks of committee chairmen (**13.29**). Thus, he suggested that the Affirmative must shoulder the burden of proving a thesis that previously had been taken for granted.

Fraser's reply was most remarkable. Instead of contending that the experience cited by Rusher was not applicable to the present case, instead of affirming that abolition of the seniority system *would* produce more youthful chairmen, Fraser declared (**13.30**) that "age is not necessarily a disability." This declaration served to split the ranks of the Affirmative, since previous witnesses for the Affirmative had insisted that age is indeed a disability.

Hasty Generalization

In everyday language it is not uncommon to suggest that somebody has "jumped to conclusions." This accusation signifies, most generally, not that a conclusion is patently false but that it does not yet deserve to be regarded as valid. The launching platforms for conclusion-jumping, so to speak, are numerous. One of these is labelled in the textbooks "hasty generalization," or the "fallacy of the converse accident."

This sort of blunder consists essentially of ascribing to a group of things, or to the group as a whole, some trait that is true of some of the parts, without pausing to ascertain whether the trait really is general. In abstract terms, a hasty generalization looks like this:

Major premise:	Class I contains elements a, b, c, and d.
Minor premise:	Element d has the property p.
Hasty conclusion 1:	Elements a, b, and c have the property p.
Hasty conclusion 2:	Class I has the property p.

In less abstract terms, a hasty generalization is exemplified in the following assertions:

Normative assumption:	Relief from pain is beneficial.
Causal claim:	Opiates give some people relief from pain.
Hasty conclusion:	Opiates are beneficial.

The foregoing example is not identical to the previous, abstract, example. Its conclusion is hasty for a number of reasons. In the first place, it presupposes that the *only* test for assessing beneficiality is "relief from pain," whereas the normative assumption is silent as to whether "relief from pain" is the sole, or just one of many, tests of beneficence. In the second place, the conclusion generalizes from *some* cases of benefit (in the form of relief from pain) to all cases, whereas the causal claim leaves room for the possibility that opiates sometimes cause, and sometimes relieve, pain.

The debate on the Congressional seniority system gave rise to at least one example of hasty generalization. This example was furnished in the course of testimony by Jack Anderson (sections 4, 5). If we overlook some nuances, we can summarize the thrust of Anderson's testimony as follows:

Premise(s):	The U. S. Congress discloses "numerous" examples of incompetent committee chairmen. These chairmen are debilitated by old age, or by coming from inappropriate electoral districts, or by both.
Conclusion:	The Congressional seniority system should be abolished.

The conclusion here is hasty for a number of reasons. In the first place, while the factual premise states only that "numerous" committee chairmen are incompetent (and thus leaves room for the possibility that "numerous" chairmen are superbly competent), the conclusion presupposes that committee chairmen are generally incompetent (or at least that the incidence of incompetence is greater than would be the case in the absence of a seniority system). In the second place, while the premise lays the blame for incompetence immediately on age and the character of electoral districts, the conclusion presupposes an underlying cause, namely, the seniority system. In the third place, the conclusion implies a normative premise to the effect that "competence-promotion" is the sole test for appraising alternative methods of selecting committee chairmen. One might insist on the relevance of other tests, such as "conflict-avoidance" or "responsiveness to one's colleagues." (Moreover, the causal claim that chairmen are debilitated by age and their districts, leaves room for the possibility that they are *fortified* by *other* things related to the seniority system.)

Of Plain and Subtle Contradiction

Among the hazards confronting participants in controversies over public policy is the presence, in one's audience, of dissensus. People do not always value the same things, in the same order of priority. If they can decide whether a given policy shall be enacted, and if they disagree about what they desire (or about the names they assign to what they desire), they must be courted artfully. They must be induced to believe that a given policy is conducive to ends they deem valuable, even if it appears to be the case that these several ends are incompatible. In effect, they challenge the advocate to argue along several fronts without visibly falling into contradiction.

Now an abstract example of contradictory argumentation would look something like this:

Normative claim	Result r_1 is good.	Result r_2, which is antithetical to r_1, is good.
Causal claims:	Policy p_1 fosters r_1.	Policy p_1 fosters r_2.
Practical conclusion:	policy p_1 should be adopted.	

If I explicitly made a case in these terms, I would quite obviously be engaging in contradiction. I would be espousing mutually exclusive values, and I would be advancing directly opposing versions of cause and effect. I would probably alienate, instead of reconciling, all my listeners.

Yet I might deem it necessary to propound a case, or cluster of arguments, that is markedly inconsistent. This would be my task if the fate of my pet project hinges on winning the support of people some of whom favor result r_1 while others favor result r_2. In these circumstances, I would need to argue in such a manner as to blur the inconsistencies. Such argumentation is feasible in real-world controversies more than in the realm of abstract logic, because real-world controversies involve tacit understandings and words that are ambiguous and/or vague. It calls for an artful use of what a political theorist named T. V. Smith has felicitously called "strategic obfuscation."* The principal weapons here include insidious omissions and foggy verbiage.

If I relied on insidious omissions to propound the kind of case that was sketched, abstractly, above, my argumentation would look something like this:

	(1)	(2)
Normative assumptions:	Result r_1 is good	—
Causal claims:	—	Policy p_1 fosters r_2
Practical conclusion:	policy p_1 should be adopted	

This argument depends for its credibility on the willingness of my listeners to fill in blanks, and to do so on the basis of (*a*) an instinct for 'closure,' or for sensible thinking, and (*b*) a desire to discern means conducive to their favorite ends. Champions of result r_1 might be induced to believe that since I have espoused this value *and* have espoused policy p_1, then I must somehow have said, and even shown, that p_1 favors r_1. Similarly, champions of r_2 might be induced to believe that since I have affirmed both that p_1 fosters r_2 and that p_1 should be adopted, then I must also be friendly to r_2. I might encourage this illusion by assigning quite distinct names to the two kinds of results, suggesting that they are merely different in character without being divergent.

The debate on the Congressional seniority system provided an example of argumentation using well-timed omissions and foggy verbiage to blur an appeal to divergent interests. This example can be summarized as follows:

The Ethics of Compromise—And the Art of Containment (Beacon Press, 1956), p. 47.

(1)	*Since*	(2)
The seniority system exemplifies "democracy" (Kilpatrick, 7.28). Committee chairmen are "representative" of nonchairmen of their respective committees, and of the regional roots of the membership at large (Ibid.; also Jones, 8.2ff and Crane, 11.12ff).	*and*	The seniority system acts as a "brake" on the "power of the Presidency," the "impulse of the people" and the "automatic power of the 51 percent" (Kilpatrick, 6.6; Rusher, 13.31). Abolition of the seniority system would augment the political influence of big outside pressure groups (Crane, 10.16).

Therefore

The seniority system should be retained.

These two versions of causation are not plainly and diametrically opposed, but they certainly strike discordant notes. If the first version of reality is true, the second cannot easily be true as well. Moreover, and most importantly, if the first version of cause and effect paves the way for a conclusion favoring retention of the seniority system, then the second cannot readily do the same job. In each case, there is an unstated normative premise. In the first case, the implicit normative premise is that "democracy" is a good thing. In the second place, the implicit normative premise is that the power of the President (who alone is elected by the national electorate), the impulse of the people, and the impulse of the majority of the people need to be curbed. This version of what is desirable, and what is circumstantially urgent, does not self-evidently amount to saying that "democracy" is a bad thing (since the nature of "democracy" is a matter of disputed definition). But it does attest, in all probability, to what most people would regard as a value orientation that is anti-democratic, or at most is quasi-democratic.*

---

*A similar element of inconsistency might be ascribed to the Affirmative side, on the basis of two passages. First, to Kilpatrick's claim that "democracy does operate" under or through the seniority system, Miller replied that "*if* it's worked, though, it's worked without voting [for chairmen]" (7.28-.29). Second, Miller intimated that a sound method of selecting chairmen would distribute authority not in proportion to the populations of various regions, or sections, but in proportion to the gravity of problems that, in his judgment, they face (9.11). These statements reflect discordant concepts of representative government. In the first case, attention is directed to the idea of accurately reflecting public opinions. In the second case, attention is directed to the idea of serving public needs.

Should the government subsidize all campaigns for office?

OVERVIEW

In the days of the Roman Republic, men who aspired to hold elective governmental office found it expedient to shower their fellow citizens with bread and circuses. Matters have not changed substantially in the ensuing centuries. In 1796, James Madison, the father of the United States Constitution, suffered a summary retirement from Congressional office when he disdained to blandish his Virginia constituents in the customary manner by "treating," or wining and dining them.* Few of his contemporaries were so fastidious.

Although "treating" no longer plays a pivotal role, enormous sums of money are still directly involved in political campaigns. In 1960, Americans spent around $175 million in connection with nominating and electing public officials.** The cost has gone up sharply since then, what with increases in the prices of advertising, manpower, and postage. By far

---

*Ralph M. Ketcham, *James Madison: A Biography* (Macmillan, 1971).

**Herbert E. Alexander, "Financing the Parties in Campaigns," in *The Presidential Election and Transition*, 1960–61, ed. Paul T. David (Brookings Institution, 1961), pp. 116–49.

the biggest portion of campaign spending goes to buy time for radio and television broadcasts and space for newspaper advertisements and billboard manifestoes. Additional outlays buy bumper strips, leaflets, transportation for candidates and their entourages, opinion polls, arenas for rallies, press agents, organizers, and buttons.

Public concern about the role of money in politics has engendered a dense—but porous—thicket of regulations. The primary aim of most of this accumulated legislation has been to minimize 'undue influence' of candidates on susceptible voters, and of interest groups upon candidates. An additional aim has been to limit the competitive advantages enjoyed by wealthy or heavily sponsored candidates over relatively impoverished rivals. Accordingly, various regulations prohibit outlays for certain types of electioneering (such as "treating" and paying individuals to register or vote), set limits on the amount a single campaign committee can spend (but not on what *all* committees devoted to a single candidate or party can spend), set additional limits on the amount an individual (but not his cousins, children, and friends) can give to a single candidate or committee, prohibit corporations and unions (but not their officers) from contributing directly (but not indirectly) to campaign committees, prohibit political "assessments" of civil servants, and require candidates and committees to account publicly for their larger receipts and outlays.

Most specialists in the subject agree that the existing regulations are less than fully effective. Moreover, specialists have lately voiced concern about another aspect of campaign finance: the problem of getting enough money *to* the candidates, so that they in turn can get their messages across to the voters. Existing regulations restrict the sources and amounts of campaign funds. They also hamper the accumulation of "adequate" funds.

Several proposals of reform have recently been advanced. One consists simply of removing restrictions on the amounts individuals can donate—restrictions, it is argued, that only inspire the proliferation of collection points. Another calls for mounting a strenuous publicity campaign in which voters are urged to contribute *en masse*, but in modest amounts, to the candidates and parties of their choice. A third plan would encourage small donations from masses of voters by means of tax deductions. A fourth would make available to each presidential candidate, or to each major-party candidate, a block of free time for radio and television broadcasting.

A fifth, and more sweeping, proposal consists of banning all private contributions to political campaigns while at the same time furnishing direct government subsidies, on a substantial scale, to the candidates. According to proponents, this sort of scheme would solve *all* the vexing problems connected with campaign finance: undue influence, unfair competition, and inadequate resources. According to opponents—as the following debate illustrates—the consequences of such a scheme would be worse than the ills it ostensibly would cure.

1   OPENING STATEMENTS

1.1   MODERATOR ROGER FISHER: Tonight the problem is the role of money in political campaigns: how candidates get campaign funds, and the effect of large contributions on the political process. [We shall] look closely at one proposal for dealing with that problem: namely, that all campaign costs for national office should be borne by the taxpayers. The question is this: "Should the government subsidize all campaigns for [Federal] office?" Advocate Miller says "Yes." Advocate Rusher says "No."

1.2   ADVOCATE HOWARD MILLER: A method of financing the election of our elected officials can open national scandal. One must either be wealthy, or have access to those who are wealthy, or have special interests, in order to run and be elected. We propose a change in that system. We propose a plan by which all Federal election campaigns would be subsidized and all private contributions would be banned. The purpose of that plan is to deny the special interests and to guarantee that our representatives represent people and not money.

1.3   The cost of getting elected to public office has skyrocketed. It now costs between 20 and 25 million dollars to run a Presidential campaign. Even an average House campaign can cost over $100,000 for each candidate in the final election. And in large States, millions can be spent on Senate races. At the same time that these costs have skyrocketed, enormous amounts of wealth in our country are created by government action: airline routes, TV licenses, the various tax laws. And what has happened is that those who benefit from government action have been those who are subsidizing and electing the ones who are supposed to watch and regulate *them*. We have built-in conflicts of interest. We have a built-in scheme where the financial interests that should be watched are the ones who elect those who are supposed to be watching them.

1.4   This is not that new a problem. In 1907 [President] Theodore Roosevelt suggested a plan for subsidizing Federal elections and cutting down on private contributions. In 1936 a Senate committee suggested the same sort of plan. It has been consistently opposed by the special interests who now have the people they want in elective office. We propose a basically simple plan, with two features: a subsidy sufficient to finance all campaigns—the average amount in a Congressional district would be $100,000 [and] the Democratic and Republican [Parties] would each get $17 million to finance their Presidential election campaigns—[and] along with that, we ban *private* contributions *entirely*. No money, however, is ever dispersed to a candidate, or passes through his hands. Those who provide services to the candidates, whether they be ad agencies or printers, present the vouchers directly to the United States Treasury and are paid directly from the Treasury. The candidate himself controls none of the money; it simply supports his bid for the office. He initially qualifies in the primary by presenting petitions with at least 2,000 ballot signatures in the Congressional district. Once he does that, he qualifies for a proportionate share of the primary money. Third parties may be formed. If they are legitimate third parties and have previously qualified in a Presidential election, or if they can get 3 percent of all the voters in the country to sign a petition (2,100,000 signatures in a presidential compaign) they, too, may be subsidized. The American Independent Party in 1972, for example, would receive over $8 million to subsidize its election. Thus, the principles are simple: finance by the [Federal] government, so [that] the peoples' representatives can be elected, *sans* special interests, so that legitimate laws may be enacted.

1.5   ADVOCATE WILLIAM RUSHER: Mr. Miller's plan will not only do great damage to the democratic process itself, but will open our elections to a flood of subsidy-hunting splinter parties and make it even easier than it is today for an incumbent to ward off a . . . serious challenger.

1.6   Let's understand that the Miller Plan . . . prohibits *all* contributions by *anybody* to a candidate, and all expenditures by the candidate himself [except] out of this special fund provided to the candidate, out of the taxpayers' money, by the Federal government. This means that in Presidential elections, Mr. Miller said, each of the two major parties would get $17.5 million of Federal money; and in Congressional contests, anybody at all who can get 4500 signatures on a petition automatically qualifies for $18,000 of the taxpayers' money for campaigning. As much as it is an invitation to every kook in the country to start running for office, it is by no means the worst damage of the Miller Plan, which is the damage that it does to the actual democratic process itself.

2. FIRST AFFIRMATIVE WITNESS: DIRECT EXAMINATION

2.1   MILLER: To talk about the problem of our current method of campaign financing, I have asked to join me tonight Journalist Britt Hume, an associate of Jack Anderson in the writing of the "Washington Merry-Go-Round" syndicated column. Mr. Hume, do special interests influence legislation?

2.2   BRITT HUME: Yes. They dominate policy in a number of areas. The best and most obvious example, I suppose, is the oil industry, where the depletion allowance enables America's oil companies to get by without paying $2.5 billion of taxes a year.* (It may be down some now, but that is a recent figure). A good example of a company which profits by this system is the Atlantic-Richfield Company, which in the last several years has paid virtually no taxes. In 1968, President Nixon was favorably disposed toward the oil depletion allowance; indeed, behind closed doors, Vice-President Agnew promised that the Administration would work to retain it. In exchange, executives of the Atlantic-Richfield Oil Company came through with $65,000 worth of campaign contributions for Republicans.

2.3   MILLER: Is that true of just one political party, or both?

2.4   HUME: I think it's on both sides, and I would point out that there are about 100 committees in Washington that have been formed for the sole purpose of being conduits for money from special interest groups to political causes, and about half of these are labor organizations.

2.5   MILLER: Don't they balance each other out?

2.6   HUME: No, . . . because they represent very narrow interests, and there is no one there to represent broad public interest.

2.7   MILLER: Is the public directly hurt in that?

2.8   HUME: Yes. . . . A good example of that would be a case of Dr. John Knowles of Boston, who was selected by the Nixon Administration to become Assistant Secretary of Health [in the Department of Health, Education, and Welfare]. The reason he was selected was that [Robert] Finch, who was then the Secretary [of H.E.W.], felt that he had a number of very imaginative proposals to deal with the skyrocketing cost of health care, which every American was concerned with; while the American

---

*The depletion allowance permits oil companies to deduct from income that otherwise would be taxable a prescribed sum that ostensibly reflects the dwindling value of their resources—namely, petroleum under the ground. The allowance thus resembles what manufacturers can deduct from taxable income as a cost of depreciation of their machines. Hume's testimony here voices the claim, essentially, that the amounts the oil companies are allowed to deduct exceed the actual depletion they incur.

Medical Association, despite his qualifications, decided they didn't want him. The American Medical Association in 1968 came through with about $2 million worth of contributions indirectly to political causes, and they succeeded in prevailing over the will of a Cabinet Secretary and changing the mind of a President. It was an extraordinary demonstration of power.

2.9   MILLER: Are there also narrowly regulated interests that—

2.10   HUME: There certainly are. A good example would be the United States shipping industry, which survives today only on the strength of about $400 million annually [in] Federal subsidy. The man who presides over this program is Representative Edward Garmatz [of] Baltimore, Maryland, who is the chairman of the House Merchant Marine Committee. Now, Mr. Garmatz is up for re-election this year [1970], and the shipping executives and their counterparts in the maritime unions have made "gratuities." They have raised about $37,000 for Mr. Garmatz's campaign. Which really doesn't sound like a lot of money by today's standards—but the fact is that Mr. Garmatz *has no opposition.*

3.   CROSS-EXAMINATION

3.1   RUSHER: Do I understand you to say that, say, Senator Long of Louisiana, who is in favor of the oil depletion allowance, would oppose it if he and others were not receiving substantial contributions from the oil industry?

3.2   HUME: Senator Long would probably be in favor of oil depletion allowance whatever the case [because oil is so vital in his home State]. However, there are Senators who now might very well oppose it if they were not so dependent upon campaign contributions from the oil industry. . . .

3.3   [For instance,] Senator Fulbright has shown that he is a man who is willing to go against what would appear to be the normal trends of interest of his constituency. A good example of that was the Carswell vote: most Southern Senators were for Judge Carswell, but Senator Fulbright rose up and voted against [Carswell's Nixon-proposed elevation to the Supreme Court]. Senator Fulbright has also been a maverick on a number of other legislative and foreign policies; and my boss, in the privacy of Senator Fulbright's office not too long ago, said "Senator, here you've been an independent man, you've been a courageous Senator, on an enormous number of issues. Why is it that you invariably go down the line in the oil and gas interest?" And he said "Well, Jack, the reason for that is that they could slaughter me in Arkansas. I need their support, and I'm just vain enough to think that I am a better Senator than Orville Faubus would be."

3.4 RUSHER: You mean to tell me that Senator Fulbright's courage—that you speak of so highly—simply deserts him on the subject of the oil depletion?

3.5 HUME: What I'm saying is this: on an issue in which campaign contributions are involved, it is extremely difficult for a United States Senator today to turn his back—

3.6 RUSHER: I'm interested in that question now [about how] Senator Fulbright's courage doesn't desert him; it "modulates" on the subject, because the oil industry, through its contributions, could slaughter him—

3.7 HUME: Listen: let me make this point about Senator Fulbright. He can defend [his vote on oil depletion] in the same way that Senator Long defended it. What I am saying is that there is a distinct possibility that Senator Fulbright might change his mind on the oil and gas issues in the absence of campaign contributions. And I would like to give him the chance to make judgments on those issues, independent of financial dependency.

4. SECOND AFFIRMATIVE WITNESS: DIRECT EXAMINATION

4.1 MILLER: One man who has thought hard and long about [problems of private financial contributions], and who has proposed a plan on which we base the plan we put forth tonight, is Philip Stern, author of *The Great Treasury Raid*, a book on loopholes in the tax laws, and author of a book on the Oppenheimer case. Mr. Stern, why did you put forth your proposal?

4.2 PHILIP STERN: Because I firmly believe that we will never have real democracy in this country and real one man-one vote, unless we reform the way we raise political funds and the dependence of political candidates [upon] contributions from special interests, who later ask for a return for their investment in the form of huge government programs and subsidies; and because I believe that the political fund-raising process lies at the heart of our skewed national priorities, makes us spend millions on oil depletion and on the SST [super-sonic transport], and impinges on housing and urban mass transit and antipollution measures.

4.3 MILLER: Do you think this proposal in any way undercuts political participation?

4.4   STERN: On the contrary, I think it *expands* it to the ultimate. Everybody talks about the benefits of spreading the base of the financial support for the parties, and this does the ultimate. It has *everybody*, every citizen of the United States, support the political process, and ends the system whereby a few contribute the bulk in hidden ways with hidden interests.

4.5   MILLER: Total cost of the plan would be $210 million for all offices in the Presidential year, $150 million in a non-Presidential year. Is that too expensive an investment?

4.6   STERN: The money costs of this are really an investment: in part, an investment in real democracy (one man-one vote), but with dollars and cents return to the consumers and taxpayer. Quick example: President Nixon's Cabinet committee recommended that he abolish oil import quotas and [said] that this would save the consumers—the people that buy oil and gas in this country—$5 billion. He had the choice of siding either with those consumers or with the oil industry. He sided with the oil industry. The $90 million a year this plan would cost is a small fraction of the $5 billion the consumers could have saved if the President had sided with them.

4.7   MILLER: If we do subsidize these elections, will different kinds of men be elected? Will it really make a difference?

4.8   STERN: I think it will make a profound difference in two respects. Number one: you will see candidates that are now in effect barred from running either because they lack the personal means or because they are unwilling to become [beholden to] special interests running for office. Secondly, you will see the political system respond to people instead of money. You will see a President side with the consumer instead of the oil industry. You will see us beginning to spend, I think, billions for housing and urban mass transit instead of the oil depletion.

5.   CROSS-EXAMINATION

5.1   RUSHER: As an expert on loopholes, would you say that your plan has none?

5.2   STERN: If it has any, they're minute compared to the chuckholes that exist in the present system.

5.3   RUSHER: We'll be coming to some of those "minute" ones a little later. Tell me this: we've heard a lot about the damages of big contributions; but what about small contributions? How do *they* damage the political process?

5.4   STERN: I don't know whether they necessarily damage it; but—

5.5   RUSHER: Then why do you prohibit them?

5.6   STERN: Because I want to take broad participation to the ultimate, and I think that the way to *really equalize* influence is to see that everybody contributes equally. If one man contributes one dollar and another contributes even 10 or 15 or 20 dollars, the man who contributes 20 has more influence—has more access to the ear of an office-holder—than the man who contributes nothing. That makes for unequal influence.

5.7   RUSHER: Are you seriously saying that if 10 dollars is contributed by someone for a candidate to Congress or [for] President, and 20 dollars is contributed by somebody else, a damage results, or an influence arises, so great that we must prohibit it by law?

5.8   STERN: I am saying that the more a person gives, the more his influence on a political candidate. I am saying that the way to equalize each person's influence and to make one man-one vote, is to—

5.9   RUSHER: Is to compel all of us to give for everybody. I understand that, but I want to know the damage. It seems to me that there is certainly an argument to be made (and we will be hearing [about it] at length) that the democratic process is very considerably helped by large numbers of small contributors. And I don't see . . . that we have all these corrupt Senators who would vote otherwise on the oil [depletion] allowance if it weren't for the situation we have. Even leaving that aside, it seems to me that there is a very great deal to be said for small contributions, and the more the merrier. And you are forbidding them, absolutely forbidding them—five dollars, one dollar—[so] nobody can give anything to a man he really likes. Isn't that your proposal?

5.10   STERN: He can still work for him, ring doorbells for him, pass out leaflets for him; and no public harm is done because everybody would have a chance to have access not only to the ballot but [also] to the voters.

5.11   RUSHER: . . . You speak of the evil of money pressure; but why is money pressure evil, or more evil, than other types of pressure? Certainly, 200,000 people milling around the Washington Monument accusing the President of the United States of murder is a form of pressure. Now this form of pressure you don't mind—I gather you think it's fine. Why then is it so terrible that somebody who doesn't go there wants to send $10 to the candidate who will stand up for the other side of the question?

5.12   STERN: Because the contributor of money has more access to the ear of the office-holder than the non-contributor; and in answer to your question earlier to Mr. Hume, I know of an instance where the oil industry came in in October and offered $10,000 to each of several candidates—Democratic Senatorial candidates in the West—provided they would support the depletion allowance. They were desperate for it. Most of them accepted it and they committed themselves.

5.13   MILLER: To even speak about the small contribution is to shift the argument. The small contribution provides a very small amount of total campaign financing. The overwhelming amount of financing is the $500-and-over—the very substantial—contribution. That is the problem we deal with; and if we are going to have genuine one man-one vote, and genuine representative democracy, the candidates will have to be financed other than the way they are now: by the public treasury.

6.   FIRST NEGATIVE WITNESS: DIRECT EXAMINATION

6.1   RUSHER: We'll be talking [of the Miller Plan's damage to the "democratic process"] first. The first witness, Congressman John Ashbrook of Ohio, is out campaigning tonight, appropriately enough. Mr. Miller and I went to Washington yesterday to tape his testimony. Here is how it went: Congressman Ashbrook, how long have you been in the House of Representatives?

6.2   REP. JOHN ASHBROOK (on film):   Since January 1961. I'm just rounding out five terms.

6.3   RUSHER: I assume you have the usual trouble, perhaps, in raising campaign funds?

6.4   ASHBROOK: I think everybody has trouble, and I have probably been a little more successful than others; but yes, it's a problem, and always has been.

6.5   RUSHER: How would you like a nice fat Federal subsidy to pay for your campaign instead of having to pay from your own money or having to go out and raise it?

6.6   ASHBROOK: Oh, I suppose, to be facetious, I would say I would like it; but the more I think about it, I'd say "No." I think it would in the long run have a very destructive consequence, and if subsidies did to the politicians what [they have] done to agriculture and some other areas, I think you can only guess how bad it would be.

6.7   RUSHER: What is to be said of the present system of raising campaign funds among their friends and supporters?

6.8   ASHBROOK: I happen to believe the problem in our country is the fact that we don't have enough people involved in politics. We have suffered in the past 20 years [from] "chronic political anemia": not enough people are active in politics. The goal is to encourage *more* people to get in and, as I see it, a subsidy, if anything, would *deaden* this interest, would make fewer people interested, on a theory that "George is doing it—it can be done by somebody else; therefore, I don't have to participate." So, to my way of thinking it moves directly opposite to our desired goal [of greater inclusion of people in the active political process and [the development of] more interest and more awareness . . . . Whenever we feel that somebody else is doing our job, that's when we all shirk our responsibilities. We have enough areas where we are already letting George do it, and if we add politics to it, this would be the crowning blow on our society.

6.9   RUSHER: In other words, you think that this business of raising funds for political office and seeking contributions is an actual *affirmative contribution* to the democratic process. Is that right?

6.10   ASHBROOK: Very definitely. In my own particular campaign for example, up to this point I have received contributions from 1,400 different individuals. The average contribution would be small, probably less than $10, but here 1,400 people in one Congressional district have actively participated. If you ever let these 1,400 people think that somebody else is doing the job for them, I'm sure they wouldn't participate. We need more people interested in politics. We need more activity rather than less.

6.11   RUSHER: Isn't it true, though, that a man is beholden to those who contribute to his campaign?

6.12   ASHBROOK: No, I don't think this is necessarily so; but I am sure we know cases where groups—labor unions or business groups, oil lobbies and so forth—have chunked great amounts in certain campaigns, and there probably is some area of connection. But I think on the whole, most people feel as I do in politics: we accept contributions on the theory that "they buy my philosophy, I don't buy theirs, and if they want to support me, fine." [Furthermore,] I think the lobbying principle is good. Many causes need an advocate in our country and, again, this is why we should have political contributions. This is proper; it is a way that people redress their grievances. I have no objections to a Mr. [John] Gardner starting a "Common Cause." To say he couldn't spend money, in my opinion, would be ridiculous.

7.   CROSS-EXAMINATION

7.1   MILLER: In 1873, a Senate committee censured Senator James Highland of Iowa because he accepted a campaign contribution of $10,000 from an officer of the Union Pacific Railroad. The Senate committee said it would undermine the Republic and could be completely contrary to public and private virtue to allow campaigns to be so financed. Today, those kinds of contributions are everyday things and you support them. Why is the public morality changed?

7.2   ASHBROOK: I don't know that the public morality has changed that much. The political facts of life have changed. I know they have changed in the 10 years I have been in Congress. It costs a lot more to run for office. You have television. We have more sophisticated candidates for office, and we have a more sophisticated public.

7.3   MILLER: Isn't it a fact [that] the cost has skyrocketed? When Abraham Lincoln ran for Congress, he got a $200 contribution in 1846, and returned $199.25 and spent 75 cents on a barrel of cider. Today, in a large Congressional district, it costs $150,000 to $200,000 to run. Now, most of the contributions come from large donors, not small donors. Over 80 percent of all contributions are over $500. Isn't there a risk of undue influence because large donors finance expensive campaigns?

7.4   ASHBROOK: There is always a risk, but by the same token we cannot make the democratic process that simple. Sometimes people want to make everything simple. If we're going to equalize finances, then we should equalize names, the way people look—

7.5   MILLER: Let's just talk about finances; because you mentioned participation, and there are many ways to participate. . . . And suppose we did bar all private contributions, as we propose. What would be the arguments against changing and going to a system of private contributions?

7.6   ASHBROOK: Private contributions, as I said before, encourage people to be active in the political process. I think of many issues over the years that have been advocated by individuals banding together. It's proper that labor unions advocate legislative programs.

7.7   MILLER: But they'd still be able to do that.

7.8   ASHBROOK: They wouldn't be able to spend money.

7.9   MILLER: But everyone who now runs *could* run. If the labor unions [wish to run a candidate], that candidate would be financed out of the proposal. So what harm would there be to those who wanted to support candidates? Those same candidates would run. What harm would there be to those who wish to support them?

7.10   ASHBROOK: The first harm I would see would be a tendency to have splinter parties. Anybody could run for office. I have an American Independent running against me who didn't get 1,800 votes in a primary.

7.11   MILLER: Exactly. Under our proposal you have to get 3 percent of the total votes in your district on a petition to even *qualify*. For example, you talk about participation. Thirty-two individuals financed a third of Hubert Humphrey's presidential campaign in 1968. Thirty-two contributions, that's all. Don't you think there's a risk when that few people finance a Presidential campaign? How can influence be avoided?

7.12   ASHBROOK: I absolutely agree with you, but I do not think it is necessary to tear down the whole structure of public participation in campaigns to accomplish this end. I happen to think it is wrong, for example, when members of a family [can virtually finance a candidate's campaign. For example, "a dozen members of his family contributed $180,000" to the election campaign of Representative Richard Ottinger of New York]. The same thing happened [in Howard] Metzenbaum's race [in Ohio]. The answers come in putting more teeth in [the laws prescribing] maximum contributions that can be made. Don't let a person give $5,000 to [each of many committees backing one candidate.].

7.13   MILLER: Well, let's look at that. We do have limits and they don't work. We limit large contributions, but by having many committees, in effect we have men contributing hundreds of thousands of dollars. The "limit" approach has not worked.

7.14   ASHBROOK: It has not worked. That's why we need a legislative remedy. But we do *not* need to make the remedy so broad that it absolutely discourages the *small* donor.

7.15   MILLER: Tell me why you favor limits. Do you favor limits because large contributions, in fact, are an evil?

7.16   ASHBROOK: I think large contributions, again, would have the same effect as what you're advocating. If I can get five to six people to subsidize my campaign, I don't have to worry. If the Federal government subsidizes my campaign, I don't have to worry. I want candidates who have to work to get the money; I want them to go out and actively get it. I think there should be some effort to put some limit on those who might improperly use their money. But I think the proposal you make would do exactly the same thing.

7 . 17   MILLER: Let's look now at who does get subsidized. In effect, running for re-election has enormous advantages through the franking privilege, [and] through subsidized television studios.* In fact, this proposal would simply equalize the challenger; that is, it is more likely that people would challenge, is it not? Isn't this proposal really a threat to incumbents?

7 . 18   ASHBROOK: I don't see it as a threat to incumbents. I think incumbents are in enough trouble in this day and age anyway. . . . But let's take that point. I think one of the things you would *dis*courage the most is the citizens' group who want to *unseat* somebody.

7 . 19   MILLER: But this citizen's group can still work. There's no limit on *participation*. They can work in precincts, they can work in headquarters, they can volunteer their time.

7 . 20   ASHBROOK: But they could not make a mailing to the State of New York, for example, saying, "We Republicans feel we should replace Charles Goodell. . . ."

7 . 21   MILLER: They cannot contribute money. Every kind of participation [would be legal] except contribution of money. Given the fact that small contributions are so few in our system—so few despite all attempts to encourage them—and that large contributions in effect finance everyone, what real harm is there to participation? Isn't there likely to be *more* participation, because more people will challenge and be able to run?

7 . 22   ASHBROOK: I don't agree. The more restrictions we place on the individual's operation in politics, his inclusion in politics—in the long run it's going to be worse for our society.

7 . 23   MILLER: You don't think that the lack of financing for challengers, the need to raise money from wealthy men, is in fact a restraint on entry into politics?

7 . 24   ASHBROOK: I don't think it's a restraint at this point. The rich obviously have an advantage over the poor. The millionaire with a mission in this day and age— [Howard] Samuels in New York, Norton Simon in California, Howard Metzenbaum in Ohio—seem[s] to have an advantage. So that, if we need remedial legislation, let's make it more difficult for individuals with a lot of money to circumvent the law. Let's *not* cut out those tens of thousands of people—the Goldwater campaign for example in 1964—the several million people who contributed.

---

*The franking privilege entitles incumbent Congressmen to send mail to their constituents without paying postage. There are some formal restrictions on the character of messages covered by the frank. Congressmen also are entitled to use broadcasting and videotaping studios on Capitol Hill.

7.25   MILLER: A small percentage of the total financing.

7.26   ASHBROOK: But this [small-sum financial support] is a good thing. I like the one-dollar contribution. I like the ten-dollar contribution. I also like the 500-dollar contribution. [*End of filmed segment.*]

8.   REACTIONS OF "THIRD-PARTY" LEADERS

8.1   RUSHER: Now we're going to look more closely at Mr. Miller's plan and some of its details. The principal beneficiaries, as we both said earlier, would be the two major parties, and each would get $17.5 million in a presidential year. But the American [Independent] Party would *also* be eligible to receive $8.5 million because, as you may recall, it ran George Wallace for President back in 1968 and got ten million votes. I don't know whether Governor Wallace plans to run again in 1972. He may not have decided. No major third-party candidate ever has run a second time. But I'm sure if he's thinking it over and hears about an offer to give him $8.5 million in taxpayers' money, it may help him make up his mind. Anyway, we asked T. Coleman Andrews Jr., the chairman of the American Party, what he thought of Mr. Miller's generous offer of public funds. Here was his reply:

8.2   T. COLEMAN ANDREWS, JR., (*on film*): Well, I must say that $8.5 million, which is the figure that's been suggested that this program would provide, would be a very healthy shot in the arm for a struggling, fledgling third party as the American Party is. I'm sure, judging from some of the problems we've had collecting a rather modest assessment from our State parties, that this would substantially help our cause. And I'm sure I'd have a difficult time if, indeed, I took the position that we shouldn't take it—of convincing the executive committee and Governor Wallace that we shouldn't take an $8.5 million subsidy.

8.3   RUSHER: Of course the American [Independent] Party did get those 10 million votes in 1968, which is why it would qualify for such a big slice of Mr. Miller's pie. But *any* person, in any average Congressional district, who can gather as many as 4,500 signatures on a petition, would *also* qualify for $18,000 of the taxpayers' money, under the plan. And this prospect has naturally excited everybody from the Communist party, on the one side, to Lar Daly, that individualistic patriot out in Chicago. Here are four typical reactions, beginning with Charlene Mitchell, the 1968 Presidential candidate of the Communist Party of the United States.

8.4   CHARLENE MITCHELL (*on film*):   What we need in the way of encouragement is only to be able to get out among the people. What it would do is to make it possible for . . . more of the people to hear us. And therefore, of course, we would have more candidates in the field.

8.5   KIPP DAWSON (*leader of the Socialist Workers' Party, on film*):   Subsidies to the candidates would enable not only the socialist Workers Party but parties like the La Raz Unida Party, which is the Chicano Party . . . in the Western States and represents the interest of Mexican-Americans— parties like that to present their views to the public and to present the reasons why they feel the Democrats and Republicans cannot represent the people of this country in their best interests.

8.6   RAYMOND MILLER (*leader of the Abolish Port Authority Party, on film*):   In 1968 I ran for Congress under the theme "Abolish the Port Authority." Just three words, "Abolish Port Authority." I was interested in the Delaware Port Authority. The money would be the key to it. I would probably be a winner if I had the money right now. [As for getting petitions], I go around and get them all the time. I got 18,000 [signatures] with no problem whatever when I wanted to abolish the Delaware River Port Authority. I got petitions every time I turned around. My people—all of them— my neighbors across the street—they sign petitions all the time. I go out every weekend and get 100 to 200 petitions signed, merely because I'm trying to do something to improve my community. I feel there would be no problem in order to get 15,000 [signatures].

8.7   LAR DALY (*on film*):   If you don't like your Uncle Sammy, why then go back to your home or the sea, to the land from whence you came, whatever be its name, but don't be ungrateful to me. And if you don't like the stars in Old Glory, if you don't like the Red, White and Blue, don't act like the cur in the story, don't bite the hand that's feeding you. I run for President four times, and United States Senator from Illinois seven times, and Congressman from Illinois twice; and I will say that if I can get Federal money so that I can reach the voters—mainly through the miracle medium of TV, and radio and newspaper ads—I feel that my policy, my America First policy, will certainly do much much better at the polls than what's been happening in the past 30 years.

9.   SECOND NEGATIVE WITNESS: DIRECT EXAMINATION

9.1   RUSHER: Now it is possible to believe as I do that people like these and others like them have the right to run for public office; but $18,000 apiece per campaign! Our next witness will be the Director of the Citizens' Research Foundation of Princeton, Dr. Herbert Alexander. I believe the Citizens' Research Foundation is the only organization in the country that devotes its full time to the study of campaign financing. Dr. Alexander, . . . I suppose [that] too large a contribution might be harmful if given by one person to one candidate or one office-holder, but is there anything inherently harmful in the idea of political contributions as such?

9.2   DR. HERBERT ALEXANDER: On the contrary. Political contributions are a positive good, an expression of citizen and group interest and concern in a democracy. The American political system has a great tradition of voluntarism. Financial contributing is a form of political participation, and it is one to be encouraged, not discouraged. . . . We need *more* [contributors]. I don't think we have . . . enough at present, but we are making great strides in the effort to broaden the base. . . . There has been a rising trend of contributors over the past decade and a half. There's been a tremendous increase in the number of contributors in 1968. There was something on the order of 10 or 12 million people who gave to some party or candidate. I don't believe in inhibiting these impulses toward participation in the democratic system.

9.3   RUSHER: What is your chief objection to the plan that we heard tonight?

9.4   ALEXANDER: By limiting campaign contributions to the amount of the subsidy, at the same time that we prohibit private contributions, we are introducing an element that favors the incumbent, that favors the person whose name is well known, that favors the group that is able to mobilize the most manpower. The American political system depends upon competition, depends upon challenge. Challenge is accomplished in part by the spending of money in order to forward political views. Incumbents have natural advantages. Challengers need to spend, most often, more money than incumbents in order to campaign effectively.

10.   CROSS-EXAMINATION

10.1   MILLER: Do you favor any kind of subsidy at all? You've simply spoken of the objection to limitation of contributions. Do you favor a subsidy for a campaign, of any kind?

10.2   ALEXANDER: I *am* in favor of doing what we can do to encourage more small contributors. I believe there are forms of *indirect* government assistance which are desirable. For example, . . . tax incentives for political contributions. . . . This is an indirect form of government subsidy in which the citizen makes the determination as to what party or what candidate he will support. The financial support by the government is not determined on the basis of an arbitrary formula that is set by a group of lawmakers in Washington or in the State capital; and there is a substantial difference in that.

10.3   MILLER: Then the amount of the contribution would depend on which party still was able to get the greatest number of solicitations even though they were a tax benefit. Isn't that correct?

10.4   ALEXANDER: Yes; but in effect the government would be sharing the amount of the contribution with the contributor. The contributor would still have some stake in the system.

10.5   MILLER: It *is* necessary, in fact, given skyrocketing costs, that the government begin to share some of the cost of election campaigns.

10.6   ALEXANDER: I'm not opposed to the notion of governmental assistance in indirect forms or in terms of services. But I think we should encourage the strides that have been made toward increasing financial support from large numbers of individuals.

10.7   MILLER: If we had a government subsidy which is sufficient for the campaign, what harm is there in denying the [private] contribution? Every candidate would still always run. Whomever you supported would still be in the race, since no one is excluded and your candidate would still always run. What is the harm in denying the contribution?

10.8   ALEXANDER: There is a constitutional harm in denying the contribution, for the reason that the First Amendment gives the individual the right of freedom of speech; and the First Amendment, by extension, gives the individual citizen the right to express his views. In order to express his views effectively, he may have to spend money on mass media, or he may be able to contribute it to candidates or to parties which, in effect, represent his views.

10.9   MILLER: But there are no cases that hold such a right. Do you think that he has the same right to bribe an official? Is that an aspect of free speech? You want to express your views, so you express them by paying him money for his vote.

10.10   ALEXANDER: Oh no. I certainly wouldn't equate bribery with political contributing.

10.11   MILLER: That's a judgment to be made. Now, you said, in terms of the challengers, we don't deny participation. You said that the person would win who mobilized the most manpower. Isn't that in fact the *greatest* way to *increase* participation: by giving a subsidy and allowing no more to be given? You positively encourage the kind of participation that counts: the doorbell-ringing, the person-to-person participation.

10.12 ALEXANDER: It's important that we recognize that certain groups in society are better able to mobilize manpower than others. Labor unions [and] college students, for example, can be better mobilized than certain minority groups, [such as] senior citizens.

10.13 MILLER: Do you think *that* differential is somehow *worse* than the differential of people who can afford to give different kinds of financial contributions?

10.14 ALEXANDER: Don't put words in my mouth. I'm not saying that the differential is worse. We have to look at the basis of the political system, which is that there are in society vested interests [and] that these interests will find expression in one way or another. One of the desirable ways is through participation as an individual: by going down to the headquarters and volunteering labor, time, service. But in an affluent society, such as we have, contributing [money] is an important form of political participation. For many people it's easier to write out a check than to give an hour's time. I don't think that we should inhibit this form of political participation.

11. THIRD AFFIRMATIVE WITNESS: DIRECT EXAMINATION

11.1 MILLER: We saw the film of Lar Daly and the other candidates who might somehow get rich on the scheme,—which of course they couldn't do, because they'd never get any of the money; it would go simply to support their campaign. The important thing is that no harm that Lar Daly or any of those other candidates could do *begins* to equal the kind of harm that we have now perpetuated by allowing special interests to finance campaigns. The point seems to be that someplace, somewhere, somebody is going to get money, which he will use for what? Simply to "express his political belief." Perhaps he even gets some for some other reason. We're here tonight talking about *grand theft*, about the grandest of grand thefts: billions from the Treasury because of special interests. And the opposition seems to oppose this plan because there might be a risk of petty larceny. As we balance the risks, the risks that "somehow, some of this money will go to people that you might not want to get it"—that unknown risk is so small compared to the risk that we *now* know about, in the misuse of special interests, that there can be no answer than to accept the smaller risk and deny the greater and the special interests.

To talk to these points I have asked to join me tonight the Boston attorney who has been active in the field of proposing legislation much like ours to ban contributions and subsidize campaigns. He is Jerome Medalie. Mr. Medalie, do you think there's a risk of squandering this money on people who shouldn't have it [to] run for campaigns?

11.2   JEROME MEDALIE: I'm more concerned about those highly qualified people who choose *not* to run for public office [and] who might be inclined to do so, except that they're not wealthy or they do not have access to wealthy friends or special interests to support them, or do not want to engage in the filthy process of soliciting contributions from special interests. [As for] the Lar Dalys and the others, I'm not terribly concerned about them. If they can muster the degree of public interest in their candidacies to qualify for public funds so that they can expound their candidacies, to me this is the essence of the political process. I have infinite confidence in the judgment and wisdom of the American public, come the election.

11.3   MILLER: We're talking about additional sums to be spent on election campaigns. Do we in effect now spend money on federal elections?

11.4   MEDALIE: We subsidize the entire electoral process. We pay for the printing of ballots [and for] expensive voting machines; we keep school buildings and fire houses open at night; we pay the heat, light, power, policemen, election commissioner; we send around absentee ballots. We spend a fortune on the election process. But when it comes to what the election exists *for*, we treat that very shabbily. It exists so that we, as voters and American citizens, can make an informed judgment on candidates who we hope, when elected, will be unencumbered by obligations to special interests. I'd like to spend a little money for that objective.

11.5   MILLER: Dr. Alexander spoke about the tradition of voluntary contributions in American life. Do you think that this plan discourages that, or that [that is in] any way an objection to this plan?

11.6   MEDALIE: First of all, I disagree with [the] simplicity in Mr. Alexander's statement about voluntarism. There is very little "voluntary" in a Senator who is campaigning for office having his campaign finance manager tap the executives of airline companies or oil industries for a contribution, when he sits on the committees which regulate them. I do not call that "voluntarism." Every effort to raise large amounts of money through small contributions [has] fallen flat on [its] face, and they're well documented in many publications put out by the Citizens' Research Foundation, which Dr. Alexander heads as Executive Director. The "10 million contributors" figure has to do with *all* elections, and that still represents perhaps 10 or 12 percent of the entire electorate.

12. CROSS-EXAMINATION

12.1 RUSHER: . . . Would you tell me, sir, if you think that making a compulsory contribution through taxation will improve voluntarism?

12.2 MEDALIE: I might answer that by stating that there is compulsory taxation of the American public for a variety of special interests which far exceed any possible cost of this program.

12.3 RUSHER: What about voluntarism, sir? Is it really voluntary if all of us are going to be taxed to pay for all of these candidacies? Is that your idea of voluntarism?

12.4 MEDALIE: I suppose either one of us may oppose an ABM system, or I perhaps may not like to spend money for an SST program. There is no voluntarism in the fact that I am taxed, and pay my taxes, to support these programs any more than this.

12.5 RUSHER: And there isn't any more voluntarism in this, is there?—in the plan that Mr. Miller proposes.

12.6 MEDALIE: It's voluntary in the sense that we are all contributing in the same way that all of us pay our taxes for every purpose.

12.7 RUSHER: It's just as "voluntary," in other words, as the income tax.

12.8 MEDALIE: That is correct. But I can't think of a better way to spend our tax money than [to] . . . preserve our free elections.

12.9 RUSHER: Mr. Miller said that the money would not go to the candidate. In any case it was thus not proved it would. But isn't it going to be perfectly easy for him to put it where he wants to? Suppose the candidate, qualified [by getting] 4,500 signatures to run for Congress in an average district, gets his $18,000 subsidy, and tells the Treasury of the United States to make a check out for a large chunk of it to his brother, who just "happens" to be in the public opinion polling business: an independent contractor whom he wants to hire to poll the district. Is the Treasury going to pay the brother?

12.10 MEDALIE: Part of this plan would create an agency which would supervise this entire process, and one of the essential elements would be that fair value would have to be given by any supplier of goods or services.

12.11 RUSHER: Surely I'm not saying the brother wouldn't give fair value. The point is the [the candidate] could give all of the money to close friends if not relatives of his. Isn't that true? If relatives were banned for some particular reason, he could certainly [give] it to his closest friends. That's perfectly obvious, isn't it?

12.12 MEDALIE: If that is the worst you can say about the system—

12.13   RUSHER: It's not, but suppose you let me say it: if that were the worst, it would have to be said, and you too would have to say it. Isn't it true it could be done?

12.14   MEDALIE: It would be possible . . . [but] today we have much more serious problems in this regard—

12.15   RUSHER: I gather you think contributing time to somebody's campaign is all right?

12.16   MEDALIE: Time and voluntary services, yes, . . . provided that they are not being paid for by someone else.

12.17   RUSHER: Would contributing property—say, a trailer or a hall or a sound truck, be all right?

12.18   MEDALIE: I would say that is a service that is a contribution, [and] . . . would not be all right.

12.19   RUSHER: In other words it's all right to contribute services and time, . . . but not a hall and not money. What's the big difference? Why should it be perfectly all right to contribute all the time you want to your candidate, but not be allowed to contribute a cent?

12.20   MEDALIE: Because the voluntarism that Mr. Alexander was talking about, I wholeheartedly favor, if people are spending their time trying to get a candidate elected, going around obtaining signatures promoting his candidacy. But when it comes to something like making a hall available that ordinarily is paid for, for rental, that is a contribution.

12.21   RUSHER: What about a person over 65, say, who doesn't have the energy or the inclination but would make out a check? Is that person just going to have to curb his appetite for voluntarism? Under your plan I guess he would.

12.22   MEDALIE: If he's paying any taxes, he's already made his contribution.

13.   CLOSING STATEMENTS

13.1   MILLER: The problem, of course, is not those who contribute halls, but those who contribute very substantial cash contributions while they themselves are regulated by the government. Those who oppose this plan are the special interests who now benefit under the status quo. Those who should favor it are every taxpayer who will be making an investment in cutting down on some of the needless subsidies that we now pay, and every American who is interested in having a government that really works.

13 . 2   RUSHER: Here is a plan that actually proposes to "improve" our democratic processes by *prohibiting* us from giving money to the candidate of our choice, and forcing us, through taxation, to give instead to candidates whom we may despise. The present system has many defects, but at least it doesn't have *that* one. In his great book, *The Costs of Democracy*, Dr. Alexander Heard put it very well when he said: "The private financing of elections, with all its imperfections and distortions, is one of the many instruments by which the organized power of government is made subservient and sensitive to the whole complex common life of society."

 *13 October 1970*

POSTSCRIPT

In late November 1971, the Democratic majority in the Senate amended a major tax bill so as to include a plan whereby a major party's Presidential nominee would be entitled, as of 1972, to $20.4 million in Federal funds as a campaign subsidy. The subsidy would emanate from a "check-off" system, whereby taxpayers could earmark one dollar of income tax for this purpose. In order to qualify for the subsidy, a candidate would be obliged to forego all other—that is to say, all "private"— campaign contributions. President Nixon announced, through White House press channels, that he might veto the whole tax bill unless this amendment were eliminated. The fate of the amendment, as of November 21, 1971, lay in the hands of conference committee summoned to reconcile House and Senate versions of the tax bill. President Nixon managed to get the bill sidetracked. But in early 1972 he signed the Federal Election Campaign Act, superceding the Corrupt Practices Act of 1925. This law involved no public subsidies for candidates. It imposed ceilings on what candidates can spend on advertising through the mass media: $14,250,509 for a Presidential candidate in 1972, $52,150 for a House candidate, a sliding scale for Senators according to size of State population. It also imposed more rigorous rules for reporting of contributions and outlays by candidates and political committees.

SUGGESTED EXERCISES

1. Cite and discuss the use of *ad hominem* argument in the debate on whether the Federal government should subsidize all campaigns for office.

2. Write a concise summary of the terms of the Miller Plan for reform of campaign finance, indicating what provisions were not made altogether clear during the debate.

3. Draw up a 'balance sheet' on effects of adopting the Miller Plan as alleged by participants in the debate. In one column list claims emanating from Affirmative spokesmen, and in the other column list claims emanating from Negative spokesmen. When contradictory or near-contradictory claims about cause and effect occur, place these adjacent to one another. Make a special effort to record *specific* claims about effects, as well as "glittering generalities" (discussed in the Commentary below).

4. From certain passages in the foregoing debate, one might piece together the following line of argument:

Normative assumption	1) Equality in the campaign resources of contestants for elective office is desirable.
Factual and causal claims	2) Such equality does not normally prevail at present.
	3) Incumbents presently enjoy competitive advantages over non-incumbents. Among other things, incumbents are better known among voters.
	4) In order to overcome competitive handicaps they now face, and thus to campaign effectively, non-incumbents must out-spend incumbents (Alexander, 9.4).
	5) The Miller Plan would prevent non-incumbents from out-spending incumbents.
Practical conclusion	6) The Miller Plan should not be adopted.

Now, if you accept the first four statements in this argument, can you still offer a reasonable case to the effect that the practical conclusion is premature?

5. From other passages in the foregoing debate, one can piece together a similar line of argument, with a different practical conclusion, as follows:

Normative assumption	1) Equality in the campaign resources is desirable.
Factual and causal claims	2) Such equality does not normally prevail at present.
	3) Incumbents presently enjoy competitive advantages over non-incumbents. Among other things, incumbents enjoy the franking privilege, access to publicly subsidized television studios, and opportunities to elicit campaign contributions from groups interested in pending legislation.
	4) The Miller Plan would prevent incumbents from out-spending non-incumbents.
Practical conclusion	5) The Miller Plan should be adopted.

Now, if you accept the first *three* statements in this argument, can you still offer a reasonable case to the effect that the practical conclusion is premature?

COMMENTARY

The debate on whether the Federal government should take over the financing of Federal election campaigns, like the debate on whether to abolish the Congressional "seniority system," served to illustrate some recurring devices of argument. Two of these devices are discussed below.

Glittering Generalities and Name-Calling

Father Charles E. Coughlin, a notorious figure in American politics in the late 1930's, once delivered a speech containing the following sentence: "Ours must be a moral platform from which there is preached a positive policy based upon the principles of religion and of patriotism."

Embedded in this sentence, according to the Institute of Propaganda Analysis, were four instances of the propaganda device known as the "glittering generality": namely, the terms "moral," "positive," "principles of religion," and "principles . . . of patriotism." Such verbiage exemplifies the use of "virtue words" so as "to make us accept and approve" a project or person "without examining the evidence."*

The counterpart of the "glittering generality" is "name-calling," or pasting a bad-sounding label on a person or project so as to encourage respondents to reject it without examining the evidence. This device was exemplified by the introductory sentence above, in which Father Coughlin was described as a "notorious" person. That adjective once meant simply "widely known" or "famous" but in common usage it now connotes "widely known to be a scoundrel."

Such generalities and name-calling not only invite us to jump to conclusions before examining relevant evidence, but also tend to prevent us from appraising evidence properly. The terms used often lack accepted meaning. Thus, no amount of examination would serve to establish, to the satisfaction of a wide audience, that a given platform is "moral" or that a given policy is "positive."

Participants in the debate on campaign subsidies were remarkably lavish in their use of name-calling and glittering generalities. From the Affirmative side came a cloud of attractive, but elusive, claims: that adoption of government-only campaign subsidies would "deny the special interests" (1.2), would "guarantee that our representatives represent people and not money" (1.2), would foster the "broad public interest" (2.6), would facilitate "genuine representative democracy" (5.13) and "real democracy" (4.5), and would engender "legitimate laws" (1.4). These glowing but elusive promises were coupled with ominous but elusive characterizations of present conditions, such as that "those who benefit from government action have been those who are subsidizing and

---

*Alfred McClung Lee and Elizabeth B. Lee, eds., *The Fine Art of Propaganda* (Harcourt, Brace: 1939), pp. 131, 23. The sentence in question also was described as exemplifying use of the "plain folks" device ("ours"), and the "transfer" device ("preached," "principles of religion"). The former is "the method by which a speaker attempts to convince his audience that he and his ideas are good because they are 'of the people,' the 'plain folks'." The latter device "carries the authority, sanction, and prestige of something respected and revered over to something else in order to make the latter acceptable. . . ." (*Ibid.*, pp. 23–24.) These definitions, unfortunately, refer not only to the content of speech, but also to the intentions of speakers. Moreover, each example presupposes consensus among respondents about what labels are good and bad.

electing the ones who are supposed to watch and regulate *them"* (**1.3**) and that we currently suffer from "skewed national priorities" (**4.2**).

From the Negative side, too, came some cloudy verbiage, such as the warning that adoption of the Miller Plan would greatly damage "the democratic process" (**1.5**). The last phrase exemplifies a glittering generality, suggesting that we now have a "democratic process" which is a kind of seamless web. On the other hand, the phrase exemplifies name-calling with respect to what it says about the consequences of adopting the Miller Plan.

The rational response to glittering generalities and name-calling surely is a suspension of judgment, pending receipt of further information.

Use of Analogies and Precedents

Policy arguments involve claims about what will happen in the future. Opposing advocates offer clashing interpretations of what will happen if a given measure is adopted by a given unit in a given context. These interpretations clash on two levels: the level of values and the factual level. If the dispute is primarily over values, the disputants may agree that policy p_1 will probably yield effects e_1, e_2 and e_3, but will disagree about the desirability of these results. If the dispute is primarily on the level of facts, the disputants may agree about what they deem desirable but will disagree about the effects likely to ensue from the adoption of p_1.

When disputes arise primarily at the factual level, disputants commonly rationalize their clashing claims by appeal to past experience. They cite cases, or *precedents* and *analogies*, as evidence on behalf of their versions of probable futures. And listeners seeking to distinguish between more and less plausible versions of what a given policy will produce must scrutinize these cases with care.

The debate over the Congressional "seniority system" furnished at least two examples of argument based on precedent and analogy. These were discussed in the Commentary dealing with burdens of proof. A further discussion will be given below, together with an investigation of how precedents and analogies were used, and abused, in the debate on campaign finance.

1. *House Speaker Elections.* In the course of the debate on the Congressional seniority system, as you may recall, William Rusher cited a precedent of sorts by way of challenging a particular causal assumption. The causal assumption was that abolition of the seniority system would produce more youthful chairmen for standing committees.

Rusher did not challenge this assumption by comparing the experience of non-Congressional organizations in selecting leaders by means other than a Congressional-type seniority system. Neither did he compare the ages of Congressional committee chairmen before and after the advent of the seniority system. Instead, he alluded to another segment of Congressional experience: elections of Speakers of the House of Representatives during the past 70 years. The Speakers had been elected by majority party caucus without reference to seniority, yet they had proved to be quite advanced in age at the time of their initial election.

This experience was not cited by Rusher as conclusive evidence against the notion that abolition of the seniority system for selecting chairmen would produce more youthful chairmen. Rusher made more modest, but argumentationally rather effective, use of this case. He offered it as the basis, as we noted earlier, for imposing on his opponents a new *burden of proof*: giving substantial reason for believing that abolition of seniority system would indeed rejuvenate the ranks of the chairmen.

2. *Congress Against the World*. Howard Miller engaged in a more comprehensive appeal to experience when he invited assessment of the Congressional seniority system by comparison with a vast array of other human organizations. He argued, essentially, that *since* no human organization but the Congress chooses leaders strictly on the basis of seniority, *therefore* the Congressional seniority system must be deemed guilty of being counter-productive until proved innocent.

This appeal to experience was more complex, and more devious, than Rusher's. It involved, first, an evasive and deceptive contrast between Congressional and non-Congressional modes of selecting leaders.* It involved, second, an important omission: a judgment as to whether non-Congressional human organizations have in general been more productive (however measured) than the Congress. Only if the latter claim is made, *and* if the contrast in quality of performance is causally related to a contrast in modes of selecting leaders, would it be reasonable to

---

*In the first place, some Congressional leaders are selected under conditions remote from what can be called a "seniority rule" or "the seniority system." In the second place, the system governing the selection of Congressional committee chairmen does not literally entail "seniority" in the sense of age, of years of membership in the Congress, or of years of membership on a given committee relative to *all* other members. In the third place, even though the seniority system of the Congress is unique to the Congress, the committee chairmen of Congress are not markedly dissimilar to leaders of other human organizations. Leaders quite commonly are older than sub-leaders and non-leaders, and are more "senior" in length of organizational membership.

conclude from the evidence of experience that the Congressional senior-ity system is of doubtful utility.

3. *The Censured Senator.* The debate on campaign finance yielded at least four examples of using precedents or analogies. One case involved the now-familiar business of shifting burdens of proof. Howard Miller argued, on the basis of a historical instance, that what is now standard practice (the funding of election campaigns from private contributions) once was considered immoral. He implied, moreover, that the earlier concept of morality really is not obsolete, so that current practice should be changed.

The evidence cited by Miller consisted of a censure imposed by a Senatorial committee on a member back in 1873. The censure allegedly was imposed because the Senator "accepted a campaign contribution of $10,000 from an officer of the Union Pacific Railroad. The Senate com-mittee said it would undermine the Republic and could be completely contrary to public and private virtue to allow campaigns to be so fi-nanced" (7.1).

This appeal to experience proved to be rather effective in the context of the debate. It elicited a lame response from Rep. John Ashbrook to the effect that "the political facts of life have changed," what with increasing campaign expenses and a more sophisticated public (7.2). But further re-flection, and a closer look at the text of the debate, suggests that Miller's description of the case of the censured Senator was deceptive. Miller does not say, in so many words, that the Senate committee was objecting *in principle* to raising campaign funds from private contributors (and was faithfully reflecting public sentiment at the time). Miller leaves room for the possibility that the Senate committee was condemning some par-ticular *aspect* of the censured Senator's conduct, such as the size of the donation or the terms of its acceptance.

This possibility gains a measure of probability among persons knowl-edgeable about American history. Such persons would know that in 1873, as well as in 1803 and 1970, candidates for elective office did in fact finance their campaigns from private contributions. Moreover, such knowledge of common practice can even be inferred from *another* case cited by Miller. This was the 1843 case in which Abraham Lincoln re-turned the *unspent* portion of a campaign contribution *he* had received (7.3). Here there is no hint of immorality in the initial *acceptance* of such a donation. To this extent, it appears that Miller has falsified past prac-tice *and* past standards of propriety. Accordingly, the question posed by Miller to Representative Ashbrook—"Why is the public morality changed?"—involves a false premise.

4. *The "Parallel" Case of Non-Electoral Subsidies.* Another instructive example of arguing from precedent or analogy was furnished by Representative Ashbrook. Here a provisional assessment of the consequences of granting campaign subsidies to electoral candidates was derived from an assessment of the consequences of granting subsidies to other classes of persons. In Representative Ashbrook's words, "if subsidies did to the politicians what [they have] done to agriculture and some other areas, I think you can only guess how bad it would be" (6.6).

This resort to analogy affords a nice example of implanting a conclusion by insinuation while engaging in multiple question-begging. Representative Ashbrook evaded the question of whether experience with non-campaign subsidies *does* serve to shed light on the probable consequences of campaign subsidies. He also gave short shrift to the question of whether, and in what ways, non-campaign subsidies have indeed produced "bad" effects.

5. *The "Parallel" Case of "Election Subsidies."* Another appeal to analogy in the debate on campaign finance served to illustrate the process of attempting to make a policy innovation palatable to people who, in the most literal sense, are conservative. People of this description mistrust novel experiments. If they are numerous and/or influential, their fears must be allayed.

The most direct way to dispel such apprehensions is to show that what appears to be a novel departure really is not new. Such a demonstration often is feasible, because a policy suggested for one government at one point in time may have been implemented by that government in the past or by other governments at other times. But if such a demonstration is not feasible, then more indirect methods of appeal must be employed.

Attorney Jerome Medalie furnished an example of this more indirect approach. In response to a question from Howard Miller, he declared that Americans already "subsidize the entire electoral process" (11.4). This version of reality served to implant the idea that subsidizing election campaigns already has been sanctified by custom. (For another method of making novelty palatable, see the Commentary on ambiguity and equivocation in the debate on low-income housing.)

This claim, however, placed Medalie in an awkward position. Having declared that the "entire electoral process" already is subsidized by the American taxpayers, he was scarcely in a position to argue that a component of the "electoral process" is *not* now subsidized and *should* be subsidized. He tried to extricate himself by drawing a subtle, if not tenuous, distinction between spending public funds on "the election process" and spending public funds on "what the election *exists for*," namely, enabling voters to make informed judgments on candidates who are "unencumbered by obligations to special interests."*

6. *"Negative" Cases.* Our final example of citing past experience involves several cases or episodes mentioned by proponents of government-only campaign subsidies. These cases had one feature in common: each sought to derive a lesson from experience with the *absence* of a proposed measure.

Such modes of argument are standard practice. It often is impossible to cite 'positive' cases, in which a preferred policy has previously been tried in some setting or another and has produced more or less discernible effects. It then becomes necessary to rely not only on oblique comparisons, but also on 'negative' cases in which a given policy, so to speak, has been conspicuous by its absence. These 'negative' cases, in other words, draw upon past experience wherein something virtually antithetical to a given policy (legality *vs.* illegality of alcohol, for example) has been tried.

Now, in assessing cases derived from 'negative' experience, a reasonable person must bear in mind two questions. First, are the past experiences described by the proponent of change really bad experiences? Second, are these bad experiences causally related to the absence of a prescribed remedy? If our answers to these questions are affirmative, then we credit the proponent of a given change with having established a need and having shown that the given change will meet the need.

Proponents of the Miller Plan cited a number of 'negative' cases. But their handling of these cases, from the standpoint of sustaining plausible inferences about cause and effect, left something to be desired. Here is a review.

---

*A less tortuous appeal to convention could conceivably have been formulated in the following terms. Many aspects of the electoral process, *including* candidates' campaign resources, already are subsidized by the taxpayers, but in a manner that, unfortunately, is covert and partial. Many perquisites vested in Congressional office, such as salaries, staff allowances, travel allowances, and the franking privilege, serve to all intents and purposes as public subsidies for electoral campaigning. But these subsidies are granted only to incumbents. If *overt* subsidies were given both to incumbents and to non-incumbents, and if all other campaign funds were outlawed, then competition for office would be conducted on more equitable terms *and* contestants would be insulated from the insidious influence of "special interests." This *way* of citing precedents on behalf of campaign subsidies, perhaps, is peculiarly unattractive to incumbents.

1) *Non-Appointment of Dr. Knowles.* In the course of testifying on behalf of the Miller Plan, Journalist Britt Hume was asked whether the public is "directly hurt" by the presence of multitudinous, private, money-dispensing interest groups (2.7). He answered "Yes," and cited as a "good example" of this damage the failure of Dr. John Knowles to be appointed, after initial Administration support, to the office of Assistant Secretary of Health, Education, and Welfare. Hume blamed this episode on the American Medical Association, and then delivered the following two-pronged judgment: "The American Medical Association in 1968 came through with about $2 million worth of contributions indirectly to political causes, and they succeeded in prevailing over the will of a Cabinet Secretary and changing the mind of a President. It was an extraordinary demonstration of power" (2.8).

Hume's testimony concerning this case can be described as an extraordinary feat of insinuation, stemming as it does from an inordinate amount of evasion. Hume suggested, but did not undertake to show, that the appointment of Dr. Knowles was in the public interest. Hume insinuated, but did not undertake to show, that the A.M.A.'s ability to thwart the appointment of Dr. Knowles emanated from its capacity and its right (under present law) to dispense campaign funds to favored candidates for office.

What is more, Hume managed to leave behind a hint to the effect that the latter inference was wrong. This hint consisted of the remark that the A.M.A. in 1968 spent $2 million "indirectly" on political causes. The term "indirectly" tells us, at a minimum, that "contributions to political causes" take at least two forms. One of these, perhaps, is donating directly to favored candidates for office. Another, perhaps, is lobbying, or attempting to persuade incumbent legislators, as well as the public at large, to support certain policies. The latter sort of activity ("indirect" political spending?) would *not* be proscribed by the Miller Plan. Accordingly, the circumstances surrounding the non-appointment of Dr. Knowles, as described by Hume, shed little light on the probable effects of adopting the Miller Plan.

2) *The Oil Industry.* The same applies to what was said, and was not said, about the power of the "oil industry." Hume *insinuated*, as did Philip Stern, (*a*) that the oil depletion allowance and oil import quotas are averse to the general interest, (*b*) that these measures attest to the exhorbitant political power of the "oil industry," and (*c*) that such power would be neutralized by a ban on private contributions to election campaigns.

None of these propositions, however, was overtly stated, let alone substantiated. The closest thing to a direct assertion was Stern's reference (**5.12**) to Western Democrats who allegedly were offered $10,000 donations to their Senatorial compaigns in return for "commitments" on oil depletion. But Stern did not say, let alone show, that these candidates would have opposed the present oil depletion allowance but for the campaign contributions. Neither did Hume ever declare that any Senator's votes on oil depletion would change in the wake of a ban on private contributions to election campaigns.

3) *The Shipping Industry.* Similarly, Hume cited the "shipping industry" as an example of a "narrowly regulated interest" that gained improper advantage from present laws governing campaign funds. The shipping industry allegedly "survives today only on the strength of about $400 million annually [in] Federal subsidy." Members of that industry made a $37,000 campaign contribution to the Chairman of the Merchant Marine Committee of the House of Representatives, even though the recipient was unopposed for re-election (**2.10**).

This case surely raises some interesting questions. It also evades some questions that are vitally relevant to the issue at hand. It evades these questions: (*a*) whether the presence of a domestic shipping industry is against the public interest; (*b*) whether Federal subsidies are necessary to maintain such an industry (assuming that its maintenance *is* in the public interest); and (*c*) whether the presence of a superfluous or unduly expensive domestic shipping industry is due to the legal privilege of making private campaign contributions to selected candidates for elective office.

On this showing, the 'negative' precedents cited by supporters of government-only campaign subsidies were quite inconclusive.

Should the federal government register voters for presidential elections?

OVERVIEW

On the first Tuesday of November in every even-numbered year, millions upon millions of American adults heed the call to elect national legislators. The votes they cast decide who shall fill all 435 seats in the House of Representatives, around 34 of the 100 seats in the Senate (each Senator being elected to serve a six-year term), and—every other time—the office of President. But millions upon millions of other American adults do *not* take part in these decisions. Accordingly, it is an illusion that American legislators are elected by universal adult suffrage. In fact, rates of turnout for United States elections, even with presidential candidates at the top of the ballot, rarely match the rates attained by many, if not most, countries that are commonly classified as democracies. Indeed the 1972 presidential election set a modern record for abstentions.

Nonparticipation has aroused alarm in some quarters and a search for causes. Some nonparticipants manifestly have been fully eligible to vote but have chosen to abstain. Many more nonparticipants have lacked eligibility, even since the abolition of restrictions based on wealth, religion, sex, and race. In most of the States (as in most countries), would-be voters must go through a formal registration procedure prior to the date of an election. Some people who are entitled to register and then vote fail to take the first step. And some individuals who qualify in other respects have stumbled against a legal barrier that is peculiarly consequential in the American context. This barrier is the requirement that individuals reside in a given locality for a prescribed length of time before they can register and vote.

Residence requirements have been imposed by State governments. Their terms vary from State to State, but until recently a typical requirement necessitated residence for one year in a given State, 90 days in a given county, and 30 days in a given precinct prior to the date of an election. Such requirements are not uniquely American, but they have imposed an abnormally severe restriction on the abnormally mobile American population.

These requirements have recently been almost eliminated. In consequence of the Voting Rights Act of 1970, few adults now are directly barred from voting in Federal elections because they are newcomers to a given locality. But an indirect barrier remains. Newcomers still must register before they become fully eligible to vote. They must register at times and places prescribed by State governments and administered by local officials such as county registrars. Existing procedures commonly make it more cumbersome and time-consuming to register than actually to vote.

Registration policies and practices vary from State to State. Rates of turnout also vary significantly, and persistently, from State to State. Low rates of turnout in certain States have been ascribed to, among other things, "negative" official attitudes toward registration. Lately it has been suggested that the Federal government take a more direct, promotional part in getting citizens registered to vote. The merits and demerits of such an innovation are canvassed in the following debate.

1.   OPENING STATEMENTS

1.1   MODERATOR VICTOR PALMIERI: The problem [aired tonight] lies at the very heart of the democratic idea: the right to vote and, specifically, the exercise of that right. We don't know how many people voted in *this* election [of November 1970], but in the last *presidential* election [of November 1968], which was decided by a margin of only 600,000 votes, 37 million eligible voters did not go to the polls. Why don't more people vote? Some experts believe that our present system of voter registration has a lot to do with the low turnout. Congressman Morris Udall of Arizona and Senator Daniel Inouye of Hawaii have introduced a bill that will change that system drastically. Tonight "The Advocates" examines their proposal, called Universal Voter Registration. Specifically, our question is this: "Should the Federal government register voters for Presidential elections?" Advocate Miller says "Yes," [while] Advocate Rusher disagrees.

1.2   ADVOCATE HOWARD MILLER: President Nixon has told us the most important four-letter word in the country is "vote." The American ideal is that all citizens vote and participate in elections. The reality, however, is that certain groups of citizens do *not* vote and do *not* participate. For example, 50 percent of those between the ages of 21 and 30 are not registered to vote. They are not registered largely because they are highly mobile and move around from place to place. Fifty percent of those with less than a fourth-grade education are not registered to vote. By and large, we have excluded people by the difficulty of registration; and that exclusion has fallen unequally. Because of the . . . requirement that a voter may have to [register] to vote weeks, months, before the election, many people do not know where to register, and are excluded by residency requirements.

1.3   We propose to narrow [the] gap between reality and ideal. Because, basically, [many] people don't vote because of the complexity and craziness of many of our registration laws, we propose a Federal registration law to guarantee that every citizen may vote. We propose . . . the Universal Enrollment Plan.

1.4   The first thing to note about the Universal Enrollment Plan is that the basic obligation may be the State's. Any State that registers 90 percent of its voters simply gets a cash grant from the Federal government to defray the expenses of that registration. Two of our States, Utah and Idaho, now register over 90 percent of their voters. For those States that do *not* register 90 percent, however, the Federal "back-up" system comes into play. That system is basically simple: a Federal Enrollment Commission appoints directors in each Congressional district; those directors arrange for a door-to-door canvass, by volunteers, over everyone in the district, and those who are not registered may be registered by the Federal Registrar; those lists are then turned in, and whoever is registered by the Registrar may vote. [And] even if someone is not registered (because he has been missed, because he didn't want to be registered, or because he's moved within a few days before the Presidential election), he may show up at any polling place, give proof of his identity, and vote on a double-sealed ballot, [its validity] subject to [a check on his identity]. The total cost of the plan: $50 million in election years; 50 cents per vote. And ultimately, when the Federal registration lists are turned over to the States, it is hoped that all States will register over 90 percent, the voting percentages will go up, and the Federal Commission will only serve as a guarantee of registration.

1.5   ADVOCATE WILLIAM RUSHER: This proposal is almost a case study in what can be wrong with a piece of legislation. Almost everything about this proposal is deceptive. In the first place, the problem [of non-voting] is not nearly as serious today as Mr. Miller [and others] have cracked it up to be. [And] the problems that it purports to solve have already in large part been solved by the Voting Rights Act of 1970. It is true that American elections tend to have a slightly lower rate of voting than those in certain British Commonwealth countries and the Scandinavian nations; and that is primarily because we have so many more elections. Due to our Federal system, we have Federal elections; we have State elections; we have city elections; we have primary elections; we have general elections; [and] we have school board elections, Constitutional amendment elections, special elections. All of these things cause, naturally, a going back and forth to the polls and a lower proportionate result, even in large elections, than you would get where elections were much fewer and further between.

1.6   And in the second place, the cure that is proposed by the Udall bill is infinitely worse than the disease. As usual with these proposals, a vast new Federal bureaucracy is called for—unnecessary, expensive, overweening, and subject to both financial and political corruption. The expense of this whole preposterous idea is going to be far greater than even Mr. Miller has conceded. [Although his estimate is 50 cents per voter and $50 million in every presidential year,] if you were lucky enough to register, say, 10 million additional individuals under this bill, you would, by a simple calculation of arithmetic, be spending $5 per person for each of those individuals. And, of course, [since they [would be] people who do not ordinarily vote, and haven't [voted] to date, it is safe to assume that they will not *all* vote when registered. It is very likely that the *actual* cost for each additional voter acquired by this process [would] rise to something on the order of $15. Moreover, there is an enormous bureaucracy involved here. You will be glad to know that Congressman Udall, however, has "frugally" provided that although there will have to be a lot of people hired, none of them can be paid more than $100 a day. We will be saved further expense than *that* per individual hired to enforce this process!

1.7   In point of fact, this bill is not a convenience for people who are unable to vote today. It is a *dragnet*, which is going to mandatorily place the names of every single individual qualified to vote in America on a specific list, and hand that list over to a political official of the local or State government, under the terms of the law, on request, without any discrimination, without any restriction, for any purpose for which [he] chooses to use it.

1.8   This is not an experiment in democracy at all. It is a scheme hatched, to tell you the truth, in the back rooms of the Democratic National Committee, where they have begun to notice that they've been losing elections; and they are doing their desperate best to tilt the pinball machine of the American political mechanism to get their poor party back on the track.

2.   FIRST AFFIRMATIVE WITNESS: DIRECT EXAMINATION

2.1   MILLER: To talk in favor of this plan we have asked to join us the man who has introduced it in the Congress of the United States: Morris Udall. Congressman, why should the government take the lead in registering voters?

2.2   REP. MORRIS UDALL: We say we are a government of the people; and the other democracies—the Swedes, the Germans, the British, the French—vote 85, 90 percent of their people in all their major elections. We don't. And I think they do that because they have [the proposed] kind of [enrollment] system.

2.3   There are really two theories involved here. One says that "We, as a society, have no stake in whether you vote at all; we really don't care; it's up to you; if you don't do it, well and good." And implicit in this argument is the idea, I think, that maybe the undereducated, the poor, the minority groups, won't register and vote. I reject that philosophy. And my philosophy is that society has a real stake in making sure that everyone votes; that we go out and encourage people to vote; that we spend enough money to make sure that every American has a right, a chance, an opportunity, to vote.

2.4   MILLER: Do current registration laws, in effect, disenfranchise people?

2.5   UDALL: Let me tell you something. In 1968, when we made this vital decision—[about] four years [of a] President [and] war and peace priorities—31 million [people, plus a few more, supported Richard Nixon,
while a few less than 31 million supported Hubert Humphrey, and] 37
million people voted for no one. Shut out of the process. And these aren't
statistics; these are people. These are people who have their sons drafted
to go to Vietnam. These are people who pay taxes. These are people who
may have a freeway run through their living room by government. We've
erected this whole series of booby traps, high hurdles, an obstacle course,
to keep them out. And it's wrong.

2.6   MILLER: Does this Federal system of registration in any way interfere with
basic States' rights?

2.7   UDALL: No, indeed. This system I propose would say to the States, "As
soon as you get 90 percent of your people on the rolls, the Federal system
won't operate." It gives the States first shot at it, and it finances the
States' operation.

2.8   MILLER: But for those States that do not achieve 90 percent, is this kind of
backup with house-to-house canvassing necessary?

2.9   UDALL: It's absolutely necessary, because you have to have registration
under State law. And we want to make sure that every American votes
for President, whether he's been in the State a day, a month, or a decade.
Under this plan, he can go to the polls on election day and be allowed
to vote.

2.10   MILLER: Under the 1970 Voting Rights Act there are different requirements
for residency for Presidential elections. They're cut back to 30 days.
Does that make this act unnecessary?

2.11   UDALL: No. I want a permanent cure. The 1970 Voting Rights Act will ex-
pire in five years, and this is intended to be a permanent system. The
1970 Voting Rights Act only *permits* people to register under the State
law. The State law still governs. Here we would have a system under
which no registration would be necessary except the Federal enrollment
certificate. The Federal government would go out through the system
three weeks before the election and give everyone, every American, a
chance to vote in the Presidential election.

2.12   MILLER: Your bill starts with the Presidential election. Where do you think
it will lead?

2.13   UDALL: I hope . . . we will have assemblymen and governors and mayors and everyone else elected by all of the people instead of 50 percent or 60 percent. Actually, I foresee that, by turning these Federal enrollment rolls over to the States, very soon the states would have the high percentages that I'd like to see: 85 or 90 percent. The system would wither away, and the Federal Enrollment Commission would simply be there as a backup, to make sure that citizens could continue to have the right to vote.

3.   CROSS-EXAMINATION

3.1   PALMIERI: What makes you think, Mr. Udall, that all those non-registered voters would vote?

3.2   UDALL: There's no guarantee that they would. But the experience has been that, when we get people registered, 85 [or] 90 percent or better of them will vote. It's the people who are not registered who are excluded from the process.

3.3   PALMIERI: And basically, [your view is] that it would be a good thing for the country if everybody who might be eligible could vote.

3.4   UDALL: At least have the opportunity to vote.

3.5   RUSHER: I presume that there would, under almost any system, be some people who choose, however, *not* to vote [and choose] not to register, even, if they [have] the choice. What about those people under your bill?

3.6   UDALL: The philosophy of my bill is simply that we give them a *chance*. We give them an opportunity. If they reject that chance, so be it. But most of the people who are shut out today are shut out involuntarily.

3.7   RUSHER: The statement that you inserted in the Congressional Record, when you introduced the bill, stated that the bill would enroll every qualified person to vote who does not refuse.

3.8   UDALL: This has been unfortunate language, of which there is considerable in the Congressional Record. [Laughter.] The intention of the bill is simply to give them an *opportunity* to vote.

3.9   RUSHER: The *intention* of the bill is, indeed, that; but in point of fact it *compels* them to register, does it not? And there isn't a word in your bill from one end to the other that says a thing about it being voluntary?

3.10   UDALL: There's a question of interpretation here. [The intention is to give such persons] the *opportunity* to register, but not *require* them to register. And I would simply say that if the technical language would be interpreted by lawyers to require them to register, we can correct that with an amendment which I would support.

3.11   RUSHER: It can be interpreted by anybody who reads English. I refer you to line 3 of page 4: "When every such determination has been made with respect to any person"—that is, the determination that he is qualified—"his name *shall* be entered on an enrollment roll compiled by the national enrollment officials for the election district concerned."

3.12   UDALL: Yes. But there's nothing in the bill that would require that person, so enrolled, to go down and vote. No one's going to haul him to [the polls].

3.13   RUSHER: I didn't say it did. But it *does* require him to register and his name to be on the list, doesn't it?

3.14   UDALL: It puts his name on a list which will permit him to vote—

3.15   RUSHER: Whether he likes it or not.

3.16   UDALL: Whether he likes it or not. And he can reject that opportunity.

3.17   RUSHER: What happens to the list, Congressman?

3.18   UDALL: The list goes to the election officials on the election day and if that individual shows up, he can demand the right to vote for [a presidential candidate].

3.19   RUSHER: And after election day, what happens to the list?

3.20   UDALL: The list is destroyed unless the State officials want that list for their own purposes. . . .

3.21   RUSHER: In other words, any State or local [election] official who asks for the list, gets it. Is that correct? . . .

3.22   UDALL: Precisely.

3.23   RUSHER: And they can get it without any restrictions on use whatever.

3.24   UDALL: No [restrictions], indeed. We hope they'll use it.

3.25   RUSHER: Show me the restrictions on their use of it.

3.26   UDALL: I don't know whether there are adequate restrictions in the bill as now written—

3.27   RUSHER: Did you read the bill before you introduced it?

3.28   UDALL: Oh, I did, indeed. [*Laughter.*]

3.29   RUSHER: Did you draft it?

3.30   UDALL: Line by line, and word by word.

3.31   RUSHER: Well, are there any words that say that the list cannot be used for any purpose whatever by the local official who takes it?

3.32   UDALL: No, but I would be glad to write such a restriction.

3.33   RUSHER: I'm sure you would. I daresay you wish you *had*. [*Laughter.*] But in point of fact, what you have got is a bill which compels every single qualified person in the United States to be registered and be placed on the list, and then provides that the list shall be given on simple request, without any restriction, without any discrimination, to anybody who is a State or local election official and wants it; and [he] can thereafter do with it what [he wants].

3.34   UDALL: Yes, sir.

3.35   PALMIERI: There seems to be implicit in Mr. Rusher's position that there is something very dangerous in the fact that State election officials would have that list. Are you agreeing with that?

3.36   UDALL: No, I'm not agreeing with that at all. Mr. Rusher's erecting a straw man here. He has great, evil uses made of this list. The idea is to give, at Federal expense, the State people a list of all the potential voters; to give the States a chance to let those voters vote in state elections.

3.37   PALMIERI: Mr. Rusher, I urge you to suggest to the Congressman what dangerous and hazardous uses [against] the principles of democracy you see in those lists.

3.38   RUSHER: I was about to do that when you interrupted. I suggest, Congressman, that there are a great many people in this country who, for reasons of their own that may or may not appeal to you, do not, in fact, want their names listed and handed out to political officials who can thereafter hand them on to anybody else they want.

3.39   UDALL: I think we should have restrictions on [use of the lists].

3.40   RUSHER: Why didn't you put them in the bill?

3.41   UDALL: They should be used for election purposes. This is an educational effort. This is a beginning. I have never seen a bill, a major bill, passed as it was originally introduced.

3.42   RUSHER: You are a member of the House of Representatives, are you not?

3.43   UDALL: I am, indeed.

3.44   RUSHER: You are used to introducing bills?

3.45   UDALL: A number of them.

3.46   RUSHER: You expect them to become law?

3.47   UDALL: I hope so, in most cases.

3.48   RUSHER: You hope that this will become law?

3.49   UDALL: I do, indeed. [*Laughter.*]

3.50   RUSHER: And that it becomes law then with the particular provisions in it which I have described?

3.51   UDALL: No. I think you're erecting a straw man in suggesting that particular deficiencies in the bill that you have pointed out—

3.52   RUSHER: And you agree are there?

3.53   PALMIERI: Yes, but my difficulty is, Congressman and Mr. Rusher, that at least . . . for me, [and] perhaps also . . . for . . . our audience, we [have not] identified precisely what those deficiencies are.

3.54   RUSHER: Let me suggest that the deficiency the Congressman is referring to, and fully recognizes [is] there, [is] . . . that this [bill] requires people to have their names placed on a Federal list which then becomes usable by any political official of the local election process who wants to use it and to hand it on to anybody else that he wants. Now, it is a fact that, for many purposes in this country today, our names are on altogether too many lists. I daresay that before this year is over, I will be hearing from Mr. Miller that we must have a Federal proposal, with a bureaucracy and a budget to match, to wipe people's names *off* lists. Just last week, he was protesting that the police were watching entirely too many people and that we all had so much to hide. Now he comes forward this week with a proposal that Congressman Udall's bill should register us all on a Federal list and then give that to any election official who demands it within 30 days.

3.55   UDALL: I have sponsored legislation over the years to allow people to get their names off mailing lists that want to get them off. [*Laughter.*]

3.56   RUSHER: But why didn't you put it in this bill?

3.57   UDALL: Because I think the major point here is are we going to give all American people the chance to vote, an opportunity to vote for their President or not. Now these are petty details . . . which in the amendment process of the legislation can be corrected. I don't want—

3.58   RUSHER: Well, I don't know whether they are ["petty details"]. I suggest [that] you correct them. Now let me go to another point, if I may. We have in this bill a proposal that the whole National Enrollment Commission will consist of nine people . . . of whom no more than five can be of a single party.

3.59   UDALL: Precisely.

3.60   RUSHER: It would be perfectly possible for either President Johnson (in his time) or President Nixon (today) to make those five—in other words the majority of the commission members of his party. [And] . . . it would probably be logical that he would do so.

3.61   UDALL: I would think so.

3.62   RUSHER: The director of the National Enrollment Commission also will be appointed by [the President] because [he would also] be the head of the

Bureau of the Census. Presumably [the director will be] a man of the same party.

3 . 63 UDALL: Undoubtedly. [*Laughter.*]

3 . 64 RUSHER: All 435 District Enrollment Directors will also be appointed by that man, would they not?

3 . 65 UDALL: Yes, they would be.

3 . 66 RUSHER: Is there anything in the bill that prevents them from all being of the same party?

3 . 67 UDALL: I think not. [*Laughter.*]

3 . 68 RUSHER: How about the volunteers under them? According to Professor Andrew Hacker, who will testify later, up to 3,000 volunteers will be required in each of the 435 districts. Are they all going to be of the same party?

3 . 69 UDALL: They may, but I don't . . . share your cynicism. . . . [*Laughter.*]

3 . 70 RUSHER: I don't share your optimism, Congressman. [*Laughter.*]

3 . 71 UDALL: The Republicans control the New York legislature and the New York governor is a Republican, and yet they haven't taken the New York political process and prostituted it so that we don't get fair elections. I have faith that [fairness] can be [accomplished].

3 . 72 RUSHER: It would *take* faith, Congressman. [*Laughter.*]

3 . 73 MILLER (*in summation*):   For the good of all of us, things are not nearly as dangerous as the tone of the questions suggest—and only the *tone*. Congressman Udall said on the House floor, as the draftsman of the bill, that the enrollment officers would visit every residence in the land and enroll every qualified person who does not refuse. Someone may simply refuse to have his name on the list. We're talking about the basic purposes of the legislation. The basic purpose is simply to see that all may vote. And this is the way to meet that purpose.

4.   FIRST NEGATIVE WITNESS: DIRECT EXAMINATION

4 . 1 RUSHER: To prove [that this scheme was hatched by Democratic leaders in order to "get their poor party back on the track,"] I will call as my first witness the distinguished [Republican] United States Senator from the State of Colorado, the honorable Peter Dominick. Senator, on the basic principle: Do you favor people who want to vote—anybody who wants to vote—voting?

4 . 2 SEN. PETER DOMINICK: Anybody that wants to vote should have the oppor-

tunity of doing so; and we *have* that opportunity now that we have passed the Voting Rights Act of 1970.

4.3   RUSHER: What then is [generally] wrong with Congressman Udall's bill?

4.4   DOMINICK: The first thing is that it's unnecessary. We don't want to pass legislation unless it is necessary, on the Federal level. [The Udall bill] is unnecessary because we passed the Voting Rights Act of 1970, which says that any person who moves into a State within 30 days before a Presidential election can vote in that new State regardless of [its] residency requirements. If [he] moves in after that 30-day period, [he] can get an absentee ballot from [his] previous place within seven days before the election. So most of the people who have been disenfranchised prior to this time [from] voting for President or Vice-President, have been *re*-enfranchised by an act that we have already passed.

4.5   The second thing wrong with it is the fact that it *does* have, within the wording as it's now phrased, a compulsory listing of everybody within this country. And I can't tell you how many people resent this. They just do not like to be on any more lists.

4.6   The third thing that's bad with it, as far as I can see, is that those lists, once that they are made, are turned over to any local election official in any area in the country that demands it. This could be anybody who is connected with the elective process, be it a watcher, a challenger, or anything else. And I don't think this is right. I think this is an invasion of privacy.

4.7   RUSHER: [What] about the cry that we must get out the vote? How are we otherwise going to get out the vote?

4.8   DOMINICK: Interestingly enough, the task force appointed by President Kennedy in 1963 brought out some very interesting recommendations which were designed along the lines which we now have, where we get the so-called "third sector" of our country—the private organizations, like the League of Women Voters and the educational associations and a group of others—working very hard to acquaint people with their rights. At the same time, the two-party system obviously is going to have registration drives, and the stronger we can get the two-party system to bring people out and to register, the stronger the country's going to be. And this is the recommendation of President Kennedy's task force.

4.9   RUSHER: It was a rather frugal one, because it didn't cost the voters a cent. Is that right?

4.10   DOMINICK: That's right. And they said in that [task force report] that they were against compulsory voting and against a Federal system.

5.   CROSS-EXAMINATION

5.1   MILLER: Senator, I know you oppose this bill. Are you as excited about it as Mr. Rusher is? [*Laughter.*]

5.2   DOMINICK: I think that any bill [in which] you try to put everybody on some kind of a master computer list is wrong.

5.3   MILLER: If you accepted the sponsor of the bill's interpretation of what he said on the House floor—that people could refuse—that at least would remove that objection.

5.4   DOMINICK: It would help, but you're still going to have an enormous Federal pressure against people. You know, if you've got a Federal official coming up to a poor fellow who is somewheres around . . . and says "I'm a Federal official and I want you to sign this," he's going to have kind of a lot of pressure.

5.5   MILLER: I doubt that's what would be said, but let me ask you: why the differences in voting in today's electorate? The Gallup Poll reports that 44 percent of those who rent their houses, who rent their apartments, who rent and do not own, are not registered to vote. Only 16 percent of those who *own* homes are not registered. Why do you think there's that difference between those who rent and those who own?

5.6   DOMINICK: I wouldn't have any idea.

5.7   MILLER: Do you think it's because of the [greater rate of] mobility of those who rent? Certainly that's one factor.

5.8   DOMINICK: It may be. There are a lot of people now who are refusing to participate in any of these Federal programs. They don't want to be on a Social Security list—

5.9   MILLER: Any of these Federal programs like voting—

5.10   DOMINICK: They don't want to be on a draft list, or anything. [*Laughter, applause.*]

5.11   MILLER: Tell me about some other differences of the vote. Fifty percent of those between 21 and 30 don't register to vote. Do you think that's because of a lack of interest in the electoral process?

5.12   DOMINICK: I don't know. The Gallup Poll of 1968 said that 15 million out of the 37 [million] who didn't vote [in the national election] failed to vote because either they were disinterested, or didn't want to, or they didn't like the nominees.

5.13   MILLER: Well, let's see *why* they're disinterested. In 1965 you supported the Voting Rights Act of 1965 to send in Federal examiners . . . to the South, to register blacks who may have been discriminated against.

5.14 DOMINICK: I did. Less than 50 percent of the total population [was] voting.

5.15 MILLER: Let's talk about a State where there is less than 90 percent registered. You can send in Federal examiners to the South, take blacks because they have not registered. What about the young and the renters and the poor and the uneducated who are not registered now? By the same principle can't we send in Federal registrars to register them?

5.16 DOMINICK: I don't think so. What we're talking about here is the basic question that anybody that really wants to vote should have the right to vote. That problem was solved by the Voting Rights Act of 1970. . . . And it would seem to me that to go beyond that is putting in a Federal imperative, or a compulsory voting system.

5.17 MILLER: Let me ask you about the Voting Rights Act of 1970. All that does is change the residency requirements to 30 days.

5.18 DOMINICK: Oh, seven days on an absentee.

5.19 MILLER: People must still register under State law, and that varies from State to State. In Delaware, for example, within that 30-day period you have to go to *Wilmington* to register, and go to Wilmington to *vote*, because you're not part of the regular registration procedure. In Texas, the regular rolls close in January. There will be special procedures where you have to go. There [are] still inhibitions even with the Voting Rights Act of 1970, aren't there?

5.20 DOMINICK: There's a lot of things that we can do to improve that, within the State and local areas. But that doesn't mean that you have to put a whole Federal program in, like a blanket and a net over everybody. . . .

5.21 MILLER: States that register 90 percent would not have to have any Federal interference at all. Why shouldn't every State in this country have 90 percent registration?

5.22 DOMINICK: They get paid $100,000 times every Congressional district that they've got in the place. And I can see any State Governor saying, "Holy smokes, I'm going to get a lot of free revenue; and we can use it for anything."

5.23 MILLER: That's exactly right. Well, use it to defray his expenses, and that's well worth the price of the 90 percent.

6. SECOND NEGATIVE WITNESS: DIRECT EXAMINATION

6.1 RUSHER: Now let's take another look at the bill about which Mr. Miller, apparently having decided that it may not be totally defensible, nevertheless feels that I have become too excited. Let us discuss some of its other defects with Professor Robert Nisbet of the department of sociology of the University of California at Riverside. Professor, in addition to what we shall call the "modest" holes in this bill which have been uncovered so far tonight, is there anything about it that particularly disturbs you?

6.2   PROF. ROBERT NISBET: The one that bothers me the most, Mr. Rusher, is Section 3F, where the National Director of Enrollment "shall collect the results of all Federal elections held in the United States, [and] analyze such results in a manner to enable the voters to better understand such results." And that troubles me. The professor from whom I took statistics a good many years ago began the first three lectures of every course with a quotation from Mark Twain: "There are lies, damn lies, and statistics." [*Laughter.*] He was not trying to disabuse us for a moment with the indispensability of statistics in modern social science, nor did he wish to be understood in that light. But the interpretation of statistics, the presentation of statistics, even when a man of an exceptional probity is involved, is still, I think, very hazardous.

6.3   RUSHER: We can certainly say, then, that this particular clause is in the bill for some reason that we may not be totally clear about; but that a political official is going to be authorized to analyze the statistics of the vote, to make them understandable to the voter and to distribute his analysis.

6.4   NISBET: Yes. I do not question the motivation behind it at all.

6.5   RUSHER: Well, I *do*. [*Laughter.*]

6.6   NISBET: Having studied and worked with statistics for a good many years, I should be myself extremely apprehensive of that particular assignment.

6.7   RUSHER: What type of person is likely to be caught by this dragnet of Congressman Udall's, now that we have the Voting Rights Act that will catch the most people?

6.8   NISBET: There have been a good many studies made of the non-voting type in the United States, whether by sociologists, political scientists, or others. Almost invariably we come up with the same discovery. Characteristically, the hard-core non-voter in the United States is a man or a woman who, in the phrase of the day, has either chosen [not to vote] or involuntarily "copped out." He is, almost invariably, low income, very low education, rarely belongs to any kind of organization where he is used to the give and take of ordinary interaction. We have discovered, in many of these studies, a high degree of a certain resentment and a certain hostility to social order. And, I may say, with excellent *reason*, in many instances, *for* the hostility.

6.9   RUSHER: Would you say that the types of person that were found occupying the former Spahn Ranch, the "extended family" there,* would fit the category? [*Murmurs.*]

6.10   NISBET: I would have to answer, bluntly: yes.

7.   CROSS-EXAMINATION

7.1   MILLER: Let me pull you back to this side of paranoia. Do you object to the Census Bureau giving [out] not only the every-ten-year report, but its weekly and monthly reports of its investigations of the populace, too, because they might be statistically manipulated?

7.2   NISBET: The Census Bureau has some of the finest statisticians in the United States.

7.3   MILLER: And this [enrollment commission] would be run by the Director of the Census, would it not?

7.4   NISBET: And the Census Bureau is dealing with demographic data that do not have the political sensitivity that the data would have in an electoral report of this kind.

7.5   MILLER: One report that [has been mentioned this evening] . . . is a 1968 report of the Census Bureau of the 1968 elections, analyzing voting by socio-economic data—the very kind of data you rely on in your testimony. What's wrong with that?

7.6   NISBET: I am not questioning for a moment the possibility of an objective analysis of electoral data. That's what modern social science is all about, in many of its key areas. I'm only suggesting that that particular item, in which the Director of National Enrollment . . . is mandated to prepare the results of the recently preceding election in such a way that they will be understood [is distressing].

7.7   MILLER: It doesn't trouble you that the Director of the Census, in fact, now *does* that as part of his duties?

7.8   NISBET: He does that for a vast range of *demographic* data; which has a slightly sterilizing and even nullifying effect upon political sensitivity. There's a great difference.

7.9   MILLER: You've talked about the kind of person who doesn't vote. I'm interested in why that person happens to fall so often into certain categories that make no sense, the ones I asked Senator Dominick about.

---

*Referring to Charles Manson and his "family" of ritual murderers.

Why is it that 44 percent of those who rent don't vote? Is that because they are all hostile? Maybe they are, because they weren't able to vote when they tried? [*Laughter.*]

7.10   NISBET: You have to begin with the fact that there will always be—and I have no objection to it—an irreducible core of people in this country, and perhaps others . . . who simply do not choose to vote. But our studies have indicated, and there have been many of these studies, starting in the 1930's at the University of Chicago under Charles Merriam—many fine studies—of the kind of people, their motivations, their social [traits]—

7.11   MILLER: And presumably that's the kind of statistical analysis which can't be manipulated. So let's focus in on the renters. How do you explain the 44 percent of those who rent don't vote or 50 percent of those between 21 and 30 don't register? Is that because they're all hostile and don't want to register?

7.12   NISBET: Oh no. In the last election, 62 percent of the electorate voted, and by the standards of many countries that is rather low. And of the remaining percentage of people, I do not question for a moment that there are many well-off, civilized, educated [persons] . . . who simply do not choose to vote.

7.13   MILLER: Well, tell me about this problem of voting lists. . . . Everyone seems to be so concerned about the voting lists getting into the wrong hands. Today, under State law, in California and other States, for example, as a requirement of the clerk keeping a kind of precinct list, anyone in the State can obtain precinct voting lists of those who have registered to vote, to aid in the political process. There's nothing wrong with that, is there?

7.14   NISBET: That's not an aspect of it that bothers me or to which I am especially sensitive. But what I *am* sensitive to is simply the increasing number of lists. And I think a list that has, well, the majesty, the power of the Federal government behind it—

7.15   MILLER: And which is turned over to the State 30 days after the election, or is destroyed—

7.16   NISBET: Even though there may well be additions to the legislation which give some protection to it, I think such a list as this comes close to being unique.

7.17   PALMIERI: Professor, I'd like to know whether you think it would be a good idea if everybody who might be made *eligible* by this proposal *did* vote. Do you think it would be a good idea for democracy?

7 . 18   NISBET: No. . . . While it is true that some thoroughly democratic nations have high voting records, it is also true that some totalitarian nations achieve 90, 95, 98 percent.

8.   THIRD NEGATIVE WITNESS: DIRECT EXAMINATION

8 . 1   RUSHER: Two points before we proceed. Mr. Miller is far too good an attorney not to know the distinction between the voting lists of California, which are today made up of people who are *voluntarily on* them, and the voting lists he is advocating tonight, which will be made up of people who are *not* in all cases voluntarily on them. That is, of course, the distinction between the two.

8 . 2   MILLER: Your repeating that is simply not going to make it true. [*Laughter, applause.*] . . .`

8 . 3   RUSHER: It is going to be more *difficult* [to move on the next witness] if I must obey the apparent wish of individual members of our studio audience not to make a point of the fact, for example, that we do have large numbers of drop-outs in this country today, and that they are among the groups that will most certainly be caught by Mr. Udall's dragnet. I will call as my last witness Professor Andrew Hacker of the Department of Government of Cornell University. Professor, what's wrong with Congressman Udall's bill?

8 . 4   HACKER: To begin with, it complicates what is at present a fairly simple process. There are going to be a series of elections, not just one election. This bill is to enroll those persons to vote in elections for President and Vice-President. It may well mean, *will* mean, that we will need a series of ballots when a person comes in in a presidental year, one at one level and one at another. Then you drop back for the next three years to the old-fashioned system. Four years later, with the new presidential year, you come into a new system again.

8 . 5   RUSHER: If we do not use the Udall system for getting out the vote, how can we then get it out?

8 . 6   HACKER: I hope we'll continue to get out the vote as we have been doing; which is to say—and I would simply take the lead from the format of this program—[through] the adversary system. Let those political parties, let those groups, let those movements that wish to, mobilize voters, knock

on doors, ring doorbells, bring people out. This has been done in Fayette, Mississippi, [and in] Cleveland, Ohio, for example. In Mississippi, the voting proportion has gone up 750 percent since 1965, as people like Charles Evers [have worked to get voters registered. Similarly, in Cleveland, Carl Stokes's] forces have gone out and actually got people to the polls.

8.7   RUSHER: Is there, in addition to its other defects, any danger of corruption of any type from this bill?

8.8   HACKER: Well, certainly I'm concerned with concentration of power here. For example, [a section of the Udall bill says,] "The National Director of Enrollment will appoint a District Director for each Congressional district." Four hundred thirty-five District Directors appointed from Washington. Each one of these, I compute, will appoint at least 3000 enrollers. They might all be from one party [and], with various degrees of alacrity, of dedication, will go around and enroll people as, well, their consciences deem that they should.

8.9   RUSHER: If Mayor Daley [Democrat of Chicago] was the one who provided the recruiters: what about that?

8.10   HACKER: I daresay there are certain Republican districts that might not receive the dedication they should.

9.   CROSS-EXAMINATION

9.1   MILLER: One reason the registration and the vote went up in Mississippi in that period of time is because there were Federal examiners there to do the registering. Isn't that right?

9.2   HACKER: This is a red herring. Of course there were Federal examiners to keep people from [being denied their civil rights].

9.3   MILLER: I wish you'd leave that red herring out of it, considering what's been said.

9.4   HACKER: A black herring. [*Laughter.*] Under Mississippi arrangements blacks were not allowed to vote. Blacks can now vote.

9.5   MILLER: But that's why it went up: because there were Federal examiners there.

9.6   HACKER: To keep people [from preventing others from registering and voting arbitrarily] on the basis of race.

9.7   MILLER: That's right. But without the Federal examiners those people would not have [gotten registered].

9.8   HACKER: I wasn't invited here to discuss the 1965 Act.

9.9   MILLER: Well, we've heard plenty about the 1970 Act so I don't know that that's excluded. Tell me, this problem of corruption and Mayor Daley—again you use Mayor Daley as an example of the fact that there is corruption there. But that's the *existing* system, isn't it? Do you think the existing system—with parties, as you say, under the adversary system of getting voters—is free from corruption? Is that your view of it?

9.10   HACKER: I fear you're confusing two things. Under your system, which is this bill, what you would have is, I figure, about 1.2 million enrollers appointed by a commission which has a majority of a single party.

9.11   MILLER: But let me ask you about the existing system. The existing system, in fact, has enrollers in various districts under a single party.

9.12   HACKER: Democrats here, Republicans there, Wallacites here—

9.13   MILLER: And you think there's no corruption in that system?

9.14   HACKER: Oh, there's lots of it; but it balances out. It's what we call "pluralism." [*Laughter.*]

9.15   MILLER: Like the judge who called in one lawyer and said, "The other side has given me $10,000, and if you do too, I'll decide it on the merits."

9.16   HACKER: That's your business. [*Laughter.*]

9.17   MILLER: Do you agree with Professor Nisbet that even if everyone were registered, there are people in this country who should not vote?

9.18   HACKER: Oh, yes. Indeed, I am quite persuaded that the decision *not* to vote can be a very rational decision. For example, the Census Bureau you keep quoting cited that over 100,000 college graduates expressed no interest in voting whatever. Now I say if they don't want to vote, if they think the system's a fraud—

9.19   MILLER: Then do you think there are people who have an interest in voting who ought to be precluded from voting because of complicated registration laws to meet that goal?

9.20   HACKER: Certainly not. But I think there's nothing wrong with walking, say, ten blocks and waiting for 20 minutes to have to vote.

9.21   MILLER: *If* it's only 10 blocks and *if* it's only 20 minutes. If you have to drive all over the State of Delaware or go to a special spot in Texas—

9.22   HACKER: Delaware actually had a 70 percent turnout last time, you know, despite that.

9.23   MILLER: Did you consider that, in view of the 85 and 90 percent turnout in nontotalitarian countries, to be something that we should point to?

9.24   HACKER: I think that 70 percent is very good. It's better than California. [*Laughter.*]

9.25 MILLER: Tell me about this problem of the voting lists. Do you fear this enormous voting list problem also? I'm interested in seeing how far this madness has spread. [*Laughter.*]

9.26 HACKER: "Madness." My own view is that if a person doesn't want to be on a list [he] shouldn't be on a list. But if a nice lady from the League of Women Voters knocks on my door with a clipboard and says "I'm here to register you," I feel that certainly I should be able to send her away. Under your bill here it says I *shall* be registered; which is a rather imperative verb.

9.27 MILLER: Congressman Udall has told us—

9.28 HACKER: That it will be changed "next year." [*Laughter.*]

9.29 MILLER: No, not changed next year; but his interpretation, as the draftsman, is that that's what the bill says. Do you think it was justifiable to send the Federal examiners into the South to register blacks?

9.30 HACKER: Definitely.

9.31 MILLER: Then again, I don't understand. The same question as to Senator Dominick. If it's justifiable for blacks, why is it not justifiable for the young, for those who rent—

9.32 HACKER: Because the young nowadays and the renters, for whom you have a great affection [*laughter*], can now go and be registered in Mississippi or any place else. . . .

9.33 RUSHER (*in summation*): Just for the record: there is nothing in Congressman Udall's bill that excludes Mayor Daley from participation in the political process under it. And you may be sure that Mayor Daley will be there and participating. This kind of bill is the sort of sloppy legislation that rains in upon the Congressional hoppers year after year after year, with a primarily propaganda effect. Congressman Udall's *intention*, whatever it was—whether he proclaimed it on the floor of Congress or not—has not the slightest thing to do with what is *in* the bill, and would not have the slightest legal *effect* if it was passed. The bill provides a compulsory dragnet to list every single qualified voter in the country on a given list and hand it out to any State or local election official who asks for it within 30 days. And there are plenty of people in the United States with good reason—and I would have thought, after last week, when Mr. Miller was all concerned about the police keeping files on dissidents, that *he* would consider with good reason—people who would rather not be on a list of that type. The next step, mark you, will be compulsory voting. Big Brother has plans for you.

10. SECOND AFFIRMATIVE WITNESS: DIRECT EXAMINATION

10.1   PALMIERI: Mr. Miller, as I understand Mr. Rusher, he thinks this is a Democratic plot and a renters' plot; perhaps a plot by Democratic renters. [*Laughter.*] But in truth, his main thrust is in terms of the adverse effects for democracy of the principle of putting people on more lists. He's made important and powerful points. It's now your turn for rebuttal.

10.2   MILLER: You have no idea what a feat it was to summarize it that clearly. [*Laughter.*] We are somewhere between the Spahn Ranch and totalitarian China, and I'm not sure how we got there. [*Laughter.*] The fact of the matter is that none of the imaginary evils of this bill *begin* to exist. We have a statistician who objects to statistical analysis when it's done by the Census Bureau under this bill—unless, of course, it's done by the Census Bureau today. We have people who object to handing out voting lists, except that's what's done today. We have enormous emphasis on the fact that people will be compelled to register, but the draftsman of the bill simply says it is a matter of interpretation, and that *isn't* what it means. In fact what we have in reality is a current system that excludes from voting those very people who we ought to most want to bring into the system: those people who feel alienated from the system. And I daresay one reason [for this attitude] may be [that] when they try and register, they don't know where or when, and when they try and vote, they [find they have] lost out on registration. The goal of politics is to bring those people into the system, not to be scared of them [for] fanciful faults that simply don't exist. As for last week, I should have thought the inconsistency was elsewhere. Last week there was no objection to keeping track of anyone in the country whom the police or the government wish to keep track of. Suddenly this week, giving a person the opportunity to put his name on a voting list has become a major evil that will destroy our society. [*Applause.*]

10.3   PALMIERI: I want you all to know that you're being punished for not seeing last week's show [when Miller supported and Rusher opposed the proposal that police be prohibited from keeping intelligence files on political dissidents].

10.4   MILLER: To talk to us about why this bill ought to be adopted, and why it is basic for the way our country works that it be adopted, we have the former Attorney General of the United States, Mr. Ramsey Clark. Mr. Attorney General, we've heard a lot of talk about how maybe there are some people who shouldn't vote. Is it important to bring into the system people who are excluded by current registration laws?

10.5   RAMSEY CLARK: It's absolutely essential. A survey that I made for a commission in 1969 indicated that 47 million Americans did not vote in 1968. Who were they? They were the young, the women, the poor, the minorities, the blacks, the Puerto Ricans, the Mexican-Americans. If we believe in democracy, we must vitalize democracy. We've got to include *all* of our people. We've practiced exclusionary politics in America since, really, the end of Reconstruction. And we can't go on like that.

10.6   MILLER: Why do people oppose this plan?

10.7   CLARK: There are a variety of reasons. Perhaps foremost is [that] those that wield political power today don't want to share it. They don't understand the frustrations of being utterly powerless in America. Politics is a source of power. And if we revitalize democracy in this country and share power with the people, create new constituencies for our representatives, why we'll see America flourish. We'll see our people included in this system. We'll see a commitment to the rule of law because they participate in its making.

10.8   MILLER: Do we have a recent example in the Voting Rights Act of 1965 about what Federal examiners can do?

10.9   CLARK: We have a lot of recent examples. But the Voting Rights Act of 1965 was based on the observation that in the 1900's we had had whole States that had voted less than 10 percent of their voting-age population in the nineteenth century in presidential elections, if you can imagine. And they tended to be in the South. And that tended to arise from the fact that blacks had been systematically excluded there. And the Voting Rights Act remedied that situation to a very substantial degree. It lifted participation of all segments of the population in the South. It's brought us scores of new black elected officials, and it can make democracy work.

10.10   MILLER: Is there any objection to this plan because it interferes with the basic State's right to run the election?

10.11   CLARK: There's an objection from States' rights in certain areas. The Supreme Court of the United States has held that this was within the constitutionally delegated powers of the Congress, and I don't think there's any real question about it. The performance of the States has been inadequate in some areas, historically; and under the powers in the Constitution that have been delegated by the people to the Congress, it [the Congress] has the capacity to do this, and must.

10.12   MILLER: Did the 1965 Voting Act, which sent in Federal examiners, involve any invasions of privacy or basic freedoms, or [any] totalitarianism?

10 . 13   CLARK: I have heard no allegations of that at all. The fact is that it really wasn't so much the Federal examiners that put a million additional black citizens of America on the voters' rolls in the South; it was the voter education projects. The mere opening up of the opportunity has proven inadequate. That's why we had 37 million people who didn't vote in 1968, in an election that may determine the future of this world. The voter education projects were funded from foundations and otherwise, and they went to the people and they said "We need you. We need you in the system. We want you to vote. Please enroll. Please register. Please vote." And they put a million people on [the rolls] that way.

10 . 14   MILLER: Why is this an important proposal?

10 . 15   CLARK: It's important because our system isn't working well. And our system *has* to work well. There is no other way. Violent revolution has been relegated to history. And we have got to vitalize the system. Political power in America has got to be shared with all of our people. And there's only one way to do it, and that's to go to the people and say, "Please educate yourself. Please inform yourself. Please register. Please be enrolled and vote. We need you."

11.   CROSS-EXAMINATION

11 . 1   RUSHER: You want to say "please" to these people. Does the bill say "please"?

11 . 2   CLARK: Well, the bill *can* say "please," can't it? Do we want to stick on the central purpose of this bill, or do you want to stick on the details?

11 . 3   RUSHER: I want to stick on the bill. Do you want to get away from it?

11 . 4   CLARK: I'm prepared to get away from it. I want the best bill we can get.

11 . 5   RUSHER: I'll bet you are. But I want to stay with it. The topic tonight is the bill, Mr. Clark; and if you don't mind, we'll discuss that.

11 . 6   CLARK: Is that right? I'm for universal voter enrolling. I think the wisdom of the Congress is adequate to provide a bill that is not mandatory.

11 . 7   PALMIERI: In point of fact, Mr. Attorney General, the thrust of the program is with respect to the principle of universal voter registration. It is in fact fair, I think, for Mr. Rusher to delineate any differences he and you may have with reference to the bill. The question is the principle.

11 . 8   RUSHER: My understanding is that the discussion tonight is on this bill. I was formally instructed that it was.

11.9   PALMIERI: My statement has just improved your understanding. So let's proceed. [*Applause.*]

11.10 CLARK: I would think you'd be prepared to discuss the principle anyway.

11.11 RUSHER: I will be glad to forgive Mr. Udall his mistakes and to proceed to ask Mr. Clark whether or not he wishes to coerce people to vote who don't want to vote.

11.12 CLARK: No; I don't want to coerce people to vote who don't want to vote, but I want to remove barriers. We've had barriers that have excluded millions from participating in American democracy. And who have they been? They've been the young Americans; they've been the women, and the blacks and the Puerto Ricans and the Mexican-Americans—the people that we need the most.

11.13 RUSHER: There's nothing that prevents Puerto Ricans and women from voting in America, and you know it.

11.14 CLARK: Don't kid yourself. Look at the history of this country.

11.15 RUSHER: I'm not kidding myself, and you're not kidding me, sir.

11.16 CLARK: Well, you don't know history, sir.

11.17 RUSHER: And you don't know politics, then. Let me suggest to you that, substantially, the Voting Rights Act of 1970 has cleared away most of the serious obstacles. But the people who Mr. Udall's dragnet bill are going to get are people who in point of fact, for reasons of their own, in most cases, do not want to vote. And what's more, the way in which he proposes to do it, [provides] a totally partisan system that could be corrupted, and would be, by either party. Isn't that a fact?

11.18 CLARK: No, that's not a fact. In the first place, the 1970 Act does nothing of significance except give the 18-year-old the right to vote; and by God, it's worth it for that, because we need the 18-year-old in the system. And the thing we'd better do when we give them the right to vote is also to give them the real opportunity. We ought to take registration right into the high schools. We ought to take voting machines right into the high schools. [*Applause.*] We ought to tell those 18-year-olds, "Vote this year and vote every year of your life. We need you."

11.19 RUSHER: How about the 30-day residence requirement limitation that was put into—

11.20 CLARK: You don't need 30 days to register. You can register on the day of the election in Presidential elections.

11.21 RUSHER: How about the seven-day absentee-ballot provision? Isn't that any good?

11.22   CLARK: It's not substantial.

11.23   RUSHER: How about—under Mr. Udall's bill, which you're here to defend—the National Enrollment Director appointing 435 District Directors without the slightest provision that there should be anything bipartisan about his choice?

11.24   CLARK: There can be bipartisanism. Even more than that: we need a dozen checks.

11.25   RUSHER: I'm aware that there *can* be; but is there any requirement that there *must* be?

11.26   CLARK: I think there are ample checks and we know—

11.27   RUSHER: What ample checks are there?

11.28   CLARK: Well, you're talking about the bill again.

11.29   RUSHER: You're talking about the checks. Where are they?

11.30   CLARK: I would like to talk about what's possible.

11.31   RUSHER: I want to talk about the ample checks that you say exist in the bill.

11.32   CLARK: You talk about what you want to talk about, and I'll talk about what I want to talk about. [*Laughter.*]

11.33   RUSHER: All right. You don't want to talk about it.

11.34   CLARK: I want to talk about what's possible. I think America has to address itself to real problems and not puny technicalities. And the real problem here is getting the people to vote. And you can do it. You can have ample checks. You can have poll-watchers. You can have Democrats and Republicans and Independents. You know that.

11.35   RUSHER: The real problem is preventing corruption—and coercion—and *filibustering.*

11.36   PALMIERI: Mr. Attorney General, let me ask you a question. Mr. Rusher, stay with us for a moment. I don't want you to leave. [*Laughter.*]

11.37   RUSHER: I'm not about to leave.

11.38   PALMIERI: Mr. Attorney General, Mr. Rusher has made a very strong point with previous witnesses with respect to the hazardous effects of the so-called lists, the listing effects of universal voter registration, which would comprise one more in a long list of computerized formulas which bring everybody's name to the attention of government. And he has, I think, asked why we should have one more list.

11.39   CLARK: Well, I'm an anti-list man. I do not like lists. But I'll tell you, you've got to have priorities in America today. And the first priority has to be democracy, and we need to vitalize democracy. And we've got millions and millions of people. If you want integrity in your voting system, you're going to have to have lists. We have lists already. A Federal list can be protected. If the Federal list can't be protected, then the government is inadequate to the times; and the government is *not* inadequate to the times. . . .

11. 40   RUSHER: Mr. Miller was terribly worried about the people—I think he said particularly renters—who were not able to find the polling place. You know, they had to travel all over Delaware. We have a great many people in this country on welfare. Have we had any trouble that you know of with them finding the place where they could get their welfare checks?

11. 41   CLARK: Well, of course we have.

11. 42   RUSHER: Oh, we have? There's a difficulty with that, too? Where was that?

11. 43   CLARK: Yes, we certainly have. Take Social Security. One in three among the poor do not receive Social Security benefits in America because they are unable to find the place—

11. 44   RUSHER: I said "welfare."

11. 45   CLARK: The contract right they have earned, and they don't get the money.

12.   CLOSING STATEMENTS

12. 1   MILLER: This proposal has become a test of our ability to open up the political system; and, I daresay, a test of our ability to discuss proposals sanely. What we are talking about here is whether we ought to open up the system by bringing in the Federal government as a backup registrar where States do not register 90 percent of their voters. That would open up the system and bring in those who today are excluded by a crazy-quilt of registration laws that even lawyers cannot understand. We have been told all sorts of "horribles" that may be wrong with it. But there are lists today, voting lists, that are open to the population as a whole. No one would be compelled to put his name on this, and in fact the system can work. It can open up the system. Ultimately with State-wide registration, no more Federal backup will be needed. And finally, we can have a system that is what we want it to be, where all of us decide: not only by the people and for the people, but of the people as well. [*Applause.*]

12. 2   RUSHER: Mr. Miller has a charming way of suggesting that anybody who opposed one of his new Federal bureaucracies and the $50 million they'll cost, and all the fine things they'll do with us, is somehow irrational or insane. It isn't necessarily true. Week by week we go through these pro-

posals, and all of them require substantially the same thing: new bureaucracies, new costs, new Federal intrusions into the lives of people. If
there's one thing clear about the tendencies in this country today, it is
that we are turning away from that kind of absurdity. If you believe that
American democracy will in fact function better when every single person on an "extended family" in a lean-to in the western United States
is dragged out by Congressman Udall and registered and coerced to
vote, then this bill is for you. If you believe that voting is a solemn act
to be carried out in a serious spirit, by people who have given it real
thought, then you will reject this travesty, this caricature, on everything
that true democracy means. [*Applause.*]

 *November 3, 1970*

SUGGESTED EXERCISES

1. From the foregoing debate, piece together a succinct summary of the
   provisions of the Universal Enrollment Plan, as drafted by Representative Udall. In writing this summary, take care to distinguish between
   provisions which were and were not subject to dispute as to their immediate sense.
2. From passages in the foregoing debate, summarize the provisions of the
   1970 Voting Rights Act.
3. Enumerate the principal lines of argument emanating from the Affirmative side of the debate on the Universal Enrollment Plan. In preparing
   this outline, you may find it helpful to distinguish between 'positive'
   arguments (claims initiated by the Affirmative) and 'disclaimers' (denials
   made in the course of rebuttal).
4. Similarly, enumerate the principal line(s) of argument emanating from
   the Negative side.
5. Can you think of any lines of argument that were conspicuous by their
   absence from the debate? In pondering this question, you may find it helpful to imagine yourself as a critic who shows how a case was weakened
   by the absence of some relevant claims about the cause and effect.
6. Did any line of argument occurring in the debate arouse in you a sense
   of moral indignation? If so, name this line of argument, and justify your
   sense of outrage.
7. Cite and discuss uses of *ad hominem* argument in the foregoing debate.

8. Cite and discuss at least one example of statistical nonsense in the foregoing debate. (To refresh your memory on statistical nonsense, see the Commentary on the Congressional seniority system.)

COMMENTARY

Arguing Beside the Point

The debate on whether the Federal government should register voters for Federal elections gave rise to at least one argumentational device that has not previously been discussed. This device goes by the Latin phrase *ignoratio elenchi,* and is conventionally translated as "arguing beside the point" or "ignoring the point." Here is a fictitious example:

> Q. Does Simas gasoline give more mileage than other standard brands?
> A. Simas contains Super Suds, and tests have shown that if you remove Super Suds you get 13 percent lower mileage. Simas Swings!

The example serves not only to illustrate a reply that is beside the point, but also to illustrate how a seemingly relevant reply is *insinuated.* The techniques for achieving the latter feat are numerous indeed.

A rather stylish example of arguing beside the point was supplied by Representative Udall, in response to a question posed by Miller. Here is the text of the exchange (2.4-.5):

> MILLER: Do current registration laws, in effect, disenfranchise people?
> UDALL: Let me tell you something. In 1968, when we made this vital decision—[about] four years [of a] President and war and peace priorities —31 million [people, plus a few more, supported Richard Nixon, while a few less than 31 million supported Hubert Humphrey, and] 37 million people voted for no one. Shut out of the process. And these aren't statistics; these are people. These are people who have their sons drafted to go to Vietnam. These are people who pay taxes. These are people who may have a freeway run through their living room by government. We've erected this whole series of booby traps, high hurdles, an obstacle course, to keep them out. And it's wrong.

Representative Udall could just as easily have given a much larger figure on non-voting in 1968, a figure such as 100 million. Perhaps he chose the figure of 37 million because it comprises the number of adults who (*a*) did not vote although they were registered, (*b*) were not registered although they were legally eligible, and/or (*c*) were not registered although they would have been eligible under rules other than the ones in existence in 1968. At any rate, Representative Udall's excursion into numbers did not furnish an answer to the question posed by Miller. Representative Udall did not differentiate the many factors that keep people away from voting booths. He did not say *how many* of the abstainers *have been blocked by laws and procedures that would cease to exist under the Universal Enrollment Plan,* and how many are "shut out" by other forces. Yet he managed to *insinuate* that vast numbers of people—perhaps 37 million people—are disenfranchised solely by current registration laws. He encouraged that inference by timing his remarks to come right after a particular causal question, and by using indiscriminate metaphors about closed doors, booby traps, and the like.

Should congress adopt president nixon's general revenue-sharing plan?

OVERVIEW

In his 1971 message on the State of the Union, President Nixon urged the Congress to adopt a package of measures which have come to be known as "revenue-sharing." These measures would alter the extent and the terms whereby the Federal government shares money it has collected from American taxpayers with units of State and local government. According to the President, the adoption of "revenue-sharing" would mark a "historic" and "bold" step, inaugurating a "new American revolution" in which government at all levels would be "refreshed and renewed, and made truly responsive."

Federal aid to State and local government is not by itself a novelty. It has long been practiced, and in recent years it has undergone a vast increase in scale and in range. Hundreds of categories of State and locally administered projects are subsidized from Washington, to the tune of billions of dollars yearly. Assistance generally is contingent on the provision of "matching" (but rarely equal) sums by receiving agencies. The subsidies are furnished either by way of semi-automatic "formula grants" scaled according to the number of persons eligible for a given form of aid in a given locality, or by way of "project grants" made if an agency applies for, and is judged eligible to receive, financial assistance in connection with an authorized type of program.

President Nixon has proposed essentially two major changes. On the one hand, many rather narrowly defined categories of projects would be consolidated under broader headings, such as "education," "transportation," and so on. School boards, for example, would gain greater flexibility in deciding how to use Federal aid to education—including, of course, the authority to eliminate, reduce, or enlarge various programs (vocational training, audio-visual aids) as they see fit. About $11 billion would be made available in this way, of which $10 billion would come from consolidating already-funded projects and the remainder would be new money. This segment of the President's proposal is known as *special* revenue-sharing.

On the other hand, $5 billion of new money would be allocated by the Federal government to States (and from them, in part, to local governments) with no restrictions on how the money is spent. This fund, which would increase in succeeding years, would be divided among the States roughly in proportion to their populations, but with variations according to the scale of the existing State-local "tax effort." Each State government—according to a deal worked out in July 1969 between governors, mayors, and county officials—would "pass through" 48 percent of its allotment to general-purpose organs of local government. This aspect of the President's proposal is known as *general* revenue-sharing. It has aroused the greater volume of controversy, and it is the topic of the following debate.

1.   OPENING STATEMENTS

1.1   MODERATOR VICTOR PALMIERI: In the last decade, Federal aid to the States and cities has tripled: from $7 billion in 1960 to $25 billion in 1970. The money was spent for specific purposes, such as housing, education, and aid to dependent children. Despite the substantial level of Federal aid already going to the States, the President [has said that] States and cities all across America [are] facing financial crisis—caught, he said, between the prospects of bankruptcy, on the one hand, and [of] adding to an already-crushing tax burden, on the other. To meet this crisis, the President called upon the Congress to enact [his two-fold] plan of revenue-sharing. . . . The President's general revenue-sharing proposal and the grant-consolidation [or special revenue-sharing] proposal will go to Congress as separate pieces of legislation. Tonight "The Advocates" will consider only the *general* revenue-sharing proposal—the proposal to distribute $5 billion to the States to spend as they see fit. Should Congress adopt [this proposal]? Advocate Rusher says "Yes." On the other side, Advocate Miller says "No."

1.2   ADVOCATE WILLIAM RUSHER: Today there are over 500 Federal programs designed to aid State and local governments [in the form of grants-in-aid], and they cost $30 billion a year. Traditionally, the Federal government has tried to keep tight control over how this money is spent; which is why, in city after city across America, gigantic office buildings have had to be built to house hundreds of thousands of Federal bureaucrats who, in obedience to their superiors in Washington, administer these huge expenditures. That is the key point that I ask you to remember tonight. The men and women who work in these buildings are not elected by you or appointed by any State or local official elected by you. You pay their salaries, but the only connection you have with their selection is that the President of the United States in Washington has appointed Cabinet members who, in turn, choose these people. President Nixon proposes to change all this by giving your locally elected State and city governments control over how a major portion of this money is spent. And in addition, he proposes to take a further 1.3 percent of the Federal income tax base—or about $5 billion in the first full year of the program—and give that, too, to the States and localities to spend on high-priority projects.

1.3   What are the objections to this? First, of course—though I doubt the other side will mention it—a good many Federal bureaucrats will have to seek other employment. Second, the special-interest lobbies in Washington, each of which spends its full time increasing its own pressure group's share of Federal aid, will suddenly find themselves forced to make new connections with officials in 50 States and [in] literally thousands of towns and cities.

1.4   So, obviously, this plan won't go through without a fight. There will be charges of State and local corruption, [and] of injustice and inequity in the formulas for distribution. But the truth is that this proposal is endorsed by a great and growing majority of mayors and governors across America, as well as by the President of the United States.

1.5   ADVOCATE HOWARD MILLER: The basic problem with revenue-sharing is the problem of "easy come, easy go." We're giving money to States and localities that they don't have to raise—giving them money that they have no responsibility for raising at all, and we [incur] the risk of what will happen when money is given without responsibility. We know something of what happens when it's given even *with* the responsibility. Tonight's proposal would take your tax dollars and distribute them to State and local officials with virtually no control on their use.

1.6   What's more, [the proposal] takes from those who cannot afford it and gives to those who do not need it. Not only does it violate the basic principle of accountability, but it's not distributed according to any normal sense of need. The needs are in the urban areas. The average amount distributed under revenue-sharing is about $24.60 per person. But it goes in vastly disproportionate amounts: some States—predominantly rural States like Hawaii, New Mexico, North Dakota, and Wyoming—get over $30 per person; other States—States with urban problems, like Connecticut, Illinois, and Ohio—get less than $20 per person. Some States benefit [by getting more than they contribute in tax dollars. Among these are Alabama, Wyoming, Utah, Mississippi, Idaho, and Hawaii]—no major urban problems there. But States like Connecticut, Illinois, New York, Michigan, Massachusetts, and New Jersey pay more into the fund than they get back. They, in fact, are penalized. The height of this is that . . . for every dollar that New York pays [in Federal taxes] it only gets back 87 cents. For every dollar that Mississippi, which had a budget surplus, pays, it gets back $2.50. The money is not distributed where the need goes—and never can be, because it requires individualized decisions to funnel [money] where the need is: not only *shared* revenue in terms of [money] going between governments, but shared *power*—the joint decisions of the Federal and the State governments as to where the money should go.

1.7   And furthermore, we don't need to talk about the absolute need. All the States have not exhausted their [resources] for revenue. As we shall see, in Colorado and other places there are substantial sources of State revenue, based upon what people pay [in tax rates] in other States.

2.   FIRST AFFIRMATIVE WITNESS: DIRECT EXAMINATION

2.1   RUSHER: [The general revenue-sharing proposal, to repeat, is endorsed by a great and growing majority of mayors and governors]. To support it we have with us tonight the president of the National League of Cities, Mayor Richard G. Lugar of Indianapolis, Indiana. From the standpoint of a mayor of a large city in America, Mayor Lugar, what is the key advantage of revenue-sharing?

2.2   MAYOR RICHARD LUGAR: The key advantage is that revenue-sharing makes it possible for American Federalism to continue to live. Essentially, in this country we've thought in terms of Federal government, State government, city government. But government is of one fabric; and at the *delivery* end, if mayors and city councilmen do not perform, then people will not receive police protection, fire protection, sanitary protection, street and road [service]; the environment will suffer—health, welfare, all the way down the line. This is where government occurs, and it's quite fallacious to assume that the Congress in any way is able to administer any of these things. Revenue-sharing alone, in my judgment, is *the* method by which vitality might come to the *delivery* end, and Americans might have some confidence that government would continue to exist.

2.3   RUSHER: What about the criticism we hear that State governments might not give the cities a fair share of these shared revenues?

2.4   LUGAR: [Such criticisms] are terribly erroneous, because the governors, the mayors, the county officials have come to agreement on formula. We'll get 48 percent [of the money] in cities. And then we may do better, as we bargain within the States for more money.

2.5   RUSHER: We hear it said that city and State governments are less efficient, and [are] even more—perhaps—corrupt, than the Federal administrators.

2.6   LUGAR: This is demonstrably ridiculous on the face of it. I have in my hand a catalogue of Federal domestic assistance. This is a digest of some of the hundreds of programs. There are in fact 1,069 categories. No Congressman has any idea of how many ways money is being distributed around the country now. Nor does any mayor have an idea of even a fifth of the money going to his city. This means the press does not know where the money is, nor does the mayor, the council, the people, or anyone. The gigantic fraud has been perpetrated on the American public under the guise of "Federal efficiency" and the thought that, somehow or other, Federal people were more honest. In fact, they're very cautious, and they make certain that no problem is solved. And the buildings [that house Federal bureaucrats] are populated by people who do not know the problems of Indianapolis or any other city.

3.   CROSS-EXAMINATION

3.1   MILLER: What is to stop jurisdictions, like the State of Indiana or your own city, from simply lowering their own taxes once they get the revenue-sharing amount?

3.2   LUGAR: There is no reason why they should *not* lower taxes if they felt [taxes] were at a confiscatory level and wished to [lower them].

3.3   MILLER: So in fact, though you're talking about additional needs of the cities and States, one of the things you envisage happening here is that, far from satisfying those needs, the State and local governments will simply substitute Federal taxes for their own taxes.

3.4   LUGAR: Quite wrong. If property taxes were lowered in Indiana, more building would come in and we would have more revenue. This has occurred three times in a row in Indianapolis.

3.5   MILLER: But there are [places] where that may not occur. There is no restriction at all on localities or States that get this money simply substituting the Federal tax dollar for their own—lowering their own taxes and not serving any more needs at all.

3.6   LUGAR: There are needs always to be served by any public official. I'm responsible to those people and if I don't serve them I will go. The substitution *can* be made, and may, in fact, be a good thing.

3.7   MILLER: "The substitution can be made." Now let's talk about what this money could go for. When it passes through to cities and local governments it can only go to general-purpose localities—that is, cities and governments.

3.8   LUGAR: That's true, yes.

3.9   MILLER: Most education in this country, for example, is administered by special school districts, *not* by general purpose localities. Therefore, I take it that none of this money under the revenue-sharing for example could go for education.

3.10   LUGAR: Oh, quite wrong. Of the 52 percent that goes to the State, a part may go for education.

3.11   MILLER: Part of it *may* go [for education], and that depends on the State's discretion. Part of it may go to lower taxes as well . . .

3.12   LUGAR: Precisely. Yes.

3.13   MILLER: If you have so much justice in the States, why is it that the mayors of this country objected, many of them, to any form of revenue-sharing until there was this fixed percentage of 48 percent? Would you agree to revenue-sharing if all the money went to your State and there were no guarantee to the city?

3.14   LUGAR: No I would not, and I participated in the agreement in July of 1969 which made this mandatory pass-through a feature of it.

3.15   MILLER: Why didn't you trust the State? Why not have all the money go to the State?

3.16   LUGAR: Historically our relationships with the States have not always been good—constitutional prohibitions, other difficulties. . . .

3.17   MILLER: So why should you trust them with this 52 percent?

3.18   LUGAR: The adjustment has been a very fine one; a compromise has been struck which is demonstrably agreeable to all of us, except the Congress. In other words, we have this position of governors, legislators, mayors, county officials, the President—everyone except the Congress of the United States.

3.19   MILLER: Let's not talk about mayors because the United States Conference of Mayors on February 11, [1971] said the revenue-sharing plan was a subversive—

3.20   LUGAR: Oh no no no; just nine mayors, and not representing anyone but themselves. . . . They were out in San Francisco on a jaunt. [*Laughter.*]

3.21   MILLER: Are you telling me that mayors would use this money to take jaunts to San Francisco? Is that what they're going to use the revenue-sharing money for? . . .

3.22   LUGAR: I'm suggesting that John Lindsay [of New York] and Joe Alioto [of San Francisco] and others were having a good time in San Francisco. The National League of Cities, as a matter of fact, and myself, and Carl Stokes [of Cleveland], our vice-president Louie Welch, and so forth [favor the plan] . . .

3.23   MILLER: Mayors *could* use revenue-sharing for jaunts as well as for other reasons. The possibility is always there.

4.   SECOND AFFIRMATIVE WITNESS: DIRECT EXAMINATION

4.1   RUSHER: Now let's hear from the other side of this team which, as Mayor Lugar pointed out, [is] enthusiastically in support of this: Gov. John A. Love, immediate past chairman of the National Governors' Conference, and Governor of Colorado. Governor Love, what do you consider the basic argument in favor of revenue-sharing?

4.2   GOV. JOHN LOVE: Beyond the first and obvious argument in favor of it—the money that would come to help alleviate in some way the present and growing fiscal crisis in the States and cities across the nation—is a further reason that may be even more important. Historically, at least for almost 40 years now, there's been a continuing concentration of governmental power and responsibility and governmental money in Washington, at the federal level. And at least two things have happened that I don't think are good for the United States as a result of this. One is that, obviously, this great proliferation of grants-in-aid that the mayor talked about, simply isn't working. You can point to housing, the welfare program, whatever you want—it simply isn't working. And, perhaps even more important, it seems to me the whole tendency to concentrate in Washington this large, remote center of power, has caused an alienation, a feeling of helplessness on the part of a great many people, [a feeling] that they indeed can't affect, let alone control, their governmental system and control their future in their society.

4.3 RUSHER: What about the criticism that State governments are not as sensitive to people's needs as the Federal government?

4.4 LOVE: . . . I think that it needs to be said that the image that perhaps State government picked up many years ago is not merited. And I call to your attention the fact that each of the State legislatures [has] been reapportioned since the Supreme Court decision, and they do, at the present time, represent the people on a one man-one vote basis.

4.5 RUSHER: How about the proposition of "legislative efficiency"? Are the State legislatures as efficient as the Congress?

4.6 LOVE: I can't help but think of the old saying that involved glass houses and how people should be a little bit careful. When you look at the Congress of the United States, as stalemated as it's been, I point with pride and confidence to State legislatures. I would suggest that, particularly in their own jurisdictions, they will be more effective and more efficient.

4.7 PALMIERI: That's a very judicious answer, Governor, since the Congress has to pass this program. [*Laughter.*] Let's hear what Mr. Miller's going to ask you.

5. CROSS-EXAMINATION

5.1 LOVE: I would suggest also—and not have it misunderstood—that the State legislatures will be redistricting for the Congressional representatives too.*

---

*Under the Constitution, the boundaries of districts from which members of the House of Representatives are elected can be changed every ten years, in the wake of changes in population that are divulged by the Census. Some States lose Representatives, while others gain Representatives. Authority to redraw district boundaries is lodged in the State legislatures, which operate under court-imposed guidelines prescribing that districts be geographically contiguous and virtually equal in population. Specific redistricting decisions are enormously consequential for the electoral fortunes of incumbent Representatives.

5.2   MILLER: Governor, does Colorado have a revenue-sharing plan? Does the State of Colorado distribute to the cities money that it raises and gives them free to use as they wish?

5.3   LOVE: We, of course, distribute to the school districts. . . . We also distribute from the highway users' fund to the cities for specific purposes.

5.4   MILLER: But you have no *plan* in Colorado by which the State of Colorado raises money and gives it for *any* purpose to the city of Denver or any other locality to use it. Why not?

5.5   LOVE: Because the problem of dealing with the city and the State is a problem [of] dealing between functions. The city has certain functions, the State has certain functions.

5.6   MILLER: And the Federal government has "certain functions."

5.7   LOVE: But what are those functions at the Federal level? Are they in housing and education, streets and so on? Isn't this a legitimate difference?

5.8   MILLER: Well, we'll hear about the Elementary and Secondary Education Act, [about] what happened in States in this country [until it passed]. [Now,] if the purpose is to return control to the local governments, why wouldn't you support such a plan, in which Colorado taxes are given without restrictions?

5.9   LOVE: You've just [given] the reason: because [of] the difference in functions. The cities and the school districts have different and separate functions.

5.10   MILLER: What function does the State government have?

5.11   LOVE: The State government has the function of supporting education. It has the function, at the present time, of contributing [to], and supporting very materially, welfare. It has the function of regulating all sorts of various activities across the State. And we could go on and on.

5.12   MILLER: But you wouldn't dream of giving money without restrictions to cities in Colorado.

5.13   LOVE: Well, I would—yes; maybe. But I say that the point you attempt to make is not relevant. The difference between the State and the city is not the same as [that] between the Federal government and the State.

5.14   MILLER: One of the State functions, of course, is to raise taxes. Now if your tax level in Colorado were at the same tax level as that of the highest-taxing State (Wisconsin), your State would raise an additional $116 million. Why don't *you* raise your taxes to that level? Other States have it at that level.

5.15   LOVE: I would quarrel with your premise. You'll find that . . . the total tax effort [of] Wisconsin [places her] somewhere in the middle of the States.

. . . I also would suggest that you look at the record of the States and the cities as far as raising taxes. While [the Federal government has reduced] taxes, States and cities have . . . found it necessary to raise taxes more than 400 percent.

5.16   MILLER: It raises the question of what [Colorado's] share would be [of] the $60 million including the pass-through. If you raised your taxes to the level of other States, you would raise far more than the $60 million.

5.17   LOVE: We're among, I'm sorry to report, the higher per-capita tax States in the nation.

5.18   MILLER: If you raised your taxes to the median of all other States, you would raise an additional $42 million.

5.19   LOVE: Not to the median. I'd quarrel with that.

5.20   MILLER: All right, we'll have figures on that; but to the high level. Certainly, if you raised taxes [to a level] as high as Wisconsin, you'd raise substantially more money. Why don't you want to raise your taxes to a level of what other States are taxing? Why get the money from the Federal government?

5.21   LOVE: Colorado's tax effort is beyond the median in the United States. But I think the broader question is this: at the State and local and Federal levels, all of them *combined*, we're now taking from the people about almost 35 percent of the Gross National Product in taxation.

5.22   MILLER: Which is a lower percentage than other industrialized countries.

5.23   LOVE: It seems to me [that the percentage] cannot go much beyond that without endangering the very system.

5.24   MILLER: But it's all taxes. This $60 million that you get back from the Federal government, that goes back to Colorado: it's not there for nothing, is it? People pay taxes. Those are taxes that are coming back. Someone is paying for that, isn't that right?

5.25   LOVE: People in Colorado; yes.

6.   FIRST NEGATIVE WITNESS: DIRECT EXAMINATION

6.1   MILLER: To talk to us about [variations in State tax "effort"], and the problems with this plan, we've asked to join us Melville Ulmer, professor of economics at the University of Maryland. Professor, have the States exhausted their tax resources?

6.2   PROF. MELVILLE ULMER: I realize that [such exhaustion] is a very frequently repeated assertion, but it doesn't seem to have any foundation in fact.

Well, not much. There are fully 13 States of the 50 that have no income tax at all, or did not have any income tax at all as of the start of this year. There are some 15 other States that have very *low* income taxes, of perhaps 2 percent as a flat rate. There are 12 or 13 States that are [rated] as having "high taxes" by the Advisory Commission on Inter-Governmental Relations. I think that that classification is somewhat generous. I personally would classify only five States of the 50 as really making a conscientious effort in this respect. These are New York, Oregon, Delaware, Minnesota [and Wisconsin]. If all 45 other States were to duplicate the income-tax effort made by the five most conscientious States, the revenue of the 50 States would be raised by $8 billion, which is a good deal more than the money provided by President Nixon's revenue-sharing plan.

6.3 PALMIERI: When you say "match the effort," do you mean in terms of Governor Love's standard of "tax per capita?"

6.4 ULMER: No. There are difficulties in using per-capita taxes. Some States are blessed with industries that are owned by people outside the State, and it [Governor Love's usage—taxes paid per capita] obscures the meaning of the statistics. I am using, in particular, income tax rates [as a gauge of tax "effort"]. . . .

6.5 MILLER: Tell us about Colorado: if Colorado were to duplicate [the income tax rate of the five "conscientious" States].

6.6 ULMER: Colorado . . . would be able to raise [$116 million more, if its State income tax were at the Wisconsin level;] which is more than the $60 million they would get under the President's plan.

6.7 MILLER: Does the distribution of funds [as proposed under the revenue-sharing plan] meet the needs that we hear about: the needs of the cities?

6.8 ULMER: The revenue-sharing plan is almost diabolically contrived to frustrate the needs of the highly urbanized States, with their ghetto poor and all their problems of poverty and crime associated with the ghettoes. In effect, revenue-sharing takes money from the highly urbanized States and turns it over to the rural States. It does this because of the peculiar formula used for allocating that revenue.

6.9 Every State contributes to the Federal income tax revenue, through the taxes paid by [its] citizens. Revenue-sharing takes part of this Federal revenue and gives it back to the States—but not in proportion to the contributions they make. This is the issue. This is why New York gets 87 cents back for every dollar it contributes; Illinois gets 60 cents back for every dollar it contributes. And these are highly urbanized States with great needs, whereas Mississippi gets $2.50 for every dollar it contributes; Alabama gets $1.56. If we went down the line of the rural States and the urban States, this is the pattern that would, in general, be followed.

7.   CROSS-EXAMINATION

7.1   RUSHER: We'll be hearing later [about] . . . statistics. I tend myself to get drowned easily in statistics; but I notice Mr. Miller has this big thing about the urban poor. Are all the poor or most of the poor in America in cities?

7.2   ULMER: Of course not.

7.3   RUSHER: Why don't we worry some of the time about the others?

7.4   ULMER: I think we do.

7.5   RUSHER: Why doesn't Mr. Miller discuss this? There isn't any shame particularly attached to being poor in a rural as against an urban area.

7.6   ULMER: Not at all; but if we want to help the poor we should do so directly, not help poor States and expect that the money given to Mississippi will filter down some day, some year, some millennium.

7.7   RUSHER: You use Mississippi, and I can understand for rhetorical purposes why you do; but in most of the poor rural States of this country, there is no reason to think that some bureaucrat by the name of Mr. Carlucci, sitting in Washington [as head of O.E.O.,] is better able to help a poor person in a small rural State than the mayor of his own city, is there?

7.8   ULMER: Mr. Carlucci sitting in Washington may be more disposed to help the poor.

7.9   RUSHER: May or may not. I don't see why, but perhaps he is; maybe he has a bigger heart.

7.10   ULMER: I don't think he does. He reflects the sentiment of the American people.

7.11   RUSHER: I wonder if he does. I think the American people are able to reflect their own sentiment.

7.12   ULMER: He's a Federal official, sir.

7.13   RUSHER: Well that doesn't make him God. [*Laughter.*]

7.14   ULMER: No; but he acts under laws passed by the American people.

7.15   RUSHER: Indeed he does. And the mayor of any city and the governor of any State does the same thing; with the special additional thing in his favor that they are laws passed by the people directly affected.

7 . 16   ULMER: That's why the poor get $35 per family in Mississippi against $250 in New York.

7 . 17   RUSHER: That's not exactly why they do. Let's find out why they do. Is Mississippi as rich a State as New York?

7 . 18   ULMER: The relative difference in wealth is not that great.

7 . 19   RUSHER: Just answer the question.

7 . 20   ULMER: Of course not.

7 . 21   RUSHER: Now, if it isn't, can you expect to get as much per capita out of its people in the form of taxes?

7 . 22   ULMER: I don't expect to get as much per capita, but I expect to get a good deal more than Mississippi's now paying.

7 . 23   RUSHER: That may well be; but you still wouldn't get as much if it isn't as rich, would you?

7 . 24   ULMER: Right.

7 . 25   RUSHER: So that it's going to have to come from somewhere. The whole idea that a State that's as rich as New York (or some of the other States that Mr. Miller constantly weeps over) has to give a certain proportion of its tax revenues, not just to Mississippi, but to the many poorer States—

7 . 26   ULMER: Do you realize that Alabama recently refused to use Federal funds for the medical care of the poor? Now, why do we expect that Alabama will raise its own funds for this purpose? It hasn't done so, so the Federal government needs to do it.

7 . 27   RUSHER: You speak as though we were discussing giving *all* Federal funds over to State and local authorities—but in point of fact, we're talking about $5 billion. Isn't it a fact that under the Nixon proposal, $22 billion will remain allocable by the Federal government as [at] present? . . .

7 . 28   ULMER: Yes, certain grants-in-aid programs [will remain as before].

7 . 29   RUSHER: So that, if Alabama were in fact suffering from a lack of a medical program, it wouldn't have to come out of the $5 billion anyway. It could come out of the $22 billion that [is] still to be allocated by the Federal government.

7 . 30   ULMER: I was simply pointing out that, if we really have regard for the poor people, whether they're in New York, Mississippi, or Alabama, we ought to *help* the poor people, not simply turn money over, free of any restrictions, to the States. I have no idea what'll be done with it. . . .

7 . 31   RUSHER: But I don't see why it should be done only by bureaucrats in Washington. Your faith in the Federal bureaucracy is touching.

7 . 32   PALMIERI: Let me test that faith with one question. Would you feel the same way if the country were in fact divided along the Mason-Dixon Line and you didn't have to worry about the historic problem of the South?

7.33   ULMER: Yes, I would feel that way. I realize that I've been using southern States, but this is simply because they have been farther down the ladder in all social welfare proposals and actions.

7.34   RUSHER: You complained about the low State tax efforts supposedly. Isn't it a fact 43 States now have income taxes?

7.35   ULMER: No. You're including States that have "special" taxes: income taxes on something like dividends and interest.

7.36   RUSHER: I'm including Pennsylvania, which was just added last week. . . .

7.37   ULMER: That brings the number [that don't have State income taxes] from 13 down to 12; but [Pennsylvania's] isn't in effect yet. . . .

7.38   RUSHER: What about the proposition [that] the State and local tax debt has doubled in the past ten years [and] that there have been 450 new or increased State taxes in the same period—in some cases, while the Federal government was lowering taxes?

7.39   ULMER: I agree that the States and cities have a financial problem.

7.40   RUSHER: I didn't say that. I said they'd been *raising* their taxes. You talked about "tax effort." They've been making that tax effort, have they not? . . . But "not enough" is your proposition.

7.41   ULMER: Right.

8.   SECOND NEGATIVE WITNESS: DIRECT EXAMINATION

8.1   MILLER: I'm delighted that the rural poor have been [mentioned]. You've heard (and it is true) [that] the mayors of this country, representing major cities, simply would not agree to a revenue-sharing plan that only gave money to States. They didn't trust them—for certain historic reasons, as we've heard. They bargained for a 48 percent pass-through, so those cities and counties do get 48 percent. *They* had the *power* to bargain. Rural poor *didn't* have power to bargain, and if there's anyone that gets hurt most by this, it's the rural poor, who will not be served by the States because the rural poor couldn't come in and say, "Give us X percentage." They simply didn't have the power the mayors have. The problem is how to help people, how to get through to the people who need the help. There are alternatives, both to help people and to help governmental units. One alternative, for example, is to federalize welfare—that is to have the Federal government undertake all the costs of welfare. If we were to do so, that would help poor people directly and would also relieve State and local governments of tax burdens of over $7 billion, returning more to their use than this proposal does. To talk to us about what is wrong with this proposal and [about] other alternatives we have with us tonight the United States Senator from Illinois, Adlai Stevenson. Senator, long before you were in the Senate, were you concerned with problems of State and local finance?

8.2   SEN. ADLAI STEVENSON III: I was. I served in the State legislature. I've also served as a State treasurer. I've seen in one State, Illinois, many of the serious financial problems that States and local governments have, all across this country. They're facing—they're coping with—serious problems involving the health, the education, the welfare of our citizens. And in many cases—not in all but in many cases—they can't cope effectively with these problems for lack of financial resources. But I've seen other problems, too, at the State [and] the local levels. I saw in the State of Illinois, for example, . . . a State reputedly teetering on the brink of bankruptcy at a time when I, as State treasurer, had $1 billion in my custody. With a little reform in the fiscal management of finances in that State we could generate, of the people's money, as much as the general revenue-sharing would give the State of Illinois in one year—money that could be used for public needs.

8.3   MILLER: Considering your concern for the State and local governments, why are you opposed to revenue-sharing?

8.4   STEVENSON: Many reasons, some [of which] have already been mentioned. Primarily, though, it's a question of accountability. The Federal government was never intended to become a tax collector for other units of government at the State and local level. To collect taxes from the people and then to, in a sense, give them away to State and local governments, would breach our responsibility at the Federal level to the Federal taxpayers—the citizens of the country. I think it would invite waste, extravagance, disordered priorities, at the State and at the local level, too. That's one reason.

8.5   [For another,] there are better ways of helping the States. I'm very concerned as a Senator about facing up to our national priorities in the country. To mention but one (I could mention many), we have a responsibility at the national level for managing the economy of the country. To give away—to distribute indiscriminately—$5 billion to be spent as States see fit [would] diminish the opportunity for the Federal government to manage the economy sensibly through a sane and sensible fiscal policy (budgeting surpluses and deficits). That's one of the problems; and if we did have a full employment economy right now, States and local governments would gain more in increased revenues from their existing tax resources than they could from additional revenues from the general revenue-sharing proposal.

8.6   MILLER: If the unemployment rate were down to 4 percent instead of its current 6.

8.7   PALMIERI: Would you feel the same way if revenue-sharing were based on per capita?

8.8   STEVENSON: Yes I certainly would. The general revenue-sharing [plan] is based on per-capita plus a "tax effort" factor.

8.9   PALMIERI: So that in fact it [would] return to the urban States a greater share than to the rural States.

8.10   STEVENSON: There's no question but what the Federal government should do still more to help State and local governments. The question is: How?

8.11   MILLER: What are the alternative "hows"?

8.12   STEVENSON: There *are* better ways. [To] federalize welfare is one possibility. That would be a possibility which gave the Federal government an opportunity to face up to a national problem, and it is a critical national problem.

8.13   PALMIERI: That would be very heavily weighted in favor of the urban States, wouldn't it?

8.14   STEVENSON: It would be heavily weighted in favor of States [which] need help and people who need help. It would solve a national problem, or at least *tend* to solve a national problem, by helping to diminish some of the inducements to migration from rural and Southern areas to our already-overcrowded cities, and [it would] save more than $1 billion a year just in administrative costs at the same time it is very effectively sharing revenues with the States and local governments which need help.

9.   CROSS-EXAMINATION

9.1   RUSHER: There was a predecessor of yours, a state treasurer of Illinois who, after he died recently, was discovered to have stashed a lot of cash away in shoe boxes.

9.2   STEVENSON: Not a state treasurer. *Secretary* of *State.* I was the last State treasurer. [*Laughter.*] . . .

9.3   RUSHER: You have, I know on other occasions, cited him as a horrible example of the type of corruption—

9.4   STEVENSON: No sir, I haven't.

9.5   RUSHER: Well, certainly you have referred to him as an example of the problem here, have you not?

9.6   STEVENSON: No sir, I haven't. What I *have* suggested is a consequence of general revenue-sharing: we would invite waste and disordered priorities in our State and our local governments. I'm as concerned as the governor and the mayor are about revitalizing.

9.7   RUSHER: I was about to ask whether you were worried about corruption in the city government of Chicago.

9.8   STEVENSON: I'm worried about corruption in every level of government. [And I'm] worried . . . about the insensitivity of government at every level. One of the principal problems of general revenue-sharing: it embalms the *status quo*. It gives us no incentive to change and to reform.

9.9   RUSHER: Certainly we have the case, at any rate, at the Federal level, of Bobby Baker, the well known case of corruption, and Sweig and Voloshen in the Speaker's office in the House of Representatives, and Billie Sol Estes in the—

9.10   STEVENSON: It's a problem, as I say—

9.11   RUSHER: The problem at "all levels of government." Precisely. Did I hear you call for higher Illinois taxes? I must not have been hearing very well this evening.

9.12   STEVENSON: For several years I supported a subsequently-adopted proposal for an income tax.

9.13   RUSHER: Do you favor Professor Ulmer's idea that the States all ought to get up to the level—as he sees it—of income taxes in Wisconsin?

9.14   STEVENSON: The decision on taxation should essentially be left to State and local governments. That's one of the problems I have.

9.15   RUSHER: But this is a proposal that they could raise this money by increasing their taxes. Do you endorse this proposal?

9.16   STEVENSON: Not all of the revenues. As I've indicated, I think the Federal government should help more. The States already receive some 20 percent of their total revenues [from Federal grants].

9.17   RUSHER: Should they raise more in higher taxes?

9.18   STEVENSON: The question is: "How."

9.19   RUSHER: The question is: "Should they?"

9.20   STEVENSON: The question is how the Federal government can most effectively help States which need help.

9.21   RUSHER: No, that was not the question.

9.22 STEVENSON: And this is my answer to the question [*laughter*]: there is a progressive and a fair tax collection system in the country, and it is the Federal tax collection system, and I think it should be used—but not by giving away Federal revenues to be spent or misspent. If I were a governor or a mayor, I might have a different attitude toward general revenue-sharing; but I don't think so.

9.23 RUSHER: Treating that as your "answer" to my question, I will turn to another question. You complained of a lack of accountability. Doesn't that in fact exist under the present system of matching grants?

9.24 STEVENSON: Exactly; and I think we should consolidate our grant-in-aid program. We should be getting away from the red tape. We should be using [grants] as a stimulus to reform and to change, especially at the local level of government.

9.25 RUSHER: Doesn't it also apply to the case of *State* revenue-sharing [revenue-sharing by States with municipalities and localities]? There is a lack of accountability *there*, too.

9.26 STEVENSON: Yes; I'm against it.

9.27 PALMIERI: Mr. Rusher, you've used that word ["accountability"; please explain].

9.28 RUSHER: The criticism, as I understand it—I do not share it—is that if you provide money from the Federal government to the States, for them to spend, there will be no accountability: no explanation of where the money has gone, what it has been spent on—that sort of thing. And above all, there will be no way in which the people who have raised the money can be effectively coordinated with the people who are going to spend it.

9.29 STEVENSON: That's a fair statement [of the "accountability" thesis].

9.30 PALMIERI: That's saying quite a bit, on this program. [*Laughter.*]

9.31 RUSHER: You spoke of the necessity for [the Federal government] to plan our national goals and so on. Take pollution. Was it a State or a Federal government that first controlled, or made an attempt to control, pollution problems?

9.32 STEVENSON: Well, there may have been some State, of 50. But I think the thrust has come at the national level.

9.33 RUSHER: What is the thrust? Why shouldn't the State that did it first get the credit?

9.34 STEVENSON: Why doesn't Senator Muskie, for example?

9.35 RUSHER: As long as we're talking about innovative governments, which do you think—the State or Federal government—first imposed a personal income tax?

9.36   STEVENSON: This is one of the features of our Federal system that I think we should do all we can to preserve. States used to be the laboratories for reform in the country. Even California once was a pioneer—

9.37   RUSHER: Which first passed a law for women's suffrage: State or Federal government?

9.38   STEVENSON: My objections to general revenue-sharing, as I've tried to indicate, are: they lock us into the *status quo*. There's no stimulus for reform. I want to help the States take initiative.

9.39   RUSHER: "No stimulus for reform"; and yet the stimulus for reform in civil rights came first in the neighboring State of Indiana, didn't it? And the first stimulus for the 18-year-old vote [from] the State of Georgia. . . . And the stimulus for women's suffrage in the State of Wyoming.

9.40   STEVENSON: Yes, and I'd like to see that [stimulation, innovativeness] continued.

9.41   RUSHER: All these are more innovative than the Federal government.

9.42   STEVENSON: More innovative for a long time. My own State experimented— it flirted once—very briefly, with a reform. That was in 1892 [*Laughter.*], in the case of railroad regulation.

9.43   MILLER (*in summation*):   The fact that one State may have done something before the Federal government simply doesn't mean anything. The fact of the matter is that the needs were totally unmet across the country in those areas until the Federal government stepped in in the other 49, 48, or 40 States that had failed to move. The kind of proposal we're talking about, in an age where we hear about fiscal responsibility, [exemplifies] the ultimate irresponsibility of giving money to a unit of government that has not raised it. And that money is allocated so that those who need it don't get it, those who can't afford it have to pay it, and it can't go to local educational districts when that may be where the greatest need is [located]. We need shared power—not the giving away of power, but *shared* power as we now have with the grant-in-aid program, where the Federal and State governments decide together how best to meet their needs.

10.   THIRD AFFIRMATIVE WITNESS: DIRECT EXAMINATION

10.1   RUSHER: Mr. Miller, under pressure, swept rather rapidly, I thought, from the urban ghettos to the rural poor; but I nonetheless welcome his understanding that this is not a matter of pitting the poor States against the rich, or the South against the North, or something of that sort. It is a problem national in scope. [I now call a witness] from the Federal government itself: Dr. John O. Wilson, Assistant Director of the Office of Economic Opportunity in Washington [and] a PH.D. in economics on leave from Yale University. Dr. Wilson, what about this charge that general revenue-sharing will favor rural over urban areas and certain States over others?

10.2   DR. JOHN O. WILSON: We seem to have been involved in a discussion that pits urban and rural States against each other, and [to have forgotten] about the people revenue-sharing's going to help. The money's going to go where the people [are] and the people are where the problems are. As a point of fact, the revenue-sharing is going to go into the urban areas where the real problems are, and that's the central cities. If you examine the ten largest central cities in this nation, you will find that [these] will receive two and a half times more, per capita, under general revenue-sharing, than the suburbs. The problems of the poor and disadvantaged are in the central cities, not the wealthy suburbs; and the senator and the professor seem to have neglected this point of view. Let's look at New York City. In Harlem, for example, residents will get $25 per capita—about the U.S. average. [People] in the suburbs will get about $8 per capita. In Los Angeles there'll be $30 per capita in the central city, $10 per capita in the suburbs. Revenue-sharing goes where the problems are. The problems are in the central cities, the ghettos, and the rural areas of America.

10.3   RUSHER: What about the argument that no general formula is going to work; that each problem must be faced individually, and that only the Federal government can do this?

10.4   WILSON: Why, this is utter nonsense. We've had 50 years of conditional grant experience; we now have over a thousand conditional grants; we've seen what's occurred. This is stating that [it is] the local governments, the State governments, who provide the basic services that really affect the quality of life of the poor and the people of America—education, sewage, highways. In fact, recall the debate in Congress over rat control. Rat control was laughed out of Congress, but at the local level where the mayors have to answer to an electorate, that's a very serious problem. The mayors can answer to those problems, and so can the governors.

10.5   RUSHER: What about Senator Stevenson's idea about federalizing welfare?

10.6   WILSON: Senator Stevenson proposed a proposal that helps the rich States get richer and the poor States stay poor. Under his federalization scheme, two States in this nation—New York and California—would get 45 percent of the total benefits. They happen to have 14 percent of the total poor. The southern States, where 45 percent of the poor live, would only get 11 percent of the benefits under the Senator's proposal.

10.7   RUSHER: Of course they lost the Civil War. Maybe he thinks it's only fair.

10.8   WILSON: The rich would get richer. Right.

11.   CROSS-EXAMINATION

11.1   MILLER: Tell me why the President's proposals for welfare—that is, his Family Assistance Plan, taking the Federal floor of the $1600 minimum—are so in conflict with his revenue-sharing plans. Why didn't the President deal with welfare by giving money to the States to totally administer welfare?

11.2   WILSON: Ah, but first of all you're wrong on your figures. It's $2,200, not $1,600.

11.3   MILLER: Counting the food stamps. All right.

11.4   WILSON: In his latest proposals, [the President calls for treating] the food stamps as pure cash—$2,200 in the latest proposal. Indeed [President Nixon has] proposed both [measures]. When you're talking about federalizing welfare, you're talking about dealing with the poverty problem at the State level, and that's why you want a national floor.

11.5   MILLER: But I don't understand. Why not give the money to the States?

11.6   WILSON: Revenue-sharing goes directly to the *other* problems: the garbage and the payment for education; the payment for streets and highways and fire protection.

11.7   MILLER: Let's stop on education. It can't go to special educational districts. We'd have to rely on the States—

11.8   WILSON: The governor of Colorado has already pointed out that the States can "pass through" [funds]; and don't overlook the fact thay you have *special* revenue-sharing that will put $5 billion [of existing money] into education. You also have $22 billion in conditional programs, of which $3.8 billion will go into education. . . .

11.9   MILLER: In welfare, the President said [the] Federal government's going to pay directly $1,600, or $2,200 now that we're going to count the food stamps as cash. We're going to federalize to that extent. Why didn't he take *all* the money for welfare, the billions of dollars, and do the same thing with it—give it to the States to administer their welfare program?

11 . 10   WILSON: The President well recognizes that half the poor live in the rural areas, half the poor live in the South; and if he federalized the existing welfare system, one-half of those total benefits would go to two States: New York and California. He's concerned about *all* the poor, not just the poor in New York and California.

11 . 11   MILLER: Tell me about all the bureaucrats, now, that we're going to lose. How many people are going to lose their jobs because of general revenue-sharing?

11 . 12   WILSON: Nobody will lose their job because of general revenue-sharing. That's all a net increase in new funds.

11 . 13   MILLER: You mean all those buildings [which house local branches of Federal agencies] are still going to be filled with Federal bureaucrats?

11 . 14   WILSON: Ah, but you're overlooking *special* revenue-sharing. That's another issue.

11 . 15   MILLER: I'm interested in getting to the problem of welfare and other things. Now welfare, I take it, has national implications. . . . Let's look at other areas. Education has national implications as well.

11 . 16   WILSON: Very definitely. That's why the President proposed *special* revenue-sharing. That's why we're going to keep conditional programs.

11 . 17   MILLER: It has national implications, and national policy in education is terribly important isn't it? And national policy in housing, affecting the housing markets and building codes, is terribly important? National policy in road building is terribly important?

11 . 18   WILSON: Right.

11 . 19   MILLER: Well, aren't all those programs, then, programs in which the Federal Government should share some of the responsibility for making the decision?

11 . 20   WILSON: Indeed, the Federal government *is* going to share that responsibility. That doesn't mean the Federal government's got to have a thousand different programs sharing that responsibility.

11 . 21   MILLER: The Federal government should share that responsibility with this $5 billion in general revenue-sharing as well.

11 . 22   WILSON: [President Nixon proposes] to share it with about $32 billion in the other [categories of aid].

11 . 23   MILLER: Why not with this five [billion]? It goes to these same problems doesn't it? They have national implications.

11.24   WILSON: The Federal government *is* recognizing that the Federal government's got responsibility to provide those services such as police, fire, highways, sewage collection, garbage collection. . . .

11.25   MILLER: Is that the "new federalism": that fire protection is part of the Federal government's responsibility?

11.26   WILSON: You're overlooking the fact that the Federal government's got to recognize that the people in Mississippi and Harlem have just as much right to those services as the people in Scarsdale.

11.27   MILLER: And that's exactly why it's a national problem, isn't it? Because they *do* have as much right.

11.28   WILSON: The national problem is how to revitalize the power of State and local governments to deal with those problems.

11.29   MILLER: And we revitalize by giving them money with no conditions that they change? To split local governments, with no condition of metropolitan government?

11.30   WILSON: Yes indeed, we *can* [revitalize these governments in this way].

11.31   MILLER: As the crime money went to Alabama under the Law Enforcement Assistance Administration.

11.32   WILSON: As the U.S. Congress laughed at the rat controll bill.

11.33   MILLER: Laughed [at] and ultimately passed.

11.34   WILSON: Because of the power of the State and local governments [that] rose up in indignation and said that that was a serious problem.

12.   FINAL AFFIRMATIVE WITNESSES

12.1   RUSHER: Illinois' junior senator, Mr. Stevenson, and Professor Ulmer of the University of Maryland opposed revenue-sharing. You've heard Mayor Lugar of Indianapolis, Governor Love of Colorado, [and] Dr. Wilson speak in its favor. Perhaps you thought that made matters even, or a little more than even. The truly striking thing about revenue-sharing is how many American political figures endorse it. Republican and Democrat, liberal and conservative, black and white—the elected leaders of the American people speak up for President Nixon's proposal:

12.2   GOV. RONALD REAGAN OF CALIFORNIA (*on film, Jan. 25, 1971*):   Federal government is too big, too powerful, and should be decentralized; and for people to dismiss [President Nixon's] idea of revenue-sharing, and to pretend that the Federal government can administer more efficiently public funds at the local level than local government and States can—this is to live in a dream world. These are different times. This is one of those moments in history in which the people are standing out there, Democrat and Republican alike, and they're looking at government and they're saying, "We didn't send you up there, Democrat or Republican, to just fight each other and have a lot of fun in a partisan political game. We sent you up to co-manage the people's affairs and settle the problems that are disturbing all of us."

12.3   MAYOR CARL STOKES OF CLEVELAND (*on film, April 16, 1970*): We just can't permit politics to interfere with the basic, fundamental, crucial needs of those of us who are trying to keep these cities of this nation viable.

12.4   MAYOR JAMES TATE OF PHILADELPHIA (*on film, April 16, 1970*): Congress should and must act on the revenue-sharing measure at this session, and before it ends. We can't stand further delay.

12.5   GOV. NELSON ROCKEFELLER OF NEW YORK (*on film, Jan. 29, 1971*): All I can say is that if we don't meet this problem, we're going to see a breakdown of services this year, in our cities and metropolitan areas, spreading throughout the country.

12.6   MAYOR KENNETH GIBSON OF NEWARK (*on film, Jan. 22, 1971*): The next step for Newark is not to be able to provide *any* services to its 400,000 people. And my question is whether America—whether it be local America in the States, or whether it be national America in the Congress—is to allow a city to completely halt the delivery of services to 400,000 people.

12.7   GOV. REAGAN (*film of Jan. 25, 1971*): I guarantee that this revenue-sharing plan will not only aid the States and the localities; and I can tell you, in California we can reduce taxes with it at the same time that we can perform some of those services better, and we can reduce the bureaucracy in Washington, if revenue-sharing is put into effect.

13.   CLOSING STATEMENTS

13.1   RUSHER: If you've ever tried to take a bone from a dog, you will understand the problems involved in trying to take control of Federal aid away from the bureaucrats who now preside over it. According to a recent Gallup poll, 77 percent of the American people favor revenue-sharing; but its fate in Congress is in doubt, because Chairman Wilbur Mills of the House Ways and Means Committee has pledged to kill it, and he has in his corner the whole vast array of Federal agencies and employees whose sole excuse for existence is the supposed need for their services in dispensing billions of dollars of taxpayers' money. Basically, it boils down to this: are we, as a nation, capable of governing ourselves, or is that a job for anonymous Federal experts who know better than you, and your neighbors and your local mayor and your State's governor, what is good for you? If you want to return power to the people of this country, I urge you to vote for revenue-sharing.

13.2   MILLER: Governor Reagan gave the game away: "We can reduce taxes." And that's what it's all about: substituting the Federal taxes for the State taxes. Who trusts this proposal? No one, unless they get theirs. The motto here is that "it's better to receive than to tax." The mayors would not agree to this proposal until they got a guaranteed percentage, because they knew what would happen if the State governments alone controlled this money, just as Congress knows what will happen. Not only Chairman Mills, but a large majority in both parties, oppose divorcing responsibility [for] taxing from responsibility for spending. There are national problems, as we've heard. There are national problems in welfare, which the President understands; national problems in education, in housing; national problems throughout the country. The question is: "Should the Federal government divorce itself, to the extent of this money, from planning in all those problems?" It should share some of the power, participate in some of the decision-making, and help both the States, the Federal government, and the people.

 *16 March 1971*

POSTSCRIPT

On Oct. 16, 1972, at a ceremony in Philadelphia's Independence Hall, President Nixon signed into law a Congressional bill providing for general revenue-sharing on a scale of $30.1 billion over a period of five years. Terms of the program differ somewhat from those that were disputed in the foregoing debate. State governments will be entitled to keep one third of the funds, while 38,000 units of local government get two thirds. Distribution among the States is according to a complicated pair of alternative formulas involving size of population, per capita incomes, and tax effort. Distribution among the localities also is according to a complicated formula. The Federal grants must not be used for general administration or for education (which is supported through other channels), and are to be used in ways that are loosely related to public safety, environmental protection (including sewers), public transportation (including streets), health, recreation, and libraries. The first year's outlays amount to $5.3 billion, State governments getting between $2.1 million (Alaska, Connecticut) and $197.1 million (New York), and cities getting between $18,500 (Poteet City, Texas) and $247 million (New York).

SUGGESTED EXERCISES

1. Enumerate the provisions of the Nixon Administration's general revenue-sharing plan as described in the foregoing debate. Indicate which, if any, significant details were not clarified.
2. Identify and appraise alternative methods of measuring "tax effort," using the debate on general revenue-sharing as a source.
3. Using the debate on general revenue-sharing as a source, discuss alternative principles for devising a "fair" formula for allocating Federal funds among the States (and do not just mutter vaguely about "need").
4. Cite and discuss examples where precedents or analogies were used in the course of the debate.
5. Write a 'balance sheet' in which the principal lines of argument emanating from the Affirmative and Negative sides in the debate, along with assertions made by way of rebuttal, are listed in adjacent columns.

COMMENTARY

Red Herring

The debate on revenue-sharing, like the debate on electoral registration, produced a noteworthy example of *ignoratio elenchi*, or arguing "beside the point." In this case the diversion was achieved by means of a device known as the "red herring." This consists of injecting a given issue into a controversy so as to divert attention, more or less intentionally, from another, more immediate, issue.

Gov. John Love of Colorado used a red herring to divert attention, intentionally or otherwise, from problems arising from contrasts in the respective States' "tax efforts." The governor was confronted by ambiguous contentions to the effect that general revenue-sharing would be superfluous because some States are laggards in "tax effort," or that general revenue-sharing under the Nixon formula would be inequitable because of inter-State contrasts in "tax effort." He responded to such claims, in part (5.21, 5.23), by voicing concern over the present overall burden of taxation in the United States, relative to Gross National Product.

Concern over the latter problem may be warranted; but the matter has no bearing on questions about general revenue-sharing arising from differential State "tax efforts." Accordingly, Governor Love's response was a red herring.

Incidentally, Governor Love's *choice* of a red herring seems peculiarly unfortunate for an avowed proponent of general revenue-sharing. The plan for general revenue-sharing, as described in the Overview, involves Federal disbursement of "new money," or funds derived, presumably, from additional taxation. The overall burden of taxation in the United States would not be eased by adoption of the general revenue-sharing plan; it apparently would be aggravated.

Testimonials

Another example of arguing beside the point was supplied by William Rusher. In his opening statement Rusher anticipated that "charges of State and local corruption, [and] of injustice and inequality in the formulas for distribution," would be hurled against the Nixon Administration's proposal for general revenue-sharing. "But the truth," said Rusher in the next sentence (1.4), "is that this proposal is endorsed by a great and growing majority of mayors and governors across America, as well as by the President of the United States."

Rusher responded to a pair of immediate issues (efficient use of funds, equitable distribution of funds) by inserting a third issue (prevailing gubernatorial and mayoral opinions about revenue-sharing). Widespread endorsement of general revenue-sharing would not dispose of the preceding issues. Perhaps the endorsements come from crooks or from prospective recipients of disproportionate amounts of Federal largesse.

Perhaps, on the other hand, the endorsing officials appreciate the problems of corruption and maldistribution, but believe that general revenue-sharing on balance would serve the public interest.

The red herring used by Rusher in this instance exemplifies what has come to be known as the "testimonial" device. This consists of inviting respondents to appraise a proposal by reference to the character, real or alleged, of its opponents or proponents. Rusher returned to this device later in the debate. He credited general-revenue sharing with support from a great many "American political figures," "Republican and Democrat, liberal and conservative, black and white. . . ." (**12.**1).*

This mode of argument serves to underscore a distinction made previously (in the Commentary on the debate on the Congressional "seniority system") between proper and improper use of *ad hominem* argument. Although Rusher used testimonials at one point as a red herring, his *choice* of testimonials, in the context of the debate as a whole, was not beside the point.

There are many standards for appraising the propriety of testimonials. Prominent among these is the standard involving the relevance of authorities cited for a given purpose. We can readily appreciate this point by recalling that when the war-time Roosevelt Administration gambled vast sums of money on inventing an atomic bomb, it acted very substantially at the advice of Albert Einstein, rather than at the advice of Alfred E. ("What—Me Worry?") Neumann. It elicited testimonials from eminently qualified authorities on the given issue.

---

*In his closing statement (**13.**1), Rusher supplied additional evidence concerning the popularity of revenue-sharing plan. He alluded to a recent Gallup poll showing that "77 percent of the American people favor revenue-sharing. . . ." This reference might qualify as an example of what propaganda analysts call the "plain folks device," in which a cause is commended on the ground that it is favored by, or emanates from, ordinary people. However, Rusher did not cite the Gallup poll explicitly as grounds for adopting general revenue-sharing. He used the Gallup reference, rather (in conjunction with his remarks about the feelings of non-Federal officials), to conjure up a conflict of wills between the people as a whole and a vast, tenacious, parasitic Federal bureaucracy.

Incidentally, an experienced student of public opinion polls would be inclined to question the validity of the way in which Rusher describes the results of the Gallup survey. At an offhand guess, it seems likely that Rusher was referring to respondents who voiced an opinion pro or con, while ignoring respondents who voiced uncertainty. Moreover, before accepting Rusher's claim that 77 percent of the respondents "favor revenue-sharing," one would wish to know precisely how the Gallup poll question was phrased.

Widespread support by elective public officials at all levels surely deserves to be counted as substantial evidence on behalf of any policy measure. It deserves respectful attention from people who believe in the principle of popular government. It also deserves attention on the ground that public officials are peculiarly experienced at assessing the probable consequences of a prospective policy decision.

Accordingly, Rusher can be credited with citing testimonials from proper sources. He did not, for example, use clergymen as expert witnesses on the physiological effects of cocaine. At the same time, two lines of adverse criticism concerning Rusher's use of testimonials in connection with the general revenue-sharing plan seem to be warranted.

In the first place, Rusher indulged in a bit of card-stacking* when he directed attention to the views of mayors and governors (as well as the President) while ignoring the views of Senators and Representatives.

In the second place, Rusher *et al.* furnished insufficient evidence on behalf of the claim that a "great and growing majority of mayors and governors across America" endorse the Nixon Administration's general revenue-sharing plan. Filmed statements by two governors and three mayors were shown, *but* only two of these contained *explicit* endorsements of general revenue-sharing. Other testimony in the debate called attention to both support and opposition (including, it would seem, opposition from the mayors of New York, San Francisco, and seven other cities). The evidence concerning the scope of mayoral, gubernatorial, and other official support for general revenue-sharing, in short, was less than conclusive. Yet one bit of evidence, in the form of a conspicuous omission, bolstered Rusher's characterization of prevailing official opinion: opponents of general revenue-sharing did not *challenge* the claim that "a great and growing majority" of mayors and governors support the general revenue-sharing plan.

---

*See Lee and Lee, *The Fine Art of Propaganda*, cited in the Commentary on glittering generalities in the debate over campaign finance.

Should the federal government compel suburbs to accept low-income housing?

OVERVIEW

America is a nation of migrants. People first arrived on the East Coast, then moved inland, farther and farther to the West. Later came massive migrations from farm to city, and from the South to the North and the Far West, especially in the wake of the Dust Bowls of the Depression and then the availability of new factory jobs created by World War II. A new pattern of migration picked up momentum in the late 1940's, and still is under way. This movement is from central cities to suburbs. The rate of increase in suburban population has lately run 15 times greater than the rate of growth in big cities. Suburbanites already out-number big-city dwellers and rural residents, by a ratio of about 36 to 30 to 34,* and the movement to the suburbs shows no signs of abating.

But the migrants to the suburbs do not constitute a cross-section of the population. Although there are suburban tracts for low- and moderate-income families, the bulk of the newcomers have been in the moderate- to upper-income brackets, and have been white. This has been

---

*Linda and Paul Davidoff and Neil N. Gold, "The Suburbs Have to Open Their Gates," *New York Times Magazine*, Nov. 7, 1971, p. 40.

the case, in considerable measure, because of policies adopted by established residents of suburban communities.

Suburban communities usually enjoy a substantial measure of "home rule." Through their organs of local government, suburbanites can decide where, and whether, to permit the construction of residential units, factories, shopping centers, business centers, trailer parks, schools, gas stations, and the like. Moreover, they exercise basic control over the character of new housing: apartment buildings vs. single-family units, large lots vs. small lots, big structures vs. small, expensive materials vs. cheaper materials. This authority can be used, and frequently has been used, to create enclaves of prosperous, privileged families. It can be used to keep vacant land effectively off the market for most uses, and thus to increase the price of other land.

Such practices have lately provoked an attack against home rule. There have been many lines of criticism, but among the more basic and frequent is the charge that restrictive zoning practices by suburban communities have thwarted the development of decent housing for low- and moderate-income families. Some of these critics argue that the Federal government should compel suburbs to accept shares of low- to moderate-income housing. This step is espoused and assailed in the following debate.

1. OPENING STATEMENTS

1.1   MODERATOR VICTOR PALMIERI: . . . As long as the local communities are given the final choice in the matter, many contend, the suburbs will remain chiefly the refuge of America's middle class, while the cities remain enclaves of its very poor. To circumvent this, housing experts and some civil rights leaders have proposed that the Federal government, which will subsidize more than a quarter of all new housing units built this year, step in and alter the suburban pattern of living on behalf of the poor. Specifically, they propose that the Federal government have the power to compel suburbs to accept low-income housing. [To this proposal] Advocate Miller says "Yes," [while Guest Advocate] Mahoney says "No."

1.2   ADVOCATE HOWARD MILLER: The national goal of a decent home for every American is today being frustrated by suburbs that arbitrarily exclude low- and moderate-income families. The land is in the suburbs. But many of those enclaves of privilege zone land out of use that builders wish to build on and that people wish to live on, and force higher costs and congestion elsewhere.

1.3   There is today enough Federal money and enough Federal programs to build low- and moderate-income housing. Between 25 and 33 percent of all housing constructed this year will be government-subsidized housing. There is money for the housing; there are builders all over the United States who wish to build; there are government subsidies to finance it; and there is land that is available. But that land is in suburbs, and many of the suburbs are zoning it out of use. How do they do this? By zoning it for non-residential use, by requiring only single-family homes, by requiring large lot sizes that the government will not finance, [and] by requiring large square footage for each house, [thereby allowing only very expensive houses to be built and] zoning out the low- and moderate-income housing that is there wanting to be built. What kind of housing are we talking about? Not the old concentrated kind of public housing tracts, but new kinds of government-subsidized housing: subsidized housing for small single-family homes, for small apartment units; subsidized housing for homeowners on scattered sites—the kind of housing that's been kept out. The answer: a national law to require that every suburb accept a minimum amount, and its fair share, of low- and moderate-income housing, spreading the cost of placing it throughout the United States, calling for a true integration of the suburbs, and bringing back into use the land which suburbs are now keeping out of use, raising costs and forcing congestion elsewhere.

1.4   ADVOCATE J. DANIEL MAHONEY: Local home rule is one of the most cherished traditions of our democratic system. Any sensible housing program must work within that system. The social engineers, however, want to replace local zoning boards with Federal bureaucrats.

1.5   The proposal for Federal zoning power over the local communities of America is a major breakthrough in the field of wrongheaded social engineering. The people of a community have a democratic right, as our Supreme Court recently held, to determine the character of that community. After all, they are the ones who have to pay the taxes for the municipal services, the police, the fire department, the schools, to support new housing that can't pay its own way. Furthermore, as I will demonstrate, the way to provide improved housing for our poor is with *housing vouchers*, akin to the food stamps we provide today. Federal zoning power is a non-answer to a very serious question.

2.   FIRST AFFIRMATIVE WITNESS: DIRECT EXAMINATION

2.1   MILLER: To speak to why this plan [for a national law requiring each suburb to accept a share of low- and moderate-income housing] should be adopted, we have with us [first] Paul Davidoff, director of the Suburban Action Institute, an organization devoted to bringing low-cost housing to the suburbs. Mr. Davidoff, is the Federal government involved now in housing?

2.2   PAUL DAVIDOFF: Oh yes; it's been involved in housing for quite some time. Throughout the world, nations for decades have recognized that decent shelter is of tremendous importance. The United States since the middle 1930's has recognized that the private market in housing has failed to provide an adequate shelter for all Americans. And in 1930 the government began a program of erecting housing for low-income families. In 1949 the Government said through Congress that every American family should have a decent home in a suitable living environment.

2.3   MILLER: Are there harmful effects from this suburban exclusion of low- and moderate-income housing?

2.4   DAVIDOFF: Oh, yes; tremendously costly effects to our society today. Not only are many millions of families deprived of the right to live in a decent shelter in the wealthiest nation of the world, while in other nations people are given this guarantee; here families live in rat-infested quarters, unsafe structures. We have many families who are deprived of decent shelter. But beyond that, we have a growth in America today of tremendous population and jobs in our suburbs; and large numbers of our population—middle class, working class, lower class, whites and blacks—are systematically excluded from the suburbs because of the controls that are employed by the suburbs, in their economic self-interest, to keep out all but the wealthy.

2.5   MILLER: Does this kind of zoning also hurt the building industry? What does *it* wish to do?

2.6   DAVIDOFF: The cost to the building industry is tremendous. In the suburbs that I am familiar with, in the metropolitan regions around the nation, it is possible for us today to be building at least twice the number of units that are being constructed annually today in the suburbs. This would mean that the building industry could be spurring our economy.

2.7   MILLER: In order to get to the problem—in order to spur the building industry and get additional housing units—[must] we prevent suburbs from having this kind of exclusionary zoning?

2.8   DAVIDOFF: We must, if America is to grow. Our country is built upon growth. . . . The suburban extremists, by their overuse of government power—the Ivy League socialists—are prohibiting development, hurting our economy at this time, and depriving people of the right to live decently where the new jobs are developing.

3.   CROSS-EXAMINATION

3.1   PALMIERI: Let's hear if Mr. Mahoney has anything to say for the "suburban extremists."

3.2   MAHONEY: . . . Let's take a hypothetical case: a builder, a Mr. Getrich, goes over to the local zoning board. He's got a tract. He wants it zoned for multiple housing and can't get it done. He goes down to see Mr. Faceless, the Federal bureaucrat, and Mr. Faceless has a decision to make. How does he determine that? What are the criteria by which he makes his mind up?

3.3   DAVIDOFF: I don't understand why you are so harmful to the builder, giving him that name. Aren't you in favor of the builders being able to make a profit? . . . The builders are the ones who are providing shelter for us.

3.4   MAHONEY: My apologies to Mr. Getrich wherever he is. But back to the question at hand. How would Mr. Faceless, the Federal bureaucrat, deal with this problem? . . . He's been denied a right to build [a low-cost tract] in the local community. He comes down there and says, "I want a variance; I want a Federal variance under the new Davidoff Law." What is the standard by which Mr. Faceless decides whether or not he gets the variance?

3.5   DAVIDOFF: It's a matter of a plan that has been created by the region of which Mr. Faceless is a part. The metropolitan region of which the suburbs are a part prepare[s] a comprehensive plan for that whole region, which shows how all of the parts of the region, working together, can join in solving the problem. And each of the communities is given its fair share.

3.6   MAHONEY: What does the plan say? We've got a tract of land. We know how many poor people there are in town. How do you make up your mind?

3.7   DAVIDOFF: I don't think it's a very difficult problem. If we know that Town X in the suburbs is a town that's gaining a lot of industry, and it's taking the taxes from that industry and presently not willing to house the workers, the regional plan would indicate that, rather than having the workers travel long distances to get to those new jobs, they ought to be able to find attractive land proximate to where they work.

3.8   MAHONEY: So is your proposal only to apply to towns with new industry, then?

3.9   DAVIDOFF: Oh, no. It applies to suburbs throughout our metropolitan areas.

3.10   MAHONEY: What about the suburb that doesn't have new industry? How do you decide there?

3.11   DAVIDOFF: It's very simple in that case. [Some] suburban areas have large amounts of vacant land proximate to the new interstate highways that are accessible to where the jobs are growing. [These areas] are suitable for residential development. There are sound planning reasons that can be given in each community as to where that housing should be constructed.

3.12   MAHONEY: Before you take away this right of zoning from the local communities that have had it all these years, wouldn't it make some sense at least to try out some of these new housing concepts that the Federal government has?

3.13   DAVIDOFF: They should be tried out, and we are trying to make it possible. But we can't do it. The zoning prohibits us from doing it.

3.14   MAHONEY: But isn't that zoning in large measure a response to the heavy housing projects? Isn't that why they've zoned out? The very projects you say you don't want to use any more have created the problem in terms of the reaction of the local homeowners.

3.15   DAVIDOFF: No, that isn't the reason why suburbs have used zoning power to exclude. They've done it out of economic self-interest to try to prevent any growth in the suburbs.

3.16   MAHONEY: They've done it because if people come in, their taxes will go up to handle all the new housing. It's one thing to say somebody can come in and put three or four people in an apartment. It's another thing to say that you're going to put in a 250-family development, and the local community is going to bear the entire burden of the police—

3.17   DAVIDOFF: People are coming into the suburbs. The suburbs are where America lives today. People live in the suburbs. People have been coming into the suburbs and once the people come in, they want to close the door and shut out everybody else.

3.18   MAHONEY: I'd like your comment on these statistics. In Nassau, Suffolk, and Westchester, three suburbs right near where you are, the increase in public assistance is dramatic: from 1960 to 1970, 7900 to 54,300 in Nassau, 14,000 to 64,000 in Suffolk, 11,000 to 44,000 in Westchester. How does that square with the notion that there are no new poor people coming in? Who *are* these people?

3 . 19   DAVIDOFF: In Oyster Bay, where the N.A.A.C.P. is suing the town because it has tremendous industrial growth—

3 . 20   MAHONEY: That isn't the question I asked you.

3 . 21   DAVIDOFF: I am responding. In a five-year period the white population grew by 30,000; the nonwhite population diminished by a few hundred.

3 . 22   MAHONEY: Are we talking about poor people or are we talking about economics?

3 . 23   DAVIDOFF: We are talking about economics and race. We are talking about both, and they are definitely related.

4.   SECOND AFFIRMATIVE WITNESS: DIRECT EXAMINATION

4 . 1   MILLER: Of course there have been objections in local communities, and we have to investigate what those objections have been. To talk to us we have here today a homeowner [and Town Meeting member] from Lexington, Mass., which has been concerned with this problem; Sumner Wolsky. What is wrong, Mr. Wolsky, with excluding, by this kind of zoning, from the suburbs, low- and moderate-income families?

4 . 2   SUMNER WOLSKY: We exclude people, [deprive them] of having a choice of where to live. We compress them into the urban area. We put them in places where they have improper educational opportunities. In fact, we bus some of these out to Lexington to provide them with better education. But that's very small; that's really tokenism. We're actually barring the door to them.

4 . 3   MILLER: As a homeowner in Lexington, are you afraid of what will happen if low- and moderate-income families begin moving in?

4 . 4   WOLSKY: I'm not afraid of poor people. I came from a ghetto area in Roxbury, and I think poor people are not undesirable. I don't make "poor" equivalent with "undesirable." I think that these people, placed in an opportunity, like myself, to have better education and have a better opportunity, will prosper, just as I did.

4 . 5   MILLER: Can't we expect, though, the suburbs to voluntarily change their zoning and accept these families?

4 . 6   WOLSKY: Absolutely not. History will show in the town of Lexington that for three years we have been trying to do that. We voted a new zoning by-law which authorized what we call low- and moderate-income housing, but we refused to implement it.

4 . 7   MILLER: Do you think it's justified, though, for the Federal government to impose this requirement across the country in all suburbs?

4 . 8   WOLSKY: I think that the Federal Government is going to have to intervene in order to make this work. For example, in the town of Lexington, the Town Meeting, by a vote of 128, a two-thirds vote, did authorize a low- and moderate-income housing development. But this was overturned by a vote of almost two to one in a public referendum.

4 . 9   MILLER: This is a national problem that justifies the Federal government coming in?

4 . 10   WOLSKY: This is definitely a national problem. I do not believe that home rule and a national problem such as this, Federal intervention, are in conflict at all. This is a national problem; it's not a local issue.

5 .   CROSS-EXAMINATION

5 . 1   MAHONEY: You mention freedom of choice. . . . I guess that's for everybody except your neighbors in Lexington. Is that right?

5 . 2   WOLSKY: No; I think we all have freedom of choice in Lexington.

5 . 3   MAHONEY: You're a fan of referendums, I gather.

5 . 4   WOLSKY: The people in Lexington have a freedom of choice. Everyone wants to be the last one in town. I would have liked to have been the last one in town. But I recognize a moral responsibility to others.

5 . 5   MAHONEY: Justice Black said recently in a Supreme Court case: "Provisions for referendums demonstrate devotion to democracy, not to bias, discrimination, or prejudice." I gather you disagree with him.

5 . 6   WOLSKY: No, I don't. I think there's an interesting fact that, again, the situation in Lexington will demonstrate. In a town meeting where we had a standing vote [to authorize low- and moderate-income housing], the vote was two-thirds in favor. Yet when people got behind the curtain where they were not seen when they had a vote, they voted "No."

5 . 7   MAHONEY: So you don't like voting booths?

5 . 8   WOLSKY: No; I think that people in the Town Meeting who have an opportunity to study the issues are better informed.

5.9   MAHONEY: Then you *are* anti-referendum. I mean, you think that the people that come to Town Meetings, the ones who turn out, the ones who take an interest in a Town Meeting, are the only ones who should really have anything to say.

5.10   WOLSKY: I think on a national issue such as this, the Federal government has to intervene. We have a history in this country of Federal intervention.

5.11   MAHONEY: Federal intervention where? In zoning?

5.12   WOLSKY: We have, in our own town, in conservation. We purchased conservation ground. We have no complaints about going to the Federal government for that money. We've put no restrictions on that.

5.13   MAHONEY: Just because the Federal government is in the conservation area, you think it's traditional for them to be in the zoning area? Maybe we studied some different Constitutional history. I don't recall it being set up that way.

5.14   WOLSKY: When the zoning [is] restrictive and restricts opportunity for people, definitely we have to have a Federal override . . . What would happen in Selma, Alabama, if we were to have a vote on desegregation? I think the Federal government had to intervene there. It's the same type of principle.

5.15   MAHONEY: In other words, the principle is that any time you think your neighbors aren't doing the right thing, you want to call the Federal government in.

5.16   WOLSKY: It's not what I think.

5.17   MAHONEY: Why isn't it what you think? They had a vote there. It was two to one against you, and now you're saying "I want a recount; let's call in a new ballot taker."

5.18   WOLSKY: I think that those in the Federal government have to look from a national [vantage point]. We're concerned with local problems. I'm saying, for one thing, I don't think in that particular situation that the electorate were that informed. But they were concerned with certain problems.

5.19   MAHONEY: You don't think they were that informed. Maybe it's their right to be uninformed. The point is: they made their decision. You just don't want to accept it. Isn't that right?

5.20   WOLSKY: I don't want to accept their decision. And I am hoping for the Federal government, through national laws, to overcome that . . . because of its responsibility for the country to do it. And I hope there will be enough people in the Congress, in the national government, to think along with me. I'll have to wait for it. I'm not too optimistic it will happen too rapidly, but I'm hopeful that it will.

5.21   MAHONEY: What's wrong with the people of Lexington deciding how Lexington is to be zoned?

5.22   WOLSKY: Because they're self-centered, self-interested. They all want to be the last one in town.

5.23   MAHONEY: Who decides that—you and Howard Miller? I'm saying, "Let *them* [the local residents] decide." Your position is that you and Howard Miller [are] going to go around and decide.

5.24   WOLSKY: No, we're not deciding. I think nothing can be decided except by national law. And national law is made by politicians. And they want to get elected. And they won't get elected until those people put them in office who want this action.

5.25   MAHONEY: Well now, nothing can be decided except on the basis of national law. And you've got them in housing; you've got them making zoning decisions. . . . What *do* you think the people of Lexington have a right, or the capacity, to decide for themselves, if anything?

5.26   WOLSKY: I think they're very right in deciding about their education system. (We accept Federal subsidies for that, incidentally.) I think they have a right to worry about where they're going to put sewers. . . . We control the type of housing we put in there. We're not letting builders come in and put anything there willy-nilly. We're controlling it. We have the [strictest] zoning bylaws concerning low- and moderate-income housing. We're not losing control.

5.27   MAHONEY: The point is: you want to *have* them *lose* control. You want some bureaucrat, who's never been in Lexington and probably couldn't pick it out on a road map, to come in and tell them how to do it. You think he would know better than the people of Lexington how the thing should be run. Isn't that right?

5.28   WOLSKY: Yes. I think they see from a total overview. Yes. I would agree with you 100 percent that, from a national viewpoint, sometimes the Federal Government has to decide what's best for the people. And historically it has.

5.29   MAHONEY: The Wolsky Total Overview Theory. Thank you very much.

5.30   WOLSKY: The Mahoney Underview. [*Laughter.*]

5.31   MILLER: (*in summation*):   I deny the power that's been graciously offered to me to order the people of Lexington what to do. The problem is that the people of Lexington or other suburbs are not the only people concerned with whether the land is used for low- and moderate-income housing. There are other people concerned: the people who want to live on the land, the builders who want to build on the land, the government and the taxpayers who are willing to subsidize the housing. And those people have no representation in that vote. So all [that] tonight's proposal says is: "You can't keep out low- and moderate-income housing. Once it comes in, . . . you plan for it, say where it should be, zone for it. You simply have to recognize the rights of others to be represented to the extent of not excluding them. Suburbs can't keep land off the market that others want to live on."

6. FIRST NEGATIVE WITNESS: DIRECT EXAMINATION

6.1 MAHONEY: The Federal zoning power contended for tonight is a dramatic departure from our basic democratic system. No case has been made, or can be made, for putting the zoning of thousands of communities across our nation into the hands of Federal bureaucrats who would have no knowledge of local conditions, no role in the local political process, and no responsibility for, or concern about, the economic and social costs of their arbitrary determinations.

I'd like now to call a homeowner from a middle class neighborhood in Greensboro, North Carolina: Cecil Rouson. Mr. Rouson has been working on the problem of the black and the poor for over ten years, and served for a time as a lieutenant of the late Malcolm X. He attends college by day, works at night, and serves as president of the Woodmere Park Improvement Association. Mr. Rouson, how do you think we should provide better housing for the poor?

6.2 CECIL ROUSON: First of all, we need to stop playing these little silly theoretical games about a very serious problem. To get to the crux of the problem we should go to the source. And that source is the poor themselves. It's what *they* think and what *they* want to have. And I'm sure— being a black person is so many times in this country synonymous with being poor—they would say that they want better job opportunities, better educational opportunities. And I think what James Brown described in his song points this out very beautifully: "And I don't want nobody giving me nothing. Just open up the door, and I'll get it myself."

6.3 MAHONEY: How did you get to live in [a] middle-class neighborhood?

6.4 ROUSON: I got there by working 16 hours a day for the Southern Railway in the snow; my wife working in Greenville, North Carolina, which was

250 miles away; my two children at the time 250 miles in another direction in North Carolina with my parents for a period of six months.

6.5   MAHONEY: Does your wife still work?

6.6   ROUSON: My wife is now working 26 miles from Greensboro, North Carolina at Thomasville, and I'm still working at night with Southern Railway.

6.7   MAHONEY: Have you had any experience with low-income housing in your area?

6.8   ROUSON: We have a 250-unit public housing project known as Claremont Courts in the Woodmere Park area. And we have two additional tracts which are in very close proximity to this particular area [that were] rezoned for more. We were able to rescind one. We are in Federal court now with the Department of Housing and Urban Development, with Urban Systems Development Corporation of Westinghouse Corporation and a local black church, Unity Zion Church of Greensboro.

6.9   MAHONEY: And the Federal government: what side are they on in that litigation?

6.10   ROUSON: They are for high concentration, high density of housing, in our neighborhood.

6.11   MAHONEY: Do you think you have the facilities (recreational, educational)— the capacity to absorb more low-income housing in your neighborhood?

6.12   ROUSON: It is virtually nil. We have none. We do have a community center promised, which was to be $250,000 at first. Now it's down to $80,000.

6.13   MAHONEY: Do you have a serious problem, in your judgment, of overcrowding in that neighborhood?

6.14   ROUSON: Most definitely. Urban planners have argued for years that lower density in housing and more open spaces provide fewer social problems.

6.15   MAHONEY: Would you want the Federal government to make this decision for your community?

6.16   ROUSON: No.

7.   CROSS-EXAMINATION

7.1   MILLER: Let's look at the limits of local zoning power. You think the Federal government should not intervene if there were a local zoning regulation that simply purported to exclude blacks and said no blacks could live in this community?

7.2   ROUSON: I don't know of any of that kind.

7.3   MILLER: Well, there were, many. Do you think that should be allowed?

7.4   ROUSON: I'm not concerned with what *was*. I'm concerned about what *is*.

7.5   MILLER: No, I think that's an important problem. Suppose we had a zoning, not a fancy zoning that said "So many square feet and so large a lot size," but that simply said "No blacks." Do you think the Federal government shouldn't intervene there?

7.6   ROUSON: Let me say this: if I'm invited to your home for dinner, and you and your guests are all dining at your table, but I have nothing on my plate, [then] I surely could not consider myself as a diner. . . . It's important to understand that just to put a person who is poor in a middle-class suburb or neighborhood so he's equal, is false. It's erroneous. What most black people or what most poor people are concerned about, as I said, is what's in their pockets.

7.7   PALMIERI: You've got a question facing you. I think you owe it to us to answer the question. I don't see anything unfair about it.

7.8   MILLER: If there were a zoning ordinance that flatly said "No blacks in this community," would you deny the Federal government the right to intervene there?

7.9   ROUSON: No, I wouldn't deny that.

7.10   MILLER: What about a zoning ordinance that said "No one in this community who earns less than $10,000 a year"?

7.11   ROUSON (*after long pause*):   I don't think that would be Constitutional.

7.12   MILLER: What about zoning, then, that has the *effect* of excluding blacks and those earning less than $10,000 a year because it requires [the lots and houses to be of such a size that] those people cannot live in the community? Isn't that exactly the same thing?

7.13   ROUSON: It could be subsidized.

7.14   MILLER: No no. Subsidized housing today covers people up in the $8–10,000 income bracket. We're not simply talking about the very poor. So we have a zoning ordinance. It uses different words. It doesn't say "No blacks and no one under $10,000." It says you have to have a 2,000-square-foot house on a half-acre lot, which has exactly the same effect of excluding people under $10,000.

7.15   ROUSON: O.K. I think that's putting the cart before the horse. I think that again the problem is not of housing, of who can live where. I think again it's opportunity, not only job opportunities—

7.16   MILLER: No, let's follow the question now. We have a man earning $8,000 a year. He's entitled to the Federal subsidy. He has the Federal subsidy. He has a builder who wants to build for him. And the community has an ordinance—it doesn't say "No blacks and no one earning $8,000," but it requires a size house and a size lot and other restrictions that mean he can't move there. Under what you've said, shouldn't the Federal government intervene there as well?

7.17 ROUSON: Well, I fail to see where this involves the wishes or desires of the people you're talking about.

7.18 MILLER: He wants to move there. He and a hundred other people want to move there. They have their application. They have their builder. They've been consulted. They've put up their money, their hard-earned money, in down payments. And now the zoning ordinance excludes them. Shouldn't the government intervene there, as it does in the race and the poor situation?

7.19 ROUSON: I think your question is still hypothetical. I don't know any people like that.

7.20 PALMIERI: Isn't there a real question in your own community? Aren't there a lot of poor people who want to move into those public housing tracts that are in your middle-income community?

7.21 ROUSON: I figure they don't have any real sayso about it. They are trapped in a situation where everybody, from the Federal government on down, is making decisions for them, and they've never been consulted. And this is the real problem.

8.   SECOND NEGATIVE WITNESS: DIRECT EXAMINATION

8.1 MAHONEY: I'd be delighted if we could get back on the subject. It's perfectly clear that both under Federal statutes and the Constitution, the kind of racial discrimination Mr. Miller is talking about is barred in this country. That's not the subject here tonight. Now, to look at some of the government problems that would be posed by Federal zoning power: Randy Hamilton, executive director of the Institute for Local Self-Government. Mr. Hamilton, why are you opposed to the proposal for Federal zoning power?

8.2 RANDY HAMILTON: For the basic reason that this country is a government of delegated powers in which local governments, as represented by their States in our early days—and still continuing in that fashion—have delegated to the central government certain powers. One of the powers that they have *not* delegated is the power to zone. And I'm aware of Thomas

Jefferson's very cogent comment on this subject, particularly with reference to the Federal bureaucrat: "Were we to look to Washington when to sow and when to reap, we should soon want for bread."

8.3 MAHONEY: Do communities have some inherent right to determine their own character?

8.4 HAMILTON: I think this is basic to the American way of life—that neighbor working together with neighbor, face to face, can determine the destiny and the character and the environment of their own communities.

8.5 MAHONEY: What about the individuals involved in these communities? What rights do they have, in your judgment?

8.6 HAMILTON: They have the right to conduct their community in particular, and in conjunction with their neighbors, as they see fit. I'm very aware of the fact that our decisions at the local level are made in what I call the Tuesday night fishbowls. That's when most councils meet. If you have a complaint, or if you have a suggestion, or if you have a recommendation to your local government, you go down there on Tuesday night and stand up on your hind legs and bray. Now it's very difficult to discuss these matters with the State legislature. It's impossible to discuss it with the United States Congress. And it is even worse than impossible to try to discuss it with a faceless bureaucrat in Washington.

8.7 MAHONEY: Now what kind of job would the Federal government do if it did take over in this zoning area?

8.8 HAMILTON: We don't know. That's a hypothetical question. I might answer your question on the basis of history. We now have 1,400 different categorical grant-in-aid programs to local government within the Federal system. If they were working, we wouldn't be here tonight.

8.9 MAHONEY: Did President Nixon make a comment about those programs in his State of the Union message?

8.10 HAMILTON: He certainly did. He pointed out, in his proposals for the reorganization and the revenue-sharing, that . . . these programs were not working; that the Federal bureaucracy could not govern the country; that it cannot be governed from a central place in Washington. It's too big, and it's too disparate.

8.11 MAHONEY: Could you comment on a couple of these programs: the urban renewal program, for example.

8.12 HAMILTON: The urban renewal program is one that is extremely interesting. Within the last 10 days, I was present when the mayor of a town—actually a budding city, a rather large city—congratulated an Undersecretary of the Department of Housing and Urban Development for the reason that their urban renewal program had finally been approved, 13 years after the city had submitted it.

8.13   MAHONEY: And how are they doing with the Federal housing program?

8.14   HAMILTON: Not very well.

9.   CROSS-EXAMINATION

9.1   MILLER: Whatever it is, it's the "faceless bureaucrat" who always gets hit. Let's talk about the principle of local control, Mr. Hamilton. A great many things that governments do override local control. The Federal government can place military bases any place in the United States without regard to zoning, can't it?

9.2   HAMILTON: Yes.

9.3   MILLER: And the freeways under Federal aid—very basic to the development of communities. Federally financed freeways are built through any community in the United States without regard to [local preferences].

9.4   HAMILTON: No sir, they are not. The present requirements for the location of Federal highways call for two sets of hearings: one is the engineering hearing, and the second is a socio-economic set of hearings.

9.5   MILLER: But the local zoning board can't stop it if that socio-economic hearing decides it's acceptable.

9.6   HAMILTON: Local zoning boards have nothing to do with highway locations.

9.7   MILLER: Absolutely right. That's the point: that the highway comes in without regard to the local zoning board.

9.8   HAMILTON: But it *doesn't* come in without regard to the local community's wishes vis-à-vis the highway.

9.9   PALMIERI: Let's move this down—you'll pardon me—the road.

9.10   MILLER: I was thinking of going into the air. Let's talk about air pollution control. Local communities do not have the power to allow their industries to put forth into the air any material they wish, not subject to State or Federal air pollution control regulations, do they?

9.11   HAMILTON: No sir.

9.12   MILLER: They do not. Now, if a local community cannot force air congestion on a neighboring community and the Federal government can step in and say "No air congestion," what right does it have to force "people congestion" on another community by keeping out people who want to live there?

9.13   HAMILTON: That's an assertion, not a question; because it doesn't force congestion on a community. And I've noted [that] in your comments and questions so far, you consistently refer to the vast amount of land available in the suburbs. Mr. Davidoff teaches from textbooks which indicate that well over 40 percent of the land *inside the central cities* is buildable. Let's talk about *that* land.

9.14   MILLER: Let's talk about the land that's being *excluded*, because the land can be bought at a price. You know very well that land in the central cities is so expensive that housing cannot be built on it, because of the cost in the central cities.

9.15   HAMILTON: I don't know that, sir. Sorry.

9.16   MILLER: Well, it is true in the same textbook that Mr. Davidoff taught out of.

9.17   HAMILTON: It is not true.

9.18   MILLER: You have to read the whole textbook. [*Laughter.*] The land for housing is the land in the suburbs. Now there are all sorts of cases where the local zoning authorities—

9.19   HAMILTON: No; I beg your pardon. The land for housing which is buildable, and which has a lower cost, is land for which the infrastructure is present: the streets, the drainage, the sanitation, the sidewalks.

9.20   MILLER: That's true in suburbs. That's true far out from the city in suburbs, isn't it?

9.21   HAMILTON: You said "far out from the city." I haven't seen very many street lights far out from the city.

9.22   MILLER: In suburbs? You don't know suburbs that have street lights?

9.23   HAMILTON: But you said *"far* out from the city."

9.24   MILLER: We *do* have to move further down the road. Let me ask you: we have all sorts of restrictions on local control. . . . We have restrictions on racial discrimination. We have restrictions on flat-out economic discrimination. We have restrictions on where freeways can go. We have restrictions on air pollution.

9.25   HAMILTON: You're back to freeways. We said that that was not so.

9.26   PALMIERI: No! That's all we're going to do with freeways.

9.27   MILLER: If the net effect of these zoning regulations is to do what is otherwise proscribed by law—now let me put to you the same question I put to Mr. Rouson—if the net effect is to exclude poor and moderate-income people, to exclude blacks, then isn't that exactly the same as suburbs flatly saying keep out?

9.28   HAMILTON: How many communities practice what you call restrictive zoning? You say "most" and "many." There are 21,000 incorporated municipalities in this country. How many have the kind of zoning you're talking about?

9.29   MILLER: Well, many more than one. Almost all have zoning that limits the character of housing to the kind that's there.

9.30   PALMIERI: In terms of principle, if *one* did, what would be your answer?

9.31   HAMILTON: If one did, then my answer would be that that would be wrong.

9.32   MILLER: And if *many* do, then it's wrong for many as well.

9.33   HAMILTON: Yes.

10.   THIRD NEGATIVE WITNESS: DIRECT EXAMINATION

10.1   MAHONEY: The question, of course, is *not* what's right and wrong, but what the Federal government has a right to compel. We ought to stay on that subject. [Our next witness will] present a practical approach to the housing problem, which respects the rights of local communities. Professor Edgar Olsen [is] an economist at the University of Virginia, formerly with the Rand Corporation and [specializing] in housing. Mr. Olsen, as you see it, what is the housing problem in America today?

10.2   PROF. EDGAR OLSEN: The problem is that there are many poor people who live in terrible housing. And the reason for this problem is that these people earn very little money and, therefore, are not able to spend very much on housing.

10.3   MAHONEY: As you see it, what is the solution to that problem?

10.4   OLSEN: In the long run the only solution that will be acceptable to both the taxpayer and the poor people is something which results in increased earnings for people: increases in productivity and greater job opportunities. But we have these people living in poor housing *now*, and we want to do something about it *now*. And for that, for the short-run solution, I think the best way to do it is through *housing vouchers* which would operate very much like food stamps. The way we would go about conducting such a program is, first, to decide who it is we want to help; second, to decide how good we want the housing that they occupy to be; then go out and look in the community and find out how much it costs to rent such housing; and then give them a housing voucher that has a face value equal to that amount, that would allow them to purchase this housing on the private market; and charge them an amount approximately equal to what they presently pay for housing, so that they wouldn't have to cut back their consumption of non-housing goods in order to consume better housing.

10.5   MAHONEY: Is this solution consistent with present suburban zoning patterns?

10.6   OLSEN: I certainly consider it to be, because if you had such a scheme, most of the people who had the vouchers would look around in their immediate neighborhood for some housing that is vacant and is better than the housing that they occupy, and which could be purchased for the amount of the housing voucher. Some other poor people with the vouchers would probably want to move into the suburbs. And I think—contrary to popular opinion—it is *not* the case that all suburbs are upper-income housing. There is lower-middle-income housing in the suburbs, and a great amount of it. And these people could simply take their vouchers and move out to these lower-middle-income neighborhoods in the suburbs.

10.7   MAHONEY: How about the proposal for Federal zoning power that we're considering tonight?

10.8   OLSEN: I don't see how that would contribute at all to better housing for poor people. It would make available a few more areas to poor people. [But] it contributes nothing in the way of adding more money to allow these people to get into these areas.

10.9   MAHONEY: And do the suburbs presently have areas now into which these people could move?

10.10   OLSEN: Yes. There *are* lower-middle-income suburbs, and people with housing vouchers would be able to pay as much as people living in these suburbs and, therefore, would be able to move there.

11.   CROSS-EXAMINATION

11.1   PALMIERI: [I hope we'll hear about] whether the effect of vouchers wouldn't be to raise prices and rents unless you had a way of bringing in more units.

11.2   MILLER: I had hoped to [get into that subject]. But my initial reaction to the testimony is [astonishment], in view of Mr. Mahoney's views of Federal bureaucrats and Federal programs. How much will this voucher system cost?

11.3   OLSEN: It can cost any amount that Congress decides it wants to pay.

11.4   MILLER: "Any amount." Billions?

11.5   OLSEN: It could.

11.6   MILLER: And how many "faceless bureaucrats" will we need to decide—

11.7   OLSEN: Very few, because there are no arbitrary requirements. The bureaucrats do not have to decide, for instance, where people will live. All they have to decide is: is the person eligible? If you are, you pay the money, take the voucher, and that's it.

11.8   MILLER: Just like in the welfare program. That's all they decide in the welfare program.

11.9   OLSEN: Just like in the *food stamp* program.

11.10   MILLER: So your opinion is that this program, which could cost up to any amount that Congress would appropriate, and would be very easy to administer, would not involve the problem of Federal bureaucrats intervening with people's lives.

11.11   OLSEN: Much less so than all existing housing programs. And certainly far less so than the welfare program.

11.12   MILLER: But what about a zoning law that would simply say that all suburbs have got to accept X percentage in its unit starts of low- and moderate-income families? Do you think *that* involves more for the bureaucrats than having to decide what housing each person needs, and what voucher he should get, and where it should be spent?

11.13   OLSEN: I don't see where that contributes anything to the ability of people to occupy good housing.

11.14   MILLER: And neither does it answer the question. Now let's talk about the question that was raised. Let's start someplace else. Instead of giving people vouchers and food stamps, why not simply give them money in a guaranteed minimum income?

11.15   OLSEN: I personally *do* favor that. That's what I would vote for. I think the reason why it is not good social policy to do that, [however, is that] many people who are willing to help the poor people don't think poor people know what's good for them.

11.16   MILLER: And so you tell them what's good for them.

11.17   OLSEN: Well, you are willing to help them.

11.18   MILLER: I wish we had Mr. Rouson back for comment on that.

11.19   OLSEN: Food stamps help them. Housing vouchers help them, conditional on certain restrictions as to how they spend them. I vote the other way.

11.20   MILLER: . . . once the vouchers are given for $50 or $60 a month, what is to stop the person who owns the apartment house, or who is selling the house on monthly payments from saying "You own a voucher worth $50 a month; therefore, the price is going up?"

11 . 21   OLSEN: You go [to] another vacant apartment where the price is $50 and it's better housing, because there are alternatives. You don't have to rent from this one guy.

11 . 22   MILLER: No; you're putting more money into the market, so prices are going to go up, aren't they? You're increasing demand.

11 . 23   OLSEN: In the short run, prices do go up any time with increased demand.

11 . 24   MILLER: What is the "short run" here? Five years, ten years?

11 . 25   OLSEN: No. We know about what the short run is in housing. You get a very quick adjustment within one year.

11 . 26   MILLER: Now you talked about people moving out, with this plan of vouchers, to lower-middle-class suburbs. In fact, they are suburbs largely composed of people in that income group, isn't that right? That's not an economic integration of suburbs.

11 . 27   OLSEN: Repeat the question.

11 . 28   MILLER: Well, let's go at it from this way. There are not people moving into the suburbs that are excluding them. With that voucher worth $50 a month, enough to pay for the housing that the Federal government and its "few" bureaucrats decide is necessary, that person could not move into a suburb that charged more than he would have.

11 . 29   OLSEN: That's right. He could not move into [just] any neighborhood.

11 . 30   MILLER: That's right. So that those suburbs that now exclude him, by requiring a maximum square footage or a maximum lot size, in effect could still exclude him.

11 . 31   OLSEN: Certainly.

11 . 32   MILLER: And what is the value of continuing to allow them to exclude him?

11 . 33   OLSEN: Since there are many other alternatives, it doesn't seem to me that that makes a great deal of difference. There are some areas that exclude. There are many areas that I can't live in because I don't have enough money. But I don't think that that greatly restricts my choice, does it?

11 . 34   MILLER: But you don't qualify for any of these programs. [Let's talk] about the cost of the housing. Isn't the effect of many suburbs keeping land off the market to raise the cost of other land by restricting supply? That in effect raises the cost of other land that's built on, doesn't it?

11 . 35   OLSEN: No.

11 . 36   MILLER: *No?* You were introduced as a professor of economics. Now, you restrict the supply of land. Doesn't that raise the cost of land?

11.37   OLSEN: There is a lot of land around cities.

11.38   MILLER: Enough so that restricting the supply doesn't affect the price at all?

11.39   OLSEN: Yes, but you're restricting supply [while] at the same time people, demanders, are going into this land. It's not that you're keeping this land entirely off the market.

11.40   MILLER: And at worse, it's a "short-term problem."

11.41   OLSEN: Right.

11.42   MAHONEY (*in summation*):   I submit that the case for Federal zoning power stands discredited. It won't do the job that needs so badly to be done. The way to do that job is with housing vouchers for the poor. If the proposal for Federal zoning power were merely useless, that would be bad enough. But Federal zoning power would be worse than useless. It would be chaotic to substitute Federal bureaucrats for local officials to make zoning decisions all over America. This proposal at least has the merit of candor. Its proponents think that the American people are either too dumb or too selfish, or both, to meet the challenge of equal opportunity in housing. These social planners have constructed a stereotype America —all the rich in the suburbs, all the poor in the cities—that really bears no relation to the complex reality around us. And now they want to revolutionize our government process, and emasculate our tradition of local self-government, to dismantle a stereotype that exists only in their own minds. That proposal deserves exactly the same contempt they so obviously have for their fellow citizens.

12.   THIRD AFFIRMATIVE WITNESS: DIRECT EXAMINATION

12.1   MILLER: It's really surprising to hear the voucher system put forth because, regardless of what was said, what we're talking about in that kind of system is another welfare bureaucracy to administer what voucher each person would get; with the increasing short-term problems of simply accomplishing nothing, because the price goes up and you're still left with the problems of suburbs that exclude people. Now let's look at that problem of suburbs that exclude people—a very tough problem, when you see what's happening. We can't exclude people because of race. Witnesses agree to that. We can't exclude them by simply saying, "You can't come in if you're poor." But communities are very sophisticated. They don't say, "You can't come in because you're black; you can't come in because you're poor." They simply say, "You can only come in if you can build a 3,000-square-foot house," despite the fact that there are builders available to build for you a 1,000-square-foot house that's perfectly appropriate to you in your economic situation. It has exactly the same effect as saying "You can't come in because you're black; you can't come in because you're poor; you can't come in because you're old; you can't come in because you don't have enough money; you can't come in because we don't like you."—all the things we don't allow [to be said] openly are said through these zoning ordinances. And that's why the government must intervene.

To talk again to why they must, we have with us Herbert Franklin, [who is] director of the National Urban Growth Program for the National Urban Coalition. Mr. Franklin, who are hurt by these exclusionary suburban zoning practices?

12.2   HERBERT FRANKLIN: Since the civil rights laws apply to subsidized housing, of course a lot of people assume that subsidized housing means housing for blacks. But in reality, white people are the majority of the beneficiaries of such housing. Elderly people, people who are on limited incomes, teachers, postal workers, farming [people]—the people who serve our suburban areas, as a matter of fact—[are the principal beneficiaries].

12.3   MILLER: What about those people now who want to move into these communities? Do they have any voice, under our existing system, in whether they can move in or not?

12.4   FRANKLIN: Actually their rights are determined in a form in which they have no representation at all. When the decision is made they are not present. And it seems to me a perversion of talk about "home rule" to assume that a suburb or a local government is something like a fraternity or clubhouse that can make decisions that, well, they don't want people.

12.5   MILLER: This Federal intervention simply requiring some low- and moderate-income housing to be built in suburbs: does that deny home rule?

12.6   FRANKLIN: Not at all. I think the phrase that Mr. Mahoney uses about a Federal zoning power is much too broad to describe what's being proposed. We're talking only about the prevention of discrimination against specific projects that have a Federal subsidy. It has nothing to do with *other* powers of the locality to control the pace and course of development.

12.7   MILLER: What about an increase in cost to the suburb, though? Would opening them up to these kinds of families increase costs?

12.8   FRANKLIN: Costs are increased by people with children generally. There is very little evidence that a moderate-income family with two children is going to bring more of a tax burden than people who are already there that have children to be educated.

12.9   MILLER: What about the costs of doing nothing, though—of simply leaving the exclusionary zoning practices?

12.10   FRANKLIN: The costs of doing nothing are enormous. The rot of our cities through congestion is certainly a cost that society generally has to bear.

13.   CROSS-EXAMINATION

13.1   PALMIERI: Let's take the case . . . where they have no desire to discriminate against anybody on account of race or social class; they simply have a community with big, rolling, green lawns, and they love 'em and they want to keep it that way. That's the case that I think perplexes people when you talk about moving in what they think of as a "project."

13.2   FRANKLIN: The answer has to lie in some kind of planning process that looks to what a metropolitan area should be. And it may be that a community of that sort has to have some equitable portion of growth that's going to take place in a metropolitan area. I believe that, if the Federal government made a new requirement for metropolitan planning processes, [then] localities would get together (just as they've done in Dayton, Ohio, for example) and apportion the share of urban growth in that whole region, pursuant to locally determined formulas.

13.3   MAHONEY: Suppose they don't want to get together. Suppose (as in Lexington) they have different views about the matter. Then somebody's going to come in and tell them what to do, right?

13.4   FRANKLIN: Somebody will tell them that they have to work affirmatively on the process. It doesn't mean that some bureaucrat—

13.5   MAHONEY: How does this work on a case by case basis? Mr. Miller says it's very simple: if you don't have a certain percentage, then you have to let somebody in. Mr. Davidoff says it's a rather complex process involving planning for a whole region and so forth and so on. Do you agree with Mr. Miller or Mr. Davidoff?

13.6   FRANKLIN: The formula would involve a determination locally as to how many units are an equitable portion for each particular locality in a metropolitan area. That may vary from metropolitan area to metropolitan area. I think there has to be a great deal of flexibility in terms of how you do it.

13.7   MAHONEY: But somebody's got to decide all this "flexibility," and that's going to be Washington.

13.8   FRANKLIN: Yes.

13.9   MAHONEY: We had a program on "The Advocates" [concerning] the volunteer Army. It seems people are for a volunteer Army these days; but *you're* for a *draft* program, to draft homeowners into a new kind of situation whether they like it or not. Isn't that right?

13.10   FRANKLIN: No; I'm for a program that would overcome the effects of coerced confinement of people of the central city.

13.11   MAHONEY: Do you know these people want to get out?

13.12   FRANKLIN: Some do, some don't.

13.13   MAHONEY: But your program is: you'll draft them, too.

13.14   FRANKLIN: No; I'm in favor of giving them a choice. Don't you believe in free choice?

13.15   MAHONEY: I believe in free choice, but there's a question involved here about who's going to make the choice. You think Washington can make these decisions better?

13.16   FRANKLIN: Washington would not make the individual decision. Washington would make the decision as to whether a decent planning process had been instituted—

13.17   MAHONEY: Oh, now wait a minute. Who would make the decision when somebody comes in there and asks for a housing development and they say "No"? Who does he go to?

13.18   FRANKLIN: He could go through your local planning processes. There may be legitimate planning objections to the project.

13.19   MAHONEY: But who has the say about this?

13.20   FRANKLIN: The final say would rest with somebody who could be appealed to if there was an allegation that there was discrimination against this project solely because of the income or race of the occupants.

13.21   MAHONEY: So you go to the local zoning board, and the zoning board says "No." Then you go to somebody in Washington and you appeal for a variance from a local zoning ordinance to Washington.

13.22   FRANKLIN: You don't have to go to Washington. You could set up regionally. Under [Olsen's plan], who would make the decision as to whether the housing in which the voucher was used was standard?

13.23   MAHONEY: They'd just go out and get what they could get in the market with the housing. Nobody trails into Bohack's [grocery] with somebody with food stamps to see what he buys with them. They go in there and they buy. They can go into the housing market and buy.

13.24   FRANKLIN: If I were some landlord, I'd get ten people with vouchers in space equivalent for five.

13.25   PALMIERI: You've both talked about freedom of choice. Mr. Mahoney's made quite a point of freedom of choice. Is he not talking also about the free right of communities to choose the character of their community?

13.26   FRANKLIN: I don't believe that the founders of the Republic designed our institutions of self-government for the purpose of permitting people to say others can't come in. If local self-government has such a high value, I think everyone should have a right to participate in it.

13.27   MAHONEY: If the founders of the Republic could have heard the testimony here tonight, they'd have carried you off in a basket. [*Laughter.*] Mr. Franklin, one last question: Don't you think we ought to try the new approaches in public housing first—all these new ideas—and then see what the suburban zoning pattern is, rather than jump into this revolutionary alteration of the zoning practices of the country?

13.28   FRANKLIN: They are being tried. And they've been frustrated.

13.29   MAHONEY: They're in a very, very nascent stage, aren't they? They just got off the ground.

13.30   FRANKLIN: Well, if you say two years is a nascent stage: yes.

13.31   MAHONEY: Two years of hardly any money appropriated.

14.   CLOSING STATEMENTS

14.1   MILLER: The new housing programs are far enough off the ground so that between 25 percent and a third of all housing this year will be Federally subsidized housing. I think it's time to say, and say clearly, that it is not an answer to any problem that we have—to simply say: "You can't do that because someone in Washington has to decide it." That is not an objection to doing things. We have here a real problem: the problem of land kept out of use. We have here false fears, fears that the wrong people will move in, fears that costs will be too high. This proposal spreads them equally. We are talking about national and human needs. We are talking about providing for every American a decent home and a decent life.

14.2   MAHONEY: The case for Federal zoning power springs from decent, if misguided, motives, for which I give full credit to Advocate Miller and the witnesses he has presented here tonight. But unfortunately, that case simply falls apart under careful analysis. You have heard practical, level-headed people demonstrate how to meet the housing needs of the poor. The way to meet the housing needs of the poor is with housing vouchers, not with some grandiose scheme based on a stereotyped view of America that is out of touch with the reality around us. In short, this dangerous proposal is the product of impatient, hasty, slipshod thinking. We do need to meet the housing needs of the poor. But we don't need the Federal Government as an absentee landlord for the suburbs of America.

 *June 1, 1971*

POSTSCRIPT

In September 1972 the Banking and Currency Committee of the House of Representatives approved a major new housing bill, providing large-scale Federal grants to support city housing but also providing restrictions against Federal authority to impose low-income housing on suburbs. According to Peter Braestrup of the *Washington Post* (15 Sept. 1972, p. A1), the $10.6 billion omnibus measure included $5.5 billion in block grants, a variant on special revenue-sharing. Local authorities could choose their own mixture of grants for urban renewal, housing rehabilitation loans, neighborhood service facilities and supportive social services. However, local governments could veto Federally subsidized low-income housing projects involving more than eight units, and were otherwise empowered to forestall low-income housing projects in locations they opposed. George Romney, Secretary of the Department of Housing and Urban Development, opposed these restrictions. The fate of this bill, at the time of writing, was in doubt.

COMMENTARY

Obfuscation: The Terms of Proposals

Among the remarkable things about the foregoing debate, in my judgment, is lack of clarity about the immediate issue. Neither the moderator nor any of the other participants in the debate specified the terms of the proposal under debate. The proposal at issue was said to be whether the

Federal government should "compel suburbs to accept low-income housing." But what sort of compulsion would be exerted, through what channels, in what degree, on behalf of what kind(s) and amount(s) of "low-income housing"? We need answers to this compound question before we can begin to argue reasonably about pros and cons. Answers were not furnished.

Howard Miller shed scarcely any light on the subject when he 'specifically' advocated "a national law to require that every suburb accept a minimum amount, and its fair share, of low- and moderate-income housing. . . ." (Paragraph **1**.3, with further clauses alluding to intended results, not to the terms of a law). What is a "fair share"? Paul Davidoff did not answer this question when he alluded (**3**.5) to the formation of a "comprehensive plan" for each "metropolitan region," in which "each of the communities is given its fair share." Apparently he did *not* mean to define a "fair share" as an "equal" portion of poor families relative to the proportion of the latter in the region as a whole. In other words, he apparently did not mean to suggest that in each region where poor families constitute 20 percent of the population, for example, each community must devote 20 percent of its housing to the poor. He eliminated *that* possibility when he alluded vaguely (**3**.7) to calculations of "fair shares" based in part on the amount of local industry, and hence the property tax base, in each community, as well as (**3**.11) proximity to highways leading *to* places where jobs abound.

Later, however, Herbert Franklin supplied a radically different version of the terms of the proposal under debate. He equated the proposal with a blanket exemption of Federally assisted housing projects from local zoning ordinances (**12**.6). In other words, locally determined zoning codes would govern "private" construction but would not cover the location or design of housing constructed with the aid of government subsidies—that is to say, 25 to 33 percent of current housing, according to Miller's estimate (**1**.3). *This* version of the terms of the proposal also is consistent with Miller's reference (**9**.1) to the precedent of Federal immunity from "home rule" in the placement of military bases.

If *this* kind of law were enacted, then Federal administrators *could* place all subsidized housing, and hence most of the low-income and middle-income families, in whatever localities they chose, regardless of proportions (or "fair shares"). Presumably they would not do so, but apparently they *could* do so, and to this extent there is scant reason to believe that the terms of the proposed policy conform to the most elemental, straightforward 'description' of the policy furnished by Miller and Davidoff.

Obscurity in the terms of the immediate issue distinguishes this debate from most of the others in this volume. In many other cases, the title of the debate is uninformative, but at the earliest point the terms of what is being proposed and opposed are spelled out.

Making Counter-Proposals

A portion of the Commentary on the debate concerning the Congressional "seniority system" dealt with conventions about burdens of proof. One of the points made there was that the advocate of innovation normally is expected to shoulder the *primary* burden of proof. The advocate of innovation must try to establish the existence of a need for change and then show that a given measure would effect the desired change. His opponent is not obliged to devise some alternative solution. It is sufficient, conventionally, for him to cite weaknesses in his adversary's diagnosis or prescription. But it is quite legitimate, and it is not uncommon, for him to adopt a 'positive' stance in which he agrees that a change is needed and then goes on to specify what allegedly is a different and superior remedy.

This 'positive' technique of counter-argument was employed rather effectively by the Negative side in the debate on housing and home rule. Advocate Daniel Mahoney, together with one of his witnesses, Prof. Edgar Olsen, proposed that poor families be entitled to receive Federal vouchers, much like food stamps, that could be used to supplement their outlays on housing (1.5, 10.1ff). Such a scheme might be quite unworkable or ineffective, in the final analysis. Its introduction can, nevertheless, prove to be quite an effective argumentational device.

Formulating a counter-proposal is apt to be an effective argumentational device chiefly because it enables an otherwise 'negative' advocate to make generous concessions on the subject of need for change. No longer is it necessary to argue that some alleged need, acute as it is, must be left unrelieved for the sake of meeting other needs. No longer is the 'conservative' advocate imperiled by the chance that his opponent, merely by painting a vivid picture of misery under present conditions, will convince his listeners that he also has devised the optimal solution.

Mahoney's bold counter-proposal threw Howard Miller off balance

(**11.1ff, 12.1**). To use the political vernacular of the day, Miller found himself being assailed from the Left rather than from the Right. Moreover, Miller was impelled to acknowledge—more openly, perhaps, than he would otherwise have done—his concern not only for improving the housing conditions of low-income families, but also for achieving racial and economic integration (**11.26, 12.1**).

The Pathetic Fallacy

In *Historians' Fallacies* David Hackett Fischer names eight "fallacies of motivation," of which one is the "pathetic fallacy." This mode of thought consists of ascribing human form and feelings to gods, to objects, or to groups, and then ascribing events to the operative intentions of these objects. The pathetic fallacy is thus one manifestation of the practice known as anthropomorphism.

Verbiage of this kind can serve a variety of purposes. One such purpose is illustrated in the debate on housing and home rule. Howard Miller employed the pathetic fallacy when he talked about the causes of inadequate and segregated housing. According to Miller, it is "the suburbs" that "arbitrarily exclude" (**1.2**); it is "the suburbs" that are zoning "available" land "out of use" and are engaging in restrictive practices (**1.3**); a national law is needed to impose certain rules on "every suburb" (**1.3**).

Such language, in which localities were endowed with human form, served in the context of this debate to *depersonalize* an issue. In ascribing wicked actions and wishes to "suburbs," Miller invited his listeners to feel free of wicked actions and wishes. Similarly, Miller's language enabled suburban*ites* to feel that they are *not* under attack for their motives and their actions, but that some impersonal entity, rather than certain individuals, would be subject to Federal compulsion under the proposal he advocated. If Miller acknowledged that he was really talking about "people who live in the suburbs"—about suburbanites who enact zoning laws—he might have incurred a loss of persuasive appeal.

Resort to the pathetic fallacy, incidentally, was not the only way in which the Affirmative side sought to relieve suburbanites of a sense of guilt, and hence of defensive posture. Another method of achieving this end consisted of picturing suburbanites less as conscious, self-interested contributors to segregation and poverty than as victims of wrong-headed manipulators. To this end, Paul Davidoff indulged in a bit of name-call-ing: he ascribed present zoning practices in the suburbs as the diabolical work of "suburban extremists" and "Ivy League socialists" (**2**.8).

Ambiguity and Equivocation

Some words are commonly used to denote a variety of things. Such words are *ambiguous*. When speakers used a given word so as to endow it with more than one meaning, they indulge in ambiguity. And when speakers build arguments around the ambiguous use of terms, so as to blur distinctions, they engage in what is known as *equivocation*.*

An example of the latter practice was furnished in the current debate. It revolved around the ambiguity of the term "involved." Howard Miller elicited from Paul Davidoff the affirmation that "the Federal government [is] *involved* now in housing" (**2**.1ff). Davidoff went on to specify that the Federal government has long engaged in providing subsidies for building residential units for low-income families. However, Miller's question to Davidoff, in the context, dealt also with Federal "involvement" in decid-ing *where* low-income housing shall be built. The latter kind of involve-ment would in fact mark a new departure in public policy. Indeed, from other passages in the debate we learn that the Federal government's efforts to house low-income families allegedly have been hampered by the authority of municipal councils to decide whether to accept low-income housing projects. Thus, it is evident that Miller and Davidoff were advocating quite a new kind of Federal "involvement" in housing and in local decision-making. But their emphasis on previous Federal "involvement" in housing served to soften the impression that they were

---

*The label "equivocal" often is used to characterize language that is elusive or question-begging. This usage is quite distinct from what textbooks on logic depict as *equivocation*, or equating things that either are not the same or have yet to be shown to be the same. When a speaker explicitly *declares* that two things essentially are the same, despite certain appearances, he is *not* engaging in equivocation. He would be doing so only if he prema-turely, or arbitrarily, operated as if his claim about identity were established. Thus, Daniel Mahoney did not engage in equivocation when he suggested (**13**.9, **13**.13) that the Affirma-tive side's proposal would, in effect, "draft homeowners into a new kind of situation. . . ." This claim amounted to drawing an analogy between a policy concerning authority over residential zoning and a policy concerning military recruitment (namely, voluntary enlist-ment vs. recruitment). The analogy is rather farfetched. Herbert Franklin invoked a similar analogy when he equated the present housing system (**13**.10) with "coerced confinement of people to the central city."

calling for a markedly new Federal authority vis-à-vis local communities. They employed equivocation so as to mask the novelty of their proposal.*

Possibly a second example of equivocation in the debate on housing and home rule arose in Part 7, where Howard Miller pressed Cecil Rouson to 'acknowledge' the practical identity of apparently dissimilar rules. Miller suggested that restrictive zoning laws, requiring large lots and large square footage for dwellings, have the *effect* of prohibiting poor people from communities, and this prohibition in turn has the *effect* of barring Negro families. Miller thus suggested that to all intents and purposes, defense of home rule with respect to residential zoning is *equivalent* to defending outright racial segregation. And since the Federal government has the authority and obligation to intervene against racial segregation, Miller went on to suggest (**9.27ff**) then the Federal government must have the authority and obligation to intervene against restrictive zoning.

This line of reasoning was adroitly selected, since it was addressed to a Negro witness who had been active in the civil rights movement and yet appeared as a witness opposed to Federal intervention in the field of housing. Rouson could have responded by denying Miller's version of equivalents. He could have observed that in point of fact 'restrictive' zoning discriminates impartially against poor non-whites *and* poor whites, and thus is *not* identical to outright racial covenants on housing. Rouson chose a different tack.

---

*Another device for relieving proposals from the curse of novelty was discussed earlier, in the Commentary dealing with analogies and precedents following the debate on electoral campaign subsidies. See the sub-section entitled "The 'Parallel' Case of 'Election Subsidies'." Incidentally, in the debate on housing and home rule, Miller *et al.* sought to relieve their proposal of the curse of novelty also by citing a precedent. They called attention to the fact that the Federal government now has the authority to over-ride local governments with respect to the location of military bases (**9.1**). This in a sense yields a precedent for Federal pre-emption with respect to housing projects. But of course it does not bear on the merits of such a measure.

Should your state adopt a pre-trial preventive detention law?

OVERVIEW

Under American law, a person who has been formally charged with committing a non-"capital" crime is entitled to release from jail, until the conclusion of his trial, if he posts a cash deposit ("bail") in the amount set by a judge. Moreover, the Eighth Amendment to the Constitution prohibits "excessive" bail. From 1789 until quite recently, judges were formally obliged to set amounts of bail solely on the basis of estimated chance that the accused person would escape before coming to trial. Thus, judges were not formally entitled to take direct cognizance of the financial resources of various defendants, or to base their decisions on estimates of the risk that defendants would commit crimes while awaiting trial for previous crimes.

This arrangement is almost unique in the modern world, and it no longer applies fully in the United States. The Bail Reform Act of 1966 entitles Federal judges to ponder the financial resources of defendants when deciding amounts of bail. Moreover, a Federal law which went into effect in February 1971 authorized District of Columbia judges to order "preventive detention"—that is, refuse to grant bail for persons deemed likely (after prescribed findings and procedures) to commit crimes while awaiting trial.

167

The rate of crime emanating from "bailees" has shown a marked increase in recent years. Several factors help to explain this change. For one thing, the time interval between charge and verdict has lengthened, what with a greater incidence of crime, fewer guilty pleas, more appeals, and more cumbersome procedures. For another thing, the range of "capital" offenses, or cases in which a judge can refuse to grant bail, has been scaled down since 1789. In addition, the 1966 Bail Reform Act has made it easier for accused persons to make bail.

This trend, at any rate, has prompted demands for the extension of "preventive detention" laws among the States. But there are serious counter-arguments, as the following debate indicates.

1.   OPENING STATEMENTS

1.1   ADVOCATE WILLIAM RUSHER: Every year there are five million serious crimes committed in this country—the great majority of them by chronic "repeaters"—men who rob, rape, and steal again and again, often while out on bail awaiting trial. Why shouldn't such men be detained pending trial, for the protection of innocent people?

1.2   In every country on earth but three (of which we are one, and Liberia and the Philippines are the other two) such repeaters *can* be detained without bail until they are tried for the earlier crime. . . . What we are proposing tonight, and all we're proposing, is merely that each State should give its citizens similar protection.

1.3   ADVOCATE HOWARD MILLER: Tonight's proposal is really the "Injustice and Crime Creation Act of 1971." For the first time, it would allow a government official, a judge, to send a man to jail on the basis of rumor or hearsay—not for a crime he *has* committed, but for a crime he *might* commit. Lawless imprisonment will send innocent men to jail, will create far more crime and misery than it can possibly prevent, and is not the way to solve the crime problem.

1.4   There are many kinds of crime. Sending an innocent man to jail is a crime. Sending a man to jail without due process of law is a crime. Allowing arrests and preventive detention, and increasing pressure on all defendants in the system to plead guilty, is a crime. And above all, it is a crime to mislead people about what the true "crime problem" is—[to mislead] with the kind of proposal that can do nothing about it, and only cause real harm. There is no way, under this proposal, to guarantee that there will not be more innocent people sent to jail than guilty—many more innocent.

2.   FIRST AFFIRMATIVE WITNESS: DIRECT EXAMINATION

2.1   RUSHER: Is ["preventive detention"] unfair or unnecessary? Let's ask a distinguished judge of the Superior Court of the District of Columbia: the Honorable Tim Murphy. Judge Murphy, I will first ask you to consider with me three actual crimes that were committed while the accused was out on bail, charged with a similar crime.

2.2   In August 1967, Thomas Janes of Milwaukee was charged with the forcible rape of a 17-year-old girl. He was freed on $25,000 bail. Two months later, Randall Scudder and his date were returning from a school dance. [According to Scudder, "a man approached my car, acting like a police officer. He wanted to look in the back seat. Upon entering the back seat, he held a knife at my girl's throat, and told me to drive and nothing would happen. While we were driving, I asked him what he wanted. He said he didn't know whether he was going to take the car or rape the girl, because people said that he was nuts. So, as I was driving, we got out into the country. I slowed the car down and tried to push the girl out. The man and I fought and I was stabbed a couple of times, and then he ran away."] Later that night the police arrested Thomas Janes. He was charged with the abduction, and convicted. He was also convicted of the August rape for which he was out on bail. He's now serving 20 years.

2.3   Or perhaps, Judge Murphy, you remember a case in Washington last summer, involving Franklin Moyler. On June 1, Moyler was charged with robbery and carrying a dangerous weapon. He was freed on $2,000 bail. On June 18, two men held up the B & G liquor store in Washington. Mrs. Adele Gotkin, the owner, pursued them, and gave Police Officer Ronald Watson the number of their Volkswagen. When Officer Watson stopped the car, and reached for the keys, he was shot twice, and the men fled. Leaning against the car, Officer Watson fired six shots, and killed one of the men. The dead man was Franklin Moyler, the man out on bail for a similar holdup just a few days before. Heroin was found in his pockets.

2.4   And finally, there's the case of Croce Centofanti, a Boston thug who had been in and out of prison since 1928, and once had staged a gun battle with 50 policemen. In October last year [1970], he was arrested for possession of a firearm and tools for burglary. He was freed on $10,000 bail. Just last month, two men robbed a bank in the Boston suburb of Medford, and in the gun battle that followed, Croce Centofanti was killed. Now, Judge Murphy, I ask you if cases of the type I have just described to you are uncommon, in your experience.

2.5   JUDGE TIM MURPHY: No, they're not uncommon. We see them with some degree of frequency, particularly where they involve a narcotics addict.

2.6   RUSHER: Would preventive-detention legislation, on a nation-wide basis, help to prevent crimes by such repeaters?

2.7   MURPHY: Yes; I believe so very much. I want to make it quite clear [that] I believe *most* people should be released, without monetary conditions. And I believe very strongly in speedy trials. But there's a select group of people that must be detained, in the public interest. And such a law is desirable.

2.8   RUSHER: What about the contention that it's hard to predict whether or not a man will be a repeater? Is it hard, or impossible, or what?

2.9   MURPHY: It's terribly difficult. But many of the things that a judge does are terribly difficult. It's terribly difficult to determine whether a man is guilty or innocent, to determine probable cause, to determine whether a person is or is not insane. Difficult decisions are faced by judges every day. But the fact that they're difficult doesn't mean that you [don't] face them. And you decide them as best you can.

2.10   RUSHER: What considerations do you take into account in determining the likelihood of a man being a repeater?

2.11   MURPHY: The past conduct is of particular significance: the present circumstances of the offense; the nature of the offense itself; his community ties; and particularly whether he has a drug problem. If he's a drug addict, you can almost be sure, to a moral certainty, that he will commit crime if released.

3.   CROSS-EXAMINATION

3.1   MILLER: The first case we saw—about Thomas Janes, the man who repeated rape—raises the question of what *percentage* of men who are convicted for rape in fact *do* repeat, and are again arrested for rape. What is the recidivism rate for that crime?

3.2   MURPHY: I do not have that statistic on rape specifically at hand.

3.3   MILLER: And what percentage chance do you think you have of being right with a person before you, as to whether he'll repeat a given crime? [Do] you think you can better 50 percent?

3.4   MURPHY: I would say that I could reasonably anticipate 90 or more percent.

3.5   MILLER: A 90 percent success rate, of predicting whether a person before you will repeat—will repeat within 60 days, which is the period of preventive detention?

3.6   MURPHY: That's correct.

3.7   MILLER: In the Court of General Jurisdiction of the District of Columbia— your district—there are two judges that have somewhat different percentages of release. Judge Halleck, for example, detains 51 percent of those people who come before him for bail. Judge Alexander only holds 20 percent. Why is it, with two judges sitting in the same courts, there's such a wide disparity in the number detained?

3.8   MURPHY: It may depend on the type of offenses they were bought before, the division of the court—

3.9   MILLER: No, they are the identical cases; it's from the Bureau of Standards study, and they're the identical criminal population. What's the explanation for such a wide diversity between the way judges grant or deny—

3.10   MURPHY: The individual judge's view as to the particular facts in the case.

3.11   MILLER: But in fact those percentages vary widely. That's not unusual. One [judge] detains 10, one detains 60, one detains 80 [percent]. A defendant is before a particular judge; he may get out with one and not with another.

3.12   MURPHY: That same defendant could never have the same set of facts in any two particular cases; so it's never quite that simple.

3.13   MILLER: But given a random sample, we have 20 percent in one, 50 percent in the other. In fact would you suspect that the judge who was harder— who detained more—was more correct?

3.14   MURPHY: The only issue under those statistics he's considering is the likelihood of flight. And that's a variable based on the people that happen to be before them. You can't say that the statistic based on random sampling in that particular situation is—

3.15   MILLER: But judges have abused the bail system, have they not? And despite the fact that detention for flight is the only reason that's given, in fact judges around the country improperly detain defendants because they think they're dangerous in many cases.

3.16   MURPHY: Higher money bonds are set than can be reached, because of dangers. In the District of Columbia, you're forbidden to consider dangerousness; and of course, after 24 hours you must put your reasons in writing, and there's an immediate appellate review in the case you're wrong.

3.17   MILLER: But today there are judges who, despite the fact they're not supposed to consider dangerousness in States around the country, *do*, and set higher bail for that.

3.18   MURPHY: I'm not sure what the laws are in particular States. But there are certainly judges that do not perform their duties in a proper manner.

3.19   MILLER: One of the problems, of course, is the delay. What is the delay now in the District of Columbia for trial in a felony? It's well over a year, isn't it?

3.20   MURPHY: I understand it's now down to about nine months.

3.21   MILLER: But it *has* been over a year, and it's a very substantial period. If we could try these defendants within 60 days, if we put our resources into speedy trial, we'd solve almost the entire problem, wouldn't we?

3.22   MURPHY: No, we wouldn't; because the [District of Columbia] Crime Commission's study shows a 50 percent recidivism rate during the 60 days, and the Hart Committee Study [shows] over 25 percent. You'd handle *some* of it, and I certainly believe everybody ought to be tried within 60 days, in or out of custody. No question about that.

3.23   MODERATOR ROGER FISHER: Judge Murphy, just let me ask [you to] clarify one point. When you said "90 percent," [did you mean] there were *categories* of defendants for whom you could be 90 percent sure? Or did you mean you'd hit 90 percent correct on the whole *group* of defendants?

3.24   MURPHY: I think [I meant 90 percent] in answer to both; because over 50 percent of the people that come before me are drug addicts. Congressman Pepper's study, that's just come out recently, says 98 percent of all the addicts support their habit by crime. Cranking in the addict figure would raise it higher than the general sampling; I think that it would approach a very high percent—

3.25   MILLER: But the question was addressed to *rape repeaters*. . . . What is your guess on rape repeaters? . . .

3.26   MURPHY: I would again use the same statistic; because I believe every decision I make, I want it to be near as right as I can. I'm not about to say that I make all decisions correctly, but I think that I have a better batting average than most. . . .

4. SECOND AFFIRMATIVE WITNESS: DIRECT EXAMINATION

4.1   RUSHER: We've heard, and we will hear, I'll predict, still more about the unfairness and the impropriety of keeping defendants in jail before trial. To deal with that question from the standpoint of the preventive detention statute that is proposed, I will call next on Donald Santarelli, Associate Deputy Attorney General of the United States. Mr. Santarelli, on this matter of the keeping of defendants in jail before trial, even under high bail, or by preventive detention: is there a problem involved?

4.2   DONALD SANTARELLI: Yes, there is indeed. Thousands of defendants are detained all over the United States by the use of the present money bond system. And the problem is that *the wrong defendants are detained.* The impecunious—those who cannot buy their way out of their detention—are detained, instead of the selected dangerous.

4.3   The solution is very simple: increase the capacity of the judicial machinery to be more consistent with our notions of due process and civil liberties; weed out the dangerous defendant for detention, and not merely the impecunious defendant who cannot buy his way out with money bond.

4.4   RUSHER: You speak of due process and civil liberties, then, as actually being *increased,* and better protected, under the preventive detention machinery. How will this work?

4.5   SANTARELLI: By actual definition. It *has* to be increased, because what is now done in the States, largely, and in the Federal system, is this use of money bond to effect detention, without due process procedures. The bill that President Nixon's Administration introduced in Congress last time would provide for a hearing, at which the defendant is required to have counsel, at which the prosecutor must put forward some evidence of the defendant's dangerousness, at which the court must make conclusions as to those facts—write them down in a finding which becomes appealable and reviewable by the Court of Appeals, and where the defendant would be detained only for a limited period of time, like 60 days, instead of endlessly, as he may now be detained, by the use of money bond.

4.6   RUSHER: And detained, I believe, even in different circumstances—

4.7   SANTARELLI: That's correct. Our bill provided that detention could occur only in a facility where he would be segregated from a convicted person.

4.8   RUSHER: If we went over to such a system of preventive detention, rather than just using money bail as the excuse, would crime tend to be reduced?

4.9   SANTARELLI: Of course. Society is entitled to a protective measure on behalf of the courts, to detain those persons who are likely to be dangerous to the society if they're released. Speedy trial is part of that picture. But detention must be had for those who are dangerous.

4.10   RUSHER: How about the charge that such a law would be unconstitutional?

4.11   SANTARELLI: That charge has been raised in opposition to every controversial proposal that's been set forth in the history of this country's legislative process. If we were to pause whenever that question is raised, we would have enacted no legislation for 180 years. The Constitution does not speak clearly to this issue. The Supreme Court has not yet ruled squarely on this issue. The Constitution was meant to be interpreted in a reasonable manner, and the rule of reason allows man to devise methods of self-preservation and self-protection that guarantee him civil liberties at the same time, as may be needed.

5.   CROSS-EXAMINATION

5.1   MILLER: You feel the system of preventive detention would in fact reduce the amount of crime?

5.2   SANTARELLI: Yes, *and* it would reduce the numbers of persons who are presently detained unfairly.

5.3   MILLER: How much crime do you think it would reduce?

5.4   SANTARELLI: That's a question that no one could answer. It would be [on a] speculative basis. Of course, it would reduce the amount of crime that occurs during a pre-trial release period, which may *not* be the great bulk of crime in the United States.

5.5   MILLER: Why is it that in the two and a half weeks or so that it's been enforced in the District of Columbia, you have not brought a single preventive detention proceeding?

5.6   SANTARELLI: For the very clear reason that we had intended this statute to be selective in its application. We narrowed its application by law to a specific number and category of cases.

5.7   MILLER: What about the problem of sending a man to jail incorrectly? Tell us about the effects. We're talking about jails now, not prisons: the short holding period. Those jails are in pretty bad condition, aren't they?

5.8   SANTARELLI: They certainly are. Deplorable.

5.9   MILLER: And hundreds of them are centuries old.

5.10   SANTARELLI: In the States that's probably true.

5.11   MILLER: What about the effect of sending a man to a jail like that, [a man] who has not committed a crime—who later turns out to be innocent?

5.12   SANTARELLI: A man who "turns out to be innocent" is not necessarily a man who did not commit the crime. You are familiar with our legal process, where the suppression of evidence often results in finding "not guilty" a man who is clearly guilty.

5.13   MILLER: And you'd like to put that man in jail even though he is found to be innocent.

5.14   SANTARELLI: The [eventual] finding of innocence is unrelated to the prediction of potential danger during a pre-trial release period.

5.15   MILLER: But you'd like to put him in jail even though he is innocent. What about the man who in fact is innocent, and gets sent to these jails that are crowded, and breeding grounds for crime, and hundreds of years old.

5.16   SANTARELLI: I would submit to you, sir, that there are thousands of people who are improperly detained under the money bond system, and that—

5.17   MILLER: This is not a contest between this and the money bond system.

5.18   SANTARELLI: Our proposal would be a selective proposal, where you select the dangerous defendant, not the impecunious.

5.19   MILLER: We assume bail reform, which cures a great many problems of the money bond system, and—

5.20   FISHER: Both advocates are suggesting that the poor, who are not threaten-[ing] or dangerous, should not be detained in jail. The question is: should the State authorize the judge to hold a man who is thought to be dangerous? *That's* the only question.

5.21   MILLER: The contrast is between bail reform without preventive detention, or whether we need preventive detention as well. Now tell me about the procedure at the trial. There is no right of confrontation of witnesses, is there, under the statute?

5.22   SANTARELLI: Oh yes, there is.

5.23   MILLER: The statute clearly says the rules of evidence do not apply.

5.24   SANTARELLI: The statute also clearly says that the defendant is entitled to present evidence in his own behalf.

5.25   MILLER: But hearsay evidence could be admitted against him; affidavits could be admitted against him—

5.26   SANTARELLI: That's correct.

5.27   MILLER: The people who charge him aren't examined. Is that correct?

5.28   SANTARELLI: Just as is now the law under the Federal Bail Reform Act in capital offender cases, where the rules of evidence do not apply, and you can detain a capital offender.

5.29   MILLER: In *capital offender* cases.

5.30   RUSHER (*in summation*):   Mr. Miller perhaps inadvertently brought out a rather interesting statistic: that in the first two and one-half weeks of the operation of the preventive detention statute in the District of Columbia, there has not been a single case in which preventive detention was applied. So that this is hardly a grand march to Siberia of all the innocents of Washington, D.C., is it?

6.   FIRST NEGATIVE WITNESS: DIRECT EXAMINATION

6.1   ⁓MILLER: It's certainly difficult to talk about these vast *benefits*, with no case being brought. . . . There are many ways to deal with crime. Most crime in this country is committed by men between the ages of 15 and 24. If we locked up all men between the ages of 15 and 24, there would be a reduction in crime. We would also be a criminal society. Of course everyone agrees that Thomas James should be detained, [and] that Franklin Moyler should be detained. The problem is that you cannot detain [such men] in any system that does not *also* detain dozens and hundreds of men who should *not* be detained, and who are, in fact, innocent. And when those men are detained, when they are innocent, when they are turned into hardened criminals, then we will have more crime and misery in this society than all the Franklin Moylers and all the Thomas Janeses can cause. In fact, only in *Alice in Wonderland* could this measure be considered as a "crime control" act. And Alice understood that:

6.2   QUEEN: There's the King's messenger. He's in prison now, being punished. And the trial doesn't even begin until next Wednesday. And of course the crime comes last of all.

ALICE: Suppose he never commits the crime.

QUEEN: That would be all the better, wouldn't it?

ALICE: Of course it would be all the better. But it wouldn't be all the
better, his being punished.

QUEEN: You're wrong there, at any rate. Were you ever punished?

ALICE: Only for faults.

QUEEN: And you were all the better for it, I know.

ALICE: Yes, but I had done the things I'd been punished for. That makes
all the difference.

QUEEN: But if you *hadn't* done them, that would have been better still.
Better, better, and better.

ALICE: There's a mistake somewhere.

6.3   Indeed, there *is* a mistake somewhere. And to tell us about it, we've
asked to join us Sergeant Hugh Williams of the Newark Police Department. [Williams has been with the department for eight years, and is
currently] a Fellow at the Center for Criminal Justice at Harvard. Sergeant
Williams, what did you do in your eight years with the Newark Police
Department?

6.4   SGT. HUGH WILLIAMS: I served in various capacities: I walked the beat; I
served in community relations.

6.5   MILLER: Can you—or do you think anyone else [can]— predict who's going
to commit a crime?

6.6   WILLIAMS: I can't—not with any substantial degree of accuracy. And I believe that those who say they can are acting out of a gut reaction—that
this will not hold water, when placed to the test of empirical analysis.
[I'm reminded of the old theory which held] that you could tell whether
a man was a criminal by the size of his chin or his arms, or the fact that
he had slanty eyes. I just don't believe that those criteria hold water; and
neither do I believe the criteria set out in the preventive detention act
hold water.

6.7   MILLER: Are there harmful effects of preventive detention?

6.8   WILLIAMS: There are definitely harmful effects. There are harmful effects
to the family of the people that are sent to jail: especially innocent people.
The problem will often call for people going on welfare. The sole sup-
porter of the family will be in jail—subsequently found not guilty, by a
jury of his peers. What kind of attitude will he have about society then?
How would he feel about our laws and the way they work?

6.9   MILLER: What about the effects of sending a man to jail who may be
innocent?

6.10   WILLIAMS: Jail is a terrible place. It's much worse than prisons. There's a
problem of placing a man in a criminal sub-culture. Not knowing about

crime, he will certainly be educated about crime inside the jails. He'll be placed in a degraded position; he'll probably be hardened when he gets out, and enraged about society.

6.11   MILLER: What will this preventive detention statute do to community relations?

6.12   WILLIAMS: It will cause a considerable amount of tension in the community. Polarization. There are many people in our society, especially blacks and Puerto Ricans, who feel that justice is not color-blind, but color-conscious, and skewed against the poor. The criteria set out in the preventive detention act [would operate so as to detain] people at the lower socio-economic end of the ladder. We have defined those people as being dangerous to society. This will affect minorities in a detrimental way.

6.13   MILLER: There *is* a crime problem. What should we do about crime?

6.14   WILLIAMS: We've spent a lot of money to find out what the causes of crime are, and to find out what we ought to do about it. We've spent millions of dollars. For two years, the Presidential Crime Commission conducted an exhaustive investigation in order to find out what ought to be done about crime. They found out that you cannot cure crime by simply adding a few more policemen, or by a slick political gimmick, like the preventive detention act. You have to deal with the root causes of crime. You have to deal with poverty. You have to deal with inadequate education. You have to deal with the sense of hopelessness that people have, [the sense] that they can't accomplish anything in a highly competitive society that doesn't equip them to deal in it.

7.   CROSS-EXAMINATION

7.1   RUSHER: I believe you do recognize that the *effort*, at least, of the preventive detention statute, is to lay down criteria which will result in the preventive detention of people who are potentially dangerous in a serious way, and in a direct way to the community. Isn't that at least its objective, whatever its success or failure?

7.2   WILLIAMS: Frankly, I think that it's the wrong way to deal with the problem.

7.3   RUSHER: I'm talking about its purpose, at the moment. You saw the three examples that I gave Judge Murphy. Would you doubt, yourself, that those men should be held under preventive detention?

7.4   WILLIAMS: I feel that they should be tried immediately. If they're found guilty then they should pay their debt to society.

7.5   RUSHER: Yes, but *other* people who are *also* up for prosecution want to be tried immediately *too*. I certainly agree with you, and Judge Murphy agrees with you: we need speedier justice than we have. But there is going to be a gap in the normal case. There has to be for preparation of a case.

7.6   WILLIAMS: Why does it have to take nine months? Why can't it take one month?

7.7   RUSHER: I don't think it *has* [to] and I don't think it *should* [take nine months]. But supposing that it takes *one* month. Must these men be out on the street during that one month: the three that we showed?

7.8   WILLIAMS: Well, frankly, I'm not certain whether you should determine that you can predict the behavior of these men once they're released.

7.9   RUSHER: Is it really impossible to tell whether such people are likely to repeat? Isn't it a fact that the great majority of those that commit serious crimes—not murder, which seems to be a rather special and "set-aside" crime—but robbery, rape, armed assault, burglary: isn't it a fact that the great majority of those that commit those crimes *do* repeat?

7.10   WILLIAMS: Depends on where you're getting your statistics.

7.11   RUSHER: I'm getting mine from the District of Columbia, where the U.S. Attorney's office indicates that of 557 robbery defendants indicted in 1968, 345 were released. The others were held, on the old high-bail system, and then of the ones that were released, 70 percent were re-arrested for new crimes. And another from the District of Columbia: the Metropolitan Police Department study showed that, in fiscal 1967, almost 35 percent of 130 indicted for armed robbery were indicted for at least one felony while out on bail for that robbery.

7.12   WILLIAMS: The National Bureau of Standards indicates that it's about 7 percent that would meet the criteria of dangerousness. [Another study, by a Harvard group,] indicates that it's only 5 percent.

7.13   RUSHER: We're coming to the Harvard study, a little bit later, if we have time. But do you feel that there is, then, *not* an important "repeater factor" in these aggravated crimes? Is that what you're telling me?

7.14   WILLIAMS: No, I'm not telling you that. It seems to me that you're making an assumption.

7.15   RUSHER: We have to make, certainly, an assumption, so that people can avoid being killed or raped, or mugged or robbed by these people while they're out on bail.

7.16   WILLIAMS: There's nobody that believes more than I, as a policeman, that people who commit crimes ought to be rehabilitated so that they will not commit them again when they get back on the streets.

7.17   RUSHER: Sure. If you're talking about crime prevention, that's something else again. But do you think that people of this type, the type that we saw on the screen again, would really learn bad habits if they got into detention? Thomas Janes, for example? Franklin Moyler?

7.18   WILLIAMS: I don't think that they would be rehabilitated, or reorientated. And that's the problem. We are generating criminals in the prison system.

7.19   RUSHER: We're dealing with a one-, or two-, or three-, or nine-month period. You're not going to rehabilitate hardened criminals in months. You're going to take a much longer period. We're trying to prevent crime—

7.20   WILLIAMS: But we're not rehabilitating them at all now. We're warehousing—

7.21   RUSHER: I'm no opponent, sir, of rehabilitation. I'm trying to do something else in addition, if you don't mind, and that is to prevent [people] from committing crimes while this rehabilitation's going on, if need be. You are aware that under the preventive detention proposal, they would actually be kept separated from convicts, aren't you? They would be maintained separately.

7.22   WILLIAMS: Well, I'm aware now.

7.23   RUSHER: You're "aware now." Doesn't that help to keep them from learning bad habits?

7.24   WILLIAMS: I don't think that hardened criminals would learn bad habits when they go to jail.

7.25   RUSHER: I agree with you, but Mr. Miller was worried that that was exactly the difficulty. Take your own State of New Jersey. In 1970, a year ago today, there were, I understand, about 1,200 people awaiting trial in jail on high bail, under the system we now have. That was 35 percent of the entire jail population of New Jersey.

7.26   Did you know that the Justice Department estimates that under the preventive detention system only 10 percent of that population—not 35—would be held preventively? Isn't that *progress*?, if we can get not more, but fewer people, and the right people, under procedures that are fairer, and into the jails preventively, until trial can take place?

7.27   WILLIAMS: It seems to be progress in a reverse direction, because you're placing definitions on people. You're going to determine that you have got the right people by a standard that I don't believe in. You set criteria: based upon a man's record, you determine what is in his mind and predict what his future behavior will be. And I have to disagree with you.

7 . 28   RUSHER: Even if the criteria were different, Sergeant, or wrong, it would be some progress of a sort, wouldn't it, if we had to keep only 10 percent rather than 35 percent in detention?

7 . 29   FISHER: That's the bail. I take it that Sergeant Williams is not defending high bail or—

7 . 30   RUSHER: No, but I'm suggesting that the proposal for reform that we're making this evening is actually going to have a result that Sergeant Williams would like. Do you favor the present system of high bail?

7 . 31   WILLIAMS: Certainly not. I think that if we could remove crime from the area of politics, and [treat it with] the seriousness that we have conducted our scientific effort with [then] we can begin to deal with the problem.

7 . 32   RUSHER: You are opposed to high bail, and yet you're opposed to preventive detention. Isn't the result going to be a much, much larger number of people released back onto the streets precisely to commit new crimes?

7 . 33   WILLIAMS: Well you're assuming that the great majority of crimes will be committed within a two or three-week period that people are [not in] jail, and I think this is contrary to the facts.

7 . 34   RUSHER: I don't think the great majority are committed within two or three weeks; but certainly a significant part—

8 .   SECOND NEGATIVE WITNESS: DIRECT EXAMINATION

8 . 1   MILLER: Don't be misled. The choice is not between preventive detention for a few or the high money bail system which keeps a large number of people in jail. We both agree that the Bail Reform Act . . . must go into effect throughout the United States. The question is: with the Bail Reform Act, which reduces the number of people in jail, do we then need preventive detention? Now of course it's easy to say that Franklin Moyler and Thomas Janes should be detained. But the argument can't stop there. That's only the premise. That fact that we now know they should be detained does not mean that we can construct a system which will single only *them* out and not hundreds of *others*. And that's the problem. In casting our net for the Moylers and the Janeses, we will pick off hundreds

of other people, necessarily, who shouldn't be caught, and who shouldn't be in jail. To talk to us about that point, I've asked to join us tonight, Alan Dershowitz, professor of law at Harvard University. Professor, I'll ask you a question I asked Judge Murphy. What is the rate of repeater for those who have committed rape?

8.2   PROF. ALAN DERSHOWITZ: It's certainly no higher than 5 percent, for those who have actually been *convicted* for rape. For those who have been *charged* with rape, it's lower than 5 percent. And if you think about the rate of recidivism for those who have been charged with rape, for the very short period of time under consideration, it's probably under 1 percent.

8.3   MILLER: Let's take that 5 percent rate figure, then, of recidivism. [Now suppose] Judge Murphy is 90 percent right, as he says. How many innocent people will he still send to jail if he's 90 percent right, as compared with guilty?

8.4   DERSHOWITZ: I've calculated this, and I still come to a conclusion that about 140 people would have to be confined in order to prevent about 45 rapes. That is "overprediction" of about 3 to 1.

8.5   MILLER: That's *even if* he's *90* percent correct.

8.6   DERSHOWITZ: And there is just no question that he is so far wrong when he says that he is 90 percent correct. It's just out of the ball park.

8.7   MILLER: Can a system be made to work? Can we really have a system that predicts who's going to repeat?

8.8   DERSHOWITZ: I've looked at every study that's ever been made of prediction. I've never heard anybody even *claim* 90 percent. I'm flabbergasted that a judge with this kind of experience would think he's 90 percent accurate all the time. The only way he could come to such a conclusion is because he's never been told he's been wrong. . . . It's like the old Thorndike study, at Harvard, where they tried to test the thesis that aim improves with experience. And they had a fellow throw darts at a board. But they blindfolded him, and never told him whether he hit or missed, and of course his aim *didn't* improve. And if judges continue to be blindfolded and continue to think that they're 90 percent accurate, when they're probably closer to 10 percent accurate in the rape area—that's the problem, not the answer.

8.9   MILLER: Is there any way we can get the Moylers and the Janeses, and these people that we've heard about tonight, without getting large numbers of other, innocent, people?

8.10 DERSHOWITZ: I would love to be able to get people like that in preventive detention. I am not a doctrinaire opponent of preventive detention. If we could come up with a system which would detain those three, frankly, even if it would result in one innocent person being confined—I know a lot of people would disagree with me on this—I would approve it. [But we] can't even come *close* to *that*. We can't even come close to any system where a judge would more likely be right than wrong in any given case. With one exception. But we have to face the exception. The exception is what Judge Murphy bases his entire analysis on: the hardcore heroin addict, who has a habit which requires him to go out and rob almost daily. If you isolate that figure, the percentage of prediction will be pretty high, because you're operating in an area with about a 95 percent rate of recidivism.

8.11 MILLER: Then shouldn't we preventively detain the hard-core heroin addicts?

8.12 DERSHOWITZ: There are better ways to deal with that problem. The District of Columbia has found such a way: a methadone maintenance program. Free dispensation of heroin to hardcore addicts. Other kinds of solutions. If we finally decide to reject these solutions, which are costlier, which are harder to advocate politically—even if we finally decide to reject those solutions, surely the most we should do is say that we should have a kind of civil commitment for heroin addicts. But don't generalize from the heroin addict to the rapist. It's a completely different problem.

8.13 MILLER: Will there be more people arrested, more people getting in the system? Will the whole system change because we now have preventive detention?

8.14 DERSHOWITZ: There's certainly a possibility that that may happen. If a prosecutor today knows that he can arrest somebody, and detain him for a period of time without the intervention of a jury, I think the possibility is—it's just speculation—that more people might today be arrested who would not be arrested under the previous system.

8.15 MILLER: Are there risks of certain kinds of defendants being singled out here, risk of certain kind of political—

8.16 DERSHOWITZ: There's a great risk of that. The statute talks about crimes like conspiracy, crimes like arson, crimes like kidnapping. For example, if a lawyer makes a speech in California and after there is some burning of banks, it is conceivable that an indictment could flow, charging him with conspiracy to engage in arson. That kind of defendant could be detained under this statute. Moreover, the statute talks about danger to the community, in addition to danger to individuals. In fact, we've had some experience under it. When Judge [Irving] Hoffman, in Chicago, detained the defendants pending appeal, the statute said the same thing: "danger to the community." A number of us at the Harvard Law School wrote a letter to the Attorney General saying, "You say you're not going to use this statute for political purposes: here's an opportunity to demonstrate your *bona fides.* Come in and say that Judge Hoffman was wrong." But no; the Justice Department came in and supported that construction of the statute, both in Chicago [in connection with the "Chicago Seven"] and in Seattle.

9.   CROSS-EXAMINATION

9.1   RUSHER: Professor Dershowitz, I would not have gotten into this except that you, I must say, speculated—at a point when he could not comment on the matter—on Judge Murphy's qualifications. You have not had judicial experience, have you?

9.2   DERSHOWITZ: I didn't comment on his qualifications. He's a fine judge, and—

9.3   RUSHER: But . . . just a moment. Have you had judicial experience?

9.4   DERSHOWITZ: You know I haven't had judicial experience.

9.5   RUSHER: I truly don't.

9.6   DERSHOWITZ: Do you know any 32-year-old judges?

9.7   RUSHER: I didn't even know you were 32, but happy birthday, if it's—in any case, the answer is "no, you haven't." And it just strikes you as "flabbergasting" and "absurd" that Judge Murphy, who has had all that judicial experience, could say what he—

9.8   DERSHOWITZ: No, it doesn't strike me. You see, I have had better opportunity to evaluate the way judges perform, . . . and so has, for example, the Harvard Civil Liberties [Union]. And so has the Law Review.

9.9   RUSHER: And so has he, as far as that goes.

9.10   DERSHOWITZ: No, I don't think so. You see, he doesn't find out when he's wrong. He doesn't find out—

9.11   RUSHER: Oh, now, now!

9.12   DERSHOWITZ: —and that person would *not* have committed a crime. What he *does* find out is if he has failed to confine somebody, and that person commits a crime—

9 . 13   RUSHER: Yes, of course. But isn't that true in the case of any judge who suspends a sentence, or authorizes a parole, or sets parole, or authorizes probation? Isn't a judge's life full of discretions in which he decides either that people shall or shall not serve sentences, or how long they shall serve?

9 . 14   DERSHOWITZ: It certainly is.

9 . 15   RUSHER: Why do you single out this particular one?

9 . 16   DERSHOWITZ: I don't. I'm critical of judges in many respects. . . .

9 . 17   RUSHER: Are you critical of the people who do not permit parole in all cases?

9 . 18   DERSHOWITZ: I'm certainly critical of the decisions to grant parole in some cases; in fact there have been some followup studies which show that the prediction upon which parole is made is often wrong. What I would like Judge Murphy and other judges to do is to be willing to test their predictions. Let's get a list of people who today were detained, and then let's release 10 percent of them at random; and let's see if he's right (90 percent) or if I'm right (10 percent) [on accuracy of predictions].

9 . 19   RUSHER: That would certainly occur, if I may say so, sir, to a Harvard professor. But it might be a little rough on the people—

9 . 20   DERSHOWITZ: Any reasonable man, it would occur to.

9 . 21   RUSHER: It might be a little rough on the people who had crimes committed by the 10 percent you and Judge Murphy released for your critical test—

9 . 22   DERSHOWITZ: And *this* system would be pretty tough on the 90 percent who would be improperly confined.

9 . 23   RUSHER: It would certainly not be possible for them to commit crimes. I don't know whether they'd be improperly confined or not. Let me ask you this: You are not altogether against preventive detention, as [you've said. Do you believe] . . . that a judge would, however, feel compelled to be over-cautious? Is that part of your point?

9 . 24   DERSHOWITZ: Yes; over-cautious [about granting bail].

9 . 25   RUSHER: . . . Because, as you say, he would learn about the crime [which] was committed, but not about the others. But what about these other cases, then, of all the other discretions a judge has? You want to limit their discretion on all of them?

9 . 26   DERSHOWITZ: I do, for the most part.

9 . 27   RUSHER: And [you would be in favor for the] most part, of the defendant, if I understand your position.

9 . 28   DERSHOWITZ: No; I'm pretty tough on crime. I would like to see defendants who have [been] proved guilty of crime serve sentences. I'm not in favor,

for example, of plea bargaining. Many defendants today get a good shake for pleading guilty.

9.29   RUSHER: We had a reference earlier to the Harvard study. Isn't it true that the Harvard study involved only defendants released on bail? And of course, since we have high-bail situations in which all of the defendants most likely to commit crimes are in jail, unable to raise bail, the Harvard study had already excluded from the study most of the people who were in the likeliest position to commit crime.

9.30   *Cross-Talk*:

DERSHOWITZ: That's possible. We—

RUSHER: Possible— well, let—

In Massachusetts—

How about—

Federal statistics study—

Unless Massachusetts is more—

FISHER: —You say that the Bureau of Statistics in Massachusetts?

No, the Bureau of Statistics study, which was authorized by the District of Columbia, came to a basically similar conclusion: 5.4 percent—

RUSHER: Isn't it a fact too that the Harvard study counted as second crimes only those that were successfully prosecuted through to a conviction? Whereas there were, in addition, crimes that were never discovered, presumably—

I think that's probably—

Tell you what I'm willing to do. I'm willing to quadruple the figures arrived at by—

I was coming to that.

and by the Bureau of Standards; and you'll still find—

9.31   RUSHER: Let's play a little game with statistics. The 140, if you estimate it on Judge Murphy's own figures, would have to be detained in order to prevent 45 rapes. Now, mind you, these would be 140 people found under the preventive detention laws to be high-risk cases, under the ten criteria prescribed by the law. They would be detained for a maximum of 60 days at most. And you [regard] that as too high a price to pay for the prevention of 45 rapes?

9.32 DERSHOWITZ: We have certainly seen the choices opposed here.

9.33 FISHER: Your position is that the certainty, as you see it, of locking up innocent people outweighs the risk of locking up some of the more dangerous poeple—

9.34 DERSHOWITZ: Of course the 140 and 45 is based on the 90 percent figure. The realities are that Judge Murphy would be 10 percent accurate. And so we get something like 1,000 people confined to prevent 45 rapes.

9.35 RUSHER: The choice I'm interested in is that, in any case in which 140 people who have high-risk potential on the basis of a ten-criteria record are put in jail for 60 days, that's "too high" a price to pay for the prevention of 45 flat-out rapes. I think that's a rather interesting statistic, whether or not you agree that that would be the actual reality.

9.36 DERSHOWITZ: It's quite clear that I *don't* agree with the "reality."

9.37 FISHER: That puts the question on the competing risks, I think.

9.38 MILLER (*in summation*): It's clear that you can't have a system which is right more often than it's wrong. In fact you must wind up with a system which is wrong far more often than it's right: 140 innocent men confined to jail, away from their families, with all that jail does to men inside the crowded jail conditions, for the 45 men who commit the rapes. *That's* with the 90 percent chance of the judge being correct. If you believe it's 90 percent, it's still 140 to 45; but of course it's *not* 90 percent. We're talking about keeping hundreds of innocent men in the most miserable conditions in this country, for 60 days or longer, in order to prevent some unknown number of crimes. In 1789 we decided that that was too high a price to pay. We have *always* decided that that is too high a price to pay, And if we understand our tradition of liberty, we *shall* always decide that is too high a price to pay.

10. THIRD AFFIRMATIVE WITNESS: DIRECT EXAMINATION

10.1 RUSHER: Mr. Miller must simply have mis-spoken when he spoke of 140 "innocent" men. Judge Murphy's assumption was, and the whole presumption of Professor Dershowitz was, that these men were *already indicted* and charged on particular crimes. Certainly they are not *all* innocent; some of them may be. It may turn out that out of 140, some may not be later convicted, but they are not "140 innocent men," or anything like it. To see how this whole system of preventive detention has worked in the rest of the civilized world, we will call upon a representative of a country that is well known for fair play: the distinguished British judge, the Honorable Sir Arthur James, a judge with the Queen's Bench Division of the Supreme Court Judicature of the United Kingdom. Sir Arthur, do you have preventive detention for non-capital offenses in the United Kingdom?

10.2   SIR ARTHUR JAMES: Have it? Yes, of course we have it. We couldn't do without it. It's common [in] every country in the world, so far as I know, apart from this country and Liberia and the Philippines, which I think follow this country's law. The Commonwealth certainly has it.

10.3   RUSHER: Does it work very well?

10.4   JAMES: Work satisfactorily? Most certainly. Recidivism is no serious problem with us. It keeps away from the public people who are shown to have been a danger, by their records.

10.5   RUSHER: Do you have safeguards?

10.6   JAMES: Of course there are safeguards. There's a right of appeal where bail is refused and preventive detention (we don't call it by that name; an order to remain in custody) is applied.

10.7   RUSHER: What about the contention that it really isn't fair? Now, you are another judge sitting on the bench with criminal defendants and others coming before you. How can you predict, sir, who will be a repeater, a recidivist?

10.8   JAMES: Well, there are two questions: is it fair? and, how can I predict? I say I *can* predict and I'd go along with the figure of 90 percent. I'll do so for this reason: when we studied the release of people from prison, we can, by computer, estimate the chances of re-offending within the period of two years from their release, and we can act on that. We use, for that calculation, figures for the gravity of the offense; the pattern of behavior of the accused when he first offended; the nature of his offenses; the isolated outbreaks (do they conform to a pattern?); what has been his reaction to former treatment, whether on probation or in custody; [and whether he has] roots in the community. Those factors can all be added up, and a reliable estimate obtained. . . . You can't expect 100 percent certainty. [But the system is] fair to the man himself and fair to the public. It's only right that he should be prevented from committing further offenses and getting himself into worse trouble.

10 . 9   RUSHER: What about the occasional innocent person, though, who, under the best of systems, with the fairest of procedures, will nonetheless get detained for a period of time? Is that fair?

10 . 10   JAMES: We're not talking about "innocent" people in the sense of new-born babes or people who are beginning to sprout wings. These are people who, by their histories, have shown themselves to be a danger to society, and of whom a judge is satisfied that they are likely to repeat that action which results in danger either to an individual or society at large.

11 . .   CROSS-EXAMINATION

11 . 1   MILLER: England is a very different country from the United States—happily, in some circumstances. There were 6,500 murders in the United States in 1965 [while in England there were 10]. Why is that?

11 . 2   JAMES: Because we are not such a volatile race.

11 . 3   MILLER: And also, you have such things as gun control, which we don't have. You have other methods which really have high priority in fighting serious crime.

11 . 4   JAMES: It just goes to show that controls keep crimes down.

11 . 5   MILLER: That *particular* control: the gun control. Now, how many people do you detain in a year [by] what we call preventive detention, in Great Britain?

11 . 6   JAMES: Altogether, the last figure which I have, for 1968, was 40,000 people received into custody for a period of time—not necessarily the whole period of time.

11 . 7   MILLER: Now, of those 40,000: after the final trial, after the finding of guilt or innocence, in fact only 22,000 were either found not guilty or released without being sent to prison. So, out of your population of 40,000, after you went through the trial and after you had your full procedural safeguards, you decided that 22,000—over 50 percent of those men—should not stay in jail.

11 . 8   JAMES: Yes.

11 . 9   MILLER: So, should those men have stayed in jail from the beginning?

11 . 10   JAMES: No, not always. But let me tell you this—

11 . 11   MILLER: You made a mistake in 50 percent of the cases?

11.12   JAMES: No, we did not. I didn't say that; you said that. Many of those who are not given custodial sentences were not [jailed] because it was felt that their experience in custody before trial taught them a lesson.

11.13   MILLER: You get to trial much more quickly in Great Britain than we do in the United States: at most, in a matter of a few months.

11.14   JAMES: That's no reason for avoiding protecting the public.

11.15   MILLER: No; but you get to trial very quickly. When you protectively detain someone, you detain them for at most 90 days. You don't have these delays of 12 and 18 months.

11.16   JAMES: We don't have delays of 12 and 18 months. There is no limit to the period of preventive detention.

11.17   MILLER: Whatever happened, [for] whatever reasons, when you got done with all your procedures and all your safeguards, out of the 40,000 people you detained, over half of them you decided not to keep in jail. Does that concern you, the over 20,000 men who were in jail that, after trial, you decided not to keep in jail?

11.18   JAMES: It does not concern me at all, because I really believe that in a number of cases, they very well may have had to go to jail, as a sentence, had they not experienced jail beforehand. This is quite often what I do. I can have reports on a man who's been in prison and learned his lesson.

11.19   MILLER: Out of those 22,000, what about the men who were found innocent of the crime? Not who were not sent to jail, but [who] were detained and found innocent? Don't they concern you?

11.20   JAMES: They don't concern me, in this sense: I think it is quite compatible with the presumption of innocence to say also that society is entitled, where an allegation is made in the name of society against a person, to hold that person in custody pending investigation of that allegation.

11.21   MILLER: On a per-capita basis, on a comparison-of-population basis, if there are 22,000 men detained, whom your system did not ultimately detain in jail, [then] we're talking about an additional 50,000 people in the United States, if we have the same. And we're talking about many thousands of men who are found innocent and yet sent to jail. Now, you're here in the United States and you tell us that, as a man of justice, and a man of the bench, and a man of compassion, the fact that tens of thousands of innocent people will go to jail when they shouldn't have doesn't concern you?

11.22   JAMES: I'm *not* telling you *that*, for one thing. I should have to reassess my situation, if I was having to do justice over here. And I should have to do it on the merits of the individual cases over here. All I know is: in my experience, I get letters complaining that I've let people out on bail; I've never had a single letter complaining that I've kept a single person in custody.

12.   CLOSING STATEMENTS

12.1   RUSHER: In recent decades, the judicial tide has flowed strongly in favor of the criminal. But the time has come to recognize that non-criminals have rights too. There are five million serious crimes a year committed in the United States. Why should a man [who is] charged with rape or robbery or some other serious crime, and who has committed such crimes before, and whose whole life history indicates a real possibility that he will keep right on committing such crimes hereafter, be turned loose to prey upon society until he comes to trial? Do you really share Mr. Miller's fear that the man will learn bad habits in jail? We say that such a man should be detained—not, as at present, by the specious device of impossibly high bail, but after a fair hearing, and for a limited time—as in Britain, as in France, as in almost every other civilized country on earth. And we ask your vote *for* such preventive detention.

12.2   MILLER: I dare say that, in 1789, there were those who said that we were the only civilized country in the world that had a Bill of Rights. We were, and we should be proud of it. We're the only ones today who do not have preventive detention, do not send those tens of thousands of innocent men to jail on some false prediction that somehow we are going to be solving some crime; and we should be proud of that. You're right; we're the only country in the world. That's why we have our Bill of Rights, and that's why we're what we are and should stay what we are.

 *23 February 1971*

SUGGESTED EXERCISES

1. Piece together the terms of the preventive detention law advocated by the Affirmative side in the foregoing debate.
2. Discuss alternative meanings of the word "innocent" and the implications of these meanings for assessing preventive detention laws, as suggested in the course of the debate.

3. Cite and discuss uses of precedents in the foregoing debate (other than precedents implied by the systematic studies that were mentioned).
4. Drawing upon passages in the debate, formulate brief arguments for and against the proposition that preventive detention will increase the incidence of crime.
5. Critically review the findings of systematic studies that were mentioned in the course of the foregoing debate.
6. Much disputation in the foregoing debate revolved around the capacity of judges to discriminate accurately between persons who would and would not commit crimes if left at liberty awaiting trial for previous alleged crimes. The issue surely is a vital one. If judges cannot make the necessary distinctions with a substantial degree of accuracy, then they could not make good use of the authority granted under a preventive detention law. They would release a great many crime repeaters, or would incarcerate many innocent persons, or both.

You are hereby invited to devise a research project that would clarify the capacity of judges to make such distinctions. What sort of investigation would you suggest? How feasible and how conclusive would it be?

Should television be allowed to broadcast criminal trials with the consent of the defendant?

OVERVIEW

If you were arrested and formally accused of committing a crime, your experience would be a matter of public record. If you were accused of committing a spectacular crime, your trial would receive lavish publicity in the printed press and in radio and television newscasts. You might even be the subject of artists' sketches of dramatic courtroom scenes. Moreover, as you entered and left the courtroom, you would be pursued by press photographers. But in 48 of the 50 States, it is illegal for proceedings *in* the courtroom to be photographed or to be directly wired for electronic broadcast.

Such prohibitions have been on the books since around the late 1930's. They were adopted in the wake of the sensational kidnaping of the son of Charles Lindbergh, the great aviator. Following the feverish trial of the accused kidnapper, the American Bar Association sponsored a ban on direct broadcasting and photographing of criminal trials. Such publicity, it was argued, creates an atmosphere inimical to fair, impartial deliberation in the courtroom. This assessment still prevails among lawyers, but it has lately come under challenge. Indeed, after rather extensive hearings in 1956, it became legal in the State of Colorado, under certain conditions, for criminal trials to be televised. Whether this practice should be continued, and broadened, is the topic of the following debate.

1.   OPENING STATEMENTS

1.1   MODERATOR VICTOR PALMIERI: [Since the adoption of the bans on direct broadcasting of criminal trials,] television has revolutionized our communications. Today we can watch men as they step onto the moon. We can watch them as they meet death in Vietnam—but not as they stand trial for violation of the criminal law. And with us tonight to argue . . . that the rule should be changed [so that criminal trials can be televised with the consent of the defendant] is Kevin O'Connell.

1.2   ADVOCATE KEVIN O'CONNELL: Law and order is a searing issue in this country today. Yet the controversy is carried on in ignorance. How many people in this country have actually seen a criminal trial? James Madison once said, "Knowledge will forever govern ignorance, and a people who mean to govern themselves had better arm themselves with the power knowledge gives." If we televise trials, the people will have that knowledge.

1.3   In Lincoln's day, the people attended criminal trials as a matter of course. Judges rode circuits. When a judge came to town, the entire citizen body came out to watch the trial and was part of it. A Frenchman, Alexis de Tocqueville, came to this country in the 1830's and was struck by how small the police forces were. Yet, he noted, rarely did a criminal escape punishment. The reason, he said, was that every citizen concerned himself personally with the process and came forward to assist in giving information and to assist in apprehending the offender.* Today, on the other hand, huge cities have grown up: no longer do the people attend trials as a matter of course, [nor do they] come forward as a matter of course, [nor] do they consider themselves part of the criminal administration. In Lincoln's day, courtrooms were large enough to hold the

---

*"In America [as of 1835] the means that the authorities have at their disposal for the discovery of crimes and the arrest of criminals are few. A state police does not exist, and passports are unknown. The criminal police of the United States cannot be compared with that of France; the magistrates and public agents are not numerous; they do not always initiate the measures for arresting the guilty; and the examinations of prisoners are rapid

entire body of citizens; just as in New England, all citizens could attend the town meeting. Today that's impossible. Cities are too large. But we do have one means of bringing the courtroom back to the people, and that is television. Unfortunately, the lawyers are keeping television out of the courtroom.

1.4   PALMIERI: [Advocate Miller feels that] this rule should *not* change.

1.5   ADVOCATE HOWARD MILLER: A criminal trial on television would be neither a trial nor television. It would, in truth, create a new event which can best be described as the "tele-trial." That new event would be characterized by criminal defendants self-passed as national heroes utilizing television for their own purposes and [by] jurors reluctant to serve because of the increased glare of publicity. Witnesses and lawyers at least as interested in playing to the stadium as concerned with the truth can have an effect on already-disturbed persons in the population motivated by the chance that by committing a crime or other destructive acts, they, too, might play center stage in yet another national drama.

1.6   Television serves its own purposes: not the purposes of man and not the purposes of justice, but its own purposes. Even in the televising of sports events, time-outs are timed so that commercials may be shown on television. In the [Billy Sol] Estes trial, which was televised in Texas, part . . . was shown on local stations in place of the "Tonight" show or the late movies. With, of course, "appropriate" interruptions: "In a moment the verdict; but first, a word from our sponsor"—that goes to the essence of television.

1.7   In a way, what we're dealing [with] here, because we have television among other things, is a kind of underlying assumption about what we do in America: [the assumption] that whatever *can* be done, *must* be done. But what we're asking tonight is not [whether] whatever can be done must be done, but what are the purposes of justice and of man? How can television best be used to aid those purposes? Not "what are the

---

and oral. Yet I believe that in no country does crime more rarely elude punishment. The reason for this is that everyone conceives himself to be interested in furnishing evidence of the crime and in seizing the delinquent. During my stay in the United States I witnessed the spontaneous formation of committees in a county for the pursuit and prosecution of a man who had committed a great crime. In Europe a criminal is an unhappy man who is struggling for his life against the agents of power, while the people are merely a spectator of the conflict; in America he is looked upon as an enemy of the human race, and the whole of mankind is against him." *Democracy in America* (New York: Vintage Books, 1945), I, 99.

purposes of television?" That's not the question we're dealing with to-night. The fact that television serves its own purposes, and has the ca-pacity to distort the events, and does so, is almost incontrovertible. It certainly did so in at least one celebrated non-judicial case. In 1963, Lee Harvey Oswald was being transported from one jail to another [after having been arrested for allegedly assassinating President John F. Ken-nedy and wounding Governor John Connally of Texas]. The question was, what route should he take? And according to testimony before the Warren Commission, a substantial part of the determination of route was made by the desire of television to cover the transfer to jail. As a result, the chaotic conditions were present that we all know about. [Out of a jostling crowd came a shot. Oswald was slain.]

2.   FIRST AFFIRMATIVE WITNESS: DIRECT EXAMINATION

2.1   O'CONNELL: Last week I discussed some of these problems [concerning] the police, public, and television with the well-known Marshall McLu-han, author of *The Medium is the Massage*. [I asked him this:] how would televising trials affect the public's participation—the public's sense of involvement in the judicial process?

2.2   MARSHALL MCLUHAN (*on film*):   You're familiar with the fact that you don't have a police force until the community bows out of the action. A police force is a specialist force—that is, comes into play when the participation in law and order is finished.

2.3   O'CONNELL (*on film*):   And television would change all that?

2.4   MCLUHAN (*on film*):   Yes, because the public automatically becomes involved in corporate, legal action. The ionoscope tube of TV fires the world at the public as its theme, its responsibility.

2.5   O'CONNELL (*on film*):   How would you relate this corporate sense of responsi-bility to trials if the public were to see trials on television?

2.6   MCLUHAN (*on film*):   The public would automatically see the individual in the box as a victim of a great big man-made environment and would point an angry finger at the big powers that create these vicious environ-ments that make these miserable victims possible. So, it would switch from its private, individual orientation to the environmental orientation.

2.7   O'CONNELL: In May 1966, shortly after the Watts riot, a black man named Leonard Deitwaller was driving his pregnant wife to the hospital. A white police officer stopped Mr. Deitwaller for speeding. After the car had stopped, the police officer accidentally shot and killed Mr. Deitwaller. The black community was obviously very upset. The District Attorney of Los Angeles County decided that the inquest on the shooting should be televised, and said why.

2.8   DISTRICT ATTORNEY EVELLE YOUNGER* *(on film)*:   At the time of the Deitwaller inquest, this community was at a boiling point. We were perfectly aware that another Watts was possible. It was our feeling that the best way to keep peace in the community, and to keep the community calm and law-abiding, was to let everybody know what was going on in the course of the inquest.

2.9   O'CONNELL: As a result of the telecast—both live, and on the evening news— the community was calm. There was no riot. I'd now like to present [as a direct witness] the Honorable Thomas Brennan, Chief Justice of the Supreme Court of Michigan. Your Honor, you're a judge and you've been a trial court judge as well. What is your opinion about televising a trial?

2.10   JUSTICE THOMAS BRENNAN: I favor it. As a matter of fact, in my view the issue is broader than merely the televising of certain trials under certain circumstances. It involves the question as to whether the courts, which have the historic responsibility of recording and reporting their proceedings to the public, are going to adopt the modern, effective, and reliable means that are available to make that reporting. As a matter of fact, most of our courts in the country today still rely on shorthand or stenotype records, and that's the official record of the court. Then we have a typewritten transcript, and that's the official publication. But in my view, every courtroom should be equipped with a television camera mounted unobtrusively behind . . . and above the jury, so that there would be a jury's eye view of the court proceedings. And this would form the permanent record—the official permanent record—of the court proceedings. Now, the publication of that permanent, official record is just a simple matter, as [is] presently the publication of our transcribed records.

2.11   O'CONNELL: What about the objection, Mr. Chief Justice, that ambitious lawyers and judges will use the camera to further their own interests?

2.12   BRENNAN: I don't think that lawyers, judges, or witnesses would act any differently with the knowledge that their words, their actions, are being

---

*Now the Attorney General of California.

recorded by the stenotype operator. As a matter of fact, everything that's said in a courtroom is on the record, and that record is now public. It's my view that if we were to have this kind of a record of those proceedings, we might . . . be able to get away from this insidious practice of trial by news conference which is now plaguing the courts and confusing the people. I think that if we had this kind of record, the people would be entitled to hear what really transpires in the courtroom—not second-hand, not third-hand, not after editorializing or condensing, but the actual record. And I think the people with that kind of knowledge would tend more to support the processes of justice and the administration of justice than they do now.

[*At this point, O'Connell plays a filmed extract from the famous Senate committee hearings that pitted the late Sen. Joseph R. McCarthy against the Department of the Army at the time of the Eisenhower administration. O'Connell apparently offers these televised hearings as evidence demonstrating that the people can arrive at reasonable conclusions on the basis of first-hand exposure*].

3.   CROSS-EXAMINATION

3.1   MILLER: Chief Justice Brennan, you favor televising trials, and, of course, we're not simply talking about storing tapes and using them on an appellate record, but the *live* transmissions of trials *as they occur*. Do you also favor the televising of *pre-trial hearings* . . . where a decision is made on whether there's sufficient evidence to hold the defendant for a trial?

3.2   BRENNAN: The kind of televising that I'm talking about should be an official record of everything that happens in open court. [But] there are always going to be occasions when the lawyers and the judges will repair to chambers to discuss matters which are not on the record or which should be considered in the absence of the jury.

3.3   MILLER: Do you think there's any problem, for example, that [if] pre-trial hearings are televised [and] watched widely, that will make it very difficult, if not impossible, to get impartial jurors?

3.4   BRENNAN: I don't hold much with this idea that an impartial juror is only one who knows nothing about the case. . . . I don't think that there's any more danger [to the procurement of impartial jurors, as a result of pre-trial broadcasting] than is the present danger from having people in the community get an improper impression about what's happening in a lawsuit from the second-hand reports that they get in newspapers and by news commentators.

3.5   PALMIERI: I understand that when [you talk about] pre-trial hearings, you're talking about the examination of potential jurors with respect to possible prejudice—where the counsel might be inquiring about any one of their habits that might bear on issues in the lawsuit. Isn't that right, Mr. Miller? I want the audience to be sure, when we talk about pre-trial hearings, that we're talking about, oftentimes, some very personal information.

3.6   MILLER: Well, that's partially it, and it's also the other kind of pre-trial hearing [in which] the defendant is being held to answer. Now . . . every trial may in effect be a pre-trial hearing, because, of course, there may be a reversal. Trail judges make mistakes—I assume, even in Michigan. You reverse them, and there has to be a re-trial. With full televising of the first trial, won't it be impossible for the defendant to be successfully tried on a re-trial if his conviction is upset?

3.7   BRENNAN: In the first place, the full public television of any trial is only likely to happen in those cases where there is already tremendous public interest in what's happening. So you're talking about the difference between whether prospective jurors are going to be prejudiced [by,] in the one case, having heard the actual witnesses under oath stating what their testimony was and, in the other case, having heard second-hand reports of what that testimony was—

3.8   MILLER: Then you think that actually seeing the entire trial—I'm sorry, I don't often get a chance to interrupt a judge—so you think that televising the trial then simply adds nothing in terms of the problem of prospective jurors on re-trial?

3.9   BRENNAN: I think it only tends to reduce the amount of misconception that people might have about what the case is about.

3.10   MONITOR*:   [In addition to advocating] television as a means of perfecting a record in the trial court, . . . do you also advocate a simultaneous broadcast of those proceedings to the general public?

3.11   BRENNAN: I'm inclined to the view that if simultaneous broadcast was something of any interest to anyone, it could be done. Yes.

3.12   MONITOR: Well, let me ask you this question, a practical one. It's common in the trial cases to sequester the witnesses so that one witness will not learn the story from the other, and thus [to] avoid the unfortunate coaching that goes on between lawyer and witness. How would you handle

---

*Joseph A. Ball, ex-president of the American College of Trial Lawyers and current member of the American Bar Association's advisory committee for television and motion pictures.

this matter, if you were a judge, if there were simultaneous broadcast and yet you still had made an order sequestering witnesses?

3.13   BRENNAN: I'd sequester the witness the same way I'd sequester a jury: by putting them up in a hotel room and keeping them from watching TV or anything else.

3.14   MONITOR: In other words, you would deprive the witness of his liberty so that the people could listen to the broadcast?

3.15   BRENNAN: Well, in a way I suppose you'd say that we deprive juries of their liberty when we sequester them. But nevertheless, sometimes this type of thing is necessary.

3.16   MONITOR: There's another question I'd like to ask also. You talk about the people getting an improper opinion about the proceedings. What's more important: that the twelve people in the jury get a proper opinion of the proceedings, or that two million people in Los Angeles County get that proper opinion?

3.17   BRENNAN: Much more important that the people in the jury get a proper view of it.

3.18   MILLER: I think that is very pertinent. I'm concerned about this problem of re-trial because of the extent that errors occur. You know the British barrister who said [that every] man is presumed to know the law—except His Majesty's trial judges, who are always reversed. And judges are constantly being reversed, and we constantly face the problem. Now, you've just said that potential jurors have to be sequestered from information, to keep them from getting a prejudiced view of the case. Isn't every member of the public watching the first simultaneous broadcast a potential juror at a second trial?

3.19   BRENNAN: I think this is true, but I suppose what you're saying is that in certain celebrated events, it's impossible to have a fair trial in this country. I don't think that's true. I don't think that it's any more impossible to have a fair trial in the United States of America, with our present instant means of communication, than it was to have a fair trial in a small town in Nebraska in 1782.

4.   FIRST NEGATIVE WITNESS: DIRECT EXAMINATION

4.1   MILLER: At least in one case, the Supreme Court of the United States disagreed. . . . Justice Brennan [has] told us the kind of trial that would be televised: not necessarily the kind of trial that may add to the public knowledge of the court, but the kind of notorious trial, or the trial involving celebrities. In fact, that's the *only* kind television *wants* to televise. It's the only kind that's commercially feasible to televise. To talk about the effect in the celebrated courtrooms, we have asked to join us tonight Mr. Grant Cooper. Mr. Cooper has been defense attorney at many notable criminal trials. He defended Sirhan Sirhan. He is also a member of the Fair Trial and Free Press Committee of the American Bar Association and a former president of the American College of Trial Lawyers. As one of this nation's most notable defense attorneys, he stands to benefit enormously from a proposal that would allow televising trials. Mr. Cooper, do you favor television in the courtroom?

4.2   GRANT COOPER: Unequivocally no. The trial of a law suit is a very serious business. It isn't entertainment. A man's or woman's life and liberty are at stake. That life or liberty should be taken away only in an atmosphere of calm, serenity, and judicial dignity.

4.3   MILLER: What would be the effect on witnesses and attorneys of wide public television at the trial?

4.4   COOPER: The effect on witnesses and all participants would be not only subtle but most explicit. You take witnesses, for example. Most of them don't want to come to court anyhow. Then you have the very timid witness. That timid witness, being nervous in the first instance about being on the witness stand, knowing that all-seeing eye is watching him, would be more timid and be reluctant to answer questions properly. On the other hand, the cocky witness, the extrovert, would ham it up. And the same thing applies to lawyers as well, on both sides.

4.5   MILLER: What about the effect on jurors?

4.6   COOPER: Here again, you have the same situation. Jurors, generally speaking, are reluctant to serve. They don't like to be taken away from their daily routines. But to know that when they're going to be jurors, the eye of the television's on them—televised to the world at large; knowing that when they go home to their neighbors, they're going to be criticized for their verdict, no matter which way it goes. The fact that kooks and cranks would stop them on the street and ask them questions and make suggestions to them: it would have a terrific effect on jurors.

4.7   MILLER: Does your opposition to television stem from the physical intrusion into the courtroom or simply from the effect of televising the event?

4.8   COOPER: Only the effect. It's no physical intrusion.

5.   CROSS-EXAMINATION

5.1   O'CONNELL: Do you think the District Attorney of Los Angeles County made a mistake in televising the Deitwaller inquest?

5.2   COOPER: Yes, I do.

5.3   O'CONNELL: You realize, sir, that the summer shortly before that, there had been the Watts riot, which had been one of the most extensive riots in the country. You realize, also, a white police officer had shot a black man bringing his wife, his pregnant wife, to the hospital. Now, it was claimed it was accidental. You realize that the black community was extremely upset about the situation, and at that time Mr. Younger said, "The only way I can get this information out to this community is by showing them what's going on." You think he was wrong to do that?

5.4   COOPER: I do, for the reasons that I've stated before.

5.5   O'CONNELL: All right, sir. Are you aware that in a survey conducted by the Kerner Commission (in other words, the National Advisory Commission of Civil Disorders), the people in the black ghettos regard television as the truest medium, the medium that they would trust more than any other medium?

5.6   COOPER: I was not aware of that. But I'm aware of the fact that the courts of this country have studied this problem and 48 States of the Union are opposed to it, as well as the Federal courts.

5.7   O'CONNELL: Mr. Cooper, could I get on [to] this part about public participation? In fact, sir, it interests me that you talk about jurors not liking to serve and that type of thing. Has it not been your experience that when jurors are actually there and see what happens—it has been my experience that they think it is an enormously impressive ceremony—a trial—and very effective? And that why shouldn't we let people know what's going on in the courtroom?

5.8   COOPER: I'd say this: I agree with you that after a juror has served, then that juror, as a result of having been a participant as a juror, enjoys the educational features of it. . . . But prior to it he's not [of that opinion].

5.9   O'CONNELL: I would like to get through this. I realize that you've had a lot of extensive cross-examinations. It's fun to be a witness. I would like to come back to this point, though, about the survey that was done by the Kerner Commission, in which the black ghetto community regards television as more reliable than any other source. They regard newspapers as part of the white press. They regard television as truer because they can see it for themselves. And my question to you, sir, would be: wasn't the

District Attorney of Los Angeles County very wise when he showed the inquest, and let the community see what was going on and what the courts were doing?

5 . 10   COOPER: My answer is still "No." I'm not familiar with the Kerner Report.

5 . 11   O'CONNELL: . . . Obviously it is a very serious matter, if the accused is [subject to being] deprived of his life or his liberty. Now, with the question as it is stated tonight, it is *he* who has the right to decide whether or not he's going to waive that right not to be televised. Is that correct?

5 . 12   COOPER: That's correct.

5 . 13   O'CONNELL: Now let me ask you this. One thing that really interested me: you said lawyers would ham it up on both sides. You defended Mr. Sirhan. He was on trial for his life. Did you play to the camera?

5 . 14   COOPER: No, I didn't.

5 . 15   O'CONNELL: I didn't think so.

5 . 16   MONITOR: I'd like to pursue this a little further. The greatest objection you've made is that the judges, lawyers, and witnesses will be seriously affected by television and try to act as actors and not in their proper roles. But that wouldn't affect a coroner's inquest, would it?

5 . 17   COOPER: Yes, it would; in the very same way. And in particular I would object to the coroner's inquest, because: suppose the coroner's jury finds that the defendant is guilty of some crime. He's got to stand trial. All of the prospective jurors have heard it.

5 . 18   MONITOR: What difference does it make whether it's reported in the newspaper or reported on television?

5 . 19   COOPER: It's wrong to report it in the newspaper, too. All pre-trial proceedings that are reported in the newspaper are wrong.

5 . 20   MONITOR: You mean you'd put a gag on television, on newspaper reporting and all types of reporting?

5 . 21   COOPER: Not a gag on lawyers; not a gag on—a gag on lawyers, yes.

5 . 22   PALMIERI: I'm interested in where you think the public's right to know about judicial proceedings becomes important.

5 . 23   O'CONNELL: I wonder, sir, if you aren't like most of us lawyers in that we sort of [think] that we have the law in this little black box, and we don't want the public to come in here. Shouldn't the public be aware of what's going on? Shouldn't they be able to see what's happening?

5 . 24   COOPER: The public are aware by virtue of what they read in the newspapers in a very general way. But to have the all-seeing eye of the television camera on witnesses, on jurors, on the defendants, has not only a subtle but a very devastating effect on them.

6.   SECOND NEGATIVE WITNESS: DIRECT EXAMINATION

6.1   MILLER: I understand why the proponents of the proposal prefer not to talk about trials, but about some other kind of proceedings. And the examples that are given are very instructive. The Army-McCarthy hearings, for example: one of the major reasons that Senator [Joseph] McCarthy had the power that he did in this country was because of his misuse of television. [And one of the major causes of the tension in Los Angeles in connection with the Deitwaller killing was the previous television coverage of the Watts riots.] In fact, it's the misuse *of* television that has often created the very problems that we now say we're going to solve *through* television.

6.2   The most important fact of the matter is that television decides to go where it wants to go. No one seriously thinks that by simply televising two trials a year—a notorious criminal case and a Chicago Seven case—we'll educate the public about how the judicial system really works. It's not like the Town Meeting, where the individual chooses to go. Television chooses to put him there. And what television chooses to do has impact on the people who watch it, very great impact. Just as, for example, the televising of the Manson criminal trial had enormous and probably harmful effect on the community as a whole—and that certainly is one of the trials, one of the only trials, the networks would choose to televise.

6.3   To talk to us about the problems caused in out-of-court conduct by the televising of trials, we've asked to join us Dr. Charles Wahl, professor of psychiatry and a psychoanalyst at U.C.L.A. Dr. Wahl, what would some of the effects of televising notorious criminal trials to the public at large?

6.4   DR. CHARLES WAHL: It seems to me that the institutions not only have to be fair and equitable themselves, but also have to take into account the nature of the human mind and of the human condition. One of the major lessons of psychiatry is that we're all impelled by enormous needs for significance, for recognition, and for acceptance. This can take very unfortunate forms, as the history of assassinations shows. Any insignificant person can catapult himself to national acclaim by putting a bullet in the head of someone of importance. There's a line of Dante that says, "If I cannot be first in heaven, by God, I can be first in hell."

6.5   And the second feature is that television is *not* the "all-seeing eye." It is run by people. It is interesting that, in matters of public issue like the

Vietnam war, I have not seen in the last two years any attempt of television to fairly represent all aspects of this complex issue. Rather, the bias of the persons who show it seems to be very evident.

6.6   MILLER: Let's talk about the effects that you're talking about, on those people who might choose to be "first in hell." Are there a large number of such people in this country?

6.7   WAHL: Happily, there's not a large number; but I think their number would be increased by seeing the enormous rewards such persons who *did* act out in that way should receive through the public medium of television of their trials. And I think they would be vastly increased.

6.8   MILLER: Would you, for example, sir, favor televising the Chicago Seven conspiracy trial?

6.9   WAHL: No, I would not have, because, in addition to those who [pursue] criminal activity and who wish for enormous significance, persons who are interested in ["revolutionary activity"] have also a propensity to seek for a public forum. The interest is not to secure justice, but to secure that forum; and such a device would immensely facilitate and re-enforce it.

7.   CROSS-EXAMINATION

7.1   O'CONNELL: Doctor, I was curious about your position that people who are publicity-hungry would go out and kill someone, or might increase violence. I would like to ask you: if a man shoots the President, assassinates the President, or if a sniper kills 13 people, is he not going to get an enormous amount of publicity anyway?

7.2   WAHL: Yes, but it would be vastly increased by the provision of seeing himself before 60 million people in a highly dramatic and infantile way.

7.3   O'CONNELL: You see, doctor, what I'm curious about is: might not there be an effect if a man goes to trial, and what he *is* comes out. In other words, if he is this infantile, insecure person that you talk about, that would be coming out over television, and people would be able to see that. Is that not true?

7.4   WAHL: I think this is true. But there is also the added effect of intensely reinforcing that behavior . . . [and] there are all the *other* persons who are motivated to do that thing.

7.5   O'CONNELL: What I'd be curious about, doctor: you're familiar with the Sirhan Sirhan trial which Mr. Cooper tried?

7.6   WAHL: Only as a layman.

7.7   O'CONNELL: When there was a psychologist, or a high school teacher, . . . on the stand testifying that [Sirhan] was [of] below-average intelligence, at that time Sirhan had an enormous outburst and wanted to plead guilty and wanted to end the trial. He did not want those facts to come out. Do you recall that?

7.8   WAHL: Yes, I do

7.9   O'CONNELL: What I would be curious about [is this:] if we had trials, rather that these people appearing as they do now in the news as perhaps romantic heroes, we would see them for what they actually are—miserable, pathetic creatures.

7.10   WAHL: I'm not certain that would follow. It seems to me that [the] added advantage of the tremendous publicity that that person would get would obviate the other advantage that you mentioned.

7.11   PALMIERI: Isn't that just incremental? Isn't [it] just a fact that a man gets tremendous publicity anyway by virtue of the other news media?

7.12   WAHL: I don't think so. Television is a very special medium that appeals to the dramatic and the infantile in us and in a way that no other medium does. . . .

7.13   O'CONNELL: Apparently though, Sirhan Sirhan himself disagreed with your opinion. He wanted to end that trial. He did not want to stay on television or anything else.

7.14   WAHL: I'm not familiar with that.

7.15   O'CONNELL: I would like to ask you, doctor: it's curious to me, your giving your opinion. It's not based on any studies, is it, of the effect of television on people?

7.16   WAHL: So far as I know, this is so new that there are no formal studies; but it is the opinion of myself and, I think, a vast number of my colleagues. Moreover, there's a phenomenon in history that this is illustrative of.

7.17   O'CONNELL: Could we omit history for a second, doctor? I just *do* want to emphasize that it did astonish me. I checked this with Dr. Schramm of Stanford and Dr. Ganz of Harvard, and I believe these are the foremost experts. It did surprise me. There are no studies of the effect of television on people. That's correct, isn't it?

7.18   WAHL: This is largely because, I think, this is so new. Give us a year and ask me that question again and I'll undoubtedly give you a different answer.

7.19   MONITOR: You take the position that televising trials might encourage people to acts of violence. Well, the televising would occur *after* the act of violence, wouldn't it?

7 . 20   WAHL: Yes, but it would profoundly affect persons in the community who are on the *edge* of some such neurotic act.

7 . 21   MONITOR: Is it your belief, or suspicion at least, that if criminal trials were broadcast then people would kill in order to get their picture on television?

7 . 22   WAHL: I most certainly believe that to be so.

7 . 23   O'CONNELL: One thing I'd be curious about, doctor. What is your feeling about the district attorney of Los Angeles County televising the Deitwaller inquest and getting that information out to the community? Do you think he was wrong to do that?

7 . 24   WAHL: I understand the motives that impelled it, which I think are laudable and advantageous. I share Mr. Cooper's views that there were many disadvantageous aspects of that [but I would not condemn it altogether].

7 . 25   O'CONNELL: Could I question you on the subject of televising the Chicago Seven trial. You realize, now, what an enormous controversy has erupted over the judicial process itself, as to whether the government and the court were fair or whether the defendants were acting horribly, or vice-versa.

7 . 26   WAHL: Yes.

7 . 27   O'CONNELL: And you are aware that they are now going to make a play and a movie out of the trial?

7 . 28   WAHL: I didn't know that.

7 . 29   O'CONNELL: That's correct. Would not it be better for the public to be allowed to see that trial for themselves and make up their own mind about what happened?

7 . 30   WAHL: There's an added disadvantage of enormously increasing the disruption in the court so that dispassion and capacity to honestly examine both sides of the issue would be infringed on.

7 . 31   O'CONNELL: What's interesting to me on that, doctor, is that in New York, in the Black Panther hearing before Judge Murtaugh, he simply ended the hearing when [disruption] was going on; and that may well be possible, and at the same time the public can see what's happening.

7 . 32   MILLER (*in summation*):   The first person to agree that television reporting is in fact different from newspaper reporting would be Marshall McLuhan. And he would make the points that not only is it different, first of all, on those who abuse; and the point is that when we have televised the trial, you get an *event*. You don't simply get reporting of what otherwise *would* have occurred, but a *different* event; and he himself would most certainly recognize that the effect on people who watch television is dramatically

different than on simply those who read the printed page. In fact, we're talking about, for the commercial purposes of television, broadcasting a few sensational trials, not for the purposes of justice, but for others entirely.

8.   NEXT AFFIRMATIVE WITNESS: DIRECT EXAMINATION

8.1   o'connell: As to what Mr. McLuhan said would be the effect of televising trials: he says that the public would become *involved*, would become *participants* in the process. . . .

8.2   monitor: Do you mean—do you and Mr. McLuhan advocate—that each neighbor spy on his other neighbor?

8.3   o'connell: What I'm saying is that, as 100 years ago when de Tocqueville mentioned it, people *should* become involved, and that, if a crime has been committed, yes, they should come forward.

8.4   monitor: Isn't that the technique of totalitarian oppression?

8.5   o'connell: No, I entirely disagree with that. If you took a look at de Tocqueville's book—and this country was certainly not a totalitarian country—

8.6   monitor: I'm thinking about the techniques used by the Nazis and the Fascists, when neighbors spied upon neighbors to gain favor with the government.

8.7   o'connell: What I'd be curious about: do you think that the public is now knowledgeable enough and interested enough in what's going on, in the problems of law administration, in the courts and the judicial system?

8.8   monitor: I do, yes.

8.9   o'connell: Let's take a look at, instead of theory, what has actually happened. I would like to point to the experience of the Supreme Court of Colorado. It was Colorado which in 1956 held hearings and then decided to allow television. And I would like to contrast that with the stand of the American Bar Association which, as far as I know, has refused to even *experiment*. They have refused a number of times. In Colorado, they held hearings and the Chief Justice of the Colorado Supreme Court who held those hearings stated: "We are concerned with realities and not with conjecture. Canon 35," which is the [A.B.A.] rule outlawing television, "assumes the fact to be that use of camera, radio and television instruments must in every case interfere with the administration of justice. For six days I listened to evidence and witnessed demonstrations which proved conclusively that the assumption of facts as stated in the Canon is wholly without support in reality."

8.10   I would like to see the American Bar Association have some experiments. I would like (to follow up) to say that the Colorado rule allows any witness to refuse to be televised. Mr. Chief Justice Moore stated, in a speech a few years ago, that not one witness refused to be televised. I would add that there has been no dissatisfaction expressed with the rule. And with us tonight to discuss the effect of television in the courtroom is Mr. Richard Jencks, who is president of CBS Broadcast Group which oversees all television and radio activities of CBS. Mr. Jencks, in your opinion will television in the courtroom be obtrusive? Will there be cables, lights, and that type of thing?

8.11   RICHARD JENCKS: There need not be. As you know, the Sirhan Sirhan trial was televised by closed circuit, and the cameras were completely hidden behind screens. There were no cables in the courtroom. The technology is perfectly able to produce a television setting without any cameras in the courtroom itself, or cables, or technicians.

8.12   O'CONNELL: Will television in the courtroom impair the dignity of the court?

8.13   JENCKS: I don't think so, unless the dignity of the court is already impaired. Trials are an immensely educational process for all those who participate in them—for witnesses, for participants, for the members of the public who see them. Smaller and smaller audiences witness trials in our large cities, and this is unfortunate because, as you mentioned earlier, there was a time when it was a common occurrence for large sections of the population to witness them. I think they're terribly impressive. They would be impressive on television. De Tocqueville, who seems to be our favorite author, spoke of the "civic religion" in America, and by that he meant a situation in which the American public virtually worshipped fair trial, free press, [and] the other constitution[al] guarantees of the nation. We need to bring that civic religion back; and one way to do it, it seems to me, would be to utilize the power of television to show the people the majesty and the fairness and the toughness of the judicial process.

9.   CROSS-EXAMINATION

9.1   MILLER: I'm interested in how you decide what to show. There are lots of parts of the system of criminal justice that either need improvement or could stand the glare of television investigation. For example, problems in juvenile detention homes, which have been severely criticized and which everyone ought to know more about. Your network has total access to those other parts of the system of criminal justice. How many programs and how many hours has CBS devoted to that problem of juvenile detention homes? or to prisons or anything?

9.2   JENCKS: "Juvenile detention, or prisons, or anything." We devoted something over 700 hours on the network last year to all subjects under the sun, just in news and public affairs.

9.3   MILLER: Well, let's strike the "or anything." Since you don't want to answer the other part of the question, let's get back to juvenile detention homes.

9.4   JENCKS: I'm sorry, but I'm not prepared on this kind of notice to tell you how much time we devoted to a particular area of controversy. We have done a number of broadcasts about criminal justice. We did a notable one, for example, about trial lawyers, in which we had some of the most distinguished trial lawyers in the nation discussing their experiences.

9.5   MILLER: Let me ask you, though, about the decision about what goes on and what does not go on. I take it [that] if you could not televise meetings of the Senate Foreign Relations Committee, you would be the first to protest and claim the people's right to know. And yet it was your network, was it not, that overruled its own president [and] instead of showing a Senate Foreign Relations Committee hearing showed reruns of "I Love Lucy?"

9.6   JENCKS: That story's usually told in terms of the sixth rerun of "I Love Lucy." I would like to point out that in that factual situation, one other network had already announced its intention to cover those hearings. The issue which was before us was whether to duplicate that identical coverage. We decided not to. I don't think that was such a bad decision.

9.7   MILLER: It led at least to the resignation of the president of CBS News. Let me ask about the Army-McCarthy hearings. How much would it cost today to televise, in full, the equivalent of the Army-McCarthy hearings, as ABC did in 1954?

9.8   JENCKS: It would cost a great deal of money.

9.9   MILLER: The estimate is $15 million. What is it you have to get for your $15 million? Don't you make money by selling commercial time at 40 to 60 thousand dollars a minute, [so that] you must have programs that people will watch?

9.10   JENCKS: We've never concealed the proposition that we're a commercial enterprise, like other commercial enterprises, and we need to make money out of what we do. But nevertheless, that doesn't keep us from carrying hundreds of hours of public affairs material each year, which is nonremunerative.

9.11 MILLER: I want to ask about the influence of that commercial necessity. Not too long ago, many of the television networks staged many quiz shows, which were represented as being fair representations of what was honestly going on at the time. And yet the neccessity for commercialization of the representation of fairness turned out to *corrupt* those quiz shows. Is there any thought in your mind that the same processes might happen in the courtroom?

9.12 JENCKS: No, there is not. In the first place, the quiz show situation—which, incidentally was one that did *not* affect the network that I happened to be employed by—occurred, as you know, many years ago; and I think it entirely inappropriate to suggest that there is, or would be, a parallel between entertainment and news.

9.13 MILLER: But, of course, you would be willing to pay the defendant for the right to televise his trial; but you would not pay him for news conferences.

9.14 JENCKS: No, we would not. We do not pay anyone for hard news interviews.

9.15 MILLER: We'll allow you to answer these questions so that it doesn't affect your position. Let's assume I'm simply talking about ABC and NBC.

9.16 JENCKS: I don't know what their practice is; but allow me to say that I think it is wrong in principle for newsmen to pay news subjects for interviews, and equally wrong for lawyers to be involved in publication . . . [of articles] for profits for defendants.

9.17 MILLER: You don't think there's any chance that the verdict would, in effect, await the commercial, do you . . . [that] the verdict would be delayed so that we can hear the next commercial?

9.18 JENCKS: No, I don't think so. I think that [suggestion is] very picturesque.

10. FINAL AFFIRMATIVE WITNESS

10.1 O'CONNELL: Let me finish my case with an interview with one of the most respected television news broadcasters in the industry: Mr. Walter Cronkite, also at CBS. [*On film:*] Mr. Cronkite, why do you believe that television should be able to cover criminal trials with the consent of the defendant?

10.2 WALTER CRONKITE (*on film*): Because I believe that television is simply the extension of the individual by electronic means anyway. And anywhere that the public is entitled to go, I believe that television should go; and our whole jury system is based upon public admission to the trial, the peers judging their peers—the public admission to the trial to constantly monitor the justice we are getting. Television is simply an extension of this right.

10.3   o'connell (*on film*):   If the Chicago Seven trial had been televised, would it have made any difference?

10.4   cronkite (*on film*):   It certainly would make a difference *now*, in the post-judgment of the trial proceeding. If the public had been permitted to be there through television, it could have judged far better by itself, on its own, the conduct of the seven in the trial and the conduct of Judge Hoffman. Now, there's going to be a great deal of rhetoric about the conduct of these two parties that we really can't judge except on the statements of the individuals concerned. That's not as good as having been there.

10.5   o'connell (*on film*):   Might also the public, the people of the country, have an interest in seeing what their courts are doing?

10.6   cronkite (*on film*):   Yes, I think you'd find that shot through this whole affair. Once you opened up the courts, there would probably be some demands for court reform, I should think. Maybe that's why it's being resisted by the courts.

11.   CLOSING STATEMENTS

11.1   o'connell: In conclusion, I would only repeat what Mr. Cronkite said. "Television is an extension of the people." Let's use it. . . . Let the people see for themselves. As Mr. Cronkite said, let them see what happened in Chicago. In order to get away from de Tocqueville, I would like to mention Socrates, who said "The unexamined life is not worth living." I would add: neither would the unexamined society [be] worth living. The courts have gotten too far away from the people. It was interesting to me to listen to Mr. Cooper, who said [that] once people get in there and are jurors, they're extremely impressed with it. That has been my experience. I say: let us show the court to everyone.

11.2   miller: Television, unfortunately, exists for itself. The mythical impartial eye, that views in the interests of the public, simply does not exist. The eye views in its own interests, and its proponents talk about a television system that simply does not exist. The system that exists changes and corrupts what it touches. Trials that are televised will be different events, to their own detriment. The system that exists chooses what is sensational and commercial, not what is educational and helpful. The system that exists would change both justice and perhaps itself to its great detriment.

 *22 March 1970*

SUGGESTED EXERCISES

1. How does the "Colorado rule" governing telecasts of trials, as described in the foregoing debate, differ from the proposal that was aired in the debate?
2. Devise a 'balance sheet' in which you juxtapose claims made by the Affirmative and the Negative in the debate about the consequences of allowing television broadcasts of criminal trials with consent of defendants.
3. Critically review the *cases* (broadly construed) that were mentioned by participants in the foregoing debate. Discuss the nature and the propriety of the inferences or lessons that speakers drew from these cases.

COMMENTARY

Reversible References

In *Historians' Fallacies* David Hackett Fischer devotes a chapter to "fallacies of factual verification," one of these being the "reversible reference," a piece of evidence that is cited on behalf of one inference, when it can just as plausibly be cited on behalf of a contrary inference. The label "reversible reference" seems applicable, loosely, to three pieces of testimony given in the debate on television coverage of criminal trials.

One of these pieces of testimony consists of Justice Thomas Brennan's argument to the effect that direct television coverage of criminal trials would be preferable to the present "insidious practice" of "trial by news conference" (**2.12**). Justice Brennan's practical conclusion starts with the premise that present press coverage of trials leaves much to be desired. More specifically, Justice Brennan is complaining about the use made by attorneys of press conferences outside the courtroom, conferences that are instigated by, among other things, prohibitions against direct electronic and photographic coverage of in-court proceedings. However, the premise can be used to draw quite different inferences. One might argue that since the newsmen now do a bad job under the present dispensation, which includes certain privileges and restrictions, they will do a worse job under a new dispensation, which would include more privileges and fewer restrictions. Similarly, one might argue that full electronic coverage of trials would merely intensify the evils stemming from "trial by news conference," especially since attorneys would still be able to use the latter device. In short, one might reverse the implications of Justice Brennan's premise concerning "trial by news conference"—as Grant Cooper implicitly does, when he tentatively advocates (5.21) more severe restrictions on the conduct of lawyers and newsmen.

Another piece of testimony that could be cited as a "reversible reference" consists of Dr. Charles Wahl's derogatory remarks about news coverage of the war in Vietnam (6.5). Dr. Wahl claims that the newsmen's biases (which were unspecified) are "evident" from their handling of Vietnam news. This experience is cited as grounds for retaining prohibitions against television coverage of criminal trials. But one might argue just as plausibly that biased coverage is a function not only of personal dispositions, but also of technical opportunities. In this vein, one might argue that the news media now can give quite biased accounts of criminal trials, because they are not allowed, much less obliged, to give quite direct, 'unmediated' coverage of these trials. If they were authorized to present direct, unmediated coverage of such trials, they would have fewer opportunities to impose their biases by way of arbitrary selection and emphasis.

Similarly, one might treat Howard Miller's treatment of the murder of Lee Harvey Oswald as a reversible reference. According to Miller (1.7), pressures from the mass media prompted the Dallas police to bring Oswald to court by a route that was congested. The ensuing confusion made it relatively easy for Jack Ruby, a bystander, to shoot Oswald. This episode was treated by Miller as an illustration of how the needs and demands emanating from television broadcasters can obstruct the administration of justice. However, one can view the same episode in quite a different light. A contrary argument runs as follows. First, present laws prohibit cameras and electronic recording devices in courtrooms. Second, this prohibition generates intense pressures to get pictures and recorded statements from participants in trials as they enter and leave courtrooms. Third, then, it was such pressure, due to such a prohibition, that led to the murder of Oswald. Thus, if direct television coverage of trials were permitted, such miscarriages would not so readily occur. On this showing, the murder of Oswald illustrates the need for allowing direct television coverage of trials, rather than illustrating the pernicious effects of such coverage.*

Pontificating

In a recent and most useful book called *Improving Your Reasoning* (Prentice-Hall, 1970), Alex C. Michalos devotes a chapter to modes of argument that "take advantage of our conditioned response to marks of authority." Among these devices he includes the practice of using "a reputable authority in one area . . . as an authority in an entirely different area." When an advocate employs this device, he engages in what Michalos calls the fallacy of "appealing to irrelevant authority." When an expert in one field lends himself to this practice by delivering pseudo-expert opinions in another field, he indulges in what can be dubbed *pontificating*.

Examples of the latter practice abounded in the debate on television coverage of criminal trials. These examples are particularly interesting because they are subtle in character. There were no cases in which a revered theologian, a brilliant quarterback, or a matinee idol was called upon to speak "authoritatively" on matters remote from his professional

---

*Closely related to the phenomenon of the reversible reference, incidentally, is a device which might be dubbed a rever*sing* reference. This consists not of offering an alternative interpretation of a given piece of evidence, but of introducing additional evidence that is related to a given case and its interpretation. Two illustrations were given in the debate.

One involved the career of Sen. Joseph R. McCarthy of Wisconsin. Kevin O'Connell cited television coverage of the Congressional committee hearings that pitted Senator McCarthy against the Department of the Army as an example of how direct coverage of events can augment public knowledge as well as support for "the processes of justices" (2.12). To this Howard Miller responded with a general reference to the career of Senator McCarthy. According to Miller, Senator McCarthy wielded excessive power "because of his misuse of television" (6.1).

The other example of rever*sing* reference grew out of the way Kevin O'Connell interpreted the direct and fulsome television coverage of the inquest into the fatal shooting of Leonard Deitwaller. Full television coverage, according to O'Connell (2.9) prevented a recurrence of rioting in the Los Angeles district of Watts. Howard Miller did not directly challenge this version of cause and effect, but he did invoke a related case. He argued (6.1) that the riots that previously had devastated Watts were causally related to the character of the television coverage given at the time.

field. The witnesses who participated in the debate were in *some* sense qualified to speaking about courtroom proceedings, about mass communication, and other relevant issues. Yet most of them indulged in no small measure of pontification.

Marshall McLuhan, a professionally trained student of literature and philosophy, has lately won renown as an essayist on mass (and particularly electronic) communication. But neither his professional training nor his research has qualified him to speak with authority on the proposition that direct telecasts of criminal trials would elicit from spectators an "environmental orientation" rather than an "individual orientation" toward crime (2.6). This assessment is far from being self-evident. Indeed, I might argue just as plausibly, and pontifically, that direct telecasts of criminal trials would magnify the "personal" elements at the expense of general patterns—would rivet our attention on individual cases at the expense of appreciation for underlying conditions that breed crime.

Incidentally, Professor McLuhan's credentials as an expert surely are impugned by his initial delivery of a piece of blatant nonsense: namely the remark—which "you're familiar with"—that "you don't have a police force until the community bows out of action" until public "participation in law and order is finished" (2.2). Members of the public at large participate in maintaining or subverting "law and order" by how they treat policemen, how they treat offenders, how they rear their children, and what they do about protecting themselves from crimes.

Kevin O'Connell indulges in a bit of pontificating, as well as conclusion-jumping, when he opined (2.9) that the absence of rioting in the Watts district, in the wake of the shooting of Leonard Deitwaller, was "a result of the telecast—both live, and on the evening news," of the Deitwaller inquest. Such a version of cause and effect is by no means self-evident. It gains only a small measure of plausibility from the following bits of evidence: a previous encounter between police and Negroes in Watts had triggered rioting; the District Attorney of Los Angeles authorized full television coverage of the Deitwaller inquest in the *hope* that this would avert rioting; the Deitwaller inquest was not accompanied by rioting; and (as O'Connell mentioned later, at 5.9) the Kerner Commission reported that television is more trusted by ghetto Negroes than are newspapers.

Thomas Brennan, as Chief Justice of the Supreme Court of Michigan, certainly is not without qualification to speak with authority on how direct television coverage of trials would affect the accuracy of records and the character of proceedings. But neither does he qualify as an expert on these subjects. He is making guesses in the absence of direct comparative experience, even as you and I. Of course, the guess of an eminent jurist properly carries more weight than the guess of a cloistered academic. But such a guess still needs to be checked against actual experience. And if direct experiences are not available for examination, the next best thing is an expert opinion, based on systematic interviews, on the *cumulative* guesses of judges and other participants in trials.

Similarly, Grant Cooper's rich experience as a defense attorney in sensational criminal trials, while not wholly irrelevant, scarcely qualified him to assess the probable impact of direct television coverage on the conduct of trials, not to mention the conduct of citizens at large. Neither was Cooper qualified as an expert to evaluate the wisdom of District Attorney Evelle Younger's decision on televising the Deitwaller inquest.

Incidentally, Cooper indulged in a bit of card-stacking when he declared that "the courts of this country have studied this problem and 48 States of the Union are opposed to it"—meaning, presumably, direct television coverage of criminal trials—"as well as the Federal Courts" (**5.6**). This claim about what the "courts" have done in the way of studies, and about how the "courts" feel about the issue, was not substantiated. Cooper apparently was using present rules (prohibitions against direct television coverage) to infer both prevailing opinion and the foundations of such opinions. But it may well be the case that many judges are receptive to direct television coverage, and that such opinions, as well as the contrary opinion, are not based on systematic studies.

Again, Dr. Charles Wahl's training as a psychiatrist does not obviously qualify him to generalize about the impact of direct television coverage of criminal trials on neurotics and psychotics in the community at large. In his case, the lack of special qualifications was eventually noted. Kevin O'Connell elicited an admission (**7.15–.16**) that Dr. Wahl was not basing his opinion on "studies . . . of the effect of television on people." Moreover, O'Connell introduced the claim (**7.17**) that "the foremost experts" on the subject at hand, "Dr. Schramm of Stanford and Dr. Ganz of Harvard," report that "There are no studies of the effect of television on people." This claim served at least to limit the authoritative character of Dr. Wahl's judgment that "television is a very special medium that appeals to the dramatic and the infantile in us and in a way that no other medium does . . ." (**7.12**).

By the same token, Richard Jencks's experience as president of CBS Broadcast Group may qualify him to give an expert opinion on how physically obtrusive or unobtrusive the physical apparatus for telecasting would be in a courtroom (**8**.10–.11), but his opinion about how television would affect the "dignity of the court" (**8**.12–.13) is no more authoritative than yours or mine.

Finally, Walter Cronkite's years of work as a newscaster scarcely qualify him to speak authoritatively on some of the topics he chose to address. Cronkite has not devoted his career to political philosophy or to constitutional law. He is strictly an amateur when it comes to the specific implications of a general doctrine concerning "the public's right to know" (**10**.2). Indeed, Cronkite is vulnerable to the *ad hominem* charge that he reflects the peculiar self-interest of a television newsman competing against printed news and against 'pure entertainment.' Moreover, Cronkite's experience as a newscaster scarcely qualifies him to speak authoritatively on behalf of the thesis (**10**.6) that direct television coverage would generate demands for reforms (positive ones, presumably) of judicial procedures.

Should colleges adopt a fixed rule expelling any student who uses obstruction, sit-ins, or other illegal physical force as a means of persuasion?

OVERVIEW

Of the many changes that have taken place recently in American colleges and universities, one of the most dramatic surely is an upsurge of violence. Buildings and equipment have been wrecked. Teachers, administrators, students, policemen, and off-campus elements have been harassed, villified, crippled, killed. Tear gas, bullets, bricks, bottles, and epithets have filled the air. It is difficult indeed to retrieve the stereotyped image of the college campus as a tree-lined ivy-covered refuge from the bustling Outside World.

Upheavals did occur in the past, but they were largely 'innocent,' or non-rancorous: a panty raid, a bonfire, a fraternity spree, a vicarious renewal of athletic competition. In the present context, the use of violence is often a calculated device whereby some students, some neighboring dropouts, and perhaps some faculty members, attempt to exert influence on campus policies or on society at large. According to some observers, these outbreaks pose a serious, and novel, threat to academic freedom, to freedom of inquiry, to the acquisition and dissemination of knowledge. In times past, threats to academic freedom were imputed largely to outside sources—governmental busybodies, imperious trustees, intolerant alumni, ignorant townies—rather than to students or to faculty members. According to other observers, however, these outbreaks can more correctly be described as rebellions against repressive and unjust elements, on campus and off.

What should be done about student-instigated violence on the campus? The possibilities are numerous, and each raises a multitude of delicate issues. One suggestion is canvassed in the following debate.

1.   OPENING STATEMENTS

1.1   MODERATOR VICTOR PALMIERI: Campus violence this year [1970] is even more widespread than last, and in more and more universities, students are resorting to unlawful physical force. They're disrupting meetings in classes; they're holding officials; they're deliberately using force as a political instrument on campus.

1.2   Tonight's debate focuses on two questions: Can it be right to use force in a university as a means of persuasion? Would it make sense to have a rule requiring the automatic expulsion of students who, after a fair procedure, are found to have used such force?

1.3   We're not debating which kinds of student protests are lawful or unlawful. We're only considering illegal actions. And the *practical* choice is this: Should colleges expel any student who uses physical force as a means of persuasion? Advocate Baker says "Yes."

1.4   ADVOCATE LISLE BAKER: If we allow physical force to displace reasoned debate as a means of settling disputes on campus, we will not only undo what a university is all about—the right to think and the right to disagree with each other—but we will also encourage the wider use of violence in society at large. For if educated men will not stand for peaceful change and against mob rule, who will?

1.5   The issue, then, is whether colleges and universities should be at the mercy of a small band of morally arrogant students. Now, in society we protect ourselves from another man's will, whether he's President of the United States or a next-door neighbor, by appealing to the higher authority of impartial law. But the problem with colleges is that many of them are now lawless: some discipline students arbitrarily, and others call in police at the first sign of trouble. We think there's a better way of doing things. Students should have clearer rules of conduct and fair hearings.

Clear rules not only protect the college, but also protect the student by keeping the college from disciplining the student except for an explicit violation of a clear rule. The most important clear rule you can have would outlaw physical force as a means of persuasion on campus. This would *not* restrict constitutionally protected speech or assembly. Nor would it prevent students from using their ingenuity to devise effective tactics for peaceful change. But it *would* keep colleges from being at the mercy of students who use muscle power rather than brain power to impose their morality. Because unless you outlaw physical force, the rule of the jungle still prevails, and the rule of law is a fraud.

1.6   PALMIERI: Advocate Semerjian says "No, such a rule would be unfair."

1.7   ADVOCATE EVAN SEMERJIAN: Automatic expulsion is unwise for two basic, fundamental reasons. First, it wrongly assumes that physical force is never justified as a means of persuasion; on the contrary, [force] is justified in many situations. Second, whether force is justified or not, automatic expulsion is unfair, arbitrary, and unreasonable.

1.8   Moreover, this proposal [for automatic expulsion] really doesn't treat students like adults at all. In fact, it treats them like nonentities and perhaps something beneath what we would call adults. I see no reason why students should be considered second-class citizens and be given rights and freedoms which are beneath those of citizens who are not members of a university.

Automatic expulsion violates the fundamental principle requiring the punishment to fit the offense and the offender. We wouldn't punish stealing a loaf of bread with deportation. And yet the automatic punishment [rule] makes no distinction between classroom sit-ins to protest university racial discrimination and wanton assault and battery to protest the color of the dean's tie, for example. There's no inquiry permitted into mitigating circumstances or background or motive. All students, whether they're straight A and honest or on probation and dishonest, are to be expelled. Such unfairness to students can't be tolerated in this country. Furthermore, the rule actually forces harm upon the college, because it forces members of the faculty to adopt an arbitrary position. It forces them to be unreasonable and, in fact, to abdicate their roles as members of the faculty and as administrators.

1.10   One other thing the rule does: it assumes that existing communication is adequate. It assumes that the university is sufficiently responsible. I think our history in the past three to five years has shown that this is not so, and is still being shown not so.

2. FIRST AFFIRMATIVE WITNESS: DIRECT EXAMINATION

2.1   BAKER: [Our first witness] is Dr. James Hester, president of New York University. We haven't quite persuaded Dr. Hester to accept an automatic rule, but he can speak to the illegitimacy of physical force on campus. Doctor Hester, is physical force ever appropriate on campus?

2.2   DR. JAMES HESTER: I don't think so. There are a couple of basic reasons that make force illegitimate. The university performs many functions, but its preëminent function in our society is to serve as our most comprehensive agency for advancing understanding and knowledge, for advancing civilization through the use of the mind, through brain power. From the experience we've had over the centuries, we've learned that the brain functions most effectively, most fully, most creatively, when it is free and unrestrained by threats and intimidation of any kind. Therefore we have worked hard, and only recently achieved conditions of maximum freedom for both faculty and students in our universities. For the faculty, freedom has been established in the last couple of decades very effectively; for the students, we are still achieving more freedom for them than they enjoyed several decades ago. Now virtually everyone in the university is free to raise any question that he wishes, to challenge the society. And this is good, because only in that kind of environment can we expect to make progress, can we expect to unearth the inadequacies of our present system and go forward.

2.3   This kind of freedom is a very complicated environment. It exists because the people in the university accept certain ground rules in their relations with one another—both explicit and implicit rules about the way people should be treated. These rules have become more explicit as violence has been introduced into the university. To introduce violence into the university, to use force, contradicts the basic assumption that the freedom that is essential for the functioning of the human mind is essential to the university; and therefore, those who use it are disqualifying themselves from being part *of* the university.

2.4   BAKER: Some students claim that they have no vehicle, that there are no outlets for their moral interests in proposing change in the university without force.

2.5   HESTER: This simply isn't true. In most instances in which violence has been used, the issues have never been adequately pushed before the existing agencies within the university. If the same amount of effort were made to persuade the faculty, to persuade other students, to persuade the trustees or the administration, of the cause that the students have in mind, much more would be accomplished than by the use of force itself. There may be instances in which there have been conservative or reactionary elements in a university, but I would argue that the use of force in order to dislodge them does not justify the great damage that is done to the essential condition *of* the university. And in many more instances, real change has come about through peaceful protest and petition within the university.

3. CROSS-EXAMINATION

3 . 1   SEMERJIAN: Do you agree that a small band of morally arrogant students are the ones responsible for the physical force that has occurred on many campuses in the past three or four years?

3 . 2   HESTER: Yes. In fact, I would say that those who have used force most often are not those interested in constructive change, but those interested in destroying the university. They realize that using force is the way to destroy the university.

3 . 3   SEMERJIAN: Is it your position, doctor, that the only students in this country who are using physical force of any kind are this small band of morally arrogant students?

3 . 4   HESTER: Not at all. There are many students who get caught up in the issues in the university, become persuaded by the violent radicals that the only way that they can effectively persuade the administration is through force; and there have been many who have been misled into violent protests of one kind or another who are not themselves dedicated to the proposition that the university must be destroyed.

3 . 5   SEMERJIAN: So in your view there are only two kinds of students who are involved in campus protest of this type?

3 . 6   HESTER: I didn't say there are only two kinds. You asked if there were two kinds, and I said there are. I would say that the major groups involved are the morally arrogant ones and the ones misled by the morally arrogant ones.

3 . 7   SEMERJIAN: All right. Now, are you saying, Doctor Hester, that physical force is never justified in a university setting?

3 . 8   HESTER: I would say so. The essential condition of the university is so important that force is never justified, because it damages that essential condition.

3 . 9   SEMERJIAN: Let me give you an example of a situation which we'll assume to be true, and you tell me whether your opinion would be changed. Assume that there is a college somewhere where there are 10 blacks who are students and that the number of blacks at the university, in proportion to the other students there, is smaller than the proportion of blacks who are available in the community. And these students, for years, appealed to the administration and the admissions office and the faculty to increase the number of blacks who are students there. And after referring it to an advisory committee, the university agrees that there are too few blacks; that, in fact, they have been admitting too few of them; and they, in fact, promise [in] the following years to admit more. The students are satisfied, and they go back and wait; and [in] the following years there are still only 10 blacks; and [in] the following years after that there are still only 10 blacks. Now, you would say, in that situation, wouldn't you, that the students have done everything they could under your system, to appeal to the college and university?

3 . 10   HESTER: Not necessarily. They could continue their effort to persuade the faculty, to persuade the administration, to persuade the trustees.

3 . 11   SEMERJIAN: How many years would you want them to continue doing this before the university changed its policy about admission of blacks?

3 . 12   HESTER: I think the integrity of the university is so important that they must continue to use every peaceful means possible in order to make their point.

3 . 13   SEMERJIAN: Well, I'm asking you, Doctor: what, in addition to appealing to the university officials, as you suggested in your direct testimony, would you suggest that they do?

3 . 14   HESTER: There are many, many devices that they can use; many forms of peaceful protest.

3 . 15   SEMERJIAN: Let's say that these students were frustrated and fed up because the university reneged on its promise to admit more blacks. And let's say the students waited a couple of years and even threw in some more pleas. Now, would you say that if they interrupted a class one of these days, and took 30 minutes to present their views to [that class], that those students would be morally unjustified in using [such] physical force in order to present their views, after the university had made that promise?

3 . 16   HESTER: There have been many instances in which students have asked permission to present their views before a class and it's been done and there's been no use of force whatsoever.

3 . 17   MONITOR*: Are you, Mr. Semerjian, going on the assumption that more blacks should be admitted because they're black, or because of their qualifications? Do you have blacks that are qualified, or do you want them to be taken into the university merely on the basis of color?

3 . 18   SEMERJIAN: I'm assuming, for purposes of my example, that they are qualified and that the university in fact promised to increase the number of blacks as students there. So the issue of whether they're qualified or not isn't really present. It's the fact that the university promised to admit them and never did anything about it that is the issue in this case.

3 . 19   HESTER: I don't know of any faculty which over a period of time, if enough effort is made to persuade it, doesn't respond to the deeply felt interests of students.

4.   FIRST SUMMATION FOR THE AFFIRMATIVE

4 . 1   ADVOCATE BAKER: The problem with force is that it's so quick and easy; and if all students waited the two years and tried every available means . . . we wouldn't be here tonight. However, force seems to be the first resort rather than the last. President Hester has told us that students who deliberately use physical force disqualify themselves from membership in the academic community. And we think expulsion should be automatic. No student should be at the mercy of a tribunal that can play favorites. And no tribunal should be at the mercy of students who would use the same physical force to intimidate that tribunal into granting them amnesty. Moreover, an automatic rule gives students and not the college the responsibility to decide whether they stay in school or not. If they choose to use force, they choose to leave.

4 . 2   MONITOR: Mr. Baker, you say that [students] should not be at the mercy of a tribunal. Are you saying that we should do away, in effect, with the jury system that we've used in this country . . . ?

4 . 3   BAKER: No no. I'm talking about in the campus community—which is a voluntary community. Nobody forces anybody to go to college, and we're proposing that students be treated like the adults they are. And

---

*Louie B. Nunn, Governor of Kentucky and chairman of the State University's Board of Trustees.

part of being adult is having the responsibility for your own decisions. If you know that your act is going to result in an expulsion immediately, then you are really responsible for your decision. It's not the college who takes the blame, who has to handle the hot potato. It's *you*. And that's what being an adult is all about.

5.   BEGINNING OF ARGUMENT FOR THE NEGATIVE

5.1   SEMERJIAN: Dissent involving force has a lot of historical precedent. To see how it's been indispensable in the achievement of many reforms in this country, let's take a look at this film:

5.2   AUDIO OF FILM: The Boston Tea Party helped establish our nation; it was an illegal use of physical force. Before the Civil War, Abolitionists smuggled hundreds of slaves north to Canada by boat, in false-bottomed wagons, and under cover of darkness; these illegal actions helped bring slavery to an end. In Flint, Michigan, in 1937, workers demanding bargaining rights held a 44-day sit-in at General Motors factories, with 50 plants being forced to close their gates and 125,000 workers being left idle. That same year, the Supreme Court upheld the right of workers to organize and engage in collective bargaining. In the southern United States, in 1964, sit-ins, marches, and other protests continued to focus attention on discrimination against black Americans. Laws considered to be unjust were deliberately violated to force the courts to re-examine them. And on April 23, 1968, Columbia University's first revolt erupted over issues of racism, war research, and lack of administrative responsiveness to students. Buildings were seized and occupied. The president's office was taken over by protestors. Occupation ended one week later in a riot that left 148 injured, 720 under arrest.

5.3   SEMERJIAN: Columbia wasn't the first use of physical force as a means of persuasion, nor was it the last. With that kind of history, a fixed rule expelling students for using the same kind of physical force as a means of persuasion smacks a little bit of hypocrisy. It contradicts our own traditions and shared values in many ways, where physical force might be justified because people's backs are against the wall.

5.4   To help us understand why students find it necessary to use physical force, I'd like to ask Tom Gerety, a graduate of Yale University and now a first-year law student at Harvard, to take the stand. Mr. Gerety, have you found it necessary to use physical force as a means of persuasion?

5.5   TOM GERETY: Yes, I have. As an undergraduate at Yale, on issues related to the war and the university's involvement in our war policies, and as a graduate student at Harvard, on issues related to the institution's racism in its hiring policies, I found myself and others in situations where I think the use of force as a political tactic was justified. Many times, when students bring issues before university communities, insofar as university communities are not totally democratic institutions, they find that they not only do not win concessions, they often do not win hearings from the administrators on their grievances and on issues which relate not only to the university government and the role of the university in the society, but to the larger questions of justice and the substantial values of our society that affect all of us as citizens.

5.6   SEMERJIAN: At Yale, what kind of physical force did you use?

5.7   GERETY: We besieged faculty meetings, we dispersed meetings called by the president of the university, and finally, on several occasions—both when I was at Yale and since—students have seized buildings.

5.8   SEMERJIAN: Did Yale punish you for that?

   GERETY: No, they didn't. I think Yale was operating under a set of reasonable rules at that time.

5.9   SEMERJIAN: And were reforms accomplished as a result of the physical force in which you engaged?

5.10   GERETY: I think there were. We didn't win everything that we wanted, but we won concessions; we won presence on the governance of the university, and we won major substantive concessions on the role of the university insofar as it's engaged as an institution in this society and on the role of the university insofar as it's an employer.

5.11   SEMERJIAN: I take it that these were reforms which would *not* have been achieved had you not used physical force.

5.12   GERETY: They might have been achieved late. I think perhaps they would have been achieved—never.

6.   CROSS-EXAMINATION

6.1   BAKER: You said, essentially—as I understand it—that you think the universities will not move on their own initiative, or even under rational persuasion by members of the community, including yourself, to do the things that they ought to do. Now, . . . how many faculty members did you button-hole when you were at Yale before you went in to disrupt the meeting? How many did you try to persuade by sitting down with them—each individually—and saying, "I think this is a good idea"?

6.2   GERETY: Not only did I button-hole faculty members, but faculty members button-holed me; and I think I must have talked to every single faculty member that I knew and met, and there were lots that I didn't.

6.3   BAKER: Did you petition?

6.4   GERETY: We petitioned. At Yale we got signatures on petitions, and moreover we had manifestations, we had demonstrations.

6.5   BAKER: Did you use student newspapers?

6.6   GERETY: Student newspapers editorialized in many cases. The *Yale Daily News* editorialized on our side on the issue of R.O.T.C. and on issues of university governance. We petitioned and demonstrated over a period of several years.

6.7   BAKER: And in the process of this, you persuaded a great many people, I assume, that your cause was just. Otherwise they wouldn't have signed that petition; isn't that right?

6.8   GERETY: Moreover, a great many students, and I think in fact a great many faculty members, supported us from the beginning. But universities are not run by students, and often they're not even run by faculty.

6.9   BAKER: We're not talking about who runs the universities tonight, we're talking about what kind of conduct students should engage in. Now, you weren't intimidated into your views. What gives you the right to try and intimidate other people into theirs?

6.10   GERETY: When questions arise which are substantial and involve the values not only of the university but of our whole society—in times of war, in times when a country is acting in a racist way towards minorities within the country—those of us who believe strongly sometimes have to risk our careers. Sometimes men have to risk their lives—and many have in this country—to put those values before their fellow citizens.

6.11   MONITOR: How much force do you think the faculty should exert on you? Should they lock you in your rooms? They obviously could exert a lot of force on you. Do you object to them exerting force?

6.12   GERETY: If I was acting unjustly towards my roommate—towards someone who lived in the dormitory—excluding someone from the dormitory, and if the faculty tried to convince me and couldn't, and if I wouldn't move, if I wouldn't alter my stand, the faculty would be very justified in doing this, just as the faculty would probably be justified in expelling a student who assaulted faculty members arbitrarily.

7.   SECOND NEGATIVE WITNESS

7.1   SEMERJIAN: With respect to that last question, one of the problems involved with what students are trying to do is that they're faced with a basic, fundamental, and very important inequality of bargaining power. And . . . the parallel between the workers in the General Motors plant in 1937 and the students in Columbia is very striking, not because their demands were necessarily the same, but because they were fighting against the facade which does not respond; and it's the same kind of problem in both cases.

7.2   Tom Gerety and other students who share these experiences are not alone in their views. Many faculty members and administrators agree with them, and one of them is Rev. William Sloan Coffin, chaplain at Yale University, whose understanding and concern for students is well known throughout the country. We asked Reverend Coffin whether students are ever justified in using physical force.

7.3   REV. WILLIAM SLOAN COFFIN (*on film*):   A lot of people think students are soft; they'd protest at anything. I think it's correct that they are soft. But it's a great Plus—that is, I don't suppose any generation of students has ever been brought up in this country being told so frequently, "You're important, you're important." And they believe it. Now, it's a Plus because by implication other people are important, too. The result is their threshold of oppression is very low. They see the humanity of human beings at stake immediately—much sooner than I would, you know, having been brought up [earlier] . . . ; you take a lot of nonsense in this world. They say, "We don't have to." That's what's wrong with the world. Too many people are taking too much nonsense. People say, "Why don't you confine yourself to reason?" We've all learned that rational persuasion is the least likely way to persuade people to be rational.

7.4   Most human beings want peace at any price as long as the peace is theirs and someone else is paying the price. Al Capone, when he had all of Chicago bottled up, used to say, "We don't want no trouble." That's a very deep human sentiment. And college professors and presidents often will say, "We will always be glad to reason, but we'll never knuckle under to pressure." But they seem to respond a little bit more when there's a little bit of clout. Human beings are human that way. And, unfortunately, it takes a certain amount of pressure to get people to pay attention.

8.   THIRD NEGATIVE WITNESS: DIRECT EXAMINATION

8.1   SEMERJIAN: There are a lot of other reasons why this proposal should not be adopted, and to tell us what some of these are I'd now like to call Dr. James P. Dixon, president of Antioch College and a member of three Presidential advisory committees. Doctor, would you ever consider adopting an automatic expulsion rule at Antioch?

8.2   DR. JAMES P. DIXON: No. In fact, the general rule should run just the opposite. The general rule should be that automatic punishment has no place in the affairs of the university. It may have a place in the affairs of two-year-olds but it does not have a place in the affairs of the adult community. And automatic punishment of this sort that's proposed is most likely to undermine the very fragile trust which permits the kind of communication that permits the university to deal with contemporary problems.

8.3   SEMERJIAN: Do you think that automatic expulsion would have any significant deterrent effect on the use of force?

8.4   DIXON: I think it would probably escalate it. You know, force occurs in small packages and in large packages, and such evidence as we have about force when it occurs in large packages suggests a counterforce, escalates the confrontation, polarizes the situation, reduces the possibility to get at the real issues.

8.5   SEMERJIAN: Doctor, what would be a better approach to the problem?

8.6   DIXON: The better approach, if you please, is to "muddle through," in the best sense of the word. To take each situation as it occurs, to try to see whether or not the demands are legitimate or whether the use of force is capricious, to try to deal with the issues in each circumstance, and to try to use each circumstance as a circumstance for learning about the problem of the use of force.

9.   CROSS-EXAMINATION

9.1   BAKER: Doesn't really putting a deterrent in an automatic situation put the burden of decision on the student rather than the faculty?

9.2   DIXON: No; it holds the student hostage to the faculty.

9.3   BAKER: Why? He's hostage right now, because when he goes before an administrative tribunal, that tribunal can play favorites. It can pick the

SDS member and throw him out, and it can leave the hot-headed liberal in and say, "You're just a good guy; you're not really destructive." What we're proposing is that you just take *conduct.* You say [to the student]; "Physical force is wrong; and if you use it, you leave. And you, the student, decide." Now what's wrong with that? Isn't that consistent with treating people like adults?

9.4   DIXON: No. It's not in the nature of the university to judge in advance—not about physical force or physical theory. It is in the nature of the university to be an institution that examines into the situation and then makes its judgment on the basis of the circumstances.

9.5   PALMIERI: Doctor, you're essentially arguing for discretion based on the particular facts of the case, as I understand it. But isn't it the peculiar thing about the use of force that it can be used against the exercise of discretion?

9.6   DIXON: Yes, and so can reason.

9.7   BAKER: But the point is that if students are willing to use physical force, to get you to hire blacks or to end R.O.T.C. or [to reach] any other particular goal, they would be willing to use force to make you give them amnesty for their use of force.

9.8   DIXON: Perhaps so.

9.9   BAKER: Isn't it useful to take away, deprive them, of that second opportunity by making the rule an automatic one?

9.10   DIXON: No. The argument that is now being presented suggests that one cannot trust students and that one has no right to trust the legitimacy of force. I think that is a false argument.

9.11   BAKER: I beg to differ with you, doctor. If you really trust students, you will say, "You're man enough to make up your own mind about what happens. If you jump in the water, there's an automatic penalty that you're going to get wet. And the same thing happens in college. If you use force, you leave the university." That puts the burden of decision on the student rather than on the faculty.

9.12   DIXON: It puts the burden on the faculty to explain why that is a reasonable way to behave in a country where the problems of force are not just inside the university but are outside, and where the problem of the university is to bring reason and care and compassion to the problems of society.

9.13   BAKER: How can the university find ways to deal with the society's problems if, instead of using reason and compassion and rational persuasion to decide what's a good idea, somebody comes and hits you over the head and says, "Let's not worry about that. I know, and I'm going to tell you, and I'm going to beat you over the head until you agree with me"? How can a university do its job if it's subject to the rule of force rather than the rule of reason?

9.14   DIXON: If the university does not have the confidence that it can deal with them reasonably and rationally, but must wipe across them in an automatic sense, then it's not in a very good position to deal with force in society.

9.15   BAKER: Doctor, doesn't really putting an automatic rule into the situation force the university to be very careful about what conduct it proscribes and what conduct it does not? For instance, if you decide you want to be merciful towards a student, you write that into the regulation. You say: "Any student who uses physical force for a morally justified end, which we define as getting us to hire blacks or getting us to end R.O.T.C. or getting us to end contracts with the Defense Department, will *not* be automatically expelled." Now, that would enable you to have the same kind of result, but it would let the student know in advance what's going to happen to him. Why doesn't the automatic rule force the university to go through that kind of mechanism?

9.16   DIXON: An automatic rule allows a university to avoid that kind of mechanism.

9.17   BAKER: It can't, though. If every student who uses physical force as a means of persuasion goes out, that means that the university has to sit there and scratch its head very hard and say, "Exactly what do we want to proscribe? Is it every kind of physical force?" Does burning down the library, for instance, warrant an automatic expulsion in your mind? Or is there something lesser which would not? You see, you have to think about it very hard when you have an automatic rule, don't you?

9.18   DIXON: You have to think about it much harder when you're faced with a variety of circumstances.

9.19   BAKER: That's after the fact when you can play favorites.

9.20   SEMERJIAN (*in summation*):   If Mr. Baker is trying to suggest that universities should not think hard and should not scratch their heads and try to resolve this problem by thinking about it, then I have a further protest to make about this particular rule. It seems to me that if anything ought to be encouraged, it's thinking. It seems to me that if there's one thing this rule does, it's that it discourages it and permits the university, as a powerful institution, to hide behind a meaningless, arbitrary set of words.

9.21   Should we throw out Tom Gerety? If he tried what he did at Yale, he'd be thrown out automatically—no questions asked. Now, there isn't a single university that has been cited here tonight that has this rule, and why is that? Because people would hesitate to adopt it, and the reason for that is: Why would anybody abrogate their discretion in determining who is a person deserving of severe punishment and who isn't? Who wants to deprive himself of the opportunity to inquire into the background of physical force to find out why somebody did something?

10.   AFFIRMATIVE WITNESS: DIRECT EXAMINATION

10.1   BAKER: Mr. Semerjian's main point seems to be that physical force is justified when you can't get colleges to pay attention to their students. Now, students have a right to be heard, but they don't have the right to win every time. And they don't have the right to intimidate people to get that right to win, especially at the cost of destroying the university. *He* says an automatic rule doesn't let universities think; *I* say students who intimidate faculty members don't let *them* think. And you've got to ask which is the bigger cause. Do you want students to think about what will happen to them and whether they should leave the college or not, or do you want faculty members to think about whether students are going to hit them over the head because they don't do what he says—or if the faculty member doesn't do what the students say?

10.2   Now, to tell us why discretion is essentially unfair in this circumstance, is Professor Alan Dershowitz of Harvard Law School. Professor Dershowitz has represented some students who've been arrested for the use of physical force. Professor, do you favor an *automatic* rule for disciplining students?

10.3   PROF. ALAN DERSHOWITZ: I do. I favor an automatic rule basically to protect the civil liberties of the students. An automatic rule regulating college discipline of students who are disruptive first requires the decision-maker to articulate with great precision exactly what kind of conduct will result in punishment. It doesn't permit a "muddling through" of the kind that the president of Antioch discussed, and "muddling through" is a terrible system. The granting of discretion to administrators, who then can exercise their discretion in any kind of discriminatory manner—which is typical of the way police and prosecutors and judges operate in our society—is very, very opposed to civil liberties.

10.4   Moreover, an automatic rule requires that fair warning be given to the students, so the students know precisely what kind of conduct is permissible, what punishment would follow; and it doesn't make it depend on what the student believes, what he thinks, what he advocates, what organization he belongs to, what race he belongs to. If you give the administrator discretion, he can consider all these factors after the fact in deciding what kind of punishment to impose. But he can't write that kind of factor into a rule in advance. And that's why an automatic rule is a good one.

10.5   Moreover, an automatic rule focuses on acts rather than beliefs, and in a democratic society it's terribly important to punish *only* for deliberately performed *acts*, and *not* for the *motivations* behind these acts. Also, the decision—what kind of conduct to punish—is less political if it's made in advance. You don't think any *harder* about a problem after the crime's been committed, necessarily. You think *differently* about it. You not only think about the crime and the moral quality of the act, but you have the man in front of you and you say to yourself, "There's that fellow. He's a straight-A student; why should I punish him?" Well, if we don't want to punish the straight-A student, let's write that into the rule. How many faculties would adopt that rule? If we don't want to punish the liberals, but do want to punish SDS students, try to write that into a rule; but don't "muddle through" with that kind of discretion.

10.6   Moreover, my experience in the criminal law indicates that when you have an automatic rule, the levels of punishment are invariably lower, because you have to face up to the fact that this is the standard punishment. You can't have a range of punishments in advance, and then punish more harshly those people you don't like and less harshly those people you do like.

10.7   And finally, it seems to me that the academic community—that is, the faculty and the students—have a greater role in deciding the moral issue of what punishment should accompany what conduct if this is an automatic rule, because when you have a discretionary rule the administrators can always come back and say, "Well, case by case, we can't reconvene the faculty every time there's a case; we can't bring in the students." But if there's an automatic rule, to be decided in advance, the students will have a much greater role to play in what punishment is for what kind of conduct; and that is, in my mind, a very desirable result.

11.   CROSS-EXAMINATION

11.1   SEMERJIAN: I take it that you are assuming that, in all these instances where physical force is used or attempted by students, the universities, prior to the use of that force, were in a position to negotiate the demands, or would have been responsive, or otherwise have set up sufficient channels of communication so that force wouldn't be necessary.

11.2   DERSHOWITZ: I'm not in favor of an automatic rule which would punish *all* uses of *force* by expulsion. There's a difference between *force* and *violence.* . . .

11.3   Three kinds of things justify automatic expulsion: physical violence against members of the academic community; destruction of academic property; and repeated disruptions of academic exercises—that is, persistent refusal of students to allow teachers and lecturers to convey knowledge. Those are the three things that in my mind would result in automatic punishment.

11.4   SEMERJIAN: And in other instances of the use of physical force, you would not apply the automatic expulsion rule?

11.5   DERSHOWITZ: No; I would want to debate this at great length before the violence occurred.

11.6   SEMERJIAN: Now, you are drawing a distinction between two kinds of force. That is true, isn't it?

11.7   DERSHOWITZ: Of course.

11.8   SEMERJIAN: All right. But with respect to a certain category of physical force which you have yourself designated, I take it that you would be in favor of automatic expulsion for those students.
        Cross-Talk:

11.9   DERSHOWITZ: I would, and I'd want it defined in advance—   SEMERJIAN: —regardless of the reasons of the use of force—

You want to have the reasons count; let's write the reasons   —fine— into the rule and define them in advance. If you want to have mitigating factors in there, write   —fine— them into the rule in advance, but don't expect the doctor, professors of the universities and the administrators to say, "Well, in some cases we will, and in other cases we won't." Equal acts deserve equal punishment. That's the adult way of treatment.

—Now, I would like you, in one five-word sentence, to tell me exactly what is your opinion with respect to this rule. I have heard two different stories.

11.10   BAKER: How many syllables can he use?

SEMERJIAN: I don't care. You can use polysyllabic words if you want; but what I'd like to know in a responsive way is: what do you believe about this proposal?

11.11   DERSHOWITZ: I want automatic rules to accompany every disciplinary decision in a college; and once we accept that rule, we then have to debate what kind of conduct justifies automatic expulsion and what kind does not. Automatic expulsion should follow certain kinds of violent activities, defined in advance, and *not* defined *after the fact*, when an administrator can consider a whole variety of impermissible factors in making his discretionary decision.

11.12   SEMERJIAN: Why do you choose expulsion? Why don't you choose fines? Why don't you choose some other kind of—

11.13   DERSHOWITZ: We should have fines for certain kinds of conduct, suspension for other kinds of conduct, expulsion for other kinds of conduct.

11.14   SERMIJIAN: Well, in order to find out exactly what your position is, we're going to have to go through the whole catalogue of student behavior, and find out which ones you would fine, which ones you would expel—

11.15   DERSHOWITZ: Is that unexpected? This is a complicated issue—

11.16   SEMERJIAN: Now, the question is that you have, it seems to me, set out a litany of different kinds of physical force—

11.17   DERSHOWITZ: But I've set them out in advance [so] you can know what you're doing. I haven't said that the litany is going to occur after the conduct is over, when it's too late to modify your behavior.

11.18   MONITOR: Professor, are you saying, in effect, that outside of the college community we have certain statutes, we have certain codes, we have certain laws to live by, [and] you prescribe the same thing for the academic community, for the college?

11.19   DERSHOWITZ: That's right.

11.20   MONITOR: And is it your proposal that once you enter college, that you should *not* be subjected to the same kind of laws as you are outside— that is, academic rules?

11.21   DERSHOWITZ: On the contrary, my position quite clearly is that under the sentencing procedures available to citizens on the outside, an automatic rule does not exist.

12.   CLOSING STATEMENTS

12.1   BAKER: People justify force because they say that peaceful persuasion won't work. But force is quick and easy and the risk is that anybody can play, and as soon as you begin to introduce the rule of intimidation rather than a rule of reason into an academic community, you're back to the jungle. Now, outlawing force on campus would free us from this fear and make students devise peaceful methods of change. Can we really educate idealistic students like Mr. Gerety if we teach them to use the lazy method of intimidation? And if educated men will not stand for peaceful change and against mob rule, who will?

12.2   SEMERJIAN: Rather than a lazy method of intimidation, I would encourage a more active method by the university to inquire and to think. I would say that, rather than throw out people like Tom Gerety and others, we ought to inquire into why the students have to do this, why their backs are against the wall, and what is causing them to behave this way, if at all. And secondly, why not treat students the way people are treated on the outside? Outside, if you burn down somebody's barn, you can get fined anywhere from zero to five thousand dollars, or be put into jail from zero to five years. But the judge decides, using his discretion, what the punishment will be. Why should a student get less?

 26 April 1970

SUGGESTED EXERCISES

1. Listed below are eight labels and 18 propositions. For each proposition, select the *two* labels that are most applicable.

Here are the labels:

> AA   Asserted by the Affirmative, through at least one spokesman
> for that side in the foregoing debate
> AN   Asserted by the Negative
> DA   Denied by the Affirmative
> DN   Denied by the Negative
> IA   Ignored, or neither asserted nor denied, by the Affirmative
> IN   Ignored, or neither asserted nor denied, by the Negative
> ADA   Asserted *and* Denied by the Affirmative
> ADN   Asserted *and* Denied by the Negative

Here are the propositions:

1. No good ever comes of using force or violence.
2. Freedom of expression is abundant in present-day colleges and universities. Dissenting opinions can readily be expressed without fear of punishment.
3. College students are entitled, as a matter of moral right akin to that of ordinary citizens, to codified, before-the-fact knowledge of the specific penalties they will incur if they are found guilty of committing specified offenses.
4. College authorities should be empowered to allocate penalties not only on the basis of the immediate character of an offense, but also on the basis of the circumstances, the aims of the offenders, and the personal backgrounds of the offenders.
5. In practice as well as in principle, citizens of the United States enjoy equality before the law, in the sense that penalties for like offenses are the same regardless of the backgrounds, motives, and resources of offenders.
6. Illegal coercion as a method of procuring changes in college policies has not worked.
7. Use of violence as a means of persuasion cripples the work of an institution of learning.
8. There are two types of violence-prone students on today's college campuses: individuals who are morally arrogant and are out to destroy the colleges, and dupes of the latter.
9. In the absence of pre-established, automatic penalties for specified offenses by students, college authorities are able to set penalties in the light of such factors as the academic and non-academic records of offenders, the nature of the things protested or advocated, and

community feelings about what disciplinary action should be taken, as well as the immediate character of the offense.

10. The incidence of disruptive violence on United States college campuses has recently increased.

11. Adoption of a rule prescribing automatic expulsion for students resorting to illegal action on campus would curb the incidence of such activities.

12. If the penalties for specified offenses are not imposed "automatically," in the sense that their nature is prescribed in advance, then physical force can be used as a pressure tactic against disciplinary bodies.

13. Unchecked use of force or violence is likely to spread from college campuses to other sectors of society.

14. Force and/or violence have proved constructive in their results in the past.

15. Many, if not most, contemporary colleges and universities are undemocratic, or at least are imperfectly democratic, in organization.

16. A system of automatic, previously-set penalties for specified offenses, including automatic expulsion for students resorting to illegal violence, would impair feelings of trust between students and teachers.

17. Reasoning is the least promising method of inducing people to be reasonable.

18. Most outbreaks of violence on college campuses in recent years have come in the wake of lengthy, fruitless, non-violent efforts at persuading established authorities to change their ways.

2. In 50 words or fewer, summarize the testimony given by James Hester, president of New York University, in the foregoing debate.

3. In 50 words or fewer, summarize the testimony of Tom Gerety.

4. In 50 words or fewer, summarize the testimony of James P. Dixon, president of Antioch College.

5. In 50 words or fewer, summarize the testimony of Alan Dershowitz, professor of Law at Harvard University.

6. In 50 words or fewer, summarize the testimony of William Sloan Coffin, chaplain of Yale University.

7. Briefly enumerate the principal *lines of argument* emanating from the Affirmative side in the foregoing debate. For purposes of this exercise, "lines of argument" are substantively distinct claims about cause and effect, or about moral propriety, that are made in relation to a policy choice. They do *not* include *evidence* adduced in behalf of such claims.

8. Similarly, briefly enumerate the principal *lines of argument* emanating from the Negative side.
9. Compose an essay defending one of the following conclusions:
   1. In the foregoing debate, the most convincing case was made by the proponents of adopting a fixed rule whereby any student who uses on-campus illegal physical force as a means of persuasion would be expelled.
   2. In the foregoing debate, the most convincing case was made by the opponents of adopting a fixed rule whereby any student who uses on-campus illegal physical force as a means of persuasion would be expelled.

Should the u.s. government make contraceptives available to every american, including teenagers, and conduct an educational campaign to limit population?

OVERVIEW

Jean-Jacques Rousseau claimed discovery, 210 years ago, of *the* method for evaluating forms of government. The highest rating goes to the regime under which, without "external aids" such as immigration and colonization, "the citizens increase and multiply most."* This approach to evaluation did not prove to be the foundation of Rousseau's lustrous reputation as a pundit.

Thirty-six years after Rousseau, Thomas Malthus published quite a different interpretation of demographic trends. The human population, he argued, is afflicted with a "constant tendency to increase beyond the means of subsistence." Indeed, populations commonly increase geometrically, while the means of subsistence increase only arithmetically.**

Malthus's specific thesis has not survived the test of experience; but

---

*The Social Contract (1762), Book II, ch. 9.

**Essay on Population (1798), Book I, ch. 1.

his more general forecast has lately evoked renewed respect. Neither plague, nor famine, nor genocide, nor fratricidal and international warfare has sufficed, singly or in combination, to thwart an immense increase in the world's population during this century. Further growth has been projected by many demographers—without, some say, proportional gains in the means of subsistence.

This trend, however, no longer bears the marks of inevitability. We have learned a great deal about preventing conception without foregoing the pleasures of copulation. We can regulate our numbers without relying on the diseases of infancy, or plague, or human slaughter. But the proper application of such knowledge involves profound moral and practical issues. Some of these issues are canvassed in the following debate.

1.   OPENING STATEMENTS

1.1   MODERATOR VICTOR PALMIERI: Tonight the problem is the threat of overpopulation. The practical choice is: "Should the U.S. government make contraceptives available to every American, including teen-agers, and conduct an educational campaign to limit population?" Advocate Miller says "Yes." Our guest advocate, Mrs. Judith Hope, will argue against the proposal.

1.2   ADVOCATE HOWARD MILLER: Mankind now faces its greatest challenge: the challenge of its own numbers. Within 60 years the population of the United States will double, and within 60 years after that [will] double again. Clearly, our expectations of ourselves for our quality of life and for our children, and the course of our population growth, are on a collision course.

1.3   There was a time, not too long ago, when nations sought to increase the size of their populations, when baby booms were in fashion and bonuses were given for boys. Today . . . that is no longer true. Truly, today, less is more. Once countries reach a certain size—and we have certainly reached that size—their strength may come from limiting numbers.

1.4   Any society can answer problems that may occur in two years. What we must do *now* [is to] plan for problems that will arise in 50 years. And today the growth of our population gives us concern for what we will be like in 50 years: the air is already polluted over most American cities; emphysema and other lung diseases already [are] on the increase; the water in the rivers and oceans is polluted, and within 10 years there may be so much sewerage in the river systems in this country that it will exhaust all the oxygen in those systems; attempts to increase our food production simply add more pollutants to the soil and make it more difficult, in the long run, to produce more food; our production of carbon dioxide may be permanently affecting the temperature of the earth's atmosphere, making it difficult for us to survive in the ultimate sense.

1.5   In addition, there are very direct [and immediate] connections between population size and what occurs in this country . . . . For example, for every one percent increase in the birth rate, school taxes must be raised 27 percent to provide schooling for those children. Given what the American taxpayer thinks he can now pay for schools, the choice may be between quality schools or limiting our population.

1.6   When we use resources, [moreover,] we don't only affect ourselves. Our country—6 percent of the earth's population—uses close to 50 percent of its resources. All the fish that we import off the Peruvian coast, mainly to feed our chickens, would [relieve] the entire protein deficiency of the Latin American continent. By using resources from around the world, by importing resources into the United States to support our population growth, we are making it more difficult, if not impossible, for the rest of the world to control *its* population growth.

1.7   ADVOCATE JUDITH HOPE: If the enemy is *us*, then the battle is over. Mr. Miller would have us destroy the people to save the village. Federal government interference in the private and very personal areas of birth control and family planning won't solve our environmental and urban problems. But it *will* trample on individual rights.

1.8   We're not against birth control. Nor are we really in favor of pollution at all. In fact, we're very concerned about it. But we *are* against tonight's proposal, for two reasons: first, there is no over-population crisis in America today; second, the government has no place in the bedroom. We have ample natural resources. We have vast unpopulated areas. In fact, . . . 70 percent of our people live in 2 percent of our land, [in an area] the size of Nebraska. The crisis of our environment is due to our affluence; it's due to our wastefulness; but it's *not* due to our birth rate.

2.   FIRST AFFIRMATIVE WITNESS: DIRECT EXAMINATION

2.1   MILLER: The question [before us] is serious. Some think it may go as far as to man's survival. The American Museum of Natural History, as part of its centennial, has been running a two-year exhibit. It seriously entitled that exhibit, "Can Man Survive?" [Let us now pose that question] to Kenneth E. F. Watt, ecologist [and professor of zoology] at the University of California, Davis. Professor, can man survive?

2.2   PROF. KENNETH E. F. WATT: Perhaps. Only if he deals with the twin problems of population and the amount of pollution produced per person. Both of these problems must be dealt with jointly, or we don't have a chance. The general risk [of not controlling our population] is that we will make the planet uninhabitable, for life by us or anything else. The three primary short-term risks [are these]: number one, we're running the world out of energy very quickly—my scenario says that if the present trends continue, we will be out of crude oil in 24 to 32 years; secondly, pollution is increasing to the point where there's a real risk of running us into an Ice Age; and thirdly, we're creating a tremendous tax burden for the middle-class taxpayer in the United States.

2.3   MILLER: Some say we can handle the problem by redistribution. [It is probably the case that] 70 percent of the United States population lives on about 2 percent of the land. Can't we solve this problem by simply redistributing the population?

2.4   WATT: That argument is bald nonsense. The most recent studies available indicate that pollution of all kinds is now being found remote from places where it was produced. There is a tremendous increase in air pollution of the sort that can affect weather over Kenya and also over the central Pacific Ocean. And DDT is being found in Antarctic penguins.

2.5   MILLER: Is there a connection between the immediate amount of our population rise and the kinds of social planning that we do?

2.6   WATT: Certainly. The difficulty at the moment is that a very small rate of increase in population can produce a tremendous increase in the tax burden on the population, merely by increasing the number of people in school tax-*consuming* ages relative to the number of people in school tax-*producing* ages.

2.7   MILLER: We're talking tonight about a program that seeks to educate and [to] dispense contraceptives, but does not apply any coercion. Can such a program, simply with education and dispensation, work?

2.8   WATT: I believe it can. It's clear that where the spirit was willing—that is, between 1929 and 1933—the birth rate of the United States dropped; and the real point is that if we don't take the choice now, we won't have a choice later. [We would then] *have* to take an involuntary program. And ultimately, if we don't have to put up with an involuntary program that man imposes, Mama Nature will deal with this in her usual fashion.

3.   **FIRST AFFIRMATIVE WITNESS: CROSS-EXAMINATION**

3.1   ADVOCATE HOPE: You said that between 1929 and 1933, where "the spirit was willing," we did control our population?

3.2   WATT: That's absolutely true.

3.3   HOPE: We didn't have a Federal government birth control program then? We didn't have the Federal government conducting an educational campaign to limit our population? We didn't have any government intervention at all in birth control at that time, did we?

3.4   WATT: No, [we didn't].

3.5   HOPE: Now, you testified before a House of Representatives subcommittee some time ago . . . that we should stop our population increase *altogether*, [and indeed that] "we would have a more salubrious climate for our people if we only had 100 million Americans instead of 200 or 300 million Americans." Is that correct?

3.6   WATT: That's absolutely true. I have a simple reason for that, too: . . . if we keep on building up our population, because of the fact that this excess in population over the number in 1800 is made possible by crude oil, atomic energy, and coal, resources which we—

3.7   HOPE: I understand all that, sir, and I want to ask you this: how are we going to reduce our population to 100 million people? How are we going to bring our birth rate down to only a zero population growth?

3.8   WATT: I suggest exactly the same way it happened between 1929 and 1933: if the public is aware of the facts, I'm confident that, sooner or later, they'll do the right thing.

3.9   PALMIERI: Are you suggesting that we ought to have an economic collapse to limit our population?

3.10   WATT: No. What really happened there was that certain facts were made clear to the public: that it was necessary to limit [family size, because of economic hardship].

3.11   MONITOR*:   [What about] the question of promiscuity and a decrease in moral values, with respect to adolescents who might be encouraged [through] the use of contraceptives to obtain the goal that you have in mind? Has that entered your point of reference at all?

3.12   WATT: There [has been] an increase in promiscuity and a startling increase in gonorrhea. However, these two things have certain causes which can be dealt with. They're not directly related to the problem of birth control.

---

*Representative Edward Koch, Democrat of New York.

3.13   HOPE: I want to ask you one sort of personal question, but it affects many people. I want a large family. I want two or more children. What are you going to do with people like me? How are you going to make me conform to these Federal standards?

3.14   WATT: I think if I had three hours to talk to you, you'd be convinced that you should *not* have more than two children. I don't have three hours.

3.15   HOPE: My husband's been talking to me for two years, and he's convinced me I *should*. Now, population growth is a function not only of how many children are born to each family, [but also] of when people marry and when they decide to have children. So, if you're going to have the Federal government in this area, isn't it a fact that you're going to have the Federal government telling us—"educating" us, if you will—that we should only have two children *and*, what's more, that we should marry later and have our children later?

3.16   WATT: That's absolutely true. But that's exactly what happened in Ireland after the potato famine.

3.17   HOPE: Did they have a Federal program there? Did they have a Federal government birth control clinic in Ireland?

3.18   WATT: No.

3.19   MILLER (*in summation*):   The best way to deal with the threat of population increase is directly through education and through dispensation of contraceptive devices. The population of women who give birth to children is growing rapidly. Because of the baby boom in the 1960's there will be 80 million women—more than twice as many as there were in the 1950's—who will be in the age to give birth to children. It is especially important to move *now*. The alternatives are, in fact, famines. The alternatives may be, in fact, depression. The alternatives are to act consciously and control our population, or to have to act in other ways to control the consequences of too large a population.

4.   FIRST AND SECOND NEGATIVE WITNESSES: DIRECT EXAMINATION

4.1   HOPE: Recently, alarmists have been saying that our birth rate is causing our pollution. Two days ago we asked Dr. Ansley Coale, head of population research at Princeton University, whether this [version of the] relationship was an accurate one. This is what he said:

4.2   DR. ANSLEY COALE (*on film*):   To attempt to control pollution by Federal intervention intended to affect the birth rate would be irresponsible, because to affect the birth rate would require measures that would have very substantial social consequences and have only an indirect effect on pollution. This increasing pollution and deterioration of the quality of our environment is more strongly associated with rising income—rising affluence—than it is with increases in population itself.

4.3   If we had only half the population that we do today, we would have many of the same pollution problems, and of very nearly the same intensity. The aspect of population that is connected with pollution is more its location than its absolute size. We are heavily concentrated into cities, and with a smaller population we would still have large urban concentrations. For example, in Australia, where the total population is only about 12 million, Sydney, the largest city, has problems of pollution and a deteriorating environment not much different from our own.

4.4   HOPE: To put the so-called "population problem" into the proper perspective, we have with us tonight Dr. Karl Taeuber, an urban population expert from the Rand Corporation. Next fall he will be returning to the University of Wisconsin as chairman of the department of sociology. Dr. Taeuber, you've heard Professor Watt's testimony that we're polluted with people. Is he right? Should we adopt the Federal Government's baby ban in this country?

4.5   DR. KARL TAEUBER: Absolutely not. With reference to the United States, Professor Watt is off base. Professor Coale was nearer the mark when he said that a program to limit population growth is an extremely "indirect" way to approach our pollution mess. I don't think that what we need is some sort of magic contraceptive potion. I don't think we need to ban babies. We need to ban the thousands of municipalities that are dumping their sewerage into our rivers. We need to ban the thousands of industries and the millions of cars that are polluting the air we breathe. We don't need to waste our taxes and our time on some sort of fancy program in which a bunch of bureaucrats turn out propaganda against pregnancies. This would be a cop-out [from] very real, and very pressing, social and environmental problems that we face today.

4.6   HOPE: We've [heard] some rather frightening testimony. Is that testimony, is that gloom and doom, correct? Are we at a crisis level in our population growth?

4.7   TAEUBER: Again, I don't see that this applies at all to the United States today. Our birth rate is now nearer the low point than it has ever reached. We're growing at less than one percent a year. I don't think that there is any justification at the present time for any sense of crisis about adoption of some kind of radical Federal program to interfere with family life.

5.   CROSS-EXAMINATION

5.1   MILLER: The growth rate for the past several years has in fact been over 1.5 percent, has it not? Around 1.8. Do you oppose this proposal, in fact, as it's stated, to dispense the contraceptives and conduct an educational campaign?

5.2   TAEUBER: Yes, I do.

5.3   MILLER: And do you think there should be any limit on the size of the population? Could we support for example, the double population of 400 million people in 70 years?

5.4   TAEUBER: I don't quite know what we can support in 70 years, because it's very difficult to see 10 or 20 years into the future. And demographers, as you know, are very good at playing this game: projecting the doubling in 70 years or 60 years; and pretty soon the mass of humanity will be greater than the mass of the earth. I think this is the wrong numbers game. We have a situation in the last 20 years in which population has gone up by one third. The number of cars has more than doubled. Our consumption of electric power has more than tripled. Our visits to national parks have gone up more than four-fold. This is the problem: the way we use our money; the way we use our resources.

5.5   MILLER: Let's focus on that use of consumption and the number of automobiles that have doubled. I take it if we have 400 million instead of 200 million people; instead of the 1,000 municipalities that you mentioned, dumping their sewerage in the rivers,—there'd be 2,000. Instead of the number of automobile trips we now have, there'd be twice as many. Won't that directly contribute, not next year but in 20 years or 30 years, to increased pollution?

5.6   TAEUBER: I don't see 400 million people in 20 or 30 years. I think we have 205 million now, we're going to be within the 250–300 million range if current trends continue. We don't know whether they'll continue.

5.7   MONITOR: It would be very helpful to know what the figures are projected to be for the world's population. Could you tell us what they were a hundred years ago, what they are today, and what—if nothing is done—the estimated world's population will be a hundred years from today?

5.8   TAEUBER: Currently we have three and a half billion people—something in that range. A hundred years ago it [was] one billion, more or less. And we are growing at a rate which will produce a doubling in the order of 35 years.

5.9   MILLER: So it's tripled. Thirty-five years would project 7 billion, and the rate will continue to increase in 50 years if the projections continue. And [the figures projected] may or may not be nonsense, but the risk is that they will, in fact, be accurate. We'll have 14 billion. There may be no sure way of knowing, but we know that the risk is that if they increase, everything else will increase. And if we do engage in a program of population control, there is no other side risk to that.

5.10   Do you agree that there may be a program of redistribution of the population in the United States, that could be better able to affect the pollution problem than population control? Do you think [that] if we spread . . . our people around more, we'd have fewer pollution problems?

5.11   TAEUBER: We would have fewer pollution problems if we managed our current cities better than we do today. We have a vast metropolitan area in New York City, which has 1,400 governmental units.

5.12   MILLER: You want to stop people from moving into New York City—decrease the size of New York City?

5.13   TAEUBER: I have no desire to do that. New York City handles more people today, in a better fashion, than it did a hundred years ago. The difficulty is that those people are consuming more, are producing more sewerage, are producing more waste, are demanding more goods, are using more automobiles, more power.

5.14   MILLER: Let's talk for a moment about the people who we will have in the future. If the studies that have been done on fertility desires are correct— [then] 25 to 45 percent of the growth in population over the past 10 years has [consisted] of children that were unwanted at conception by their parents—

5.15   TAEUBER: The figure I've heard is 25 percent.

5.16   MILLER: Let's accept your figure. . . . Now, if that is true, would it contribute to our national well-being to give people the means *not* to have children they don't want, while we reduce the population size? Is that a positive good?

5.17   TAEUBER: Yes. There are many ways to *approach* that, however. One is the current Federal program we already have, to bring family planning to the 5 million poor women in this country who do not have access to medical services [as do middle-class women]. I favor [*this* program]. We are implementing it right now. We don't know how to implement it nationally—

5.18   MILLER: So you think it's fine for the five million poor but you wouldn't want it, on a national basis, for those who don't happen to be poor?

5.19   TAEUBER: Those who don't happen to be poor can go to the drug stores, can go to doctors, and find out all that they need to know.

5 . 20   MILLER: The evidence is that half of the unwanted children, in fact, are born in the middle class. If that is accurate, do you think that such a program is not necessary?

5 . 21   TAEUBER: Such a program is perhaps important on the part of voluntary organizations. I don't think that this kind of program can be effective from the government—in the same way that Prohibition was not effective. We can't get people to stop smoking even though it's going to kill them. We can't get people to buckle seat belts even though [not doing so] is going to kill them.

5 . 22   MILLER: [Anti-smoking propaganda] *has* materially reduced the incidence of cigarette use in the United States.

5 . 23   TAEUBER: It has slightly reduced it over a period of time; but not over the five-year period that Professor Watt is talking about.

5 . 24   MILLER: Suppose our population *does* increase to 400 million. (Let's assume that risk, because the question is "What if we're wrong?" . . .) What kind of controls do you envision to keep people from congregating in the large cities? Isn't it possible that we have to prevent them from living where they want to live, because of the population increase?

5 . 25   TAEUBER: I don't see any threat of that. What we'd have to ban, instead of banning people, is . . . the automobiles [and] perhaps some of the sources of energy. Many people would rather have children, and fewer cars and fewer resources, if it comes to this. I can't see 70 years into the future to know about this.

6.   THIRD AND FOURTH NEGATIVE WITNESSES: DIRECT EXAMINATION

6 . 1   ADVOCATE HOPE: A baby ban is not going to have much of an impact on our pollution problem, according to Dr. Taeuber. But it *will* have a devastating effect on the *morality* of our country. We asked Billy Graham to give us his views.

6 . 2   REV. BILLY GRAHAM *(on film)*:   The problem of government involvement in the question of sex education, and in dispensing contraceptives and information on controlled families and family planning, is getting into a very serious moral and spiritual question that the American people ought to examine very carefully. Now there have been some countries that have experimented in sex education from a humanistic point of view, making the sex act nothing but mechanics or a mechanical act, an animal act,

and not giving the moral and spiritual guidance that is very important in the matter of sex education. And this goes over into the whole realm of whether the government should get involved in telling us how large our families should be, and in giving us contraceptives and other information that now the government is giving some consideration to doing. I'm against it. I'm against it on moral and spiritual grounds—at least in the present situation—because I believe that one of the greatest needs in America is for people to understand the rules and regulations that govern marriage, and I believe that the bedroom is a place that the government ought to stay out of. I think the bedroom is between a man and his wife and God. Let's keep government out of the marital bedroom.

6.3   HOPE: As Billy Graham suggests, the government policy of birth control is going to make some very serious changes in this country. And he poses another problem: what about those of us who want larger families—larger than Federal standards allow? Will we be thought of as unpatriotic? Will we be shunned by our community? I want you to meet now a housewife, a mother of eight children, who can tell us how she feels: Mrs. Carl Cohan of Washington, D.C. Mrs. Cohan, if tonight's proposal becomes Federal law, do you think that there will be subtle governmental and social pressures brought to bear against those like yourself who have large families?

6.4   MRS. CARL COHAN: Your question takes me back a quarter of a century to the time when I was having my children. Dr. Graham set the keynote for something that I'm going to say—it's something that's not said in public, it's just not mentioned—and that is faith in God. When I had my children, it was in the depths of the Depression. And I had them one right after another. I had five in five years. I was known as "that woman down the street with all the children." People would commiserate with me. "How was I going to educate these children?" "How was I going to raise them?" I had no answer. My only answer would be, "I have to leave that to God."

6.5   My husband lost his work. We were dependent upon my parents for food. When I was pregnant with my fifth child and told one of my close friends, she said to me, "Is it too late to do anything about it?" And when I looked at her in horror she said, "You might as well know that every time you walk down the street you're going to be talked about." And as my children came, I would have questions like "Are you going to call this one quits?" When my husband went to register our children for the sugar ration coupons and he named them all—6, 5, 4, 3, 2, 1—the registrar, who was a schoolteacher, stood up and said, "You should be ashamed of yourself." And who was she to say who is to have children and who is not to have children?

6.6   Those children that everyone wrung their hands over are now contributing members of society. My oldest son is one of the leading attorneys in Washington. My second son is an outstanding internist. My third son is an urban planner. My fourth son is serving his country in Vietnam. And the fifth one, who is sitting over there in the audience—who medical science said I couldn't have, and it was a miracle he was born—is there as a living proof of what a family can do and what it can amount to. So I feel that, definitely, there would be these terrible pressures that are very hard to fight against.

6.7   HOPE: They'd probably be worse, wouldn't they, than what you experienced?

6.8   COHAN: They'd be very much worse, because today—and when I say this, I feel like David standing up to Goliath—we are being brainwashed. The great majority of American people don't realize what the most successful lobby and pressure group in modern times has done to brainwash people. We have taken the whole concept of population out of the proper perspective. I wonder how many people here tonight know that all of the world's 3.5 billion people would fit in the state of Texas and each family would have a quarter-acre of land.

6.9   PALMIERI: Which lobby is that?

6.10   COHAN: The Planned Parenthood lobby.

7.   CROSS-EXAMINATION

7.1   MILLER: I understand, and a great many people understand, the warmth of a large family, and why a mother would want to have many children. But each of these children uses five acres of land to have beef grown, consumes 16 barrels of crude oil a year, takes up a fifth of an acre in living space, and diminishes the ability of the other children to have quality education (because of the increased need for education for a larger number). Putting it on another kind of moral level, do you think that having a large family, with that number of children, which diminishes the capacity of other children to live effectively, [is] a moral question also?

7.2   COHAN: If I believed you, I would say "Yes." But I deny what you say is true.

7.3   MILLER: Believe me.

8.   A DRAMATIZATION BY THE NEGATIVE

8.1   HOPE: Two hundred years ago, Jonathan Swift put forward a plan to limit population and improve the quality of life for the poor. He suggested that the poor sell their children to the rich for food. He called his plan "A Modest Proposal." The baby ban put forth here tonight is a modest proposal only in *this* sense. As Mrs. Cohan's testimony indicates, it will, at the least, require a massive propaganda campaign to indoctrinate all of us. And if that doesn't work, what will the government do next? By 1976, only six years from now, the news might look like this:

8.2   ANNOUNCER: Washington announced today the start of another population control program. We talked to Dr. James Barlow, western regional director of the Federal Population Control Bureau.

8.3   DR. JAMES BARLOW: We found that over the past five years, the U.S. birth rate is not decreasing enough. Many women have stopped taking the Pill because they're afraid of it. Condom, diaphragm, and loop never were very acceptable or reliable. Now, in order to reach our 1990 goal, the Population Control Bureau is, first, raising the legal age of marriage to 25; secondly, in the event of a third child, we're strongly recommending vasectomy, that is, sterilization of the male, and abortion for the female; and third, we are adding fertility depressants to the water supplies in all urban areas.

8.4   ANNOUNCER: We have a report on the Los Angeles sterility campaign.

8.5   REPORTER: This morning, artificial human hormones were added to the water of all the reservoirs in Los Angeles. Just one glass, like this, will temporarily sterilize anyone who drinks it.

8.6   ANNOUNCER: Of course this is not the end of the race. Antidotes carefully manufactured and distributed will allow each family to have at least two children. Baby certificates from local population centers, good for two babies, have been mailed to all holders of valid marriage licenses. Finally, the Internal Revenue Service reminds us that, beginning January first, the normal $800 deduction for each child will no longer be granted; and Representative Thompson of California announced today he's introducing a bill that will increase your tax with each child. That's the news this day.

8.7   HOPE: Imaginary? Yes, that's an imaginary newscast. But it's not impossible, because all of the suggestions found in the newscast were taken from the writings of those who urge us to limit our population growth to a zero rate.

9.   FIFTH NEGATIVE WITNESS: DIRECT EXAMINATION

9.1   One man who feels very strongly about such government policies is the president of Reed College, Dr. Victor Rosenblum. Dr. Rosenblum, are you in favor of the government program which would limit population by dispensing birth control devices to every American, including teen-agers?

9.2   DR. VICTOR ROSENBLUM: I'm, of course, speaking only for myself; but I'm very much opposed to such a program. I regard the program as having a great potential for becoming coercive, despite its claim that it would be purely voluntary. In addition, it would be a program that is *elitist* in its conception, because it would fail to take into consideration the very deeply held feelings of many religious groups in this country, and the very deeply held feelings amongst black people in our country.

9.3   It would also expect of teen-agers a level of behavior that runs entirely contrary to our past expectations and traditions. It would sanction a degree of promiscuity, and a degree of the materialism of sex, rather than the spirituality and individuality of the individual human being in which we so much believe.

9.4   And finally, it is the wrong priority at the wrong point in history. The priorities of this country, at this juncture, ought to be the priorities of justice, the elimination of war, and the elimination of racism. . . .

10.   CROSS-EXAMINATION

10.1   MILLER: Let's talk about the priorities of justice. What is the justice of American children who are unwanted at conception utilizing resources from other places in the world that make it more difficult for other countries to control their population?

10.2   ROSENBLUM: I make the point that this is an *elitist* program, because the deeply held feelings of many American people are that they *do* wish to have children. And as the Supreme Court of the United States said 28 years ago, "This is a basic right." The right of procreation is a basic right of all Americans.

10.3   MILLER: Is it also a right *not* to have a child if you don't want to have a child?

10.4   ROSENBLUM: In a voluntary program, it certainly would be. I believe that there are voluntary organizations in this country that are doing an excellent job and that have no threat or danger of becoming coercive in their operation.

10.5   MILLER: Now let's talk about that danger of coercion. As the population grows, the pressure for coercive measures will increase, will it not?

10.6   ROSENBLUM: I know as an educator that many government programs that begin as "mays" become "musts." The many that start out with carrots soon develop sticks; and we've seen in education that the government is today—after having first encouraged us to apply for all kinds of assistance—prescribing standards of student behavior and of school management that I find essentially incompatible with the private system of education.

10.7   MILLER: That's a good answer, but not to the question.

10.8   MONITOR: Dr. Rosenblum, what you're doing is using the *reductio ad absurdum* argument in saying that the government ultimately will do more than what it now projects. But if it did no more than that which is proposed, would you oppose it?

10.9   ROSENBLUM: These are not *reductio ad absurdum* arguments, for at this time we have many pressures that are being brought to bear upon people who are presently receiving relief payments, to practice birth control or to get off relief. We've even had a decision, in the last few days in Massachusetts, in which a judge prescribed a requirement for sterilization of an individual if he couldn't make the payments to his child that he was required by the court to make.

10.10   MONITOR: Let me ask you another question in the same area. You mentioned religious groups who would oppose it. What is your position with respect to requiring vaccinations and polio shots even against the wishes of those who believe that that ought not to be done for religious reasons?

10.11   ROSENBLUM: There are certain things which must be done in the interest of public health. But I think that the statement by the Supreme Court 28 years ago is just as valid today as it was then: that the right of procreation is one of the basic civil rights of all Americans.

10.12   MILLER: I still want to get back to that question, because I think it's terribly important. The pressure for the kind of coercive devices that you fear will grow as our population grows, will it not?

10.13   ROSENBLUM: That's not at all clear. The pressure for those devices may well come from well-meaning taxpayers who think that such a program is going to save them money by eliminating people from the relief rolls.

10 . 14   MILLER: And you think that, as the population goes up to 400 million or 500 million, there will be no proposals as have been put forth in the imaginary, *wholly* imaginary, newscast?

10 . 15   ROSENBLUM: I think there are grave dangers of our reducing ourselves to a kind of neo-malthusian conception in which we say that aid should be eliminated totally to the poor on the grounds that the poor will simply reproduce themselves if we feed them.

10 . 16 .   MILLER: . . . 70 percent of population growth comes from groups not classified as poor. It comes from the middle class. So when we talk about the total population control, or total population planning, we're very much talking about a middle-class problem. And the idea of middle-class people talking about the rights of the poor, when they are the ones that are causing the growth rate, has some odd rings about it.

11.   SECOND AFFIRMATIVE WITNESS: DIRECT EXAMINATION

11 . 1   MILLER: Dr. Rosenblum apparently is for vaccination, for all public health measures, *except* too many people and pollution. We have to look at what this proposal does. . . . The pressure for coercive measures comes as the population grows. The larger the population grows, the more that pressure will develop. This kind of program, relying on education and voluntary distribution of contraceptive devices . . . to reduce the un-wanted births [and] hold down the population, is the *only* device that has a chance of preventing *those* kinds of coercive measures. By fighting this kind of program, and doing nothing on this kind of basis to check the population growth, we are *building* the very pressures that will lead to a demand for a *more* coercive system.

11 . 2   This is the way we can control our population without having the fears that were expressed. To do nothing now is to lead exactly to those fears that were expressed. In fact, we *do* plan for children *now*. We have tax exemptions. We have welfare costs. We have school costs, medical costs. The government is involved in all sorts of expenditures. The call for this kind of expenditure to limit population growth, especially among those who do not want the children—and that includes the middle class as well as some of the poor—is the best way to allocate these risks. If we are right, and if the population will continue to go up if we do nothing—and perhaps to destroy us all—then certainly we should move. If we're wrong, if in fact there would be no great harm to unchecked population growth,

but the policy is still instituted, what will have been lost? Nothing. The population can always be increased. The risks call for instituting the program.

11.3   To talk about that kind of problem—to talk about why it is that perhaps people should not have children, and why it is that this program should be instituted—we have asked Miss Stephanie Mills to join us tonight. Miss Mills is the editor of an ecology magazine, *Earth Times*, and she also, last year at the valedictory address at Mills College, said that as her contribution to the world she was going to have no children. Miss Mills, why did you say you would have no children?

11.4   STEPHANIE MILLS: Because I feel that the birth of a child has more consequences than just those that are felt in the nuclear family. The birth of an American child, especially the birth of a middle-class American child, means that there'll be a fantastic consumption of fuels and foods and metals and everything else. And this consumption means that there'll be children in other parts of the world who will have less of a chance of living a healthy and happy life. I also feel that it's an obligation of people who have their wits about them to recognize the problem and to be able to conceptualize a future: to adopt children who would otherwise have no chance in life.

11.5   MILLER: Does not having children offend your concept of being a woman?

11.6   MILLS: No more than not eating watermelon should offend the black.

11.7   MONITOR: Do you think that your husband will have some rights in this matter?

11.8   MILLS: He'll have as many rights as I should have. And the way I feel about this, in terms of his rights, is simply that I wouldn't marry a racist who disagreed with my ethical and ideological commitments, because it would make for a lot of friction. I certainly wouldn't marry a man who is ignorant of the dangers in this crisis and who wanted to impose his will upon me against my will.

11.9   MONITOR: But if, at a subsequent time after your marriage, your husband decided—for whatever reasons he came to that conclusion—that he *did* want to have children, you would consider that an obligation to be worked out between the two of you. Is that correct?

11.10   MILLS: Yes, certainly; in full cooperation and with understanding. I would hope that he could be persuaded to realize that love of children means love of children, and not necessarily procreating.

11.11   MILLER: Do you want to keep the government out of the bedroom?

11.12   MILLS: Absolutely.

12.   CROSS-EXAMINATION

12.1   HOPE: Miss Mills, as a mother I just don't agree with you but—

12.2   MILLS: How many children do you have, Mrs. Hope?

12.3   HOPE: I have one. I hope to have more, as you know. But let's talk about something that you said in the *San Francisco Chronicle*. My understanding is that you have sort of a five-year plan for fertility control. You think that we've got to reduce our population today, and that we should have, immediately, a tax plan to make children a liability; that we should have an intensive propaganda campaign to work a radical change on our ideas of reproduction; and that if, after five years, these two methods don't work, we should have involuntary sterilization for all men after they've had two children.

12.4   MILLS: To the best of my knowledge I have never said such a thing.

12.5   HOPE: All right, the newspaper was wrong. Let me ask you this question, then. Dr. Paul Ehrlich,* [like] many of his followers—and I assume you are one of them—has had himself sterilized in support of his beliefs. Have you, or do you intend to, when you marry?

12.6   MILLS: No. It's a radical surgical operation, and it would be much simpler for my husband to have *himself* sterilized.

12.7   HOPE: So you would advocate that your husband would do this when you married?

12.8   MILLS: I wouldn't make it a requirement for marriage, but I would rather he do *that* than subject me to the risk of taking a contraceptive for all my life. I think, in terms of relative values, that if the man really has a sense of his own virility, then the ability of producing children really isn't going to make that much difference. And incidentally, I really don't "follow" anybody.

12.9   HOPE: All right. You would say that it would be your husband's freedom of choice on whether or not he would sterilize himself?

12.10   MILLS: It's his freedom of choice to marry me or not, also.

12.11   HOPE: And it is, in fact, *your* free choice that you decided that you would not bring children into the world?

12.12   MILLS: That is right. I'd like very much to *raise* children, however.

12.13   HOPE: I understand that; and if it is this kind of a free choice that you're talking about and that you believe in so strongly, would you deny to any

---

*A Stanford University professor who heads a pressure group called Zero Population Growth.

other American woman the same free choice to bring as many children, or as few, as she wanted into this world?

12.14   MILLS: I would hope that, through a program of vigorous education, women would feel a social responsibility not to procreate irresponsibly, not to behave like rabbits. I would also hope that women could see that they could find dignity in other places besides motherhood, perhaps such as law or editing—

12.15   HOPE: I'm sure you don't mean to imply that Mrs. Cohan behaved like a rabbit. I'm sure you wouldn't insult her in that way. But I would like, if we can, to change the subject a little bit. There's been a lot of talk here tonight about the "unwanted" child—[talk to the effect that] if we can just eliminate the "unwanted" child from our population, we'll have gone pretty far to solving our problems. And I would suggest this to you. We have nearly 500,000 immigrants coming into the country every year. We have millions of people who are senior citizens. Rather than ban babies, why don't we say, "No more immigrants to the United States." And why [not] say, "Let's just dismiss our senior citizens; let's not give them medical help now; let's have our population be a young, growing population, not an old population with old ideas living in old houses?"

12.16   MILLS: That's a fairly convoluted statement you just made. In the first place, nobody is talking about banning babies. In the second place, if we do not educate the people to a generalized social responsibility—which means a consideration for all the other inhabitants of the planet—we may well have to institute measures such as banning immigration, such as denying medical care, not just to the old but to the poor. The thing about the population problem is that if we don't find the solutions humanely, the solutions will find us, and it will be either plagues, famines, wars, or governmental measures which might [be much more coercive than to-night's proposal].

13. CLOSING STATEMENTS

13.1   MILLER: If we do not move now in this program, we may, in fact, face the horrible alternatives that have been put forth. There may be a natural de-sire to have a large family, but in fact that desire today conflicts with what is socially necessary in the country. We must face that choice—a difficult one, but we must face it cleanly. Any society can answer the easy questions. Those that survive are those that answer the difficult ones, that face the need for doing things like limiting their own population.

13.2   HOPE: The proposal tonight is to attack man's problems by attacking man himself. This is no solution to population, and the results, if adopted, would be a sterile society—sterile in physical terms and sterile perhaps in moral and human values. We oppose it. We ask that you do the same.

 *8 March 1970*

SUGGESTED EXERCISES

1. According to the 1961 edition of *Webster's New Collegiate Dictionary*, a *reductio ad absurdum* is a mode of argument in which a given proposition is traced out to what purports to be a logical conclusion that is absurd. In the course of the foregoing debate, Monitor Edward Koch claimed (**10**.8) that Witness Victor Rosenblum was engaging in this mode of argument. Discuss the propriety of Koch's contention.

2. Critically review the notions of justice and/or human rights that were invoked by each side in the course of the foregoing debate.

3. Critically review the analogies and precedents that were invoked in the course of weighing the merits of the policy proposal that was aired in the foregoing debate.

4. Devise a "balance sheet" in which arguments (divorced from evidence) emanating from the Affirmative and Negative sides in the foregoing debate are juxtaposed and are organized under three headings: "The Need"; "Meeting the Need"; "Other Considerations."

Should criminal penalties for the use of marijuana be abolished?

OVERVIEW

Cannabis sativa is the technical name for a weed that is related to hemp and is most commonly known as marijuana. It bears resinous leaves that can be used as tobacco is used. Marijuana smoking lately has proliferated in the United States, especially among the youth. According to an estimate emanating from the National Institutes of Mental Health, more than 12 million Americans currently can be counted among the users, at least once, of marijuana.

These users—like the consumers of bathtub gin in the days of Prohibition—are committing a serious crime. It is a felony to use, as well as to possess, to grow, to distribute, to transport, or to sell marijuana in the United States. The volume of cases has escalated. In California alone, according to a recent report by the San Francisco Committee on Crime, whereas in 1960 4,245 adults and 910 juveniles were arrested for violations of the marijuana laws, by 1969 the figures had climbed to 38,670 adults and 16,000 juveniles.

Present laws make no distinction between marijuana and "hard" drugs. According to most if not all authorities, however, there are substantial differences in the chemistry and the effects of marijuana, a hempish weed, and opium, a narcotic juice-giving poppy which produces morphine and heroin. The existence of this distinction, among other things, has prompted appeals for a relaxation of the laws concerning marijuana. A specific change is discussed in the following debate, which demonstrates that forceful arguments can be mounted on each side of the issue.

1.   OPENING STATEMENTS

1.1   MODERATOR VICTOR PALMIERI: [Some people contend] that in a world of high tension and deep anxiety, marijuana provides a pleasant and apparently harmless respite. For many, though, the fact that marijuana is used so predominantly by the young provides cause for alarm. Some people consider any penalty unrealistic and unfairly harsh for the use of a "harmless weed." Other people say marijuana may not be harmless: well-controlled studies on the subject are very limited [and] at best give information on the effects of short-term use; many drugs, including morphine and thalidomide, were also once considered harmless.

1.2   Present laws specify felony prison terms for mere possession [as well as for] growing, importing, and selling [marijuana]. The narrow question we are discussing this evening is whether to remove criminal penalties for *using* marijuana. This question assumes that [Federal and/or State] laws would still prohibit *commerical* activities like production, importation, advertising, and sale. Should we abolish criminal penalties for the use of marijuana? Advocate Greenberg says "Yes." Advocate Miller says "No."

1.3   ADVOCATE MAX GREENBERG: I've never smoked marijuana. I wouldn't advise my son or daughter or anyone else to smoke it. But the question tonight is whether we should imprison anyone who does smoke marijuana. And my answer to *that* is an emphatic "No." Marijuana is nothing more than a mild intoxicant, less addictive than either tobacco or alcohol. Criminal penalties against its use don't work and they needlessly shatter the lives of many young people.

1.4   ADVOCATE HOWARD MILLER: Mr. Greenberg's advice to his children would be good advice. Marijuana is a dangerous drug. To legalize it at this point would validate it as a permanent part of our culture, and set in motion social forces—including vastly increased use, in amounts and doses, by the young—that would seriously harm our society.

2. BEGINNING OF AFFIRMATIVE ARGUMENT

2.1 GREENBERG: I'm not here tonight advocating the use of marijuana, just as President [Franklin] Roosevelt was not advocating the use of alcohol when he spoke out in favor of the repeal of the Volstead Act [which prohibited its use].

2.2 Marijuana and alcohol are both unnecessary drugs. I would advise my own teen-age children, by word and by example, not to turn on with any drugs. There are thousands of ways to get joy out of life without artificial stimulants. Just because we of the older generation can find our pleasures without marijuana does not, however, justify the imposition of our tastes on our young people, particularly by [the exercise of] harsh criminal laws. The only rational bases for law—especially criminal law, which directly restricts individual freedom—are facts which justify these restrictions: not fears and prejudices, and certainly not myths. Now, the existing prohibition is based on several fallacies.

2.3 Myth Number One: that marijuana is physically harmful. The fact is that "there are no lasting ill effects from the acute use of marijuana, and no fatalities have ever been recorded." This is a direct quote from Goodman and Gilman, a standard medical reference work. A rigorous study conducted last year at Boston University by Drs. Zinberg and Weill, concluded that marijuana is a relatively harmless intoxicant.

2.4 Myth Number Two: that marijuana is addictive. Doctor Roger Egerberg, Assistant Secretary of Health, Education and Welfare, testified on October 20 of this year [1969], "Its use, under ordinary circumstances, does not lead to physiological dependence, as do narcotics."

2.5 Myth Number Three is the old domino theory: that smoking marijuana leads to the use of heroin and other hard drugs. The truth, as stated in a famous article in the *American Journal of Psychiatry* by Doctors Allentuck and Bowman, is that there is no evidence to suggest that the continued use of marijuana is a stepping-stone to the use of opiates.

2.6 Myth Number Four, that smoking marijuana leads to violent crime, is refuted by the famed Mayor's Committee on Marijuana in New York City. They reported, after five years of detailed study, that . . . no direct relationship [was found] between commission of crimes of violence and marijuana. And Dr. James Paulsen of Stanford University said last year, "If anything, all experience indicates that marijuana is actually anti-aggressive."

2.7 The final fallacious myth is that smoking marijuana leads to loss of motivation and dropping out from society. Here are some quotations from real life:

2.8   FILM CLIPS: [Five persons testify that they have been occasional or regular marijuana users for several years, have not been adversely affected by its use, and have enjoyed its use—in the way that salt, as one says, "brings out the flavor" of a "good situation" and "makes it even better." These witnesses include an art director for an advertising agency, a clergyman, a businessman, a computer operator for a large financial institution, and an editorial assistant in a publishing house.]

2.9   GREENBERG: Our criminal laws label these young people as felons. Can we honestly say that a criminal record would be less harmful to their lives than smoking an occasional marijuana cigarette? Here to help explain the medical and social aspects of marijuana is Dr. Joel Fort, who's been described as one of the world's leading authorities on drug abuse. Dr. Fort is a medical doctor specializing in public health and youth problems. He has just published *The Pleasure Seekers*, a book on alcohol, tobacco, marijuana, and other drugs. Doctor, do you recommend the use of marijuana?

3.   FIRST AFFIRMATIVE WITNESS: DIRECT EXAMINATION

3.1   DR. JOEL FORT: I don't *recommend* the use of marijuana, alcohol, tobacco, or any other potent, mind-altering, drug.

3.2   GREENBERG: Are you in favor of abolishing the criminal penalties against use and possession of marijuana?

3.3   FORT: I am in favor of abolishing those, and I consider that when we criminalize the user or private possessor of marijuana it is as barbaric and inhumane . . . as burning witches at the stake or [throwing the] mentally ill into dungeons [is now considered], and as ineffective.

3.4   GREENBERG: What do you recommend our marijuana laws ought to be?

3.5   FORT: American society has to face up to the fact that there is no simple, one-dimensional solution for any complicated problem. We've been trained that the way to solve problems is simply to pass a law, and then, when that doesn't work, to increase the penalties, build more jails and prisons, and so on and so forth. So we have to approach it on many different fronts.

3.6   The first major reform is to take the drug user—the private possessor of drugs who is not engaging in anti-social behavior—entirely out of the [realm of] criminal law; and concentrate a public health and preventive approach on the widespread use and abuse of alcohol [and] tobacco—a whole range of drugs [for the use of which nobody] would be handled as a criminal.

3.7   Then, we should ban all advertising of drugs such as alcohol and tobacco, and certainly not permit the widespread promotion of any other drugs through mass advertising.

3.8   . . . the major trafficking in drugs considered unwise or evil by this society should be handled through criminal law, but . . . the main emphasis of criminal law should go to crimes against a person, crimes against property, most of which do not involve drugs and, when they do involve a drug, mostly involve alcohol.

4.   CROSS-EXAMINATION

4.1   MILLER: Do you think there should be no penalties for the use [of] marijuana [by] young people—say, 14-year-olds? 15-year-olds?

4.2   FORT: I do not believe that the proper approach to them or to anyone else is to destroy their [lives] by making them criminals.

4.3   MILLER: Is that true for all dosages of marijuana? Say, taking its higher dosage form, the joint that may contain 10 percent THC.

4.4   FORT: The proper approach for all doses or all substances that may be harmful is through education, prevention, and through providing positive alternatives, rather than through blind punishment and destruction.

4.5   MILLER: What about the use of heroin? Should the use and possession of heroin be a crime?

4.6   FORT: The private drug user, I do not believe, should be treated as a criminal, with heroin or other drugs. But I do believe each drug should be handled as a separate issue, and with heroin the major thrust should be to prevent its growth, its distribution. And great emphasis [should be placed] on the trafficker in heroin. That is one of my main points.

4.7   And my second main point is, with marijuana, that as compared to other risks and dangers in society, it is particularly barbaric to continue to use our present approach.

4.8   MILLER: Do you think the sale of high-potency marijuana—again, let's say 10 percent THC, a fairly strong joint—should be illegal, to a young person, for example?

4.9   FORT: Yes, I do think so.

4.10   MILLER: And you say you think that a marijuana law should say that the sale is illegal but the use is legal? Is that going to increase respect for law?

4.11   FORT: Greatly, because the present law is wholly hypocritical. It's irrational in its priorities, ignoring the massive use and abuse of alcohol and tobacco, and putting the brunt of enforcement on the private user while failing to apprehend the major distributor.

4.12   MILLER: Suppose [the laws against the use of marijuana] were changed and entirely taken off the books, so there were no [penalties]: neither the present penalties nor lesser [ones] like misdemeanors. Do you think the use of marijuana would increase?

4.13   FORT: Not significantly. I don't think any drug, including marijuana, is so inherently desirable or important that 200 million Americans would suddenly rush out of their homes to use it. We have greatly oversensationalized it, glamourized it, made it seem much more interesting.

4.14   MILLER: Let's not talk about 200 million. Let's talk about several additional million. Do you think there is a substantial number of people who would use marijuana if there were no penalties for its use?

4.15   FORT: There are a substantial number who would use it *less*, because one of the causes in present use is the hypocrisy and absurdity—irrationality —of our present approach. So that would balance out. Certainly there would be some who would use it; but many of those would find that they get nothing out of it and would go on to do other things.

4.16   MILLER: So on net gain, you don't think whether marijuana is legal or illegal to the user makes any difference in the rough total quantity that's used?

4.17   FORT: Probably not, because it's escalated so much, as we know, in direct association with (and often caused by) the present extreme laws and enforcement policies.

4.18   MILLER: Suppose we remove penalties for the user. Would not that create an incentive for the illegal seller of the drug to sell more expensive drugs, to push the drugs harder, because now the user in effect can use it without penalty, so his market has been opened up to him?

4.19   FORT: Not at all. In fact, that shows a misconception about how marijuana is disseminated. It is not a big-time pusher, for the most part, who is passing it around, but rather people who are making it known to their acquaintances and friends, and usually amateurs or somewhat-professionals—

4.20 MILLER: So . . . you advocate that if 10 people go out and chip in to buy a kilo of marijuana, the one who buys it for the use of his friends is a seller and should be punished, but the others who simply use it . . . should not be?

4.21 FORT: Well, I advocate first of all that . . . our whole approach be reversed, become a constructive, positive attempt to provide meaningful alternatives to drug use, and that, secondly, no user—particularly where you're dealing with alleged or imagined evils as compared to real or proven evils—be criminalized.

4.22 MILLER: There are some people for whom marijuana, especially in the higher dosages, is, in fact, harmful?

4.23 FORT: It *may* be harmful. I think [that] is the best way of putting it.

5. BEGINNING OF NEGATIVE ARGUMENT

5.1 PALMIERI: All right, now it's your chance [Mr. Miller] to present your side of the case for retaining the penalty.

5.2 MILLER: We are dealing with the new myth-makers, and the problem is not the old myths but the new myths. Because we now realize that marijuana is not as bad as heroin, we hear people say that it's like salt. Because liquor causes [an] enormous [sum of] deaths in this country—40,000 deaths on the highways alone, 30,000 deaths in other accidents—we hear people say that other things, simply because they may only be *that* harmful, should also be legalized. We hear talk of "marijuana," a myth itself, as though there were some single dosage of marijuana that is uniformly used when, in fact, as our experts will testify, the marijuana that is most widely used in this country is very weak. But to remove the penalties would open the door to much stronger and harsher and more hurtful kinds of marijuana. We hear talk about enormous numbers of people who use the drug. But, in fact, the enormous growth in the number of users is fairly recent—over the past five to ten years—and probably is not as extensive; but even if [this is] so, [use] has moved into a different level of the population. And as soon as people who are not terribly used to being exposed to criminal penalties—the white middle class—became exposed to this, suddenly it became a great issue. Millions were using it before, and of course the fact that it was harmless escaped the attention of many who now urge repeal of laws against it.

5.3   The final myth we're dealing with is that this is just an issue for the individual—that, after all, if it may not be harmful for any individual, those who use it and who think it's like salt may have the repeal of laws which will cause its more widespread use in society.

5.4   We're dealing with societal mechanisms here. Dr. Fort thinks that the repeal of criminal laws [would have] very little effect on the number of people who use it. In fact—especially among the young—the repeal of the criminal laws would have very substantial effect, and, as our expert psychiatrists who work with the young will testify, is a very material factor in limiting the use.

5.5   Finally, a great deal of what's been said about marijuana most recently is not relevant to how we can measure it, because it was just two years ago that a substance in marijuana that causes harm, THC, was synthesized. And it is only now that we can effectively measure the effect of dosages. We have with us here Dr. Reese Jones, a professor of psychiatry at the Langley-Porter Clinic, University of California Medical Center, who had the first National Institute of Mental Health grant to do research solely on marijuana. Doctor, what is the normal burden of proof in whether we're considering that a dangerous drug ought to be introduced into society?

6.   FIRST NEGATIVE WITNESS: DIRECT EXAMINATION

6.1   DR. REESE JONES: Good medical practice in this country and all countries indicates that one must prove a drug is harmless before it's introduced into society, and laws are written to make for this [result]. . . .

6.2   MILLER: Are there, in fact, different dosages of marijuana?

6.3   JONES: American, or the domestic marijuana that's available in most of our large cities, is little more than an active placebo, in terms of this tetrahydracannabinol content you referred to. It's very weak material. More potent forms are available.

6.4   MILLER: Have you done experiments with more potent forms?

6.5   JONES: We have used a variety of forms, ranging from materials [with] no THC to hashish that has up to 20–25 percent THC, by weight; and the results varied greatly.

6.6   In the low [concentrations], not very much happens; [marijuana] looks like a harmless drug. But this is material that's very, very low in THC content. When one gets up in the range of materials with 10–15 percent, one sees psychotic reactions, grossly impaired motor performance, memory impairment, a variety of behavioral deficits.

6.7   MILLER: That's an amount of marijuana that could be taken in how many joints?

6.8   JONES: If one had available some of the better quality materials [such as] Panama Red: two or three joints, in some subjects.

7.   CROSS-EXAMINATION

7.1   GREENBERG: You said "if you get up to a high enough dose, you'll find motor impairment in anyone," and that sounds very impressive. But isn't it equally true of alcohol? If I give even a confirmed drinker a high enough dose of alcohol, won't it show some impact on the way he behaves?

7.2   JONES: This is true of any drug. . . . There are some important differences between alcohol and marijuana, however. With a high dose of alcohol, you fall asleep, generally, or you get sick and start vomiting. High doses of marijuana quite often, instead of producing motor impairments, produce psychological impairments. . . . Within the toxic range of the *cannabis* products, in a number of laboratories and in the real world, the medical [reports show] a paranoid, delusional, anxiety-ridden picture that's quite different than the drunk in the gutter.

7.3   GREENBERG: Have you done any studies involving smoking in a social setting?

7.4   JONES: In contrived social settings. At present our results, however, are consistent with the reports, the isolated reports, of toxic reactions one reads about—most recently in the journal of the American Medical Association and other medical journals.

7.5   GREENBERG: Mr. Miller said it's only recently that we can do a study of *cannabis*. How many years has *cannabis* been in common use somewhere in the world as a means of smoking, or being ingested?

7.6   JONES: Thousands of years.

7.7   GREENBERG: Thousands of years! And isn't it true that the United Nations estimated in 1960 that there were 200 million *cannabis* users throughout the world?

7.8   JONES: I'm not sure of the figures, but it is possible.

7.9   GREENBERG: If there have been *cannabis* users for thousands of years, and [if] there were 200 million of them throughout the world in 1950 or 1951, and if we've had a sharp increase (up to 12 or 20 million users, are the estimates that I've read, in the United States in the last five or ten years), [then] aren't there some studies that could be made about the impact of the use of *cannabis?*

7.10   JONES: There's a variety of studies dating back; there are some very fine ones done in the latter part of the nineteenth century, in the French literature and in a number of Middle Eastern countries. The results uniformly indicate that the use of *cannabis* in these countries is quite analogous to the situation that alcohol is causing [in our country]. In France they claimed, rightly or wrongly, that the hospitals were full of chronic hashish users, around 1890.

7.11   GREENBERG: Was that the finding of the Indian Hemp Commission, which made a very responsible report in 1894?

7.12   JONES: The Indian Hemp Commission found a significant number of people impaired through the chronic use of hashish, albeit a significant number *not* impaired.

7.13   GREENBERG: Oh well, impaired by the use of hashish. Let's examine that. There are three grades of *cannabis* being used in India at the present time, aren't there?

7.14   JONES: At least three.

7.15   GREENBERG: Yes. And the one that's comparable to the marijuana being used in the United States is not hashish but bhang, isn't it?

7.16   JONES: Bhang. Yes.

7.17   GREENBERG: So when you talk about studies of hashish, you're talking about an ingredient that is not widely used in the United States at the present time.

7.18   JONES: Usually the hashish users first began with bhang; a certain percentage of the bhang users go on to using and seeking out the more potent forms of material. This is the usual history of the patterns of drug use.

7.19   MONITOR*:   Do you think that as these drugs get more and more publicity through public discussion, possibly more and more people . . . would be tempted to experiment with them?

---

*George Murphy, U.S. Senator from California.

7 . 20   JONES: I would think that's a tremendous influence. With the publicity these drugs have gained, it would be a rare person who wasn't curious enough to try it.

7 . 21   GREENBERG: Is alcohol responsible for a very high percentage of the people in our mental hospitals?

7 . 22   JONES: Yes.

7 . 23   GREENBERG: And is alcohol addictive? Do people become physiologically dependent upon it?

7 . 24   JONES: Some can.

7 . 25   GREENBERG: Do they get cirrhosis of the liver from drinking excessive amounts of alcohol?

7 . 26   JONES: Yes.

7 . 27   GREENBERG: Do you know any *cannabis* user that has cirrhosis of the liver from using *cannabis*?

7 . 28   JONES: If one takes some of the foreign literature at the highest-dosage forms of it, the potent form, they speak of "chronic debilitation." I don't know what this means.

7 . 29   GREENBERG: Is that marijuana used as you know it in your work?

7 . 30   JONES: I think we are talking in this country in a very naive way. We're talking about an active placebo, by and large.

8 .   SECOND NEGATIVE WITNESS: DIRECT EXAMINATION

8 . 1   MILLER: We have reached the nub of the question, which is a political question, not a scientific question. Assuming that what the testimony says is correct (that what is used in the United States is perhaps an active placebo, or very mild marijuana) and [assuming] also (which I think is [established] by the scientific studies) that more potent forms of the same drug, marijuana, do cause serious effects (especially, as we hear, among the young); the question, then, is—and it's a political question, a question for a law-maker—what will be the social effects of now removing penalties and legalizing the drug?

8 . 2   Everything tells us—and our psychiatrists will testify—that the social effect will be increased use throughout society: especially increased use by the young. Second of all, we will be creating an enormous market (because [marijuana] will no longer be illegal to use)—a market which those who import marijuana into this country will not be slow to exploit,

especially for the potent forms. It's a question of the social effect of re-moving the law, and that is the kind of question we must answer.

8.3 What are the alternatives? Once it is legalized there is probably no way to control the dosage. . . . Think of the situation if only beer and wine were legal and hard liquor were not: the enormous demand for hard liquor. And I certainly hope the new myth-makers are not—[a four-way, incoherent colloquy, roughly related to Prohibition and bathtub gin, ensues.] We have here, to make a personal statement on the use of mari-juana on him, Philip Quellet. Mr. Quellet, were you a regular user of marijuana?

8.4 PHILIP QUELLET: Yes, I was. I noticed variable effects from the use, some of which were quite undesirable, both in myself and in other people. Among them I noticed, in certain cases where there was a strong dosage used, a panic on the part of the user, because of the unusual effects that can sometimes occur due to the use. Another effect that I noticed, in myself and in others who used marijuana—especially in heavy amount, over a regular period of time—[was] something you'd call apathy: a tendency to talk about social, political, economic problems, but really to remain very passive about them.

9. THIRD NEGATIVE WITNESS: DIRECT EXAMINATION

9.1 MILLER: I would now like to have speak to us Dr. Thomas Ungerleider, professor of psychiatry at U.C.L.A. Dr. Ungerleider has seen thousands of people—spoken to them personally, on a one-to-one basis, especially the young—who have used marijuana. And in questioning Dr. Unger-leider, I will not be talking simply about the heavier dosages, but the normal amount used in the United States today. Doctor, what are the effects that you've noticed of marijuana on the young?

9.2 DR. THOMAS UNGERLEIDER: What we see has been variously described as the "amotivational syndrome," [as] being "strung out," [as] a loss of what we call "goal-directed behavior" (a diminished "frustration tolerance"). In some cases we're beginning to see now what we would even call "emotional cripples" resulting from prolonged, continuous use of the drug.

9.3 MILLER: In your opinion, from speaking to those who use marijuana, would the use be increased if there were no penalties for use?

9.4 UNGERLEIDER: Use would be increased tremendously by our young once the culture accepted it. No question. For every person I've talked to who's used it, there are many who have refrained from using it simply because of the penalties—although the present penalties I'm not in favor of, the felony penalties.

9.5   MILLER: Neither am I. We're talking about criminal penalty: a misdemeanor.

9.6   UNGERLEIDER: Right. So once our culture accepts it, then the use would really mushroom, really increase. And we would have the same situation we have with alcoholics: maybe six, maybe eight million "marijuana-holics" to go with our eight million alcoholics.

10.   CROSS-EXAMINATION

10.1   GREENBERG: Doctor, do I understand . . . that you have personally talked to thousands of marijuana users face to face?

10.2   UNGERLEIDER: Yes.

10.3   GREENBERG: And it's your impression that the law and the existence of the criminal law did not have some impact on *making them users*?

10.4   UNGERLEIDER: Some people have used [it] precisely because of the law. Many *more* have *not* used [it] because of the law.

10.5   GREENBERG: So that you talked to thousands of users and you talked to many thousands of non-users also?

10.6   UNGERLEIDER: Yes.

10.7   GREENBERG: In a statement in January of 1969, didn't you say, "We can only deplore the legal situation with regard to marijuana"?

10.8   UNGERLEIDER: The felony situation. That's right. The felony penalty is as disastrous as legalization would be. Absolutely. [I advocate reducing the penalties for using and possessing marijuana from felonies to misdemeanors.]

10.9   GREENBERG: Didn't you conclude in that statement that, because of the present harsh penalties, the law has lied to the youth in subtle ways, and that as a result of this situation many youths tend to disregard the law?

10.10   UNGERLEIDER: The marijuana laws have lied . . . by calling [marijuana] a narcotic. They've lied by not differentiating between the dealer and the pusher, the pusher being the one who tries to make a profit, the dealer being your friendly local supplier. Yes, the law has lied in many ways.

10.11   GREENBERG: And because the law has lied to them, they've lost their respect for it, and they may tend, indeed, to use marijuana as an example of that disrespect?

10 . 12   UNGERLEIDER: Many people: long hair and marijuana are the symbols now, in our culture, of the young.

10 . 13   GREENBERG: Did you read in the papers recently, as of last Wednesday, a statement by Weldon Smith, coordinator of narcotics programs for the California Department of Corrections, where he said that marijuana use pervades almost every sector of our society and that, as a result, we've lost the battle, and the more rational approach would be to establish controlling and regulatory procedures similar to the laws relating to alcohol?

10 . 14   UNGERLEIDER: I don't recall the statement, but I disagree [with it]. I think this is a tragic manifestation of so many of us adults who become very guilty because the law did lie, and the narcotics officials did lie, for years, to people about marijuana. We've suddenly become overwhelmed with guilt, and therefore feel that we should say "The situation is hopeless and lost, and let's have the culture accept it; let's encourage millions more to use it, and try to regulate it." That's a tragic situation.

10 . 15   GREENBERG: Wouldn't we have a more intelligent regulatory scheme if we didn't try to penalize the victim of this crime—the user himself—and instead used harsh penalties for those who traffic in the drug commercially and who sell to the young?

10 . 16   UNGERLEIDER: Certainly that's an important part of it—

10 . 17   MILLER (*in summation*):   What we're dealing with is a kind of over-reaction rather than overkill. Because marijuana is not heroin does not mean it should be legal. The way to increase respect for the law is not to legalize use but punish the seller who sells to the legal user. That creates just as much disrespect for the law. The problems in marijuana are very real. They do cause harmful effects, sometimes more than alcohol, as Dr. Jones testifies. But, most important, Dr. Ungerleider testifies that, based on personal experience with thousands of individuals—young people—there would be many *more* who use marijuana if the penalties were removed. We should prevent those people from receiving the harm they would if they used the drug.

11 .   BEGINNING OF AFFIRMATIVE REBUTTAL

11 . 1   PALMIERI: The testimony from Mr. Miller's side of the case shows the really basic question relating to this: whether making the drug legal in terms of the use is going to stimulate a great deal more use *and* a great deal

more use in terms of higher dosages. I think that's the question you have to meet on rebuttal right now, Mr. Greenberg.

11.2   GREENBERG: I intend to meet that, but I must say that we should examine the impact of the present criminal penalties; and you have to balance the benefits and the costs of any situation where you're talking about what laws to enact.

11.3   The startling recent increase in marijuana use by many young people has intensified the conflict between generations and posed enormous problems in the enforcement of drug laws. Our laws treat marijuana as a narcotic despite all existing evidence to the contrary. Penalties for its sale and use in most States are extreme. In one State the penalty is two years to life imprisonment for a first offense of possession.

11.4   MILLER: I do not support any such penalties. I think those penalties are far too hard.

11.5   GREENBERG: Thank you. This patchwork of Federal and State law—no, I mean that [word of thanks to Miller] sincerely, because I think the American people should know that in most States in this country the penalties are unduly harsh—now, this patchwork of law, inconsistent as between Federal and State, and often unenforceable on its merits, has led to an essentially irrational situation. Since many of our youths believe marijuana to be relatively harmless, and yet are faced with legal sanctions, they're led into a practice of law-evasion which contributes to general disrespect for the law. The situation is reminiscent of the problems encountered in enforcement of Prohibition during the 1920's.

11.6   These are not only my views. I've been quoting from a statement issued last Wednesday by the Eisenhower Commission on the Causes and Prevention of Violence. . . .

12.   SECOND AFFIRMATIVE WITNESS: DIRECT EXAMINATION

12.1   GREENBERG: We're fortunate to have with us here tonight a world-renowned scientist and teacher, former president of the World Federation for Mental Health, professor of anthropology at Columbia University. She has specialized in the study of adolescents and their values for more than 40 years. Dr. Margaret Mead. Doctor, do you advocate the abolition of criminal sanctions against mere possession and use of marijuana?

12.2   DR. MARGARET MEAD: I do, [and] for several reasons. One: we have tied marijuana, which is not a narcotic and not addictive, in with narcotics and addictive drugs. We've created a false connection that leads marijuana users, because of the connection we've made, into the use of hard, dangerous, addictive drugs. I want to break that tie, and I think we could break it by separating marijuana out from narcotics laws. . . . .

12.3   The second point is that it's leading to disrespect of law, just as we found in the days of Prohibition. If one sector of the community seeks to impose its attitudes on a large sector of the community that does not share them, we then get a tremendous break in this country between those who are respecting the law and those who are not.

12.4   And third: it's leading to a sense of grievance of young people against older people, in the cases where older people say "Let us have our alcohol and our tobacco"—age-tested menaces—"but we won't let you have marijuana." It's important to recognize that those Americans who do not smoke, drink, or use tea or coffee, are in a fine position vis-à-vis their children. At least they're not hypocrites. But the bulk of the society is defending the use by adults of one set of chemical substances and denying it to young people while they're reserving it for themselves. This is increasing in young people a sense of grievance and a sense that the adult society is hypocritical.

12.5   GREENBERG: Do you think that the use of marijuana would increase substantially if the criminal laws against use and possession were repealed?

12.6   MEAD: Well, . . . there might be more use, but it would be mild use in social settings instead of the present use in criminal settings, where we cannot control the marijuana, where it's being doctored with heroin, doctored with LSD, doctored with all sorts of drugs; so that young people are now, under present circumstances, being led into terrible situations. They might, you know, smoke a little pot on Saturday night in a pleasant group instead. [*Applause.*]

13.   CROSS-EXAMINATION

13.1   MILLER: Dr. Ungerleider, who has worked personally with thousands of young users of marijuana, says that his conclusions, based on the clinical evidence, are that the use would substantially increase if the penalties against use, were removed. You disagree with that?

13.2   MEAD: I disagree with that; and I disagree with it as a student of society over the last 45 years. Also, I was very puzzled about these "thousands" of young non-users that came to his attention. You know, this puzzles me. [*Laughter.*]

13.3 MILLER: That's because Dr. Ungerleider moves generally in society and happily meets people who do what you want them to do, that is, not smoke marijuana. But tell me: Dr. Ungerleider has spoken directly to the young people involved; he's a scientist, a respected scientist. Let's forget about—you know, we're in an adversary situation here—but let's forget about the cross-examination and talk about it.

13.4 MEAD: Oh, why? I thought that's what this was called. [*Laughter.*]

13.5 MILLER: Basically because I'm afraid of you.

13.6 PALMIERI: You mean you won't be lured into the cool pursuit of truth with us?

13.7 MEAD: Nobody ever said advocacy was cool. [*Laughter.*]

13.8 MILLER: Dr. Jones says that, based on clinical observations, two or three joints of high dosage [can] produce harmful effects. Do you disagree with that?

13.9 MEAD: He didn't say that. What he said was that there were forms of very intense, concentrated *cannabis* which could be put (he said that, when you asked him), if necessary, into three joints. He did not say this would necessarily be the case. I think it's a great mistake to say "If people use *cannabis* in extreme forms over a long time it may be bad for them," or say "There's some people that it's bad for." There are a lot of people aspirin's bad for.

13.10 MILLER: Dr. Jones, could . . . we have this cleared up?

13.11 JONES: There's a series of case reports in the journal of the American Medical Association of about three or four weeks ago where two or three joints of Vietnamese marijuana, or *cannabis* if you will, produce psychotic reactions.

13.12 MEAD: Yes. I just wanted to keep clear, though, if you would, the difference between these very intense hashish-style doses and the fact that some people have a psychotic response to marijuana and to many other things.

13.13 MILLER: Have you spoken to numbers of young people who have used marijuana, and asked them whether or not the legalization inhibits or does not [inhibit] the use?

13.14 MEAD: I've talked to great numbers of young people, and they feel they might as well be hung for a sheep as for a lamb. And therefore, under the present situation, they smoke defiantly, and they know that they're running terrible risks, so they go into higher and higher drugs. This is the point that I'm making.

13 . 15   MILLER: You think that if the *use* of marijuana were legalized, while at the same time the *sale* [remained illegal]—that was the situation of the Volstead Act; it was the manufacture and sale that was illegal—there would not be a significant industry in this country, growing because of the continued demand, [with] an incentive then to push the harder doses and more marijuana on the young?

13 . 16   MEAD: The first step that we have to take is to repeal these penalties on use and possession. That is the first step. We may have to take other ones.

13 . 17   MILLER: But . . . you would care if . . . anything were done to cause significantly larger numbers of American young people to use marijuana. You would be concerned?

13 . 18   MEAD: Not if they used the mild form in social situations which were decent and were not subject to felonious attack . . . through associations with gangsters and to exposure to drugs that are unregulated and contaminated by every dreadful drug loose in this country.

14 .   CLOSING STATEMENTS

14 . 1   GREENBERG: Dr. Fort emphasizes that marijuana poses little if any threat to the individual user in society, and Margaret Mead has told us that the present criminal penalties threaten to shatter the lives of many young people and make them lose confidence in our legal system. Just this week [the] head of the narcotics program for the California prison system stated, "We've lost the battle to prevent the spread of marijuana." He says the more rational approach is to place marijuana into the same type of controls that are applied to alcohol; and we agree.

14 . 2   MILLER: We are simply dealing with new myths, and it may take us as long to get rid of the new as the old. The new myths are that marijuana is relatively harmless. The new myth is that anything that is simply less harmful than alcohol (causing the enormous [quantity of] deaths it [does]) should be approved. The new myth is that when you remove the penalty on something it doesn't change the use, and significantly more people don't use it. The facts are, as a legal matter, as a political question: to

remove the penalties would increase the use; there are significant numbers of people harmed by it; and in our over-reaction to the old myths, to go to the new would cause even more harm.

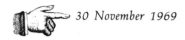 *30 November 1969*

SUGGESTED EXERCISES

1. Which of the following statements, if any, express(es) the principal issue aired in the foregoing debate?
   1. Whether to imprison everyone who smokes marijuana.
   2. Whether to increase legal penalties for trafficking in narcotics.
   3. Whether users of marijuana ought to be criminalized.
   4. Whether to eliminate all legal penalties for using marijuana.
   5. Whether marijuana is a narcotic drug.
   6. Whether marijuana ought to be accepted as part of American culture.
2. Which of the following statements, if any, received assent on both sides of the debate—not necessarily *overt* assent by *all* speakers, but tacit or expressed assent by at least one speaker on each side?
   1. Respect for law is desirable.
   2. Marijuana resembles heroin in its effects on users, if not its chemistry.
   3. Marijuana resembles alcohol in its effects on users.
   4. If a substance is harmful, and if legal action to prevent use of the substance is warranted, then similar prohibitions and penalties should be applied to the manufacture, the sale, the purchase, the possession, and the use of such a substance.
   5. Present laws governing marijuana ought to be changed.
   6. Marijuana use commonly leads to the use of "hard" drugs.
   7. The recent spread of marijuana use in the United States is cause for alarm.
   8. Present United States laws treat marijuana and heroin alike, with respect to the legality of production, distribution, sale, possession, and use.
   9. Legal penalties for trafficking in marijuana should be stiffened.
   10. Commercial promotion of alcoholic beverages, tobacco, and marijuana should be prohibited.

11. Legalization of marijuana use would lead to a broadened incidence of use.
12. Legalization of marijuana use would lead to use of more intense doses of marijuana.
13. Present laws encourage individuals to ignore the real differences between marijuana, on the one hand, and such truly dangerous drugs as heroin, on the other.

3. Which of the following statements, if any, can be deemed true, on the basis of evidence and/or testimony given in the marijuana debate?
1. The Volstead Act, like present laws governing marijuana, prohibited the manufacture, the sale, and the possession and consumption of a substance (alcohol) that was considered to be dangerous.
2. The Indian Hemp Commission found that marijuana, or *cannabis sativa*, does not lead to physical impairment of users.
3. The physiological effects of marijuana resemble those of opium and heroin.
4. The psychological effects of marijuana, used in substantial doses, resemble the effects of alcohol, used in substantial doses.
5. Dr. Margaret Mead has conducted elaborate studies showing that the present laws encourage, more than they deter, the use of marijuana.
6. Investigation has indicated that the legalization of marijuana use would bring about the ingestion of relatively intense dosages or forms of this drug.
7. Dr. Reese Jones found that marijuana produces dangerous psychological effects on users only when the dosages are in proportions close to what is physically impossible for an individual to ingest.
8. Marijuana is addictive, in the sense that its use creates a condition of physiological dependence.

4. Debates generally disclose agreement as well as disagreement between participants, on certain matters of fact and on some standards for deciding on the merits of a given course of action. The participants disagree about what should be done, while they agree, in some measure, about how to *determine* what should be done—that is, about what *tests of value* to apply to alternative policies, what *goals* are worthy of being pursued, what *values*, in short, are valuable. Briefly identify some terms of the underlying value consensus among the participants in the debate on marijuana law, by completing the following statement: *Laws are good if they encourage:*

1.
2.

3.

4.

5. Name at least one non-trivial argument or proposition emanating from the Affirmative side of the debate that was weakly substantiated, and explain your selection(s). (The following remarks may serve to clarify what is being asked here: An argument, or proposition, or line of argument, is an alleged reason for drawing a conclusion, including a conclusion about what course of action is warranted. An argument is trivial if it evokes a response like this: "Even if the factual element in your statement is true, the statement helps little, if at all, to support the conclusion you advocate." An argument is well substantiated, or weakly substantiated, according to the extent to which appropriate evidence and testimony are supplied on behalf of the factual claims, including claims about cause and effect, that are imbedded in the argument.)

6. Similarly, name at least one non-trivial and weakly substantiated argument emanating from the Negative side of the debate, and explain your selection(s).

7. Fifty-minute debates rarely supply all the materials a reasonable man would need in order to reach a confident conclusion about the merits of a proposed policy concerning an urgent problem. Such debates can go far, however, toward clarifying some crucial *standards* for choosing between alternative policies, as well as toward identifying what *matters of fact* need to be settled beyond a reasonable doubt. Having studied the debate on marijuana law, briefly itemize, as specifically as you can, what you consider the crucial questions which remain to be resolved preliminary to arriving at a rational public policy concerning use and possession of marijuana.

Should the trans-alaska pipeline be constructed?

OVERVIEW

Americans are approaching an energy crisis. They also face a pollution crisis. And the two perils are intertwined. Demands for energy—for heat, air conditioning, light, and propulsive power, from electricity, oil, gas, and coal—increase as the population increases. The *rate* of energy use, moreover, tends to increase *geometrically* with population, as an effect and a cause of prosperity. At the same time, increases in energy output often involve increases in pollution. These increases, in noxious fumes in the atmosphere, in oil spills, in dangerous heating of rivers and streams, in disfigurement of terrain, are not necessarily proportional to increases in the rate of use of energy, but they suffice to arouse concern. The drive for increased sources of energy has collided frequently of late with the drive to protect and clean up the environment, as well as to protect people.

One such collision, or dispute over value-priorities and facts, involves our burgeoning reliance on nuclear power plants as a source of electric power. Another such collision involves whether—and how—to tap the supply of oil that lies beneath the North Slope of Alaska. The quantity of oil there is enormous, relative to most other prime sources in the world. The technical problems of extraction and transportation also are enormous.

This pool of oil was discovered early in 1968, on public lands. More than a dozen companies subsequently offered to pay some $900 million to the State of Alaska for commercial rights to the oil. But the reserve is useless unless the oil, once extracted, can be moved economically to market. One possibility is the use of specially designed tankers. Humble Oil Company spent some $40 million to modify the U.S.S. *Manhattan* for a trial run through the ice-packed Northwest Passage. Steel belts were installed around the ship's hull, and a special ice-breaking bow was devised. The giant tanker made the run from Philadelphia to Alaska's North Slope and back, but this method of moving the oil proved to be very expensive. On the trip home, moreover, an iceberg tore a gash in the Manhattan's hull, suggesting that heavy use of tankers through the Northwest Passage entailed a high risk of massive oil spills. Industry experts have concluded from this experiment that the preferable means of transportation is a combination of an overland pipeline, from the North Slope down to southern Alaskan port of Valdez, with conventional tankers which would then carry the oil to West Coast refineries.

Seven major oil companies have formed a company, Alyeska, to build such a pipeline. The pipe would be four feet in diameter and 800 miles in length, and would cost at least one million dollars per mile. It would be the costliest construction project ever attempted by a private company. The pipeline must be built through wilderness lands owned by the Federal government. Authority to grant the necessary permits, or to veto the project, is lodged in the Department of the Interior.

The wisdom of granting these permits has been a topic of intense controversy. At the instigation of Interior Secretary Rogers Morton, hundreds of witnesses have given testimony. As of this writing, the Interior Department had not yet made its momentous decision.

1. OPENING STATEMENTS

1.1   MODERATOR VICTOR PALMIERI: Should the Interior Department grant the leases? Should the Alaska pipeline be constructed? That's the question before us tonight. [Our guest advocate, John Havelock, the Attorney General of Alaska,] says "Yes." Advocate Miller says "No."

1.2   ADVOCATE JOHN HAVELOCK: Alaska and America need the trans-Alaska pipeline. America needs the energy it brings to the national economy. Alaska
needs the royalties to supply essential social services. [The pipeline] can
be built safely, and we in Alaska have the greatest stake in that safety.

1.3   I didn't come all the way from Alaska to lead a charge for the spoilers
against the forces of conservation. The environment is just as popular in
Alaska as it is anywhere else—maybe more so. Many like myself came to
Alaska because we didn't like what was happening in the part of the
United States where we lived before. To a point, the environmental
movement has been helpful to Alaska's pipeline. It has encouraged and
enabled us to insist upon the best-engineered, the best-planned, and the
safest petroleum delivery system anywhere in the world. Today we face
a much different fight: not [whether] to do it *right*, but whether we are
going to be allowed to do it *at all*. America has been asked to turn off
economic growth, and the first selected victims of the new experiment
in economic and social theory are to be the people of Alaska. Maybe we
will one day achieve the Environmental Millennium; but it isn't going to
happen just from jamming the existing system, or from attacking what's
best in it instead of what's worst. It isn't going to happen from cutting
the American economy off from its own vital energy resources, or from
ignoring the needs of the poor for public revenue, or from treating the
poor, just because they're Eskimos, as "noble savages" instead of human beings.

1.4   ADVOCATE HOWARD MILLER: We bought Alaska from the Russians for
$7,200,000. Tonight's proposal is that we sell it for oil. But the Alaska
wilderness that we would destroy is irreplaceable; it is one of the last
great wilderness areas left on an earth we have already defaced too much.
And the oil is oil that we don't need now.

1.5   We can turn the Alaska wilderness into billions of barrels of oil, but
there's no way in the world we can take billions of barrels of oil and
turn it back into the Alaskan wilderness once it is gone. And, despite
the assurances that we always receive about perfect construction—and
that nothing will ever happen in Santa Barbara, or off the coast of England, or in the Gulf of Mexico, or in San Francisco Bay—things *do* happen.
And they have happened in Alaska itself. There has been an oil spill . . .
in Prudhoe Bay. Oil spills in the Alaska subzero temperature cannot so
easily be cleaned up. Normal operations [also involve dangers, such as
what has come from a] drilling rig in Prudhoe Bay, [with] its sludge pit
leaking pollutants into a nearby stream. Nor is there [only] the risk of

ordinary operations. Alaska is a major earthquake zone. Faults criss-cross it constantly, and there are over 4,000 earthquakes a year. The most significant one of them occurred in 1964 in Valdez: a magnitude [on the temblor-measuring Richter scale] of 8.5, totally destroying the town. . . . [The danger] is not simply the earthquake risk, but the risk of tankers as well. Tankers that have run aground—the *Oregon Standard* in San Francisco Bay, and the *Torrey Canyon* off the coast of England—had displacements of 16,000 and 117,000 tons. We are now building tankers of 250,000 tons and planning them for over a million tons. They will be constantly coming down the coast. A tanker of that size, at 12 knots [of speed per hour], requires one and a half miles to stop. We are endangering the entire Western continental coast by the tanker traffic.

1.6   The pipeline itself is an insult to the wilderness and the environment. It contains major risks of earthquakes. There are major tanker risks. And it is the ultimate cynicism to suggest that it should be built for the poor, when Alaska—a State whose per-capita income is 16 percent above the national average—has never seen fit to really do what it ought to toward the Eskimo. And now it and the oil company use the poor as an excuse to build the pipeline. The insult here is not only to the environment, but to the people as well.

2.   FIRST AND SECOND AFFIRMATIVE WITNESSES: DIRECT EXAMINATION

2.1   HAVELOCK: [On the matter of treating the poor as "noble savages" rather than as human beings,] listen to Eban Hobson, former Arctic legislator and executive director of the Alaska Federation of Natives.

2.2   EBAN HOBSON (*on film*):   The development of the pipeline and the oil being pumped out of the North Slope [is] going to have some impact [on our way of life]. To some extent, over the last 20 or 30 years, there has been some change in our everyday way of life, from a native culture to what you might call a modern way of living. There has to be a change. In the process of many years, only the means to make a living to perpetuate the native culture is going to change. [In consequence of the pipeline, the native population] will have some housing programs. We will have some educational programs; scholarships; water and sewer [projects]—and there's all kinds of problems. And let me make this one point: even if we were to receive a billion dollars tomorrow, in one lump sum, and make a distribution to all of the villages, it wouldn't halfway solve all problems the villages have. That's how serious the living conditions are.

2.3   HAVELOCK: Now, to speak for all Alaskans, the senior Senator from the State of Alaska: the honorable Ted Stevens. Senator, as an Alaskan, why do you want to see the Alaska pipeline built?

2.4   SEN. TED STEVENS: This country needs energy to expand its job potential. And Alaska needs those jobs more than anyone else. We have a very high rate of unemployment, and we have very serious social problems insofar as our native population is concerned. They have the highest infant mortality rate. They have the highest unemployment rate. And they have the greatest need for education; for, as Eban Hobson said, water and sewer projects, housing projects. And this resource will give us the stability we need in our economy to provide those.

2.5   HAVELOCK: Does every Alaskan understand the relationship between these revenues and the answering of social needs?

2.6   STEVENS: I'm not sure they do; because in Alaska, the mineral resources belong to the *State* and the royalties will go to the *State*. And I believe that until they start coming in, [the people] are really not going to realize how important they are.

2.7   HAVELOCK: Speaking as a national senator, Senator, how fast are the energy needs of this country growing?

2.8   STEVENS: It's been predicted that our energy needs are going to grow 50 percent in this coming decade. I don't think it's really important whether it's 5 percent annually, 3, 4, [or] whatever you want to pick. The important thing is that our energy needs are growing very rapidly. Even more importantly, the *world*'s needs are growing very rapidly. We used to consume a considerable portion—I think it was almost 50 percent, ten years ago—of the world's energy resources annually. We're down to 35 percent now; which means the rest of the world is growing at even a more rapid pace than we are. And if we're going to have stability, we have to have domestic reserves.

2.9   HAVELOCK: What does this oil mean in terms of price to the American consumer?

2.10   STEVENS: With the increase of the Middle Eastern oil to its recent price of about $3.45 a barrel, it means that Alaskan oil is even more "on the market," you might say. We thought it would be expensive oil, but it's not expensive oil any more. There is not much advantage to using imported oil any more, from an economic point of view. And it means that we will be able to hold the line, and the consumer should not have to pay anything more for his gasoline or his energy resource in the future.

3.   CROSS-EXAMINATION

3.1   MILLER: Do you think there are ecological problems raised—possible damage to the environment on the North Slope—because of this pipeline?

3.2   STEVENS: There will be some environmental problems, but we have the opportunity to *enhance* our countryside, too, as we build this pipeline.

3.3   MILLER: On August 30, 1969, you said to the American Association of the Advancement of Science that, by your understanding of the dictionary, "ecology" deals with the relationships between living organisms; but there are no living organisms on the North Slope.

3.4   STEVENS: That's not quite exactly true. That's the way it was reported, Mr. Miller; and I don't blame you at all for quoting that. I read from the dictionary, as a matter of fact. And it's too bad the reporter didn't quite quote it correctly.

3.5   MILLER: [Let's talk about] energy. Needs change. For example, one estimate is that the SST [supersonic transport], had it been built, in a period of ten years at full fleet use, would have used substantially all of the total North Slope oil at Prudhoe Bay. Now that we're *not* building the SST, that diminishes our energy needs, doesn't it?

3.6   STEVENS: I don't think so. Now that we're not building the SST, we're going to have to use just that many more *smaller* aircraft; and we'll have an increasing demand just the same.

3.7   MILLER: Why not use *other* reserves first, given this ecological risk? We have a billion barrels in a naval reserve at Elk Hills. Since we have an ecological risk here, as we shall see, why not use our other reserves first and keep *this* in the ground until either it's absolutely necessary? Or perhaps we shall find other oil.

3.8   STEVENS: The nation decided a long time ago that we needed naval reserves, just as we need forest reserves and we need wilderness reserves and all other kinds of reserves; and we're keeping those petroleum reserves for emergencies. That's what they should be used for.

3.9   MILLER: But why not keep the Alaskan reserves, where there are ecological risks, for emergencies, and use those *other* reserves *before* we take those risks in Alaska?

3.10   STEVENS: We have 25.8 million acres of the North Slope set aside as Naval Petroleum Reserve Number Four to satisfy that.

3.11   MILLER: But why not do it with *all*? Really. Since you have the risks there, and there are other reserves where there are no risks, why not use the reserves where there are no risks and leave the Alaskan oil alone?

3.12   STEVENS: Well, those other reserves aren't usable. They've been set aside by Congress, and I think they're needed.

3.13   MILLER: And Congress could take them out. Well, let's talk about non-naval reserves. We have 30 billion barrels generally in the ground in the United States. . . . Why not use the [25-billion-barrel or so *non*-Alaskan reserves] first? Why go to the high ecological risk first?

3.14   STEVENS: Well, I imagine you could. But as a practical matter, we're importing now about 23 percent of our [present annual energy needs], and the estimate is [that] we're going to go up to 44 percent within five years. . . . The difficulty [with this] is the tremendous leverage it gives the foreign nations over our economy. If they shut it off, as they did in Algeria or as they did in the Middle East, then our economy, our jobs, stop just like that.

3.15   MILLER: Only 3 percent of our oil comes from the Middle East. When we talk about foreign oil, we include Canadian oil as foreign oil, don't we?

3.16   STEVENS: Do you know where the Canadian oil comes from? It's imported through Portland, Maine, *into* Canada and *then* shipped *back* to us, as a practical matter.

3.17   MILLER: And we count Latin American oil as "foreign" oil. It's not just the Middle East that's "foreign."

3.18   STEVENS: It's Venezuelan. But basically, it's an interchange in terms of the total world crude stream as the exchanges go on.

3.19   MILLER: Tell me what's really going to happen to this Alaskan oil. Because of a United States act, the Jones Act, which requires ships between American ports to use American seamen, the cost of transporting on tankers this Alaskan oil to a West Coast port [will be high, so] the total net cost of the oil will be about the same as bringing it from any place else in the world.

3.20   STEVENS: Yes.

3.21   MILLER: It would be, however, cheaper to send it to Japan. And there are reports that a large amount of it will *go* to Japan. Isn't that really where it's going?

3.22   STEVENS: No. But I'm glad you mentioned that; because we're going to use American tankers and American crews, and the total economy is going to be improved by using Alaskan oil. It will mean more jobs for everyone.

3.23   MILLER: Despite the fact that it could be sold at greater profit to Japan?

3.24   STEVENS: I don't think it could.

4.   THIRD AFFIRMATIVE WITNESS: DIRECT EXAMINATION

4.1   HAVELOCK: To find out how safe this oil pipeline is, let's ask the man who's going to build it . . . : Ed Patton, president of the Alyeska Pipeline Company. Before I ask you about safety, Mr. Patton: is North Slope oil particularly risky to get out of the ground, or more dangerous than other oil reserves?

4.2   ED PATTON: No, it is not.

4.3   HAVELOCK: How about this pipeline? Does this compare with the SST? Is this a publicly subsidized program?

4.4   PATTON: It is not. There is no public money whatsoever involved. In fact, the flow of money is in the opposite direction.

4.5   HAVELOCK: How can you be sure that this pipeline is safe, and it won't leak or crack?

4.6   PATTON: We spent over 2,000 man-years of engineering and scientific talent to ensure just that. This will be the best-engineered and the safest pipeline in the history of the world.

4.7   HAVELOCK: Is safety the only factor you considered in this design?

4.8   PATTON: No, it isn't. We are in the forefront of the environmental climate in this day and age. We recognize that this pipeline will travel through some of the best scenery in the world, and we intend to keep it that way. This pipeline will be so inconspicuous that a hiker won't know it's there until he encounters it.

4.9   HAVELOCK: We've heard a lot about permafrost. Will the heat of the pipe melt the ground support, resulting in sag?

4.10   PATTON: There's a great misconception about permafrost in the lower 48 [States]. Actually it's any material that has existed for two or more years below the freezing point of water. This can include solid rock [or] gravel, as well as materials that are high in ice. Our core sampling program of thousands of samples shows that well over half the route will be in soil like rock and gravel where no hazard will exist. Where there *is* a hazard, the pipe will go above ground. We will not bury in any soils which will be unstable.

4.11   HAVELOCK: Will an earthquake break this pipeline?

4.12   PATTON: No, it won't. The pipe is designed to the tightest specifications, again, in the history of pipeline. We have taken this pipe to the University of California at Berkeley and tested it there. A 31-foot test section, under a compressive force of 2.5 million pounds and a lateral force of a half-million pounds, bent 33 inches before it even developed a hairline *crack*; and not yet a *leak*.

4.13   HAVELOCK: How about the Denali Fault, the most active seismic area in the route? What have you done there in design?

4.14   PATTON: On each side of the Denali Fault we will have automatic remote-control block valves to isolate the fault in case a leak should occur. These block valves are but two of the 73 up and down the line. In addition to that, we will cross the fault above ground in what we call a trapezoidal zig-zag pattern, which will give the pipe the ability to absorb any energy from earthquakes.

5.   CROSS-EXAMINATION

5.1   MILLER: Mr. Patton, I wish you'd been the man who built the oil wells off Santa Barbara.

5.2   PATTON: I wish I had, too. [*Laughter, applause.*]

5.3   MILLER: Of course, there are others who disagree with you [about the Alaska pipeline]. Why are you putting 48 percent of the pipeline above ground? Because the Department of the Interior *required* that you do so.

5.4   PATTON: We're putting it there for the reason I just stated: because our soil samples indicate that the soil would be unstable if thawed. And therefore, we do not thaw it; we go above ground.

5.5   MILLER: And the Department of the Interior put that in its "impact statement" as a requirement. Is that right?

5.6   PATTON: Whether the Department of the Interior had ever existed, this would have happened.

5.7   MILLER: What about the Corps of Engineers' doubts? They have great doubts, and have indicated there are environmental risks in terms of issuing you a permit. Are their doubts to be dismissed?

5.8   PATTON: I read the Corps of Engineers' statement to Secretary [of the Interior Rogers] Morton, and I didn't find any such criticism of the project. The Corps simply stated that we would have to come to them for permits to cross rivers and to build berths in navigable harbors.

5.9   MILLER: What about the Department of Transportation, that indicated that there are other alternatives, and that they ought to be considered because of this risk?

5.10   PATTON: The Department of Transportation brought up the old chestnut about railroads which, of course, are ridiculous [as means of] transporting this amount of oil that distance. . . .

5.11   MILLER: I see. *That* would contain risks or high cost. Tell me, do you think there are any risks at all? Is there a risk this pipeline might break, for example?

5.12   PATTON: About the same risk that you will encounter when you fly to Boston on your next trip. I doubt that you ever heard of the trans-Alpine pipeline which has been in operation now for about three years. It has about the same topographical features as the Alaskan pipeline and has been exposed to only one significant leak.

5.13   MILLER: One "significant" leak! And what happens if there is one "significant" leak on the Alaska tundra? Who's going to clean that up?

5.14   PATTON: We are, with our emergency crews. We have employees. This "significant" leak in the trans-Alpine pipeline was 2,000 barrels, which would cover less than one acre.

5.15   MILLER: So you're convinced, and are telling us, that there will not be a leak of any kind.

5.16   PATTON: I'm telling you that the risk of leak is minimal.

5.17   MILLER: What about the risk of an earthquake? Now suppose we had another earthquake like in Valdez: a [Richter] magnitude of 8.5 that totally destroyed Valdez. Would your pipeline sustain an earthquake of 8.5?

5.18   PATTON: We think it would. The trans-Andes pipeline has done that. It has been deformed, but it has not been destroyed.

5.19   MILLER: Tell me about tankers. Is no tanker coming down from Valdez to the United States, or wherever else it goes, going to run aground and crash? No *Torrey Canyon*? No oil spells?

5.20   PATTON: There'll be fewer of them run aground than you can imagine. There has been no American flag tanker lost since 1967.

5.21   MILLER: But will you tell me, then, why there were over 1,500 significant oil spills in United States coastal and inland waters in 1970? Can you prevent all of that?

5.22   PATTON: I can prevent all of that in the area that I am operating, yes. But I can't do it all for the rest of the United States.

5.23   MILLER: I wish you did have more power. You can do what no one else has done, Mr. Patton.

5.24   HAVELOCK (*in summation*):   Senator Stevens has said that the energy require-ments of the nation must be met. And Mr. Patton, I think, is the kind of man that can build a safe pipeline. If you watch this show regularly, you saw Mr. Miller just a few weeks ago point up the problems with atomic energy as a substitute. If we allow environmental problems to run our costs up, it's going to run up your cost of living, too.

6.   FIRST AND SECOND NEGATIVE WITNESSES

6.1   MILLER: This pipeline not only violates the environment, but through the environment, violates the people of Alaska.

6.2   WILLIE WILLOYA (*Alaska native, on film*):   The pipeline ignores the fact that things were happening all over the Arctic before they came. They're tak-ing a short-term view of the thing, and they're not saying, "All right, what's the long-term effect of us having come here?" And they're say-ing, "There's nothing wrong now." But I say "There's plenty wrong," and they're not listening to me. They're listening to themselves. They're telling the American public that it's all right. And I'm saying, because I live there: things are happening that are bad.

6.3   LLOYD ELASANGA (*Alaska native, on film*):   The pipeline deal would, I suppose, be good in some ways. But to whom? The big companies. How can *we* benefit by it? They haven't told us how we're going to benefit by this pipeline.

6.4   WILLOYA (*on film*):   There's been a report by an ecologist that the caribou would not be altered in any manner. But this is a short-term thing, and we've been here for 8,000 to 16,000 years, and we don't like to have somebody who's been up here for four or five years telling us that the interference with the patterns of caribou or reindeer aren't going to hurt us. We've had 50 years of exploitation of our reindeer industry, and that really hurts.

6.5   ELASANGA (*on film*):   The main thing that we do back home is hunting, and we carve the ivory from the walrus. The polar bear doesn't come around, and why? Because of the people that go out and kill them in the plains. But how would it affect us to, you know, get all of this money and then afterwards, when there is no more, how are the people going to live when they forget how to carve and hunt?

6 . 6   WILLOYA (*on film*):   I doubt if they have any idea about what the cost/benefit ratio is to a native villager: to give up his whole life, you know, for a pipeline—to be destroyed. I don't think there's any way you can estimate that. Because if you're losing your life, your life style and everything, there's no way that you can say there's any benefit. My village is also gone, too. And I know how bitter the feeling is when a village suddenly disappears from the face of the earth, and you have no place to go back to. You only have Anchorage, which is nothing to me.

7 .   THIRD NEGATIVE WITNESS: DIRECT EXAMINATION

7 . 1   MILLER: The pipeline will have environmental costs and it will have human costs. To talk to us about those we have with us tonight David Brower, one of the nation's leading conservationists and president of Friends of the Earth. Mr. Brower, why is the wilderness important?

7 . 2   DAVID BROWER: The wilderness is a refuge for many living things besides man, a sanctuary for them against man and his technology. And now and then it's a fairly good place for man to go to get fixed up a bit. I think that it's quite often understood to be sort of something frivolous to many people or just a special thing for bird watchers or for people to go hunt and camp in. But it's a great deal more than that. The wilderness traces right back to the beginning of life on earth. And it is really right now the one "computer readout" we have on all the information that the earth has been forming. It's uninterrupted by technology. It's the only readout we have. It is sort of the incredible memory bank. The way Nancy Newhall describes it, it holds answers to questions man has not yet learned how to ask. Or the physicist J. H. Rush, who said that if we eradicate wilderness, we obliterate the evolutionary force that put man on this planet.

7 . 3   MILLER: But is this Alaskan wilderness a fragile thing?

7 . 4   BROWER: It's a fragile thing, and it's really the most fragile kind of wilderness we have. The farther north you get, the more fragile the wilderness becomes. And this is fragile because it *is* that far north, because it has extremely delicate population balances that are very easily upset.

7 . 5   MILLER: What are the risks to that wilderness of building this pipeline?

7 . 6   BROWER: The risks start right at the beginning, where you go across, of course, a mountainous region. And you go, for 70 percent of this route, within 25 miles of major [earthquake] epicenters. And 25 miles is not the

extent to which earthquakes can cause damage. So, the earthquake threat is very real. The tanker threat: I think we hardly need more than read the daily papers to know how often these tankers crack up; there is not enough safety built into them; I don't know whether it is feasible to do that. The threat to the fisheries: we have the richest fishery in the world— or one of the richest fisheries, at any rate—off Alaska; and to spill in any of those 320 streams this pipeline crosses, [or to] spill from tankers, is a major threat to a major source of food. And it's a threat, as Willie Willoya was saying, to take a people who have been learning for millenia how to live with the land and to just sever that, to dissipate it, to scatter it beyond recall. Twenty years of exploiting for oil and getting out is, I think, a totally immoral thing to do.

7.7   MILLER: Is the pipeline itself an insult to the wilderness? Simply having it there?

7.8   BROWER: It certainly is. And you wouldn't have much trouble finding that out if you were just to go into that area to see what the pipeline would do in permafrost. And a great deal of it *would* have been built in permafrost if the suit against the pipeline had not come into court.

7.9   MILLER: That raises another point. Mr. Patton is very confident about the safety of the pipeline. Do you share that confidence? And what about government agencies? Do they share it?

7.10   BROWER: I certainly do not share it, and I know a good many government agencies who do not. Mr. Ruckelshaus* does not. The Corps of Engineers does not. And I think Secretary Morton of the Interior Department has doubts. Then there are the doubts at the lower levels of the bureaucracy, and report after report that [has] been suppressed. And we have lists of people who, if we do not use their names, would like to tell us what the threats are.

8.   CROSS-EXAMINATION

8.1   HAVELOCK: In evaluating the risk involved in building this pipeline, did you rely on the facts which are set out in an ad in the *New York Times*, published over your name on February 17 and put in other newspapers around the country? Perhaps you're familiar with it.

---

*Head of the Federal Environmental Protection Agency.

8.2   BROWER: I know the advertisement very well, and it has one error, where we talked about gallons instead of barrels, a mistake that was corrected subsequently—a correctible mistake, whereas a spill would not be.

8.3   HAVELOCK: I gather you took full-page ads to correct that error? Each mile of the new pipeline, you stated, will contain 500,000 barrels of oil at temperatures of 150–180 degrees. You also stated that there were only 12 shutoff stations planned for this. Is it not a fact, sir that there are only 11,000 barrels of oil in each mile of pipeline—an "exaggeration multiplier" of 45? That 73 shut-off valves are planned—"an exaggeration multiplier" of 6? And that although *design* temperature is as high as 180 degrees, actual temperature *expected* is closer to 100?

8.4   BROWER: These figures, of course, bounce around quite a little bit. The main point that should be remembered is that there are two "Santa Barbara-potential" disasters per mile of pipe. That's the point that counts. Also, when you talk about cutoff stations, you're talking about quite a few: you're mixing in numbers of remote-control stations.

8.5   HAVELOCK: Who's mixing in numbers, sir?

8.6   BROWER: I'm afraid you were. They're mixed up there with the pumping stations, which can be controlled, as opposed to the remote-control stations, which must be reached somehow, whatever the weather may be. And it's very uncertain whether you could reach them in a major disaster in bad weather.

8.7   HAVELOCK: But you did misstate the number of shutoff valves that were on the pipe. And in your second "Highlight" you stated that on the cold tundra landscape, the pollution will last for centuries, and that Alaska oil is particularly toxic. How did you arrive at the conclusion as to this special toxicity?

8.8   BROWER: This was reported in a British magazine, and I'm sure that the trans-Alaska pipeline people must have that story in their own documents. I hope they do.

8.9   HAVELOCK: I wonder who ate it in order to establish the toxicity. I think that this is the first time that issue has been raised. It's low-sulfur oil, as you probably know, in terms of burning.

8.10   BROWER: No, you'll find out in that article, if you look it up, that there's a great deal of variety in the toxicity of oils. The Alaska oil is apparently quite toxic, and spills at low temperatures are particularly devastating.

8.11   HAVELOCK: Also, in your ad, you stated that the tank-farm storage complex at Valdez is "actually located in an area totally destroyed in the '64 Alaska quake." That is false, too, isn't it?

8 . 12   BROWER: No, I would not say so. Valdez *was* destroyed. And if you move a few hundred yards or a mile or two outside, I don't think you're very safe.

8 . 13   HAVELOCK: A few miles down the side to a location on bedrock which was totally untouched by the earthquake, which I lived through, sir.

8 . 14   BROWER: I'm glad you lived through it; but I think that the problem is that—for example, Whittier, Alaska, is several miles away from Valdez, and they lost their airstrip; it went under water. So I don't think that a mile or two in that kind of country is going to save you. I hope you don't count on it.

8 . 15   HAVELOCK: I was there myself, and I know what it means. You also stated that the tanker traffic in Valdez was coming into one of the stormiest harbors in the world. Now I've visited there, and I've talked with the mayor and harbor masters. Nobody can remember when a ship had been unable to dock because of winds or bad weather. Where on earth did you get this fact that it's one of the unsafest places in the world?

8 . 16   BROWER: I hope such a ship won't be trying to dock where a friend of mine had the experience of coming out of a hotel in Valdez to mail a letter, and was blown down the street. He had to crawl back to the hotel. Now that kind of wind is not the kind of wind a tanker should be docking in.

8 . 17   HAVELOCK: You get winds like that in the town, sir. Your friend was on the street.

8 . 18   BROWER: I don't think the winds are any lighter offshore, not in any water I know of.

8 . 19   HAVELOCK: The conscious exaggeration such as has been illustrated in this ad is, in fact—as was pointed out in a profile in *New Yorker* on you—a conscious tool of the conservationists. Would you agree with that position on your kind of conservationists?

8 . 20   BROWER: No, I wouldn't bite. Because in the example you're referring to, they're talking about an advertisement that I didn't run. It was not a Sierra Club ad. And the fact that was used as a headline was an unfortunate one. But there was a mistake on the *New Yorker's* part. It was not our ad. It was not my exaggeration. I do not believe in it.

8 . 21   PALMIERI: Mr. Brower, [Havelock] . . . has made a point that the resources of the State are needed to meet the needs of the State. He has said, in effect, that there are many people counting on these resources and they've done their best to ensure the safety of the environment, although I suppose he would admit that it isn't 100 percent. Can't they exploit their resources?

8 . 22   BROWER: I think they should. But they should budget this. The pipeline is a formula for exploiting it in about 20 years, and it should last for centuries. *That's* what the Alaskans need.

9. FOURTH AND FIFTH NEGATIVE WITNESSES: DIRECT EXAMINATION

9 . 1   MILLER: If the issue tonight is whether Mr. Brower's ad is accurate—though of course that's not the issue—but if it is, the answer is "Yes." If the issue is, "Should the pipeline be built?"—as it is—the answer is "No." Mr. Brower talked about the fishing industry, and he talked about harm to Alaska. And though we've heard about the needs of Alaska's economy, in fact this pipeline will hurt many people in many parts of the economy in Alaska. For, as we have unfortunately learned many places in the world, oil can be dangerous to children and other living things.

9 . 2   ROSS MULLINS (*member of Cordova Fish Union, on film*):   As a fisherman who is concerned with a very major resource in Alaska, I feel that it's seriously questionable whether or not enough information is available to determine whether or not the State's interest will be best served by promoting this terminus in Valdez with the speed that it's being pushed at this time. Chronic everyday pollution from the ballast discharge plant and from small spillage from the terminal daily, which you find in every oil port in the world, is going to seriously affect the Valdez fisheries area. And this is an area where up to as high as 20 percent of the salmon in the Prince William Sound environments find their spawning grounds. So you take 20 percent off the top of the resource, and you're not left with a whole lot for the fishermen to handle. I feel, from talking with many people up and down the coast, that they feel seriously that there are a lot of unresolved problems that yet have to be dealt with in a satisfactory manner, before we can come up with a real determination whether the coastal shipping route is the best alternative.

9 . 3   MILLER: Those are the risks to the environment and to the people. And the question is: Why take those risks? Do we need the oil? To talk to us about that, we have with us tonight Congressman Les Aspin [of] Wisconsin. Congressman, do we need this Alaskan oil?

9 . 4   REP. LES ASPIN: The need for the Alaskan oil has really been greatly overstated. The people who are in favor of the oil pipeline have overstated the demand and understated the supply. For example, the pro-pipeline

people say that the need for oil will grow at 4 percent a year. But other sources, other industry sources, other government sources, predict much lower rates. They predict, for example, 2.34 percent to 3.12 percent. So it's really overstated.

9.5   MILLER: Does national security require that we use this oil now?

9.6   ASPIN: No. We're really being sold a bill of goods on this national security issue. First of all, of course, imports come from some places which are perfectly safe: Canada and Venezuela. A very small percentage comes from the Middle East. But even then, suppose we were really worried about that small percentage: the thing to really do is to preserve the oil, not to develop it; to keep some safe; to keep some that we can use some time in the future.

9.7   MILLER: What do you say, though, to the people of Alaska who say they need this resource for their development, who need the money?

9.8   ASPIN: There's a system that we can devise that would help the people of Alaska [while] still not building a pipeline. And I think you do it by the way we change our import policy. Right now, for example, oil sells at $3.90 a barrel in New York in the Eastern Coast. [On] imported oil, the price varies, but it's usually between $2.25 and $2.90 a barrel. Now what happens is, *that* difference—the $1—$1.65 difference—is now just a profit of the importers. It's a sheer subsidy on behalf of the government to the importers. What we *should* do, if we're going to help the State of Alaska, is to import an amount of oil equal to the amount that would be coming out of the Alaska pipeline: two million barrels a day. But instead of giving that oil away, the government should sell the *rights* to import it. Therefore the government would get the difference. [It] would get the $1 to $1.65, or at least up to that amount, and they would use it. They could use it in a number of ways. They could give some of it to the State of Alaska: 50 percent to the State of Alaska, 25 percent to the national security [forces]; store some oil; 5 percent to the balance of payments—and we'd still be better off. We'd still have a 20 percent surplus.

9.9   MILLER: We've talked about the need for the oil. The other side is the risk. We have a "confidence" that nothing will go wrong. As a Congressman, knowing what government agencies are talking about, do government agencies share confidence that this pipeline will be safe and that nothing will happen?

9.10   ASPIN: No. The government agencies which are really responsible for the environment have a lot of reservations about it. [Among these are] the Environment Protection Agency, the Corps of Engineers, some people in the Department of the Interior.

10. CROSS-EXAMINATION

10.1   HAVELOCK: [Regarding projected needs:] if you look at the actual experience, don't we find that in 1970, there is a 4.10 [percent] increase in the domestic requirements; in 1969, 5.56; in 1968, 6.63; and in 1967, 3.94? I could go on. But isn't there, in fact, a history of this, regardless of your predictions? And I think you would admit there are other predictions that would say differently.

10.2   ASPIN: That's right. All I'm saying is that the majority of people who are not tied up with the pipeline in one way or another predict much less need for the oil in the long run than the people who are tied up *with* the pipeline.

10.3   HAVELOCK: As the Department of Commerce stated a few days ago, as I recall, it was a 4 percent increase that they were predicting. Do you say that they're under the control—

10.4   ASPIN: No, not control. They are *for* the pipeline. They are *for* the oil companies. The Secretary of Commerce, Mr. [Maurice] Stans, was one of the people on the Cabinet task force on oil who took the pro-oil line. He's a pro-oil man.

10.5   HAVELOCK: Do you think that even if this question is in doubt that we should rely upon your figure in undertaking a policy that affects national security?

10.6   ASPIN: It's not my figure. It's a figure of experts. . . . It's a combined estimate of people who know what they're doing.

10.7   HAVELOCK: As against other estimates which are higher.

10.8   ASPIN: One other estimate.

10.9   HAVELOCK: Has [your] plan been endorsed by large numbers of Congressmen and Senators?

10.10   ASPIN: No. It's a modification of the plan, though, that is a very, very good plan, which is that we should go to tariffs instead of quotas on the oil imports.

10.11   HAVELOCK: Your plan depends, does it not, on the differential in market price: the foreign oil being cheaper?

10.12   ASPIN: Certainly.

10.13   HAVELOCK: . . . [It won't always be] the case; as you're probably aware—are you not?—Alaskan oil will frequently be cheaper than imported oil. What does Alaska do *then*?

10.14   ASPIN: The Alaska oil would *not* be frequently cheaper than import oil. The cost of imported oil—the cost of transportation—is going down. Imported oil is going to be cheaper.

10.15   HAVELOCK: I think you're using the wrong figures, sir. And in any case, over a market life of a decade, how on earth are you going to predict such a thing? And as Senator Stevens says, what happens when foreign countries decide they want to use their own oil?

10.16   ASPIN: What we're trying to do is to get some money for the State of Alaska to tide them over this short run. The State of Alaska is in tough shape financially, I agree. But other States are in tough shape financially. Alaska is not the only State that's got financial problems. But maybe the problems in Alaska are a bit more severe. In any case, what we would be trying to do is to tide them over while we study alternative methods of getting the oil out.

10.17   HAVELOCK: If I may say so, sir, it sounds grossly impractical to think that 55,000 taxpayers and 60,000 natives, of whom 85 percent are unemployed, are going to wait around for you to pass this act for which you have no support in Congress that's visible.

10.18   ASPIN: It's no more impractical than saying that we can build a pipeline down to Valdez and tank it down the coast without an oil spill.

10.19   PALMIERI: I had a feeling, listening to Mr. Brower, that he would object to this if it were not oil with the risk of spill and irreparable damage to the tundra. He objected, I think, to the fact that we were invading the wilderness, a unique wilderness. Do you share that? Would you go that far? Suppose there were gold there that could be mined?

10.20   ASPIN: I don't know. That's another subject for another "Advocates" program. What are the alternatives? We're discussing the oil pipeline now, and I'm against the oil pipeline.

10.21   PALMIERI: Are you also against a coal mine or a gold mine? Are you against invading that wilderness? That's really the philosophical question that lies behind this. I want to get this out of an exercise entirely in economics. Let's see where you stand.

10.22   ASPIN: All right: yes, I'm against invading the wilderness.

10.23   HAVELOCK: As [for] the tanker traffic, sir: isn't all your plan doing is just transferring our environmental problems to other countries which perhaps aren't quite as conservation-minded as our own in the development of their resources?

10.24   ASPIN: I don't think so. You see, at least in those cases we've got tanker traffic that we've dealt with for years. It's over established routes and that kind of thing.

10.25   And right now, with the tanker traffic up and down the coast of North America there, off the State of Washington, it's dealing in uncharted waters. It's dealing in areas where the water doesn't flush out very easily.

It's dealing in an area where there's a lot of fog. It's dealing with a lot of problems that we don't have on the ordinary tanker runs now.

10.26 HAVELOCK: I'm sure it will come as a great surprise to the Coast Guard to find out that those waters are uncharted. [*Laughter, applause.*]

10.27 ASPIN: I'm sure the Coast Guard has charted them. I'm worried about the oil companies.

10.28 PALMIERI: Gentlemen, I'm worried about the time. In the meantime, thank you, Congressman, for being on our show.

10.29 MILLER (*in summation*): This is not simply a resource for the people of Alaska to develop. The people of Alaska can no more despoil the North Slope wilderness than the people of California could cut down all its redwoods, or the people of Wyoming subdivide Yellowstone, or the people of Florida fill in the Everglades. It's a resource and a wilderness for all of man and for the entire country. What we need is a new concept of profit that includes in it the cost of despoiling this wilderness. If that cost were in— if the risk the government agencies have seen—if the risk of invading this wilderness and forever ending it were included, the cost would then be so great . . . that no one would build this pipeline.

11. FOURTH AFFIRMATIVE WITNESS: DIRECT EXAMINATION

11.1 HAVELOCK: We have now heard from Mr. Brower, who first visited Alaska in 1970, and from Congressman Aspin who, to the best of my knowledge, has never visited Alaska at all. Now let's here from Ed Fortier, who has been living in Alaska for 29 years and writing about life on the last frontier. [*He is executive editor of* Alaska *magazine*]. Mr. Fortier, why do you live in Alaska?

11.2 FORTIER: I love the wilderness, and I couldn't live there without access to it, without restoring myself. And it's still there, and I'm still there, and I expect to be there for quite awhile, I hope.

11.3 HAVELOCK: You've heard testimony that in the wilderness damage is irreparable. Is the wilderness really as fragile as it's made out to be?

11.4 FORTIER: I can show you communities that had several thousand people in them, near Anchorage, that are completely covered up. They just disappeared in a matter of 30 or 40 years.

11.5 HAVELOCK: How many of the 4,000 earthquakes which were cited in this program [did you feel last year]?

11.6 FORTIER: I must be getting numb to them, because I didn't feel 4,000, believe me. [*Laughter.*] I felt the big one in '64. I was in Anchorage. My natural gas kept coming into my home. The pipelines kept operating on both sides of Cook Inlet. As far as I know, there were no breaks caused by the earthquake.

11.7   HAVELOCK: What do you see is the role of the wilderness in American civilization?

11.8   FORTIER: It makes you feel small in a good way. It gives you a proper perspective. I *don't* see it as a gentle lady. If you've lived up there, nature and the elements are pretty harsh, pretty demanding. Life isn't easy. It's tough.

11.9   HAVELOCK: Won't the access that comes with this pipeline destroy the wilderness?

11.10   FORTIER: If you lock it up and nobody gets access to it, nobody sees it, they're never going to be enriched. I have no objection whatever—and I'm a member of the conservation society—to a road to the North Slope so that the average middle-class American can get up and look at it. Otherwise he's never going to see it.

11.11   HAVELOCK: Have the roads into Mt. McKinley National Park destroyed it?

11.12   FORTIER: To my knowledge they haven't. There are thousands and thousands of people who say it's one of the high moments of their life.

12.   CROSS-EXAMINATION

12.1   MILLER: Not simply as an Alaskan, but as an American: why take this oil out now when there's other oil we can use for years?

12.2   FORTIER: That's the nation's problem, Mr. Miller. My problem is Alaska. I'm a member of the nation, but I'm first an Alaskan, and I want to see that my people eat, put beans on the table.

12.3   MILLER: But let's talk about the national policy. For the nation, why take this oil out now when there is enough oil that we can take out elsewhere and ensure sources for years and years and years?

12.4   FORTIER: I can't imagine that the oil companies would have spent all the money they have up there just to harass and irritate myself and other conservationists, and yourself, without a justifiable reason for it.

12.5   MILLER: But we *know* why they spent it: of course, for the *profit*, the estimated 43 percent profit on their invested capital. But from a national standpoint now—not from the oil companies' standpoint, not the Alaska standpoint, but for the people watching this throughout the country— why should people around the country who perhaps are not Alaskan—

what do you say to them when they ask, "Why take this oil out now when there is so much other oil?"

12.6   FORTIER: It's there. It's available, and I personally am convinced that it can be moved very safely.

12.7   MILLER: What would happen—you talked about the hardy environment—if there were a spill? How would a spill be cleaned up? A major spill?

12.8   FORTIER: In the first place, there are about five or six Alaskas. Alaska is arctic, subarctic, panhandle, almost semi-tropical. The area you're talking about encompasses from the top to the bottom of the State. I imagine if there were a spill someplace, the president of the pipeline company would throw his coat right on it. I don't think it would happen.

12.9   MILLER: The president would "throw his coat on it"?

12.10   FORTIER: The vice-president. I don't think he, Mr. Patton, would.

12.11   MILLER: I don't understand that. You mean he would cover it up, wouldn't announce it, wouldn't let us hear it?

12.12   FORITER: They'd never let it happen.

12.13   MILLER: They'd never let it happen?!

12.14   PALMIERI: It's in the spirit of Sir Walter Raleigh. [*Laughter.*]

12.15   FORTIER: This is right.

12.16   MILLER: Let's talk about if there is [a spill]; talk about the damage. Because we're talking about *permanent* damage. Now, there's a spill high on the North Slope; 70 below zero. That's not a temperature in which oil is bio-degradable. That stays here, doesn't it? There are still scars on the Alaskan landscape from people who walked across it 20 years ago, aren't there?

12.17   FORTIER: I don't know. I didn't walk across it. To me the North Slope is the most desolate area in the world. If I never see it again, it's fine with me. [*Laughter, applause.*].

12.18   MILLER: And if you never see it again, and it's destroyed by a serious oil leak, it wouldn't concern you either.

12.19   FORTIER: I wouldn't want to see the geese, the caribou, and such get hurt.

12.20   MILLER: But you rank that very low. If you never see it again, it wouldn't concern you.

12.21   FORTIER: I say that you can love the wilderness without hating humans.

12.22   MILLER: Can you love the wilderness without preserving it?

12.23   FORTIER: We call ourselves "the last frontier." Certainly you're killing part of the American Dream if you're going to create a vast park, and it's practically a park now—you can't homestead or buy any land—and deny young Americans to go up there and maybe take a crack at their dream. I had it, and I'm grateful.

12 . 24   MILLER: We're not talking about cracks at dreams. We're talking about drilling this oil and why we have to do it now. You don't care if you never see it again. How much do you care if there would be an oil spill?

12 . 25   FORTIER: I certainly would care.

12 . 26   MILLER: Why?

12 . 27   FORTIER: I wouldn't want to see another earthquake either, but there's not much I can do to stop it.

12 . 28   MILLER: No, up on the North Slope. Why would you care?

12 . 29   FORTIER: Why would I care? Because it would tarnish our image pretty badly. Because we say we care and we *do* care. And that's why I don't think we'd allow it to happen.

12 . 30   MILLER: So you're concerned because it would tarnish your image.

12 . 31   FORTIER: Well, we don't have a good image, obviously.

12 . 32   MILLER: I see. Tell me about what Alaska is now doing. We've heard that Alaska needs this money desperately to help the poor. What has Alaska done? Alaska per capita income is about $3,700, which is 16 percent higher than the national average.

12 . 33   PALMIERI: I hate to take this out of the conservation and philosophical area and get back into economics. [But] Mr. Brower feels, I think, that there are places in the world where nothing ought to take place, because they are unique and man's activity represents an intrusion on the last refuge of nature. Do you share that view—as a conservationist and an Alaskan?

12 . 34   FORTIER: Yes; and I think we're getting it with the so-called Wilderness Areas Act. A number of them are marked for this right now in Alaska. They may not be as large as Mr. Brower would wish, but they're there.

12 . 35   MILLER: You share it, except where there is oil.

13 .   CLOSING STATEMENTS

13 . 1   HAVELOCK: Because it is far away and only a few people live there to defend it, and because this dark energy is a convenient symbolic focus for the nation's anxiety, national ecological progress has been defined by a noisy minority as slaying the Alaskan dragon. The irony is painful. The environmental care and safety engineering which have gone into this project is staggering. The construction, maintenance, and operational requirements imposed by my state, by the Federal government, and, yes, even by the industry itself, are without parallel. The trans-Alaskan pipeline should stand for years to come as an example of what can be done to

build environmental protection into economic progress. Man and his environment are compatible. As Woody Guthrie sang it, "From the redwood forest, to the Gulf stream waters, This land was made for you and me." You and me as well as God's other creatures. There is an anti-human streak in some conservationist philosophy which bears watching. And while the energies of the environmental movement are focused on this hope for clear victory in Alaska, environmental degradation continues in almost every facet of American life in the continental United States. The loss of the pipeline will be a tragedy, a personal tragedy, for many Alaskans. For American conservation, it also will represent the continuing serious problem: the creation and maintenance of the *illusion* that in blocking this pipeline, which will be the very best of its kind in America, one of the real issues of our time has really been faced.

13 . 2   MILLER: "Everyone," of course, is convinced about the safety features of the pipeline—except the Environmental Protection Agency, the Corps of Engineers, the Department of Transportation and other government agencies. Under tonight's proposal, thousands of miles to the north, which seems far away, in the name of oil, we will once again scar the land—inevitably, simply by entering, and almost certainly by accident. What are we fighting about? It's not simply a fight for the North Slope. It's a fight for what kind of standards we apply to the things we develop, to include in our estimates of cost the cost of destroying the wilderness. It is a fight not simply for the North Slope, it is a fight under our standards, in fact, to save the earth. For every act of pollution in Alaska which we ignore, there are hundreds throughout this country. What we're fighting for and applying these standards in Alaska [for] is to stop the pipeline and to reclaim the earth for man.

 *11 May 1971*

POSTSCRIPT

On Aug. 15, 1972, United States District Judge G. L. Hart Jr. ruled that the Interior Department had met all legal requirements for issuing a permit allowing the Alyeska Co. to build the projected trans-Alaska pipeline. Judge Hart thus vacated the temporary injunction he had issued in April 1970. His new ruling held that the Department had complied with the terms of the National Environmental Policy Act and of the Mineral Leasing Act. His ruling was made orally, so as to speed the case to the Court of Appeals and thence perhaps to the Supreme Court. Plaintiffs in the case were the Wilderness Society and the Friends of the Earth, joined by the Canadian Wildlife Federation and the Cordova District Fisheries Union. Final judicial action as of this writing was pending.

SUGGESTED EXERCISES

1. Identify and discuss at least one example of *ad hominem* argument in the foregoing debate.
2. Identify and discuss at least one example of anthropomorphism in the foregoing debate. (You may find it helpful to review the Commentary on *pathetic fallacies* in the debate on housing and home rule.)
3. Discuss the nature and the quality of evidence cited for and against the proposition that Alaskans sorely need the money they would get from commercial development of the oil reserves in their State.
4. Critically, review "national security" considerations that were invoked in favor of, and in opposition to, the trans-Alaska pipeline.
5. Using the "trial balance" format, juxtapose the claims (factual and otherwise) that were made in the course of the foregoing debate in support of, and against, the following proposition: *If* we could safely assume that the trans-Alaska pipeline and the connecting tanker traffic would be ecologically safe, *then* we could confidently conclude that the trans-Alaska pipeline should be constructed.
6. Analyze the topic of "safety" (or "ecological risk") as it was canvassed in the foregoing debate. In other words, break this topic into its constituent parts, naming the specific questions that arise under the general heading of "safety" (or "ecological risk").

Should there be a moratorium on the construction of nuclear power plants?

OVERVIEW

American use of petroleum products has increased at a dizzying pace during this century, but the use of electricity has accelerated even more rapidly. Electric power consumption has doubled every ten years, and the pace shows little sign of slackening. In some areas, such as the Northeast, demands already have surpassed supplies at peak times of use, producing brownouts. Additional facilities apparently are needed.

Shortages can be met by building more electric power plants of the conventional type, but not easily. Conventional plants are essentially of two kinds. One is the hydroelectric plant, which uses water falling over dams to turn giant generators. The other is the steam plant, which uses coal, gas, or oil to heat water and thus to turn generators. Economically choice sites for hydroelectric power are running out. Domestic fossil fuel supplies also are dwindling. In the meantime, segments of the public have shown intensified concern about the adverse environmental by-products of conventional methods of producing electric power: overheated streams, air pollution, ecological changes wrought by dams, messes produced by mining, and so on. These pressures, coupled with gains in technology, have impelled utility companies to place greater reliance on nuclear reactors, which utilize power extracted from uranium to drive electric power generators.

This prospect has not been greeted with universal acclaim. Grave concern has been expressed, in some quarters, not only about the environmental costs involved in nuclear power (such as dangerous heating of streams used to cool uranium cores), but also, and primarily, about alleged dangers to human life. More specifically, anxieties have been directed to the genetic effects of "normal" emissions of radiation from nuclear power plants, and to the likelihood of catastrophic accidents unleashing prodigious explosive power, fire storms, and massively fatal doses of radiation.

Are these risks serious? Are they greater than the risks involved in using non-nuclear sources of electric power or in letting power supplies dwindle in relation to demands? These and other questions inevitably arise in a debate on whether the construction of nuclear power plants should be suspended.

1.   OPENING STATEMENTS

1.1   MODERATOR VICTOR PALMIERI: Tonight the issue is the energy crisis, and specifically our question is this: "Should there be a moratorium on the construction of nuclear power plants?" Advocate Miller says "Yes," but Advocate Rusher says "No."

1.2   ADVOCATE HOWARD MILLER: "The rash proliferation of atomic power plants has become one of the ugliest clouds overhanging America." That is not my conclusion, but the statement of David Lilienthal, former chairman of the Atomic Energy Commission. In principle, nuclear reactors are dangerous. "In my mind," [says] Dr. Edward Teller, the father of the hydrogen bomb, "nuclear reactors do not belong on the surface of the earth." Why have Dr. Teller [and] Mr. Lilienthal joined winners of the Nobel Prize and other scientists in talking against nuclear power plants? Because the hasty commitment of the Atomic Energy Commission to nuclear power threatens us all. Just one accident in any one of the projected several hundred plants—not a nuclear explosion, [but] an overheating, a conventional explosion, other kinds of accidents—could release into the atmosphere enough radioactivity to devastate entire metropolitan areas and cause tens of thousands of deaths.

1.3   We are all being asked to cross the Atlantic on the *Titanic*, courtesy of the Atomic Energy Commission. Now, of course, the *Titanic* was "unsinkable", the *Hindenburg* "could not crash." [Just as we have been told that] planes do not crash and boats do not sink, [so] we are told there will never be a major accident at a nuclear reactor facility. Based on that premise, we today have 29 such plants operating in the United States, close to 100 more planned, and, by the end of this century, several hundred [anticipated]—one of them near the city in which you live. Each of those plants, if there were an accident, would release radiation [equivalent to that of] 1,000 Hiroshima bombs. And according to a study of the Atomic Energy Commission—called by it an "academic study"—if there were such a major accident, there would be caused 3,400 deaths, 43,000 injuries, [a need, in an area of normal density of population, for] the evacuation of about 460,000 people, and [devastation covering] 150,000 square miles.

1.4   What are the chances of such an accident? When the stakes are so high, [and] when the cost is potentially so great, the chances do not have to be large. One percent would do. And, in fact, there *have* been close-to-accidents: in 1966 at the Fermi reactor in Detroit; at the Hanford reactor in Washington [State]; at Oak Ridge, Tennessee—near-accidents [averted], as Edward Teller said, by luck. And just last month a Strategic Air Command bomber that was using the Big Rock plant on Lake Michigan as a target base for practice runs crashed and exploded 40 seconds away from the nuclear plant.

1.5   Those who risk their money [on such plants] know what the risks [of nuclear accident] are. The public utilities know. They would not build a single reactor until Congress passed the Price-Anderson Act, removing them from all liability in the event of any accident. There is virtually no insurance available for nuclear accidents. The utilities know the risk. They simply want to pass it on to you. Those who risk their money know what the odds are; and we who risk our lives should calculate them just as closely.

1.6   ADVOCATE WILLIAM RUSHER: In the history of man's long upward climb from barbarism, there have been few chapters more dramatic than the story of how the atom was unlocked and its vast energies harnessed for the use of mankind. And not a moment too soon, for the growth of the world's population and the vast proliferation of huge, energy-consuming machines have created a vast and swiftly-growing demand for more and more energy. Fifty years ago it seemed inevitable that this demand would have to be met by conventional energy sources, notably by the burning of such fuels as coal and oil. We were faced with the grim prospect of belching into the earth's already-polluted atmosphere a constantly increasing tonnage of combustion products to provide the additional energy we have to have. Then nuclear power came to the rescue: a whole new technology—silent, clean, obedient, immensely powerful; the best friend of mankind and of all animate nature.

1.7   Now, in a spasm of hysteria and . . . groundless fear, we are suddenly asked to stop the wheel of progress in its tracks, to halt the construction of every nuclear power plant in America, and to go on indefinitely drawing our energy largely from the burning of coal and oil.

1.8   If I may take you into my confidence for a moment, the real problem in arguing a case like this one is its technical aspects. There is no serious question about the need for a bigger energy supply in America in years ahead, and not even any real doubt that nuclear power plants can provide that power more cheaply and more cleanly than either coal or oil. But nuclear physics is a mystery to most of us. We know only that nuclear radiation can, under certain circumstances, be dangerous. It is undetectable to the human senses, and yet it can kill. I'm afraid that it was all too predictable that some scientists could and would be found tonight to attack the collective judgment of virtually all the rest and to predict in firm tones [as witness-to-be Gofman has done,] that under the present safety guidelines [concerning permissible levels of radiation] there could be as many as 32,000 additional deaths from cancer in America every year. What can I do with statements like that? What can I reasonably ask *you* to do with them, except to freeze all nuclear power plant construction, just as Mr. Miller demands? You cannot check [the dissident scientist's] data or even his arithmetic. Even if the odds are overwhelming that he is wrong, there remains some small chance that he may be right; and common sense seems to say, "Play it safe." But I invite you to be a little bolder than that—to listen with me to what the representatives of the overwhelming majority of the international scientific community have to say, and then vote for the future, for a stronger and healthier America made possible by, and *only* by, the rational and intelligent use of nuclear power.

2.   FIRST AFFIRMATIVE WITNESS: DIRECT EXAMINATION

2.1   MILLER: With me tonight to explain how nuclear reactors work, and what the danger is, I've asked to join us Dr. John Gofman, professor of medical physics at the University of California [who] has also worked for 21 years as a nuclear reactor engineer. Dr. Gofman, how does a nuclear reactor work?

2.2   DR. JOHN GOFMAN: Uranium rods [are] the fuel of a nuclear reactor. The fuel is in a pressure vessel surrounded by additional containment structures, usually topped by a dome. Energy produced by uranium fissioning can drive the temperature of the fuel upward extremely rapidly. In one year, the fissioning produces as much radioactivity as 1,000 Hiroshima bombs. Lowering control rods between the fuel elements prevents a runaway chain reaction and lowers the temperature. Movement of control rods requires an extremely complex control system. Heat generated by fission is carried off by water, finally producing steam to drive the turbine. Failure of the control rod system (which has occurred) or blockage of coolant (which has also occurred) are the two possibilities experts fear. Either failure can lead to steam or chemical explosion, rupture of all the containment, and release of massive quantities of radioactivity to the surroundings.

2.3   MILLER: What is the real worry about nuclear reactors: low-level radiation or this threat of accident?

2.4   GOFMAN: The heart of the problem is the nuclear accident. Let us assume that all routine operations go perfectly, that no one is exposed to low-level radiation, and that the radioactive waste is perfectly disposed of. While we may have reservations on all of these assumptions, why argue about them? There is *one* problem that is undeniable: nuclear accidents *can* and probably *will* occur.

2.5   MILLER: What would be the cost of such an accident?

2.6   GOFMAN: The cost, assessed by the Atomic Energy Commission's 1957 Brookhaven Report (when reactors were five times smaller than those currently planned and built) included up to 150,000 square miles of agricultural land contaminated and probably unusable. And in addition, based on this report: 3,400 deaths due to radiation overexposure; 55,000 premature deaths due to cancer—and here I've only included *high*-dose radiation; up to 460,000 people requiring evacuation, and fast, and perhaps not returning for a year; and 3,800,000 people having to be under surveillance to avoid overexposure.

2.7   MILLER: What is the *chance* of such an accident occurring? Is it a *genuine* risk?

2.8   GOFMAN: The chance? No one really knows. Let's listen to the experts. Professor Teller: "What people should really worry about is the reactor accident. Reactors belong deep underground." Dr. Ralph Lapp: "Before the year 2000, it would appear a certainty that we will have a serious accident." Dr. Walter Jordan, a member of the Atomic Energy Commission's Safety and Licensing Boards: "Our total present accumulated experience with all reactors falls a hundred times short of answering the accident question."

2.9   MILLER: Can't engineering and quality control and normal construction satisfy these requirements and give us safe reactors?

2.10   GOFMAN: No. Dr. Milton Shaw, AEC's director of reactor development, testified to Congress as follows: "Seventy-one utilities and 20 architect engineering firms are working on nuclear power plants. Most of these personnel are trying to build the first nuclear plant they ever built. They have to get their nuclear plant education with this plant." What a chilling reassurance. The A.E.C.'s top man is telling us nuclear reactors will surround us built by apprentices and novices.

3.   CROSS-EXAMINATION

3.1   RUSHER: Let us get, if possible, more chilling still. Didn't you predict, in a book you wrote not long ago, that it was possible that exposure to the present allowable level of radiation could result in a 5 to 50 percent increase in the death rate?

3.2   GOFMAN: I predicted that in our book. But that's not the issue we're raising tonight. We're talking about high-level radiation.

3.3   RUSHER: We are talking about *all* levels. The issue tonight is whether there should be nuclear power plants, and I'm going to talk about what might be called "normal" levels. You predicted that those allowable levels would produce from 150,000 to one and a half million additional deaths each year, did you not?

3.4   GOFMAN: That has nothing to do with the nuclear reactor problem. I would have no reason to discuss the present allowable levels, because I'm concerned with the serious high-level exposure from a nuclear accident.

3.5   RUSHER: I'm testing, doctor, your capacity for measured [scientific judgment]. You stated that there would be a 5 to 50 percent increase just from the allowable levels, and such crippling diseases as diabetes, rheumatoid arthritis, and even schizophrenia. Is that right?

3.6   GOFMAN: That is correct.

3.7   RUSHER: And yet, isn't it a fact that the National Council of Radiation Protection and Measurement, a non-profit corporation chartered by Congress to study and provide information on radiation problems, just on January 25th concluded that there was no need for changing most of the limits set to prevent overexposure? And that, when asked about this by the *New York Times,* you said that you were aware of the new report and you concluded from it the Council should either be "abolished or disregarded"?

3.8   GOFMAN: The Council has at no time, ever, in any way, challenged or refuted a single item of evidence which I have presented.

3.9   RUSHER: Because of your disagreement with its views as to the present allowable levels of radiation, you think it should be "abolished or disregarded."

3.10   GOFMAN: I think that is totally irrelevant to the question of nuclear power plants.

3.11   RUSHER: And when the Atomic Energy Commission disagreed with you, you observed, in a letter dated May 14th of [1970], that it seemed to believe that a stupid set of lies will enable it to ram ill-considered atomic programs down the throats of the American public.

3.12   PALMIERI: Mr. Rusher, I think we're ready to stipulate that there is a matter of dispute between Dr. Gofman and these critics with respect to allowable levels. I want now to bring the discussion to the question of nuclear power plant risks.

3.13   RUSHER: We are discussing the statement of the National Council on Radiation Protection and Measurement, a statement that the present allowable levels are perfectly safe. And Dr. Gofman has stated of the head of that council that the opinions stated by Dr. Taylor were fraudulent, hypocritical, and incompetent. Now, this gentleman is presented as an expert and the "wise man" on the subject of nuclear physics, and he has denounced *seriatim* the Atomic Energy Commission; a non-profit commission of the Congress set up to investigate these matters; and the head of that, Dr. Taylor. I think that I'm establishing that [Dr. Gofman] feels matters in an extreme way, and states them that way, and has done so tonight.

3.14   GOFMAN: No. I'm very cool and conservative, Mr. Rusher. I am not debating the issue at all tonight about low-level radiation. No one disagrees with me concerning *high*-level radiation. . . .

3.15   RUSHER: Wait and see. May I ask you: isn't it a fact that the atomic energy guidelines that are applicable to all of these power plants, and the safety requirements, are actually provided through the Environmental Protection Agency most recently and, before that, by the Federal Radiation Council? Isn't that true?

3.16   GOFMAN: The Environmental Protection Agency has just taken over, and right now is under sweeping reviews. No guidelines are set. And we should have a moratorium (if for no other reason) because the Secretary of HEW has ordered a total and sweeping review of these guidelines, because the radiation standards are in doubt.

3.17   RUSHER: However, isn't it true that the recommendation which it will provide will be drawn from figures based on the National Council of Radiation Protection and Measurement and the International Commission of Radiological Protection [studies]?

3.18   GOFMAN: I should say not. They will have the full opportunity to have a full review of all the evidence from everyone who has some information to provide. But in any event, that's totally irrelevant to the question tonight.

3.19   RUSHER: If they do disagree with you, Dr. Gofman—as they have in the matter of allowable present levels of normal radiation hazard—will you denounce their conclusions as frauds and lies?

3.20   GOFMAN: Everyone agrees concerning the effects of high-dose radiation, which is what we are talking about tonight.

3.21   RUSHER: No. We are talking about the *risk* of that happening. And virtually everybody, sir, disagrees with you, as we will find out tonight.

3.22   MILLER *(in summation)*:   You'll notice there were no questions on the point of the direct testimony: the risk of the accident. Except the statement that no one agrees with Dr. Gofman—except, of course, Mr. Lilienthal, Dr. Teller, Joshua Lederberg, Linus Pauling, and hundreds of other scientists around the world. There really is no dispute about the risk of the accident. The A.E.C. itself says that in the event of an accident, there will be damages of $7–$50 billion. Yet, despite that cost for each possible accident, the amount of insurance available is only $571 million. Thus, if there's a nuclear accident, for each person in the range there would be only the highest recovery of seven cents on the dollar. There is no insurance. If you look at your home-owner policy, you will see that the policy does not insure against loss by nuclear reaction, radiation, or radio-active contamination, whether controlled or uncontrolled. Insurance companies know the risks; they don't want to collect the premiums, because they know they may have to pay. The utilities know the risks; they wouldn't build until Congress removed their liability; they simply want the risk to be on you.

4. FIRST NEGATIVE WITNESS: DIRECT EXAMINATION

4.1   RUSHER: To place the technical problem in its larger setting, I call upon the former chairman of the Federal Power Commission, presently the chairman of the New York State Public Service Commission: Joseph Swidler. Mr. Swidler, how does America produce the electric energy it needs?

4.2   JOSEPH SWIDLER: There's a mix of generating plants. About 15 percent is hydro[electric]. We've used up all of our good hydro sites, substantially. About three-quarters of it is derived from fossil fuels: gas, coal, and oil. And of that, three-quarters, or more than half of the total, comes from coal.

4.3   RUSHER: Is that enough electricity for our present and future needs?

4.4   SWIDLER: It isn't enough even for our *present* needs. We are running power shortages practically on a national basis. In my own State, voltage reduction [and] appeals for conservation are the order of the day. [And] the long-range historical growth is about doubling every ten years, or about 7.2 percent. Recently the growth has been *more* than that—8 or 9 percent a year; which means a quadrupling, say, by 1990.

4.5   RUSHER: How are we going to produce this energy, then?

4.6   SWIDLER: We can't produce it from fossil fuels, in my opinion. Fossil fuels are limited in nature, and no more are being made. Whatever is used up is gone forever. We've got, perhaps, one generation left of natural gas; possibly two generations, under our own soil, of oil; somewhat more than that of coal. Any shortfall so far as nuclear generation is concerned will have to come from coal.

4.7   RUSHER: So the nuclear part of the mix is going to be considerably greater by 1990. Is that correct?

4.8   SWIDLER: By 1990 we will be generating over half of our requirements from nuclear energy.

4.9   RUSHER: Why can't we produce this power by burning the fuels like coal and oil—the ones we've always used?

4 . 10   SWIDLER: There just isn't enough. We're already importing 23 percent of
our oil, and it goes up every year. So far as coal is concerned, it would
take an additional *billion* tons [to produce the power needed without
nuclear power by 1990]. This is in addition to the 600 *million* tons of coal
—or approximately twice what we are now using—that will be burned on
the basis of present projections. We're *not* assuming that *all* new power
plants will be nuclear. There will continue to be a mix.

5 .   CROSS-EXAMINATION

5 . 1   MILLER: The current power shortages in New York have nothing to do with
the shortage of fuel do they? Certainly not a shortage of *nuclear* energy.
The fuel is there. The plants just haven't been programmed and managed, themselves, to deliver it.

5 . 2   SWIDLER: There is a fuel shortage as well.

5 . 3   MILLER: There's not enough oil, gas, coal in the United States now to keep
New York City with enough energy? That's a problem of construction
and planning.

5 . 4   SWIDLER: There certainly isn't enough gas. And I think it is a great administrative problem for each utility to be sure that it has an adequate supply. [Tennessee Valley Authority], for example, which normally keeps
a 90-day supply of coal, at one time was down to about a 15-day reserve.

5 . 5   MILLER: Let's talk about the management. In your own State of New York,
for example, why is it that companies, despite the need for what you say
is further fuel and new methods of development, spend more on advertising than on all their research and development? Consolidated Edison
Company, for example, spent $1,600,000 a year on advertising and
$1,300,000 on research and development. Do you justify that record as
progressive management?

5 . 6   SWIDLER: I've criticized the research record of the utility industry myself.
Most of the research is done by the manufacturers. I've urged the industry to go much more deeply into research. There is a great deal of it that
needs to be done. But most of the promotion does not come from the
utility companies. It comes from the fact that electric power is so essential
in modern life.

5 . 7   MILLER: . . . Let's talk about the management record. In 1965, there was
the famous [blackout] in the Northeast. . . . And it was later calculated

by statisticians that the events that caused it were so unpredictable that the odds defied calculation. Yet it occurred. Why?

5.8   SWIDLER: This was an electrical hazard that resulted from a relay that was maladjusted in Ontario, and there was a backup of power flows that kind of—

5.9   MILLER: But *now* it's understood. It took a long time to figure out what happened. Testimony afterwards was that the events that caused it were so unpredictable as to be beyond calculation. You would have given us assurances in 1964 that there would be no 1965 blackout. Will you give us the same assurances tonight that there will be no major nuclear accident?

5.10   SWIDLER: I wouldn't have given you assurance before that there would be no blackout. There is always a residual risk.

5.11   MILLER: There is a "residual risk" of a nuclear accident.

5.12   SWIDLER: There is a residual risk of a nuclear accident, which [risk] I consider to be something that is tolerable and acceptable in light of the fact that I see no other source of energy supply that will take care of the needs of the American people and maintain our economy over the long haul.

5.13   MILLER: As long as you're not in the city next to the explosion.

5.14   SWIDLER: I would have no concern about living near a nuclear plant.

5.15   MILLER: So you disagree with Mr. Lilienthal. When a nuclear plant was proposed in Queens he said, "If there's a nuclear plant built in Queens, I wouldn't live there." The former chairman of the Atomic Energy Commission. You disagree with that?

5.16   SWIDLER: Yes, I do, and I think that I ought to point out that he left the Atomic Energy Commission in 1950. There's a lot of water under the bridge since then.

5.17   MILLER: And a lot of water through nuclear plants as well. [*Laughter.*]

6.   SECOND NEGATIVE WITNESS: DIRECT EXAMINATION

6.1   RUSHER: I really think that Mr. Miller ought to devote himself to the safety of Richard Nixon, whose home—the Western White House, and his retirement home—is about 3,000 feet from . . . a nuclear power plant.

6.2   MILLER: Another mistake by his advisers. [*Laughter.*]

6.3   RUSHER: Apparently Mr. Nixon is not as worried about it as [Mr. Miller] and Dr. Gofman. And I expect he has advisers, too. . . . As I said earlier, the principal problem is to put this whole issue of safety in perspective.

Absolute safety—"zero risk," which is what you're being asked to go for tonight—is impossible this side of the grave. But what are the major risks we really live with today? Death by auto accident: one in 4000. Death by the Pill: one in 25,000. Death or serious injury from accidental electrocution: one in 200,000. Of death from radiation caused by living within 50 miles of a nuclear reactor: somewhere less than one in 10 million—a figure so small we can't even calculate it more accurately than that.

6.4   To discuss further what Dr. Gofman rather arbitrarily claimed [was] the *only* subject here for discussion tonight—and that is the risks, the nuclear risks in a power plant, and the accidental hazards—I have called upon Dr. Leonard Sagan, associate director of the Department of Environmental Medicine of the Palo Alto [California] Medical Clinic. Doctor, what is the *real* risk of nuclear explosion in a civilian nuclear power reactor?

6.5   DR. LEONARD SAGAN: First of all, we have to say that the reactor is quite different from the atomic bomb. They just don't explode the way bombs do. That's physically impossible. [There is] zero risk from nuclear explosion.

6.6   RUSHER: How about a *mechanical* explosion, of the type that Dr. Gofman appeared to be talking about?

6.7   SAGAN: That's possible. You know, one hesitates to say "zero." But in my own view, that risk is quite *close* to zero. Perhaps I could give you an example to describe what I mean by "close to zero." If a man were worried about his trousers falling off, he might put on a belt. And if he wanted to be super safe, he would want to put on suspenders as well. And then if he were very cautious, he might put on a second belt and a second pair of suspenders. Now it's very unlikely under those circumstances that his trousers would fall, but the risk couldn't be zero. The situation is like the reactor.

6.8   RUSHER: Let's talk about normal radiation hazards, the problem of living near a nuclear power plant. Anybody in the United States, just from the food they get in an ordinary year and eat, without any contamination at all, suffers how much in terms of radiation units?

6.9   SAGAN: About 25 units.

6.10   RUSHER: We all walk around on the ground. From the soil around us, how much additional do we absorb?

6.11   SAGAN: From that source, another 45 or so.

6.12   RUSHER: And then, from outer space there are always coming in cosmic rays, and they make us absorb how much additional radiation units?

6.13   SAGAN: They're another 50 or so.

6.14   RUSHER: The materials of the houses we live in might add an additional how much, would you say?

6.15   SAGAN: About 50.

6.16   RUSHER: Now suppose one of those houses was built adjoining a nuclear power plant—not like Mr. Nixon's, 3,000 yards away, but right next to it; and the man stood outside all year to make sure he didn't get any shielding at all from that particular plant's radiations. How much would he absorb, could you tell me?

6.17   SAGAN: The doses are so low that they're difficult to measure, but we calculate that it's about five units additional.

6.18   RUSHER: On the other hand, if he goes to the mountains on vacation or, like Senator Gravel, makes a transcontinental trip from Alaska to Washington, how much additional radiation does he absorb?

6.19   SAGAN: About five from each of those.

6.20   RUSHER: And if, on top of that he works in a tall building made out of granite, how much does he absorb?

6.21   SAGAN: He might get another 50 from that.

6.22   RUSHER: And if he takes care of himself medically and gets an additional X-ray every year, and things like that?

6.23   SAGAN: About 100.

6.24   RUSHER: All this much more, but less than five for living right next door to a nuclear radiation plant?

6.25   SAGAN: That's correct.

6.26   RUSHER: Do you have a last statement with regard to [Dr. Gofman's testimony]?

6.27   SAGAN: Well, I'm afraid that I can't agree with his statement that most scientists are in agreement with his estimates of risk from high levels of radiation.

7.   CROSS-EXAMINATION

7.1   MILLER: Dr. Sagan, no matter how embarrassed you get when your pants fall, there's nowhere near the risk involved as in a nuclear explosion. Let me make clear what we're talking about. I never said that there would be a nuclear *explosion*. We said there would be an *accident*, perhaps a conventional explosion, which would release radioactivity into the air. Now *that* is one of the things you have said was "possible."

7.2   SAGAN: It is "possible."

7.3   MILLER: If there were an accident, and there were a massive release of radioactivity, what did the Brookhaven Report say would result?

7.4   SAGAN: Well, it didn't say what you said it said.

7.5   MILLER: There would be massive deaths?

7.6   SAGAN: That report began with a number of situations, the first of which was the unlikely possibility [and "impossible situation"] that you'd have a reactor with no shielding at all, no containment. . . . And they said, "Well, what would happen if we took all those fuel pellets out of their clouding and just scattered them to the air?" There would be the consequences that were mentioned. But that's *not* what a reactor *is*. It *has* "clouding" around those pellets. It has two containment vessels, the inner one of which is eight inches of steel, the outer about ten feet of concrete. So: the Brookhaven Report concludes that with *that* kind of reactor, not only would there *not* be 10,000 deaths, there'd be *zero* deaths.

7.7   MILLER: No, no. If there were an accident—which you said was possible—let's get to the question—then the massive levels of radiation that would result and cause harm bear no relation to those low levels [you mentioned]. That's a different problem, isn't it?

7.8   SAGAN: It's a different problem; but I object to the word "massive."

7.9   MILLER: No, no. If there were an *accident* in which radiation escaped—we can argue about the chances, but *if* there *were* an accident, and radiation escaped—that's what we talk about. Are you willing to give us a guarantee there will be no such accident?

7.10   SAGAN: I can't guarantee that this building won't collapse in the next 30 seconds.

7.11   MILLER: But will you explain to me, then (because there is insurance on *that*), why no public utility in this country would build a single nuclear reactor until Congress thoroughly removed its complete liability?

7.12   SAGAN: That's an unproved assumption, you know. . . . we haven't . . . asked utilities if they'd be willing to build reactors without Price-Anderson legislation.

7.13   MILLER: [The utilities] were the ones who testified *for* the Price-Anderson legislation; and there were not any [nuclear plants] built before; and the only building came after.

8.   THIRD NEGATIVE WITNESS: DIRECT EXAMINATION

8.1   RUSHER: Mr. Miller seems profoundly concerned about the supposed dangers of this explosion in a nuclear power plant, but you'll notice he says very little indeed about the *status quo* he is defending. What are the alternatives? What are the real choices that we have? [*Films of pollution from*

smokestacks and non-nuclear power plants and strip-mine coaling are shown.]
Those are not imaginary pictures. Those are *real* pictures of *real* things
that will happen. And to discuss the environment in the brief time we
have, I call upon Dr. Merril Eisenbud, professor of environmental medicine at New York University Medical Center. Doctor, will you say
whether the building of additional nuclear power facilities, on balance,
damages our national environment?

8.2   DR. MERRIL EISENBUD: If we had the correct story about how a reactor operates and what the safeguards are, one would have to conclude that the
environment is *not* in jeopardy. As a matter of fact, the thing that's going
to jeopardize the environment is if we *don't* have nuclear reactors.

8.3   RUSHER: How about the charge, though, of *thermal* pollution [from] nuclear
reactors?

8.4   EISENBUD: Discharging waste heat is characteristic of *all* power plants,
whether they use coal or nuclear power. At the present stages of development, the nuclear plants discharge about 30 percent more heat; but
this is narrowing down, and within the decade this will even up.

8.5   RUSHER: What would you say of the comparative environmental effects of
burning coal, on the one hand, and operating a nuclear power plant, on
the other?

8.6   EISENBUD: Generally speaking, it's quite clear that the objections to nuclear
power plants have *not* come from the "public health community." These
[nuclear] plants are clean. The radioactive emissions are miniscule. As a
matter of fact, it is a curious thing that *coal* and *oil* plants discharge more
radioactivity to the atmosphere than many *reactors*. This comes about
because in the fly ash that is discharged to the atmosphere you have a
whole witch's brew of trace elements, many of which we know very little
about. And some of them are radioactive.

8.7   RUSHER: How much fly ash goes into the atmosphere in a year?

8.8   EISENBUD: Twenty million tons. [And] 15 million tons of sulfur dioxide,
which is a highly toxic gas [go into the atmosphere in a year].

8.9   RUSHER: How much radiation comes from a nuclear power plant?

8.10   EISENBUD: The Public Health Service just did very detailed studies in the
vicinity of two plants that were among the first to be [operative], and
found that the environment was essentially undisturbed. They couldn't
measure the difference.

8.11   RUSHER: Can you give us an example of just how much radiation is involved in a nuclear power plant?

8.12   EISENBUD: In the one plant, they could find no difference with instruments
because the instruments just aren't that sensitive. It turned out, upon

calculation, that the risk of the radiation dose would be about equivalent to that that one would receive leaning against a granite building for 15 minutes or a half-hour in a year.

9.   CROSS-EXAMINATION

9.1   MILLER: Let's not talk about thermal pollution or low-level radiation. Let's talk about this risk of accident. Now last month when the Strategic Air Command bomber missed the Big Rock plant on Lake Michigan by about 40 seconds, what would have happened if that plane which exploded had crashed right into the plant?

9.2   EISENBUD: I don't know the details of the incident you're talking about. But I do know that the contemporary reactors, for example, are designed for impact of the [Boeing] 707.

9.3   MILLER: And to withstand Strategic Air Command planes as well? Tell me about what happened at the Brown's Ferry Reactor near Florence, Alabama, where there were over 5000 welding errors not found by the A.E.C. until it was disclosed by an engineer. And the spokesman for the A.E.C. said, hopefully, "We would have delved deeply into welding and found the mistakes without the report."

9.4   EISENBUD: Now you're picking details out of context, [details] which can't be discussed in a few minutes. The fact of the matter is that we have 28 years of experience with about 500 reactors throughout the world.

9.5   MILLER: Well, let's talk about one of them, forgetting about the details: about the problems at Brown's Ferry (which, I take it, means there would have *been* a problem if the welding faults hadn't been found). [Concerning] the atomic reactor plant—the Fermi Plant, in Detroit, Michigan: the A.E.C.'s own advisory committee recommended against building that plant, did it not?

9.6   EISENBUD: There was a difference of opinion about it, but the plant was built.

9.7   MILLER: Yes, the A.E.C. went ahead. In 1966 there was overheating of uranium in the Fermi Plant. In fact, people have said it was very lucky, with the overheating of uranium. The plant had to be shut down. Something went wrong—not enough to cause danger, but something went wrong.

9.8   EISENBUD: All of the safeguards worked. Nobocy was hurt. There was no exposure to the public.

9.9   MILLER: And at Hanford, Washington, they had 86 safety rods, and all 86 failed to operate; but the backup system of so-called "boron balls" worked. The safety system "worked" there, too?

9.10   EISENBUD: You're picking things completely out of context. These things have no meaning. The fact of the matter is we have a track record that goes back 28 years. And no member of the public has been exposed to radiation from the reactors in this country.

9.11   MILLER: No "member of the public"; just those who work in it. Let's talk about the Hanford plant. In Hanford the 86 rods didn't fall, but the boron ball safety system worked. At Oak Ridge—

9.12   EISENBUD: You have picked certain details out of a two-billion[-dollar-]a-year program, [details] that I have no familiarity with.

9.13   MILLER: Now wait a minute. I picked the plant at Brown's Ferry, in Alabama. I picked the Fermi plant in Detroit, Michigan; the Hanford plant in Washington; the Oak Ridge plant in Tennessee, where there was a failure of the backup system. We've covered the country pretty well. . . .

9.14   EISENBUD: This is blatant nonsense.

9.15   MILLER: Well, that occurred. We have testimony on it. We have covered the country, don't you think? That's a pretty fair geographic mix,

9.16   EISENBUD: You can't identify a single incident in which any radioactivity left any of these reactors. There are all kinds of mechanical problems you can run into. These are dealt with.

9.17   MILLER: They are dealt with, *hopefully.* You just want another chance to see if one will *really* escape. Let me ask you what your explanation is for why public utilities would not build a single plant until they were absolved of all liability by Congress.

9.18   EISENBUD: I personally have no sympathy for that position. And not all the utilities felt that way. It so happens that the atomic energy industry, I think, has been advanced in many respects, including the ecological aspects; and they decided way back that the ability of the private insurance industry was simply inadequate—not just the atomic energy industry. But there are many aspects.

9.19   MILLER: The risks were too great for the entire private insurance industry and the utilities industry to assume the financial burden.

9.20   RUSHER *(in summation):*   Sherlock Holmes once said of the barking dog in the nighttime that the significant point was that the dog *didn't* bark in the nighttime. And in that horrendous series, that geographic trip that you just took around the country, did you notice that there was no nuclear explosion? There was no death. There was nothing except here and there one safety factor that didn't work and an immense number that *did*, as Dr. Eisenbud pointed out. Note that Mr. Miller and Dr. Gofman here tonight have not even *tried* to suggest—which is interesting and concessive—that radiation hazards in *normal* operation are serious or even worth worrying about. Both of them have conceded that a nuclear *explosion* is out of the question—despite all those artful references to how many "Hiroshimas" there are in an ordinary nuclear plant. You are being led up the garden path to a deliberate decision to freeze all nuclear power plants in America for a future that is going to be led right back into the coal and fuel grind of an unsatisfactory present. I suggest that we join forces to prevent it.

10.   SECOND AFFIRMATIVE WITNESS: DIRECT EXAMINATION

10.1   MILLER: You must be very precise about what you say. Safety factors *have* failed all over the country in these nuclear plants. We just haven't had the kind of occurrence that occurred in 1965, in the Northeast power blackout, where the odds were incalculable, but the event occurred. When we are calculating risks, you must remember the risk of *what*. We're talking about the risk of utter devastation which no one is willing to assume the financial responsibility for. But is it really true that our only alternative is to go with atomic power? It most certainly is not. In fact, we have sufficient oil and coal reserves. You'll notice Mr. Swidler talked about generations: one generation of [one] fuel, two of another, more of another. The coal industry says there's enough coal at present levels for 1,600 years of operation. In fact, there is technology on building clean fuel plants. [It is] much easier to clean up the fossil plant than risk these nuclear plants. And there are other sources of energy: solar energy, tidal energy, magnetohydrodynamics—things that we have made no investment in. What we need is a national energy policy, a *national* energy commission—not an *atomic* energy commission, but an *energy* commission; to stop atomic energy now and put the billions of dollars of the investment in other kinds of energy that simply [do] not bear this kind of risk. To testify to that point is the man who will introduce a bill to establish this kind of moratorium, Sen. Mike Gravel of Alaska. Senator, will the air-conditioners and the lights go out if we don't build atomic energy plants?

10.2 GRAVEL: Of course not. We're only dependent about one or two percent on atomic energy at this point in time.

10.3 MILLER: But if we don't use these atomic plants, will that force us back on these dirty coal and oil plants?

10.4 GRAVEL: Of course not. Also, we haven't begun to spend the necessary amount of money to clean up these plants that you talk of. In fact, if we spent all the money that we did on nuclear energy right out of the Federal appropriation, we could clean up all the existing ones.

10.5 MILLER: Why do you think a moratorium, a stop, is necessary now?

10.6 GRAVEL: We've got 20 plants now already invested in, and we'll probably have 100 in ten years and 1,000 by the year 2000. And we've got to stop this juggernaut at this point in time, and reevaluate the course that we're taking.

10.7 MILLER: Won't a moratorium simply delay the ultimate building of the plants; or will it end it?

10.8 GRAVEL: We don't know. This is what it's all about. We want to make a study. We want to evaluate alternate sources and assess the risk and then take a course of action.

10.9 MILLER: If we stop the atomic energy industry now, will that create unemployment, chaos, disruption?

10.10 GRAVEL: Quite the contrary. Under my plan, what we'd do is probably pick up more employment, particularly from areas like Southern California, where we have a lot of scientists that are unemployed at the present time.

10.11 MILLER: You come from Alaska. There was a recent big oil find in Alaska. Are you here opposing atomic energy because you want to sell oil?

10.12 GRAVEL: I would hope not. Our oil needs in this country are known. They have been testified to before. In the year 1985 we will be dependent on exterior imports for about 35 percent. Even if we put Alaska on a line, it would be 45 percent. But by and large, we don't use oil to generate our electric energy.

10.13 MILLER: Your legislation would place a moratorium and also repeal this Price-Anderson Act, wouldn't it? It would make the companies financially responsible.

10.14 GRAVEL: That's the triggering mechanism to create a moratorium. Of course, from the testimony I've heard here, we can assume that we won't have any opposition to this amendment to require insurance.

11.   CROSS-EXAMINATION

11.1   RUSHER: Senator, I don't want to get you in trouble with any constituents in a State which has this new, huge, newly-discovered oil field. But have you considered the environmental and the pollution effects of coal- and oil-burning?

11.2   GRAVEL: I would say we haven't. And if we took some of the money that we've been spending on nuclear reactors as a direct appropriation, and spent more money on cleaning up the environment, cleaning up our existing plants, we wouldn't have the problem we have today.

11.3   RUSHER: I can understand that in the future all sorts of good things are going to happen. But right now, the pictures that you saw a little earlier [of air pollution and other eyesores]—

11.4   GRAVEL: It will only happen if we develop a game plan that has some intelligence. We've been presently launching into this nuclear development without any sense or logic.

11.5   RUSHER: The trouble with your game plan, Senator, is that you tell us it's perfectly easy to spend money to develop clean coal-burning and clean oil-burning plants, but that it *isn't* possible to do the same thing in the future for the protection from the nuclear hazards of which Dr. Gofman was complaining.

11.6   GRAVEL: Well, we could, of course. We've been spending 83 percent of our Federal dollar doing just what you're saying. What I'm saying is "Let's spread that dollar around." We may well find, and it appears likely, that we can probably heat and provide all the energy for west of the Mississippi from a thermal source.

11.7   RUSHER: Thermal source? What thermal source did you have in mind?

11.8   GRAVEL: Well, we have a plant right here in California.

11.9   RUSHER: And it can provide energy for all west of the Mississippi?

11.10   GRAVEL: No, I think that they have finds—

11.11   RUSHER: You *hope.*

11.12   GRAVEL: Well, not "hope." If you have some time after, I can show you some maps that go all the way to Mississippi that can show you thermal sources—

11.13   RUSHER: But, practically speaking, Mr. Miller was [claiming] a moment ago [that] 1600 years of burning coal lie ahead of us [and that] we don't need to worry about that at all. And you heard Mr. Swidler, President Kennedy's Chairman of the Federal Power Commission, and the other scientist that we had on, state that this kind of thing would require by 1990 the burning of a billion additional tons of coal per year, on top of a doubling of the present coal-burning. Now, is that the future that you predict for the United States, and want?

11.14   GRAVEL: Well, I think the issue you make—and it's a very good one [*Laughter*]—is that we should broaden the spectrum of analysis in solving the energy crisis which is upon us and will continue to be with us. . . . What I'm suggesting, with this moratorium and legislation, is to create a commission that will not be only an *atomic* energy commission, but will be an *energy* commission looking at all facets of the problem.

11.15   RUSHER: It would be wonderful to have a commission "to look at all facets of the problem." But you're proposing much more than that. You're proposing to freeze nuclear power plant construction into this moratorium. And I'm saying to you that the choice available to the American people *now*, and not involving some maps you're going to show me after the show about pie in the sky 20 and 30 years from now—[our] practical choice is either nuclear power or coal and oil, by and large. Isn't that the truth?

11.16   GRAVEL: Of course not. It would take ten years to develop what you're talking about. And what I'm talking about is to develop an orderly plan on how we will proceed in that 10-, 20-, and 30-year period.

11.17   RUSHER: Do you know that, as Dr. Eisenbud testified, one type of nuclear power plant actually emits *less* radioactive material than an oil-burning or a coal-burning plant? *Less radioactive material.* Did you know that?

11.18   GRAVEL: I don't get your point.

11.19   RUSHER: Well, don't you think, then, if we're going to prevent the emission of radioactive materials in the future, that it would be useful not to burn coal and oil?

11.20   GRAVEL: I think you're talking about low-level emission. And, of course, the issue here is whether or not you can have an *accident* that would cripple a major portion of the United States.

11.21   RUSHER: That is precisely the question.

11.22   GRAVEL: Just imagine what would happen if we had an accident that would occur in the BosWash [Boston-Washington] area. You're talking about evacuating thousands of acres where hundreds of millions of people live. This is a fantastic cost.

11.23   RUSHER: The key word is "imagine," Senator.

11.24   PALMIERI: Let me ask you this: as a Senator, how do you view the operations of the Atomic Energy Commission, supporting, as you do, Mr. Miller's position that there are grave risks involved so far in these plants that have been constructed?

11.25   GRAVEL: I've been opposed to the present operation of the Atomic Energy Commission because it's charged, one, with prosecuting a goal to *develop* atomic energy. At the same time, it *also* has responsibility for *licensing* these plants. So it sits as its own judge. You can't ask any honest, intelligent person to have such a dichotomous role.

11.26   PALMIERI: Do you think they're creating risks?

11.27   GRAVEL: Very much so.

11.28   RUSHER: Have you considered the fact that on the record to date, a billion tons of coal, such as would be required if we're burning coal in 1990 in the quantities projected, can be mined only at the cost of the lives of 600 coal miners?

11.29   GRAVEL: I don't know. That's what I plan on trying to get the study made for, so we can find out what the alternatives are to coal, to atomic energy—

11.30   RUSHER: One of the alternatives we know is nuclear power, isn't it?

11.31   GRAVEL: Very much so.

11.32   RUSHER: And this would not require the lives of 600 coal miners a year in 1990.

11.33   GRAVEL: We don't know how many lives it might require, because tomorrow we might have an accident—

11.34   RUSHER: "Might."

11.35   GRAVEL: "Might" is a part of our lives.

11.36   RUSHER: And "imagine" and "projection" and "mañana." But today and now, the problem is the power requirements of the United States. In the BosWash area you mentioned, where I happen to live, we are having brownouts right now.

11.37   GRAVEL: The failures on our requirements are basically because atomic energy has not turned out to be what everybody thought it was going to be. That's the reason why the game plan has failed.

11.38   RUSHER: Not according to the chairman of the New York State Public Service Commission.

11.39   GRAVEL: All I'm suggesting is that we can have an orderly development in this problem area. And presently we spend 83 percent of our dollar on one item, and that is atomic energy. And I think it's foolhardy, particularly when we have other sources that could meet this energy crisis. Now you've painted a picture that we have an energy crisis, and you show us an alternative of belching smokestacks. We don't have to have belching smokestacks as a solution.

11.40   RUSHER: And your solution is to appoint a committee to study the problem.

11.41   GRAVEL: To do something about the problem.

11.42   RUSHER: Well then, the thing to do is to do what can be done, and not to rely upon vague imaginings of what might happen in some visionary future.

12.   CLOSING STATEMENTS

12.1   MILLER: There's an old Indian proverb that he who mounts a tiger often winds up inside. [*Laughter.*] We have mounted the tiger of nuclear power development. But we still have time to dismount. The risk we're talking about is not just the low-level radiation which people keep coming back to, which is in dispute. The risk we're talking about is the risk of an *accident*: a "1965 blackout," only in a nuclear power plant, perhaps in New York City, or Los Angeles, or where you live. There is one question that comes up repeatedly, and that those who oppose this moratorium must answer—have not, but will not: if there is no risk, why won't the utilities accept the risk financially? How can the utilities decline the risk financially and pass it on to you? Until that question is answered, until the utilities accept their own risk, there must be this moratorium.

12.2   RUSHER: Consider the witnesses you have heard tonight. Senator Gravel, from an oil-producing state, naturally favors a moratorium on nuclear power: the "long think" about the whole thing. And Dr. Gofman is here threatening 1,000 Hiroshimas and denouncing everyone who disagrees with him as liars and frauds. On the other side you have heard Mr. Swidler, President Kennedy's Chairman of the Federal Power Commission; Dr. Sagan, a leading environmental physician; and Dr. Eisenbud, fresh from two years as administrator of New York City's Environmental Protection Administration—all telling you quite calmly that, while the "zero risk" is a pure theory in human affairs, nuclear power is absolutely essential, wholly acceptable from the standpoint of safety, and by far the cleanest available source of power that America must have. Hysteria aside, it is really a question of choice. Which shall it be? Nuclear power, the energy source of the future—clean, powerful, and obedient—or coal and oil, the energy sources of the past and the grimy present, the chief agents of industrial pollution and of untold death and misery every year? Mr. Miller reminded us of the *Titanic*. But would he recommend a moratorium on ocean-going ships? Perhaps he would. But would you? Vote for san... Vote for the future. Vote for a cleaner America. Vote NO on a moratorium on nuclear power.

 *16 February 1971*

SUGGESTED EXERCISES

1. Briefly summarize the line(s) of argument provided by the Affirmative side in the foregoing debate.
2. Briefly summarize the line(s) of argument provided by the Negative side.
3. Discuss the use and abuse of statistical data in the foregoing debate.
4. Enumerate, specify, and assess the *types* of evidence invoked by Affirmative spokesmen on behalf of their principal line(s) of argument concerning nuclear power plants.
5. Identify and discuss the techniques used by William Rusher in his effort to discredit testimony given by witnesses for the Affirmative side of the debate.